GHOSTS
ON THE
ROOF

GHOSTS ON THE ⫼ ROOF ⫼

Selected Journalism
of Whittaker Chambers
1931-1959

Edited and with an introduction by
TERRY TEACHOUT

Regnery Gateway
Washington, D.C.

Library of Congress Cataloging-in-Publication Data

Chambers, Whittaker.
  Ghosts on the roof.

  Includes index.
  1. Chambers, Whittaker—Political and social views.
I. Teachout, Terry. II. Title.
PN4874.C426A25 1989   818'.5209   89-10268
ISBN 0-89526-765-9

Published in the United States by
Regnery Gateway
1130 17th Street, NW
Washington, DC 20036

Distributed to the trade by
National Book Network
4720-A Boston Way
Lanham, MD 20706

Manufactured in the United States of America

10 9 8 7 6 5 4 3 2 1

It seemed to me as I watched him leave that the most important thing I could do for him was to report for him how his father had viewed certain aspects of our reality, what I believed the forces of reality to be, and how I saw their origins and development, which pulverized individual men, and caught peoples, like shovelfuls of corn in a hammermill.

Whittaker Chambers, 1955

CONTENTS

Editor's Note   ix

Introduction: The Forgotten Career of Whittaker Chambers   xiii

ONE   A MEMBER OF THE REVOLUTION

Can You Make Out Their Voices   (1931)   3
You Have Seen the Heads   (1931)   22
Our Comrade Munn   (1931)   30
Death of the Communists   (1931)   40

TWO   NIGHT THOUGHTS

Intelligence Report   (1939)   49
Night Thoughts   (1939)   50
The New Pictures: "Ninotchka"   (1939)   56
The New Pictures: "The Grapes of Wrath"   (1940)   58
The Revolt of the Intellectuals   (1941)   60
Silence, Exile & Death   (1941)   63
Peace & the Papacy   (1943)   66
Historian and History Maker   (1944)   74
Literary Autolysis   (1944)   80
Santayana, Poet of Dissolution   (1944)   86
The Anatomy of Fascism   (1944)   92
Area of Decision   (1944)   98
Crisis   (1944)   104
The Ghosts on the Roof   (1945)   111
The Old Deal   (1945)   116
Christmas 1945   (1945)   119

THREE   A LENTEN AGE

Problem of the Century   (1946)   123
Crossroads   (1946)   126

In Egypt Land   (1946)   134
The Challenge   (1947)   141
The Tragic Sense of Life   (1947)   150
Circles of Perdition   (1947)   156
The Devil   (1948)   166
Dr. Crankley's Children   (1948)   175
Faith for a Lenten Age   (1948)   184

FOUR   THE HISTORY OF WESTERN CULTURE

The Middle Ages   (1947)   197
Medieval Life   (1947)   204
The Glory of Venice   (1947)   209
The Age of Enlightenment   (1947)   217
The Edwardians   (1947)   223
Age of Exploration   (1948)   233
The Protestant Revolution   (1948)   242

FIVE   LETTERS FROM WESTMINSTER

The Sanity of St. Benedict   (1952)   257
Is Academic Freedom in Danger?   (1953)   265
The End of a Dark Age Ushers in New Dangers   (1956)   279
Soviet Strategy in the Middle East   (1957)   291
The Coming Struggle for Outer Space   (1957)   300
A Westminster Letter: The Left Understands
    the Left   (1957)   304
A Westminster Letter: "To Temporize Is Death"   (1957)   308
Big Sister Is Watching You   (1957)   313
A Westminster Letter: Springhead to Springhead   (1958)   319
Some Untimely Jottings   (1958)   326
Letter from Westminster: A Reminder   (1958)   328
A Republican Looks at His Vote   (1958)   331
Some Westminster Notes   (1959)   333
Missiles, Brains and Mind   (1959)   335
The Hissiad: A Correction   (1959)   340
Foot in the Door   (1959)   345

Index   351

EDITOR'S NOTE

Ghosts on the Roof is a selection from essays, articles, reviews and short stories by Whittaker Chambers originally published in *Time, Life, National Review* and other magazines between 1931 and 1959. Most of the pieces reprinted here have never before appeared in book form. I have omitted the poems Chambers published in various magazines between 1926 and 1931 and the juvenilia that appeared in *The Morningside*, an undergraduate literary magazine of Columbia College, between 1922 and 1924. A partial checklist of Chambers's early writings appears in Allen Weinstein's *Perjury: The Hiss-Chambers Case* (New York: Alfred A. Knopf, 1978).

Articles published in *Time* during Chambers's tenure there were unsigned. Prior to 1948, Time Inc. publicly identified only one piece, a 1946 cover story on Marian Anderson, as having been written by Chambers. The Time Inc. Archives no longer contain any records specifically identifying Chambers's contributions to the magazine. The *Time* pieces reprinted here were identified from references in Chambers's books *Witness, Cold Friday* and *Odyssey of a Friend;* from an examination of Allen Weinstein's research archive for *Perjury,* which contains some 60,000 pages of material relating to the Hiss-Chambers case; and from other verifiable references in the published primary and secondary literature on Chambers.

John Hersey has said that *Time* writers like Chambers and James Agee had "such distinctive voices, even in stagy, anonymous timestyle, that I could tell at once, reading each issue, who among them had written what." Issues of *Time* published between 1939 and 1948 contain numerous pieces that appear to bear out Hersey's claim. With one exception, however, I have not included any unsigned pieces in *Ghosts on the Roof* for which some form of verification cannot be provided. The exception is "The Tragic Sense of Life," an unsigned 1947 review of Max Brod's *Franz Kafka*. The length of the review suggests that it was a product of the Agee-Chambers "Special Projects" department rather than a regularly assigned book review; the tone and content of the review strongly resemble those of other contemporary articles by Chambers, who admired Kafka and wrote about his story "The Hunter Gracchus" in *Cold Friday*.* I include this review for purposes of comparison with other pieces known to have been written by Chambers for *Time* during the late Forties.

---

* Chambers kept four books in the top drawer of his desk at *Time:* Kafka's *Parables and Paradoxes,* Burke's *Reflections on the Revolution in France,* Dostoevsky's *The Possessed* and *Coriolanus.*

The texts used in this volume, including all footnotes, are those of the original magazine publications. Obvious typographical errors have been corrected. Crossheads have been deleted from the *Life* and *National Review* pieces. The text of "Can You Make Out Their Voices" is that of the version published in the *New Masses* in 1931. The 1932 pamphlet edition of this story published by International Pamphlets was retitled "Can You Hear Their Voices?"; Chambers uses the latter title, by which the story is now generally known, in *Witness*.

Since no surviving manuscripts were made available to me by the Chambers family, it was impossible for me to determine the precise extent to which Chambers's writings were altered by editors prior to publication. According to William F. Buckley, Jr., Chambers's essays for *National Review* required next to no editing. Matters were different at *Time* and *Life*. According to T. S. Matthews, managing editor of *Time* during the Forties:

> Almost all *Time* writers had to resign themselves to having their copy cut and also to being hacked about ("edited") and often largely rewritten by an editor. From the very first, Chambers made it quite clear that he objected violently to this convention and would never resign himself to it. Whenever I edited his copy, if I cut a sentence or altered a word, I could always expect his protesting presence or, more effectively, an eloquently despairing note (often quoting Dante, Milton, or some German poet—usually in the original) to the general effect that his story was now ruined and . . . completely senseless and not worth publishing.

Chambers, however, was not offended by "*Time* style," the elaborately artificial house style described by Westbrook Pegler as "a nervous disease of the typewriter" and famously parodied by Wolcott Gibbs in his *New Yorker* profile of Henry Luce. In *Witness*, Chambers described *Time* style as "a discipline of expression, and not a horseplay with queer words and elliptical phrases." Chambers eventually learned to bend this eccentric style to his own literary ends, aided by the fact that he served as his own editor throughout his later years at *Time;* most of his identifiable unsigned pieces, despite the obvious quirks imposed by *Time* style, are recognizably the work of the man who wrote *Witness, Cold Friday* and the letters collected in *Odyssey of a Friend.**

Many people aided me in assembling this collection, starting with Alfred Regnery, my publisher; Glen Hartley and Lynn Chu, my agents; Patrick Swan, my research assistant, whose assistance in identifying magazine articles by and about Chambers was invaluable; and Hilton Kramer, who first encour-

---

* Two of the *Life* pieces reprinted here, "The Edwardians" and "The Protestant Revolution," underwent substantial editorial alterations of which Chambers is known to have strongly disapproved. The editing of "The Edwardians" is described in *Witness;* the editing of "The Protestant Revolution" is discussed in my introduction.

aged me to edit a collection of Whittaker Chambers's journalism. I hope he finds the results gratifying.

I also wish to thank William F. Buckley, Jr., who spoke to me at length about Chambers's tenure at *National Review;* Allen Weinstein, who allowed me to examine his research archive for *Perjury;* Ray Cave, formerly editorial director of Time Inc., who gave me access to Chambers's confidential employee files; Geoffrey Colvin of *Fortune* and Elaine Felsher of the Time Inc. Archives, who were unfailingly helpful; Andrew Ferguson, who edited the shorter version of the introduction to *Ghosts on the Roof* published in *The American Spectator;* and John Chambers, Henry Anatole Grunwald, John Hersey, Barbara Kerr, T. S. Matthews and Ralph de Toledano, who shared information about Chambers with me.

Such private papers of Whittaker Chambers as may still exist remain in the hands of the Chambers family, which has been understandably reluctant to cooperate with researchers. After lengthy consideration, the family chose not to permit me to examine Chambers's papers in preparing *Ghosts on the Roof.* I therefore look upon this volume as a purely preliminary undertaking, and I hope that a more complete edition of Chambers's writings prepared with the full cooperation of the Chambers family will someday be made available to the public. As Housman said of his edition of Juvenal: *Editorum in usum edidit.*

New York
April 1989   Terry Teachout

INTRODUCTION

THE FORGOTTEN CAREER OF
WHITTAKER CHAMBERS

*A writer's reputation often reaches a point in its career where what
he actually said is falsified even when he is correctly quoted. Such
falsification—we might more charitably call it mythopoeia—is very
likely the result of some single aspect of a man's work serving as a
convenient symbol of what other people want to think.*

—Lionel Trilling

THE PUBLIC LIFE of Whittaker Chambers revolves endlessly around two
dates. In 1938, Chambers, then the courier for a Soviet spy ring based in
Washington, D.C., broke with the Communist Party and went into hiding. In
1948, he testified under oath before the House Un-American Activities Committee about his activities as a member of the Fourth Section of the Soviet
Military Intelligence. In the course of his testimony, he told the committee
that Alger Hiss, president of the Carnegie Endowment for World Peace and a
former high-ranking official in the State Department, had been one of his
agents.

For many people, Chambers's story stops with the first date and resumes
with the second. Yet during the intervening decade, Whittaker Chambers did
what for most men would have been the principal work of a lifetime. Starting
out in 1939 as a book reviewer for *Time*, Chambers rose to become a senior
editor of the most popular newsmagazine in America. He edited *Time*'s "Foreign News" section from 1944 to 1945, giving it a strongly anti-Soviet slant at a
time when the American public was being officially encouraged to view the
Soviet Union as an ally; he was later assigned, together with James Agee, to a
department of his own, the "Special Projects" unit, that produced cover stories
on politics, culture and religion; and he wrote the text for seven chapters of
Life's "History of Western Culture" series.

It was only because his *Time* articles were unsigned that Whittaker Cham-

xiii

bers was not more widely known prior to his HUAC testimony. Given the extraordinary controversy that surrounded Chambers after he left *Time* in 1948, one would naturally expect that his articles for *Time* and *Life*, as well as his later essays for *National Review*, would be far better known than they are. In fact, Chambers's journalism, early and late, is all but unknown, even to scholars specializing in the Hiss-Chambers case, who invariably cite the same half-dozen essays and articles in discussions of Chambers's life and work.

Why is Whittaker Chambers's career as a journalist ignored? One reason is because the inherent drama of his role in the Hiss-Chambers case naturally overshadowed what he described in *Witness*, his 1952 autobiography, as "the tranquil years" he spent working for Time Inc. Of equal importance, however, is the fact that virtually none of the hundreds of articles Chambers published between 1931, when he became a contributing editor of the *New Masses*, and 1959, when he resigned from *National Review*, has been reprinted in book form. The bulk of Chambers's journalism has heretofore been accessible only to well-equipped researchers. As a result, it is chiefly as the author of *Witness* and, to a lesser degree, of *Cold Friday*, a collection of unpublished writings, and *Odyssey of a Friend*, a volume of his letters to William F. Buckley, Jr., that Chambers the writer is remembered.

The author of those books was understandably obsessed with the ultimate meaning of his anti-Communist witness. By contrast, though Chambers the journalist shares the same philosophical concerns and the same distinctive prose style, his range is much wider. Chambers, for example, wrote at length for *Time* about such diverse topics as *Finnegans Wake*, Arnold Toynbee's *Study of History* and the theology of Reinhold Niebuhr; not surprisingly, his journalism offers a more complete view of the man who is too often remembered solely as the persecutor of Alger Hiss.

To be sure, Whittaker Chambers *is* the Hiss-Chambers case for most of his enemies and, interestingly, many of his friends. He will always be remembered as the enduring symbol of a crucial moment in postwar American politics. But it has become increasingly clear in the last few years that Chambers's historical significance transcends the particulars of his association with Alger Hiss. Posthumously awarded the Medal of Freedom by Ronald Reagan in 1984, Chambers is now generally recognized as a key figure in the development of modern American conservatism. Surely this fact alone justifies closer scrutiny of the published writings of so interesting and problematic a character.

Moreover, Chambers's journalism is also worth examining for its intrinsic literary merit. "The book was not written as literature," John P. Marquand said of *Witness* in *The Book-of-the-Month Club News*, "but literature it is of a high order." Most of the original reviewers of *Witness*, even those who found Chambers's political views repellent, echoed Marquand's appraisal. At its best, Chambers's journalism is of comparable quality. To read his contributions to *Time* and *Life* is to marvel at the implicit compliment that Henry Luce was paying his readers in publishing literary criticism and cultural commentary of such erudition and high seriousness; it is difficult to imagine such criticism appearing even occasionally, much less week after week, in the newsmagazines of today.

Whittaker Chambers's journalism also deserves to be remembered for the same reason that William F. Buckley, Jr., decided to publish his letters from Chambers:

> [Chambers's letters] will help the reader to judge the plausibility of the attacks on Whittaker Chambers's character. . . . it was I who opened the envelopes that brought these communications, finding in them a sublimity which I most frankly acknowledge as having been as much influential as the goddamn Woodstock typewriter in convincing me of the credentials of Whittaker Chambers.

Allen Weinstein's *Perjury: The Hiss-Chambers Case* settled for most reasonable observers the narrow question of whether or not Whittaker Chambers told the House Un-American Activities Committee the truth about his relationship with Alger Hiss. But the question of Chambers's character, as Buckley suggests, still remains open for many Americans—not all of them sympathetic to Hiss. This uncertainty is at the heart of the continuing fascination the Hiss-Chambers case exerts on people who were not yet born when Chambers said to the members of HUAC: "I know that I am leaving the winning side for the losing side, but it is better to die on the losing side than to live under Communism."

In the absence of a full-scale biography, Chambers must inevitably remain in large part an enigmatic figure. But anyone seeking to better understand the character and motives of the man who testified against Alger Hiss will find many of the answers in the forgotten career of Whittaker Chambers, journalist.

Journalism, a "profession" of uncertain standards, has long served as a refuge for gifted individuals lacking any clear sense of what they want to do with their lives. It is made to be drifted into—and out of. Such was the erratic course that Whittaker Chambers pursued as a young writer. It is the aimlessness of his early years that stands out in a biographical statement that appeared in the July 1931 issue of the *New Masses* and was probably written by Chambers himself:

> [B]orn in Philadelphia in 1901. Boyhood in eastern U.S. Youth as periodically vagrant laborer in deep South, Plains, Northwest. Brief Columbia college experience, ending with atheist publication. Formerly member Industrial Union 310 I.W.W. Joined revolutionary movement 1925. Contributed to numerous publications. Former staff member of the *Daily Worker*, contributing editor to *New Masses*.

The facts behind this bald and evasive passage are now well-known.* After a *Wanderjahr* spent laying rails in Washington, D.C., and living hand-to-mouth in the red-light district of New Orleans, Chambers enrolled as a student at Columbia College in 1920. He was immediately recognized as a writer of talent by his undergraduate friends and acquaintances, who included Lionel Trilling, Meyer Schapiro, Louis Zukofsky and Clifton Fadiman. Trilling recalled shortly before his death in 1975 that the young Chambers "wrote with an elegant austerity."

But Whittaker Chambers was not destined for the literary life. In 1922, he published "A Play for Puppets" in *The Morningside*, an undergraduate literary magazine. The religious skepticism of the play attracted the unfavorable attention of several New York newspapers, and Chambers subsequently withdrew from school "voluntarily" and spent the following summer touring Europe with Meyer Schapiro. He remained sensitive about this episode in later life; in *Witness*, he made a point of insisting that he left Columbia "entirely by my own choice," and he said nothing of his years at Columbia in his *Time* employment application.

Chambers returned to Columbia in the fall of 1924, but dropped most of his classes by semester's end, distracted by his chronically unstable family and struggling with a growing sense of pessimism about the state of the world. Like so many other young intellectuals of his day, Chambers became interested in Communism; lacking the anchors of ambition and career, he committed himself far more completely than most of his contemporaries, joining the Communist Party in 1925. "The dying world of 1925," he would later write, "was without faith, hope, character. Only in Communism had I found any practical answer at all to the crisis, and the will to make that answer work."

Whittaker Chambers quickly gravitated to Communist journalism as a way of earning a living. He began by making newsstand collections for the *Daily Worker* and later joined the staff of the paper, whose amateurishness he mordantly described in *Witness*. ("Each desk was a triumph of chaos. Editorial and human relations were much the same.") His literary gifts were quickly recognized, and he rose through the ranks, becoming an editor in 1927. But he left the *Daily Worker* in 1929 during the period of ideological turmoil which followed the expulsion of Jay Lovestone from the Communist Party for "right-wing deviationism."

Though Chambers had grown disillusioned with the sheer pettiness of party politics, he retained his eager faith in the Communist ideal as he then understood it. Late in 1930, he wrote in *Witness*,

---

* This account of Chambers's early years is based on Allen Weinstein's *Perjury: The Hiss-Chambers Case* (New York: Alfred A. Knopf, 1978), the most factually reliable discussion of Chambers's life available.

[i]t occurred to me that . . . I might try writing, not political polemics, which few people ever wanted to read, but stories that anybody might want to read—stories in which the correct conduct of the Communist would be shown in action and without political comment. While I was brooding on this, a small group of Midwestern farmers raided some stores for food. . . . All that I wanted to say fell into place at one stroke in my mind. I wrote through one night and by morning had completed a rather long short story.

The story, titled "Can You Make Out Their Voices," was published in the *New Masses*, a Communist-controlled literary monthly, in 1931. Chambers followed it with three more short stories on revolutionary themes. Edwin Rolfe, writing in the *New Masses* the following September, noted that "Can You Make Out Their Voices," the most popular of the four stories, "has been acclaimed both here and abroad as perhaps the most mature piece of working class fiction ever written in America." Moscow's *International Literature* said of "Can You Make Out Their Voices": "For the first time [in American writing], it raises the image of the Bolshevik."

Two decades later, Chambers noted that "it is easy to see that the stories are scarcely about Communism at all. . . . What they are really about is the spirit of man in four basic commitments—in suffering, under discipline, in defeat, in death. In each, it is not the political situation, but the spirit of man which is triumphant." Lionel Trilling, who saw in the *New Masses* stories the beginning of an irreversible decline in Chambers's writing, also linked them with the anti-Communism of his maturity: "Later, beginning with his work for the *New Masses*, something went soft and 'high' in his tone and I was never again able to read him, either in his radical or his religiose conservative phase, without a touch of queasiness." Trilling's discomfort with the course Chambers's writing had taken is understandable. While the *New Masses* stories are clearly the product of a writer of considerable technical skill and a genuinely poetic sensibility, they are marred by Chambers's sentimental portrayals of the Communist Party and its members. Chambers himself dismissed them in *Witness* as "scarcely . . . worth dwelling on." Still, they were several cuts above the general run of left-wing fiction in the Thirties, and the unmistakable narrative talent they display might well have developed, given time, into something more mature and fully formed.

But Whittaker Chambers had not joined the Communist Party to become an artist, and he was soon to abandon writing altogether. Invited to join the staff of the *New Masses* as a result of the popularity of his stories, Chambers shortly thereafter received another invitation—to become an underground courier for the Communist Party. No more articles would appear under Chambers's byline, in the *New Masses* or anywhere else. His budding literary career had been interrupted for more important things.

When Chambers broke with the Communist Party and resurfaced in 1938, he quickly began to look for a "visible identity" as a means of preventing his former colleagues from killing him before he had a chance to testify about his underground activities. Penniless and terrified, Chambers grabbed at the first opportunity that came his way: an offer from his friend Robert Cantwell to introduce him to T. S. Matthews, then a senior editor at *Time*. Cantwell, Matthews recalled in his memoir *Angels Unawares*,

> told me that [Chambers] was an extraordinarily talented writer (Cantwell likened him to André Malraux), an experienced journalist, and a Communist who was about to leave the party. Cantwell showed me a short story Chambers had written, and it *was* something like Malraux: it was shot through with the same murky flashes of rather sinister brilliance.

Matthews hired Chambers on the spot at a salary of $100 a week to review books for *Time*. At the age of 38, Whittaker Chambers was more than ready to put his underground days behind him and begin yet another new life. He cannot have imagined how new this one would be.

Time Inc. in 1939 bore little resemblance to the conglomerate that today serves as corporate umbrella for such varied enterprises as *People*, *Sports Illustrated* and Home Box Office. But the biggest difference between Time Inc. then and now was the fact that Henry Luce was very much alive and well when Whittaker Chambers went to work for *Time*.

It is difficult for younger readers to imagine just how much power Luce, the founder and editor-in-chief of *Time*, *Life* and *Fortune*, wielded during the Thirties and Forties. Luce's contemporaries had no such difficulty. Immensely popular with the general public, the Luce magazines were dismissed by progressives as vulgarly written, profoundly reactionary and dangerously influential. Luce himself was something of a popular celebrity. He was regularly criticized in articles like "Time . . . Fortune . . . Life . . . Luce," Wolcott Gibbs's viciously catty 1936 *New Yorker* profile of "ambitious, gimlet-eyed, Baby Tycoon Henry Robinson Luce." By the late Forties, a cadre of ex-*Time* writers had created an entire subgenre of novels about frustrated Luce hirelings who, seduced by grotesquely high salaries, spent their days slanting the news to suit their boss's Republican preferences. In Kenneth Fearing's *The Big Clock*, the most imaginative of these books, Luce was transmogrified into Earl Janoth, a publisher who accidentally kills his bisexual mistress and then attempts to pin the death on an unknown witness—who turns out to be the editor Janoth has assigned to investigate the killing for *Crimeways*, one of Janoth's magazines.

That this paranoid fantasy was later made into a successful Hollywood movie is ample testimony to the degree to which Luce had insinuated himself into the American consciousness, and Fearing neatly captured in his frenzied prose the fashionable attitude toward *Time* and *Life:*

What we decided in this room, more than a million of our fellow-citizens would read three months from now, and what they read they would accept as final. They might not know they were doing so, they might even briefly dispute our decisions, but still they would follow the reasoning we presented, remember the phrases, the tone of authority, and in the end their crystallized judgments would be ours.

In some ways, this description of Janoth Enterprises is not so very far from the truth about Time Inc. "The earliest prospectus for Time the Weekly Newsmagazine admitted to bias," Luce said in a memo to his staffers, "and we have never since that time submitted to any emasculating operation." Furthermore, Luce was in a position to peddle his biases to a huge audience. The total audience in mid-1944 for the various Time Inc. publications, including *Time*, *Life*, *Fortune* and the popular newsreel *March of Time*, was estimated by Luce biographer W. A. Swanberg as being "at least a third and perhaps considerably more of the total literate adult population of the country."

Luce's influence extended to culture as well as politics. *Time* devoted generous space to unsigned essays, articles and reviews dealing with the arts, and Luce's stable of house intellectuals during the Thirties and Forties included such unlikely employees as Dwight Macdonald, James Agee, Archibald MacLeish and Robert Fitzgerald. Fitzgerald, who edited the "Books" section of *Time* in 1939, remembered the workings of his department with obvious fondness thirty years later:

> We managed nevertheless to hack through . . . a fairly wide vista on literature in general, including even verse, the despised quarterlies, and scholarship. . . . One week we jammed through a joint review of Henry Miller, for which Jim [Agee] did *Tropic of Cancer* and I *Tropic of Capricorn*, both unpublishable in the United States until twenty years later. Our argument that time was that if *Time* ought to be written for the Man-in-the-Street (a favorite thought of the Founder), here were books that would hit him where he lived, if he could get them.

Peter Drucker, who worked at *Fortune* in 1940, observed that Luce ran his magazines "by working around people who had the title, office, and responsibility; by encouraging juniors to come to him but enjoining them not to tell their bosses; and by keeping alive feuds, mutual distrusts, and opposing cliques." Luce's managerial style may have increased the incidence of alcoholism among his employees and the frequency with which he was portrayed in third-rate novels, but it also helped make *Time*, *Life* and *Fortune*, for all their biases and factual misrepresentations, among the most consistently interesting magazines of their day.

Time Inc. was a company made for strong personalities, and Whittaker Chambers filled the bill with ease. A dozen of Chambers's colleagues at *Time* have recorded their first impressions of him, in most of which the adjective

"Dostoevskian" figures prominently, and drama critic Louis Kronenberger's description is as good as any:

> There was something about his—then not famous—appearance which was, to begin with, at odds with itself. The short, stocky, bullet-headed, barrel-chested, black-garmented figure had something almost stagily drab about it, something to make you wonder who would dress like that—a man on call as a pallbearer? An enthusiast of a sternly cheerless sect?

Chambers's behavior was as peculiar as his demeanor. According to Matthews, "there was such an air of suppressed melodrama about him that I should not have been greatly surprised if one day a Communist gunman had shot him down in one of the office corridors. . . . he always walked fast from the elevator to his office and, once inside, always shut and often locked his door." Understandably suspicious of strangers, Chambers made friends slowly, though the ones he finally made were invariably loyal. More often, he antagonized colleagues by his appearance and behavior and, most of all, by the militant anti-Communism which permeated his thinking—and writing.

"The driving force of my work at Time," Chambers wrote to Henry Luce in 1948, "has been a sense of mission, of calling." This mission, Chambers explained in *Witness*, was to take every possible opportunity "to clarify, on the basis of the news, the religious and moral position that made Communism evil." Anti-Communism was anything but popular in the early Forties, especially among *Time*'s staffers, whose Communist contingent was sufficiently large to publish a newsletter called *High Time*.* Not surprisingly, Chambers's enemies at *Time* were legion. "I had not been at *Time* a fortnight," he remembered, "before the Communists went to work on me. The fortnight's grace was due merely to the fact that the Communist Party had not yet discovered my presence at *Time* and warned its local members."

Two things kept Whittaker Chambers afloat: his talent and the steadfast patronage of Henry Luce. Chambers claimed in *Witness* that he was hired by *Time* "because I began a review of a war book with the line: 'One bomby day in June. . . .'" That review, published on May 1, 1939, was followed in the next issue by a cover story on James Joyce's just-published *Finnegans Wake*. New writers at *Time* rarely found themselves assigned to write cover stories on any subject whatsoever, much less on topics of such manifest opacity, but Chambers, T. S. Matthews wrote, "cleared this hurdle not only creditably but with extraordinary style."

Luce first noticed Chambers as a result of his 1940 review of the film version of *The Grapes of Wrath*. The child of Presbyterian missionaries to China, Luce was extremely receptive to Chambers's religious brand of anti-Communism.

* "For some goddamn reason," Luce allegedly replied when asked why he employed so many left-liberal types at *Time*, "Republicans can't write."

In 1942, Chambers sent Luce a memo on the subject in which he set forth at length what would later become familiar as the central theme of *Witness:*

> Tentatively, I am calling what I have written: The irreconcilable issues—Belief in God or Belief in Man. . . . I wish to show that these issues are the real line of cleavage in the modern world between conservative and revolutionary, cutting across all lines of economic class and political party; binding together proletarian and capitalist in a common belief in the primacy of God, just as they inexorably throw together those who believe in the primacy of secular Man no matter what their superficial differences or pseudo-religious trappings.

The *Time* writer who found Chambers's grim *Weltanschauung* most sympathetic was James Agee, Chambers's closest friend at *Time* and a man who, according to T. S. Matthews, was fully as difficult as Chambers himself. ("They were not only subject to temperamental tantrums but prey to fits of despair; and they had absolutely no feeling about going to press, one way or the other.") In spite of their erratic work habits, Chambers and Agee together transformed the "Books" section of *Time* into the magazine's most widely read department.

But Chambers continued to make enemies at *Time* with pieces like "The Revolt of the Intellectuals," in which he coolly surveyed the behavior of American intellectuals in the wake of the Nazi-Soviet pact and concluded that "it remains to be seen . . . whether the U.S. literary liberals will bring their intelligence to bear effectively on the side of democracy." Such assaults on the literary left were a staple of the "Books" section under Chambers. "Every week," one of his friends told him with unconcealed pleasure, "that mortar goes off in the last five pages of *Time.*"

Chambers's mortar was exchanged for a howitzer when T. S. Matthews, now managing editor of *Time*, made him editor of *Time*'s "Foreign News" section in the summer of 1944. It was the assignment he had been waiting for since his arrival at *Time*. As he told Luce:

> I have spent some 15 years of my life actively preparing for FN. Some of those years were spent close to the central dynamo that powers the politics of our time. In fact, I can say: I was there, I saw it, at least in a small way, I did it . . . in dealing with international affairs, I feel like a man in a dark but familiar room: I may bump against the furniture, but I'm usually sure where the door and windows are.

Chambers's new assignment immediately caused consternation among *Time*'s left-wing writers and editors. "Out of his earshot," a sympathetic colleague remembered, "the gibes, digs and cracks aimed at him showed that half his writing and research staff were ready not merely to dislike him but to hate him." Chambers understood what he was up against. "The fight in

Foreign News," he wrote in *Witness*, "was not a fight for control of a seven-page section of a newsmagazine. It was a struggle to decide whether a million Americans more or less were going to be given the facts about Soviet aggression, or whether those facts were going to be suppressed, distorted, sugared or perverted into the exact opposite of their true meaning."

Chambers fought back with the zeal of a practiced revolutionary, unhesitatingly rewriting stories filed by *Time*'s foreign correspondents to make them accord with his anti-Communist views. "The anti-Chambers faction ganged up," recalled Craig Thompson, a "Foreign News" writer from 1944 to 1945:

> By obstruction, slipshod work and endless arguments, they undertook to shut him up or push him out. . . . When necessary, Chambers did their work as well as his own. Not once or twice, but numbers of times I saw him beat his deadline only by working straight through from Saturday morning to Monday night. During this period I asked him one morning how he felt. It was purely a casual greeting. But the answer was savage: "Like a man in purgatory."

Typical of the battles over "Foreign News" was the imbroglio that began when Theodore White, then *Time*'s China correspondent, filed a lengthy cable from Chungking about the recall of Gen. Joseph Stilwell. The cable, White claimed in his autobiography *In Search of History*, told the story of "the chaos, decay, misery, sadness and dissolution in China," all of which he blamed on the corrupt regime of Chiang Kai-shek. But the story which appeared in *Time* on November 13, 1944, as rewritten by Chambers, explained that while Chiang was governing China "high-handedly," he was doing so "in order to safeguard the last vestiges of democratic principles in China" against the Chinese Communists. Luce, White wrote, "let the story of the crisis be edited into a lie, an entirely dishonorable story."

Chambers's most controversial exercise in interpretative journalism, however, was not a rewrite of an irate correspondent's cable but an original piece written in response to the news blackout surrounding the Big Three Conference at Yalta. "The Ghosts on the Roof" was a fable in which the shades of the murdered Czar Nicholas II and his family, having converted posthumously to Marxism, convened on the roof of their old palace and predicted with relish that the Soviet Union would engage in wholesale territorial expansionism after the war:

> "And now," said the Tsar, peering through the chink in the roof, "the greatest statesmen in the world have come to Stalin. Who but he would have had the sense of historical fitness to entertain them in my expropriated palace! There he sits, so small, so sure. He is magnificent. Greater than Rurik, greater than Peter! For Peter conquered only in the name of a limited class. But Stalin embodies the

international social revolution. That is the mighty, new device of power politics which he has developed for blowing up other countries from within."

Chambers nonchalantly dropped "The Ghosts on the Roof" on T. S. Matthews's desk one day, "saying that I might like to read it but that it was certainly not for *Time*." Matthews, who by that time had come around to Chambers's way of thinking on Communism, promptly scheduled the piece for publication as an unsigned *"Time* essay." The result was as swift as it was predictable: "I was visited by an unofficial delegation from the staffs of both *Time* and *Life*, urging me strongly not to print the piece: it would drive a wedge between the Allies, it was biased and bitter, irresponsible journalism, et cetera." Shaken by the fervor of his staff's opposition to the piece, Matthews delayed publication of "The Ghosts on the Roof" for a week before sending it to press.

Time was inundated by hostile letters after the piece appeared. Several letters were published along with a mollifying editor's note explaining that "The Ghosts on the Roof" notwithstanding, *Time* "neither said nor thinks that Soviet-U.S. collaboration is 'doomed to failure.' " Three years later, after the Iron Curtain had descended on Central Europe, *Time* reprinted "The Ghosts on the Roof" with an accompanying editor's note explaining that the piece "will repay a second reading as the world enters the new year, 1948."

When Henry Luce asked Chambers what he wanted to do at *Time* after the war, Chambers responded: "I should like to edit Foreign News for a long time to come." His wish was in vain. On August 23, 1945, Chambers blacked out on a train from Baltimore to New York. A serious heart attack had already forced him to take an eight-month leave of absence from *Time* in 1942. Fearing a relapse, Matthews promptly relieved Chambers of his duties as "Foreign News" editor and temporarily reassigned him to book reviewing. "From Foreign News," he wrote in *Witness*, "I fell down the whole flight of editorial steps."

What seemed at first a disaster soon proved a tremendous opportunity. Matthews assigned Chambers and James Agee to form a "Special Projects" unit designed, in Chambers's words, "to provide *Time* chiefly with cover stories which, because of special difficulties of subject matter or writing, other sections of *Time* were thought to be less well equipped to handle." Relieved of the pressures of weekly editing, Chambers embarked on a lengthy series of memorable cover stories. He described his new beat to Luce as "religion, culture, history, with a strong consciousness of current political forces and implications." His 1946 profile of the black contralto Marian Anderson provoked such an enthusiastic reader response that *Time* broke with its long-standing policy of anonymity and identified Chambers as the author in a "Letter from the Publisher":

The preliminary work involved talks with Miss Anderson, her mother, friends, teachers, impresarios, etc. But the important work was done, the writer claims, one afternoon when he shut himself up with a phonograph and a heap of records of Negro spirituals and played them over & over. . . . Marjorie Kinnan (*The Yearling*) Rawlings wrote: "My belated obeisances for the magnificent story on Marian Anderson. It was so beautifully written (my guess would be Whittaker Chambers) and gave such a spiritual lift." Novelist Rawlings guessed right.

Whittaker Chambers's last major writing project for Time Inc. was the text for *Life*'s illustrated "History of Western Culture." Though the first seven chapters were written by Chambers, *Life* also engaged a team of outside consultants led by Jacques Barzun, and Chambers regularly ran afoul of their advice. His essay on the Reformation, for example, was substantially rewritten by other hands as a result of what Chambers described as "a head-on clash of historical viewpoint—between the economic interpretation of history and the humane interpretation of history." This clash was the climax of a growing exasperation with Time Inc. editorial policy that was evident as far back as 1944, when Chambers wrote a series of book reviews for *The American Mercury* (under the pseudonym "John Land") in which he vented his historical pessimism with an explicitness that had no place in the confident pages of *Time* and *Life*.

Henry Luce's admiration for Chambers remained unshaken by the difficulties surrounding the writing of the "History of Western Culture" series. Late in 1947, Luce even asked Chambers to write his first signed piece for Time Inc., a dark fantasy in the manner of C.S. Lewis's *The Screwtape Letters* called "The Devil" which drew hundreds of admiring letters from the readers of *Life*. But after nine years of loyal service to Henry Luce, Chambers was beginning to chafe at the constraints of mass journalism. "The years are running out on me," he wrote to Luce on July 31, 1948. "I think I have something to say and little time to say it. . . . Has a man who has something to say and the ability to say it any real place at Time?" He told Luce that he wanted to resign from *Time* as of January 1, 1949, and thereafter write strictly on a freelance basis. Luce and Chambers, as was their custom, decided to meet for coffee at a corner drugstore on August 2 to discuss Chambers's future with the magazine.

The meeting took place as scheduled, but the agenda was changed due to circumstances beyond Chambers's control. On August 1, the House Un-American Activities Committee subpoenaed him to testify about his Communist past. "It seems to me that you will not want me around here any longer," Chambers told Luce the next day. "Nonsense," Luce replied, "testifying is a simple patriotic duty." On August 3, Whittaker Chambers went before HUAC and, in the words of Arthur Koestler, "committed moral suicide to atone for the guilt of our generation." His testimony made the front pages of every newspaper in America. It also brought his career as a journalist to an abrupt halt.

Public reaction to the revelation that a senior editor of *Time* had been a Communist was swift and negative. *Time* received 877 letters about Chambers between August 1, 1948, and January 14, 1949, including 103 subscription cancellations. But Luce initially remained faithful to his old friend, allowing him to take a leave of absence and picking up his legal fees. On September 6, *Time* published the following reply to the anti-Chambers mail it had received: "TIME was fully aware of Chambers' political background, believed in his conversion, and has never since had reason to doubt it. . . . TIME believes that Chambers's penetrating knowledge of the ways of Communism, at home and abroad, has been extremely valuable to TIME—and to TIME's readers."

Time's support of Whittaker Chambers was short-lived. The revelation that Chambers had actively engaged in espionage against the United States put more heat on Luce than he was prepared to tolerate. On December 10, eight days after he turned over the "pumpkin papers" to HUAC investigators, Chambers resigned from Time Inc. He retreated to his Westminster, Maryland, farm, spending the next four years testifying at Alger Hiss's perjury trials and writing his autobiography.

Early in 1950, an abortive attempt by Henry Luce to offer Chambers a job at *Architectural Forum* fell through when, at the last moment, Luce lost his nerve and told T. S. Matthews to withdraw the offer. "Our enemies can never do these things to us," Chambers wrote to Matthews. "Only our friends can drive the knife quite through our vitals." Though Chambers's anger was temporary, Luce's decision not to offer him a job left him convinced that he would never work again. "Due to my past," he wrote to a friend, "I was permanently unemployable, as I had more than once rather badly learned, in the one kind of work for which experience and ability fitted me."

Fortunately, Chambers was rehabilitated by the publication of *Witness*. Serialized in the *Saturday Evening Post* and chosen as a main selection of the Book-of-the-Month Club, *Witness* quickly became one of the biggest sellers of 1952. Whatever tension remained between Luce and Chambers was resolved by Luce's congratulatory letter of July 18: "I salute you, as of old, as a great writer. I salute you, too, of course, as a great warrior of the spirit—and as a friend."* Chambers subsequently published two articles in *Life;* he also contributed an essay on St. Benedict to Clare Boothe Luce's 1952 anthology *Saints for Now.* (His fellow hagiographers included Evelyn Waugh, Rebecca West and Thomas Merton.) But his real return to journalism took place not under the

---

* "He didn't like to talk about Harry Luce very much," William F. Buckley, Jr., says of Chambers. "It was a combination of a sort of affable sense of the person, the human being, combined with a feeling that Luce simply hadn't understood the apocalyptic nature of the challenge—which, of course, by Whittaker's standards very few people did."

comparatively respectable auspices of Time Inc. but in the thoroughly disreputable precincts of a right-wing magazine.

William F. Buckley, Jr., met Whittaker Chambers in 1954. The two men promptly began a friendship which lasted for the rest of Chambers's life. "I myself believe," the young Buckley had written three years earlier in *God and Man at Yale*, "that the duel between Christianity and atheism is the most important in the world. I further believe that the struggle between individualism and collectivism is the same struggle reproduced on another level." This passage could have come straight out of *Witness*, and soon after their first meeting, Chambers was deep in discussions with Buckley and Willi Schlamm, another old Time Inc. hand, about the possibility of starting a weekly conservative magazine.

Precisely because of the way in which it linked religious faith and anti-Communism, *Witness* had been enormously influential in the early days of the conservative movement. For Whittaker Chambers to have affiliated himself with the Buckley-Schlamm magazine would thus have lent it immediate prestige on the right. But Chambers was concerned about the predisposition of his potential colleagues to criticize Dwight Eisenhower and Richard Nixon. ("I shall vote the straight Republican ticket for as long as I live," Chambers later told Buckley. "You see, I'm an Orgbureau man.") Nor was the ideological thrust of the proposed magazine quite to Chambers's liking. As Buckley said in the first issue of *National Review:* "It stands athwart history, yelling Stop, at a time when no one is inclined to do so, or to have much patience with those who do." This statement was sharply at odds with Chambers's view of the proper role of conservatism in America:

> Escapism is laudable, perhaps the only truly honorable course for humane men—but only for them. Those who remain in the world, if they will not surrender on its terms, must maneuver within its terms. That is what conservatives must decide: how much to give in order to survive at all; how much to give in order not to give up the basic principles.

Whittaker Chambers finally decided not to take part in the founding of *National Review*. But he gradually changed his mind about the new magazine as it began to prosper. "He very definitely believed in the function of an enterprise," Buckley says, "and we were an enterprise. He wanted to be engaged, not merely a solipsist sitting and burning manuscripts on the farm and milking the cows. I think that [working for *National Review*] fulfilled in him, at least for a while, a sense of his spiritual requirements." Whatever his reasons, Chambers decided to sign on in the summer of 1957, and Buckley chartered a private plane and flew to Westminster to close the deal, agreeing to pay Chambers $125 a week.

On August 31, 1957, *National Review* issued the following statement: "We are honored to announce that Mr. Whittaker Chambers will resume his career as a journalist to join the staff of *National Review*. Mr. Chambers will write regularly, beginning in the next few weeks." Two months later, Chambers's first piece appeared, an essay called "Soviet Strategy in the Middle East." It was the first of a dozen full-length essays Chambers would contribute to *National Review* in the course of the next two years. Several other pieces were started but never finished, for Chambers, according to Buckley, "very definitely suffered from the sin of scrupulosity," and he preferred to burn articles that he considered unsatisfactory rather than submit them to *National Review*. "Let *us* judge whether what you write is publishable," a frustrated Buckley wrote to Chambers. "You have no judgment on such matters." By far the most influential of the pieces Chambers allowed *National Review* to publish was "Big Sister Is Watching You," a 1957 review of Ayn Rand's *Atlas Shrugged* in which Chambers, in Buckley's words, "read Miss Rand right out of the conservative movement," in the process provoking enormous controversy on the right ("Chambers the Christian communist," one angry reader wrote, "is far more dangerous than Chambers the Russian spy") and foreshadowing the great libertarian-conservative schism of the Sixties.

In the summer of 1958, Chambers began to travel from his farm in Maryland to New York on alternate Mondays to assist in preparing *National Review* for publication, writing unsigned paragraphs for the magazine's "The Week" section in addition to his regular signed essays. Unafraid of hidden conspiracies among the staff, Chambers relaxed in the congenial company of his new colleagues. ("I was astonished to discover," *NR* publisher William Rusher told John B. Judis, Buckley's biographer, "that he was this great corpulent ho-ho sort of guy.") But another heart attack felled Chambers in November, and though he continued to write for the magazine, he never took part in the production of *National Review* again.

While Chambers's relationship with Buckley remained close and unstrained, his connection with *National Review* was always fitful, and he never lost his initial skepticism of what Buckley called the magazine's "schematic conservatism":

> I am not a conservative. Sometimes I have used the term loosely, especially when I was first called on publicly to classify myself. I have since been as circumspect as possible in using the term about myself. I say: I am a man of the Right.

Whittaker Chambers's last *National Review* piece appeared on June 20, 1959. In September of that year, he enrolled in Western Maryland College as an undergraduate. "I feel the crying need," he told a friend, "of formal, intensive training in history, philosophy and economics." Fully occupied with his classes and increasingly dubious about the magazine's editorial policies, Chambers reluctantly resigned from *National Review* on November 2, 1959.

*   *   *

Whittaker Chambers died on July 9, 1961. "I always felt that Whittaker was the most misunderstood person of our time," Arthur Koestler said. "I loved him. I pitied him. The witness is gone, the testimony will stand." *Time* was not so loyal to its old senior editor. Its obituary dismissed *Witness* as "a work in the classic confessional mold, its fire somewhat dampened by its self-pity."

More than anything else, that curt judgment reflects the extent to which the Hiss case transformed Whittaker Chambers into a purely political symbol—a transformation that inevitably obscured Chambers's literary abilities. When thinking of Chambers's writings, it is hard not to recall the poem George Orwell wrote about himself in 1935: "A happy vicar I might have been/Two hundred years ago . . . But born, alas, in an evil time,/I missed that pleasant haven." Born in the same evil time, Whittaker Chambers, unlike Orwell, was unable to fully realize his great talent as a writer.

As a political figure, Chambers's legacy is equally ambiguous. Though John B. Judis argues in *William F. Buckley, Jr.: Patron Saint of the Conservatives* that "Chambers's insistence on a politics that maneuvered between what was possible and what was merely ideal . . . had an impact" on Buckley and, through him, the entire conservative movement, Buckley himself disagrees:

> I never embraced, in part because subjectively it's *contra naturam* to me, that utter, total, objective, strategic pessimism of his. Among other things, I think it's wrong theologically to assume that the world is doomed before God decides to doom it. So I never drank too deeply of his *Weltschmerz*. . . . It would be hard for me to trace any direct historical or intellectual influence that he had on me.

Except for *Witness*, Chambers himself appears to have had little regard for his own work. He made no attempt to collect his essays and articles; he left unfinished at his death a book called *The Third Rome* which, according to his friend Duncan Norton-Taylor, was to have been "a supplement to *Witness*."* In his journal, Chambers explained that he was writing *The Third Rome* for his son, believing that "the most important thing I could do for him was to report for him how his father had viewed certain aspects of our reality, what I believed the forces of reality to be, and how I saw their origins and development, which pulverized individual men, and caught peoples, like shovelfuls of corn in a hammermill."

It is one of the innumerable ironies of Whittaker Chambers's life that he never realized he had already written that report, not merely in *Witness* and in his letters but in the pages of *Time*, *Life* and *National Review*. What is surprising is not that his work remains a torso (given the circumstances of his life, one could hardly have expected anything else) but the degree to which his journal-

* The surviving fragments of *The Third Rome* were edited by Duncan Norton-Taylor and published in *Cold Friday* (New York: Random House, 1964).

ism was in fact worthy of his talent. "I've always been conscious of beautiful prose," William F. Buckley, Jr., said recently, "and in some of [Chambers's] prose I saw what I thought was journalistic perfection." Many of Chambers's later essays for *Time* and *Life* could be cited in evidence of this claim; Buckley had in mind a passage from "In Egypt Land," Chambers's 1946 profile of Marian Anderson:

> [The Negro spirituals] were created in direct answer to the Psalmist's question: *How shall we sing the Lord's song in a strange land?* For the land in which the slaves found themselves was strange beyond the fact that it was foreign. It was a nocturnal land . . . alive with all the elements of lonely beauty, except compassion. In this deep night of land and man, the singers saw visions; grief, like a tuning fork, gave the tone, and the Sorrow Songs were uttered.

Chambers's essays and articles are inevitably fragmentary in their impact, and it is impossible to know what directions his writing would have taken had HUAC not subpoenaed him immediately after his decision to break with Time Inc. Even so, to encounter Whittaker Chambers's journalism, for all its obvious imperfections, is to see Chambers not merely as a political martyr but as a critic and commentator of unusual power—to see, at last, the whole man.

ONE

A Member
of the
Revolution

CAN YOU MAKE OUT THEIR VOICES

(*New Masses*, MARCH 1931)

"IT'S LIKE A FIRE," said the young dirt farmer, Frank Frances, who had been on the prairie only a year. "Everything burns up. Now my cow's sick, and if *she* dies! Why is it? Why is it?"

"Oh, it's—on account of the sun," said the dirt farmer, Davis, whose smile seemed a part of his drawl. "Ever notice it up there, Frances? Warms the earth, makes the farmer's crops grow, ripens the apple on the bough! Just now it looks like a red hot silver cartwheel. Better take a long look at it, it's about the only 'cartwheel' you'll see this year. The drought won't stop with your cow, Frances. First *all* the water'll go, then the corn and the alfalfa. If there's anything left, that'll go, too. Then winter'll come—"

"And then?"

"Then," with a mock in the drawl as he looked the younger man over, "well, then—I don't know about you—but some folks ain't going to starve. Not so long as they have guns."

"Oh, you mean hunting."

"Yeah,—I mean hunting all right."

Davis was right: the water went first in the shallow holes in the range-lot. The bottoms blistered in blunt diamond shapes of dry mud, peeled, and the edges rolled up till they met in the middle.

The grass dried, the alfalfa burnt to stalks. The corn was stunted and never developed ears. What wheat there was never developed in the heads. The vegetables in the kitchen-garden died.

You could see the bottom of the wind-mill shaft, though it stood surrounded by aspens at the back of the farm-house: the leaves were thinned out as if it were autumn. And as less and less water was pumped up, it was cloudier and cloudier and tasted sickeningly of alkali. The poor farmer, Wardell, his wife and two boys, began to envy the aspen roots that went down and sucked up whatever water there was: they ended by hating them.

Animals overcame their fear to seek water near the houses. The Wardell boys found a gopher, a pair of jack-rabbits, dead. A red-headed woodpecker lay on the front path, its wings spread out. The boys took it into the house. In the shade it revived. They gave it a drop of their water; it uttered its single sharp scream; batting itself against the windows that were always shut now, to keep out the hot wind that blew the length of the prairie, and dried the saliva out of your mouth.

In front of the house the eldest boy killed a four foot rattler that put up no fight. The boys wanted to see if it would die before sundown; it hardly twitched after its skull was crushed.

Hearing the blows and the boys' shouts, their father came out. "The drought killed it, like everything else," he said, "no insult to your courage, John."

The two boys stood at either side of their father, looking at the snake. In their overalls both were lean, bony and tall, but shorter than the man. Like his, their hair was burned white by the sun and wind, but his had turned sandy. Their faces were tanned, but smooth and unwrinkled. His had three deep lines on either side. One where the ends of his mouth went down. Two, curving parallel, on either side, ran to his smooth, long jaw-bone whose end was part of the rough angle of his chin. His long curved nose ended almost on a line with his mouth, the nostrils running back sharply, almost parallel with the bridge, and lying close to his face.

His brown eyes had seldom been afraid. They had never been dismayed except by death. Both boys' eyes were blue.

"That shows what the drought has done," he said. "They never come out of the hills. I remember when Purcell started his mines there, the men drove the snakes down, but when he closed the mines, they went back again. There hasn't been one killed around here since I was your age. It's dead all right. If the drought hadn't weakened it, it'd twitch. Of course, it's all superstition that they don't die till after sundown. It's their nerves keep them twitching. They die hard, but this one's too weak."

By afternoon a crowd in dungarees had collected to see the snake. It was a pretext. There was no work for the men to do in the heat, with the crops burnt. They wanted to talk in a body.

They stood around the dead snake in a rough circle, mostly keeping their eyes on the ground.

The sun blazed just as mercilessly in the sky, going west, as it had at noon.

They talked about the dry spell.

"How long will it last?"

"Do you think there's any chance of rain?"

"The papers don't tell you, they say there's *hope*."

"They've been saying that a long time," said Wardell. "Besides, it don't make any difference if it does rain. The corn's done for."

"My cow died this morning," said the young farmer, Frances. He was considered a newcomer in the district, having been there only a year. They thought him a bad farmer, and unsteady, and they didn't like his whine.

So Davis turned and said drily, over his shoulder, "Mine died a month ago."

"Your wife hasn't got a baby," said Frances.

They ignored it. "What do you think, Wardell?" they said partly to shut off the young man's personal plaint—(Hell, you're worse off than us!)—"will the government help us?"

Wardell smiled. It was the first time any of them had ever asked *his* advice.

"What do you think the government'll do for you? Think you're the only poor farmer in the country?"

"They'll have to make the banks give us some kind of loans," said glum Davis.

"They'll have to give us some kind of credit to live."

"If the cows keep on dying, they'll have to do something about milk."

"They'll have to make the banks give us some kind of loans, worse! Much worse!" A Bohemian named Drdla spoke. Round, smooth face, and full lips smiling while he added his drop of gloom.

"What about winter coming? What are we going to do if there ain't any food? How are we going to feed the babies?" asked Frances, panicky.

"Anyway, *you've* got one less mouth to feed," said Davis, again over his shoulder.

Everybody laughed.

"A dead cow ain't no joke," said Frances.

Everybody laughed again.

"Well, the government ain't going to do anything, if you want to know," said Wardell. "At least, I'm not counting on it handing me anything. Of course you can look at things like Mort Davis: we don't have to feed the cows that die. On the other hand, they might feed the babies."

"They're stopping credit at the stores in Paris."

"Think they'd give it through the winter? To all of us? They've got to make a living, too."

"You mean there ain't going to be nothing to eat?"

"There's plenty to eat in the stores in Paris. All you've got to have is the money to buy it. In fact, you can eat like a hog—if you're a storekeeper," said Wardell. "We only *grow* the food—when we can: they *sell* it. But as I haven't got the money to buy and neither have you, I guess we'll take it or starve."

They understood only slowly.

"You mean you'd steal it?" asked an alarmed voice.

"I mean that when I'm hungry I like to eat. And when my wife and children are hungry, I'm likely to take food where I can get it. If that's stealing, then you say I like to steal. Does that hurt your feelings?"

Most of the men had driven over in flivvers. A heavier car drew up. A heavier man got out and came over.

Purcell had been a colonel in the war. "Talking about the drought?" he asked, eyeing each face in turn.

"Wardell's John killed a rattler in front of the house," said Davis. "The folks came over to find out just what a dead snake looks like. Would *you* like to see?"

A voice as vibrant and deep as Purcell's was a surprise, issuing from the small slit of his lips, while his full angular jaws worked up and down. He spoke deliberately, with his own emphasis.

"This 'drowt', or 'drooth' as Wardell calls it, has been a lucky break for you, Wardell. You were running pretty low in your line of knocks when this bad luck came along." Little gray eyes glared gleefully on either side of his small, fighty wedge of turned-up nose.

"The 'general' got his chip on his shoulder," one of the Wardell's boys whispered to the other.

"On his face, you mean, to keep his eyes from running together," John Wardell said aloud, staring at Purcell's nose.

"Some of us call it 'drowt' and some of us call it 'drooth'," said Wardell, "but they both mean that the crops are done for, water and forage are dried up, the cattle are dying, and we'll be needing food when our credit gives out at the stores in town. Unless, of course, the banks want to make us long term loans."

Purcell, the richest farmer in the district, had a finger in the Bank of Paris, of which his son-in-law was cashier.

"The trouble with Wardell is," Purcell said, preserving his good temper, but talking rather to the gathering than to Wardell, "the trouble with him is that he spends too much time nights reading those books he has in the house, and looking up the long words in the dictionary. So he gets sleepy and sore at the world, don't you, Jim?" The men smiled, being let in on the joke by the big boss. "What was that book, in that package of yours that came undone in the post office that time?" Purcell was also post-master. " 'Socialism *Yew*topian and Scientific'!" He laughed. "Well, every man's got a right to read what he wants to in his own house, I guess, if he don't try to force others to think his crazy ways, too. But I went to school with Jim Wardell, didn't we, Jim, and I know he's still the same wild Jim, wild ideas, but a heart of gold. So if you get hungry, and he tries to feed you Socialism *Yew*topian and Scientific, if you don't feel full, and I guess you won't, I think the Red Cross will do more for you all. I got to go. So long, Jim. So long, boys."

"The Red Cross!"

"The Red Cross!"

"They did fine work in the Mississippi flood!"

"The Red Cross!"

They began to drift away from Wardell's to town or home.

"So it's the Red Cross next," thought Wardell. "I know you dirt farmers! You've got to find out for yourselves. So it's the Red Cross you'll find out about now! And when you have, and I guess you'll get your chance this time, you'll be ready to show them a few things—"

"Say, Frances," he said when they were the last two left, "we can spare some of our milk for a baby, I guess. While the cow's still giving any. Drop in after milking. Throw that snake off the path, boys," he called from the porch, not to hear the young man's thanks.

Two days later the snake was a length of shrivelled skin and spinal bones. The sun had dried it up.

It dried up the last "pot-hole" in that stretch of prairie, too, and the alkali sparkled thick on the bared bottom, with a likeness to snow strange under the red hot sun.

The "yellow-heads" from the "pot-hole" gathered in great flocks, and the farm people would stop to watch them escaping through the sky, deserting the country, as in the fall when they feel the cold coming.

"Say, Lil," said Purcell to his daughter at supper one night, "I thought Frances' cow died. I thought he'd be buying milk from us now. He's got a baby, ain't he?"

Purcell had been one of the first farmers to turn to dairying when the borers gnawed away the margin of profit the banks and railroads left on corn in that section. He had a fine herd of Holsteins and, as he could afford to ship in ensilage and water by the tank, had preserved them through the drought, leaving it to the dry spell to carry off the few heads owned by his small competitors.

"See, you don't know everything down at the bank," said his daughter, a fair, fat girl with big breasts, glasses and a gold incisor. "I happen to know that Jim Wardell is *giving* Frances milk."

"*Giving* it to him? I wonder if Frances has ever seen the way Wardell keeps his cow? I wouldn't give any baby of mine that milk. I guess Jim's got to give it away. He couldn't sell it. Well, it's only a few cents anyway."

Frances used to come a little early and sit in the kitchen a few minutes in the evening while Wardell was milking the cow.

"And how's the baby and how is Hilda today?" Mrs. Wardell would ask.

"It's very bad up there. Since she lost her milk, it's terrible. And then the cow dying. Yours is the only cow left around here, except Purcell's."

"Take this home to them," she would say when he went, his milk-can full. Wardell never asked her what was in the nameless parcels. But even the boys were going oftener to bed hungry, after eating everything there was. Sometimes there was no milk on the Wardell's table.

"The cow won't last much longer at this rate," said Wardell to his wife one night. Such a ridiculous sentence to make her heart almost stop beating!

One evening Ann Wardell thought Frances looked as if he hadn't eaten for two days, so she set some boiled dried beans, part of supper's only dish, before him. Wardell came in without the dribble of milk, and sat down.

"Don't you think the time is coming, Frank," he said, "when the poor farmers, people like you and me and the Davises and Wiggens and Drdla, will have to go and take the food out of the store-windows in Paris? There's always plenty of it there."

"You're a Socialist, ain't you?" Frank asked, ever so slyly, over his spoonful of beans.

("The branding reproach of Communism!")

"I'm a Communist, Frank."

"What does that mean?"—the beans suspended midway to the mouth.

"In this case, it means that I'm for unlimited free groceries and meat to all poor farmers. No rent for two years. Free seed. Free milk for babies."

"I guess you Reds want everything free," said Frank.

"I guess you will, too, before the baby's dead." Hard and bitter to hammer it home.

"Jim!"

"I know what I'm telling him, Ann. We're both dirt farmers, poor men, both came from the same class, so there's no reproach in your taking something from me when you need it, Frances. And there's no reproach meant, in my telling you that your kid would be dead but for your getting the milk from my cow. You couldn't buy it. Not from me, I wouldn't sell it to you. And you couldn't buy it from Purcell because he *would* sell it to you, and you haven't got the money to buy it. Well, my cow's dying. Now what do you think about having milk *free?*"

"Dying? Your cow's dying?" Frances was the color of milk himself.

"She'll be dead by morning. Now I'm going out to see what I can do for her. There won't be any milk tonight or from now on. But don't forget that it was the dirty Communist, the Red, the Bolshevik who wants everything free for every poor farmer, who kept the kid alive till now."

Frances stumbled, with the empty milk-can, out the door Wardell had left open, past the barn where he saw a light, and the cow lying on her side, and Wardell bending over her.

"Jim's cruel, but Jim's right," said Mrs. Wardell. Her husband did not come back into the house, and she waited half an hour before she slipped out and across the field paths, with another milk-can.

Lily Purcell came to the door. "Oh, hello, Mrs. Wardell." The gold tooth haloed in a golden smile.

"Our cow's died," said Ann, holding out the can.

"Oh, she died, huh? Mr. Frances said she was going to."

"Did Frank get some milk?"

"Well, we milked early, Mrs. Wardell, and we had only enough for ourselves. Mr. Frances didn't have no money. There's so many like that now."

"I've got some money," Ann said.

"Well, I'll see if mother could spare a little. Give me the can."

Ann walked in the open door where it was plain to see the chickens also walked.

They didn't hear her come.

Hilda Frances was not crying. She was walking the bare floor, saying, "Baby, baby, baby, baby!" When she reached the wall she would stop. When she paced back, she would begin again, "Baby, baby, baby!" It was Frank, with his head in his arms, on the table, who was crying.

"We did get some milk, after all," said Ann Wardell.

Hilda stopped. "Milk! God bless you, Mrs. Wardell, God bless you! Oh, God bless you!"

"A funny God that brings babies into the world, and takes away their mother's milk, and kills the cows that feed them, Mrs. Frances. But let me have a look at the baby before I go."

"You got milk for them at Purcell's!" Jim said when she came in.

"Yes."

He frowned but said nothing.

"You've got to stop," he told her a week later. "You can't do it. The cold's coming. We've only got so much. You're taking the food from John and Robert."

"You can't let a baby die."

"Worse things will happen before this winter's over. What good does it do? Keep it alive another week. You'll *have* to stop then. And you're only taking it away from the boys. They'll be up against it soon enough. That's the trouble with your charity. You can't keep it up, and it only makes Frank and his wife hope it's forever. It makes them content. And they can't be. When he sees the baby's going to die, he'll cry for milk and food along with the rest of us. He's got to. It's coming. It's coming soon."

"Say, are you really a Socialist?" asked Davis, driving his Ford up to the house.

"What do you want to know for?" asked Wardell with his foot on the running board. "Bunch of the boys want to lynch me?"

"Not yet, Jim," grudging a lop-sided smile since his face was lop-sided. "Hell *is* going to break loose around here soon, if things don't get any better, and they may be wanting you then. But this here I came about, is personal business. There's a family of greasers squatting on my land, and they won't get off. They've got four kids, and the woman just had twins last night. No doctor! They haven't got no food, and the man says they ain't got no gasoline so they can't go on, they've just got to stop on my place. Well, they ain't going to. We can't feed the white men up there now, let alone greasers. Of course, I can have them run in down in Paris. But on account of the woman having those kids last night, I thought maybe—some of your Socialist ideas—you'd let them stay on your place."

"I'm not a Socialist," said Wardell.

"What the hell are you then?"

"I'm a Communist."

"What's that?"

"Well, just now it means I want free food for every farmer that can't pay for it, free milk for the babies, free rent, and if we can't get free food, I'm going and taking it."

"What did you say you called yourself?"

"A Communist."

"That's like a Red, Russians, huh?"

"No, workingmen and poor farmers, like you and me."

"Do you have a secret society?"

"The Communists are a political party, called the Communist Party of the United States."

"And they believe in free food?"

"Yes."

"I'll be over tonight," said Davis, "I've got to go to Paris now. Goodbye, Jim. I'll tell those Mexicans to come down here."

"If you won't let them on your own place."

That day it began to snow, suddenly, before dark.

"Ann, I think Davis will come over to us," he said as he sat down to the boiled beans.

"Come over?"

"To *us*. He's coming here tonight."

"Jim, be careful."

"I'll be as careful as I can. The time is past when we can afford to be too careful. Stay up tonight, boys, and listen to what Mort Davis and I talk about."

The deep snow separated the farms, but it made starvation general.

At first they burned the fence-posts, those who had them; the others, the floor boards in the barns. Those who had no barns burned their hen-coops. But after charcoal, what?

The men took out their guns, the pretext being to hunt jack-rabbits, though most of them had died in the drought. But the women had no pretext and no will to escape the wailing of the babies, for whom there was no milk, and the whimpering and gaunt eyes of the older children.

The men made an honest search for game, but by afternoon most of them drifted into Paris, with their guns under their arms.

Many of them passed the bank windows, never suspecting what was going on within. Purcell saw them as he leaped to his feet in the fury of wrangling with his son-in-law, the cashier, and old Dr. Jesperson, the president, and walked to the front window of the Bank of Paris.

"They're walking around the streets with guns now, and you talk about closing the bank! I knew you'd do this," he screamed, shaking his fist at his son-in-law, the heavy jaws turkey red. "I knew you'd do this, I knew you would! You and your damn fool farm mortgages! And now the bank will crash, and so will you, and so will the Doc! But I won't! I took care of that!"

The main road entered Paris after turning a right angle, around an osage hedge, and crossing a creek, dried up in the drought, on a wooden bridge. It passed the double row of store-fronts, and returned to the prairie on the other side. Two tracks led south and north to scattered farms. The latter had once been busy when Purcell worked his ground-level mines in the hills, twenty miles to the north. They had been closed down for years.

Wardell and Davis found about thirty armed men on the main street.

"I don't know what to do," said a little man named Shays, "my baby's dying. He's dying all right, dying. And we haven't milk."

"Neither have we!"

"We haven't had any for two days. My baby's dying."

"We got some but my credit's gone. We can't even get any food. But milk comes first."

"There's only one place you can get milk around here," said Wardell.

"Where's that?"

"At Purcell's."

"We know that! Where are we going to get the money? He's not giving it away, and he don't trust now."

"Did you say your kid was dying, Dan?" Wardell asked Shays.

"Yes, he'll die if I don't get him milk."

"I'm glad you got a rifle with you. Will you come with me to Purcell's and make them give you milk?"

The little man blenched. "Take it from Purcell, you mean?"

"That's what I mean. Will anyone else come with us? Will you, Doscher?"

"No, I won't. I know your Socialist ideas! What do you think I am, a thief?"

"Will you lend me your gun, Doscher?" asked Davis. "I'd like to go with Jim and Shays. You know, our farms are too near together, and I can't stand listening to your baby scream itself to death, even if you can."

"I'll go!"

"I'll go!"

"I'll go!"

In the end, Doscher went, too.

They tramped out the western side of the town, fighting their way through the snow, and, in half an hour, were at Purcell's.

Wardell led them to the back door.

"Lilian," he said, "some of these men have babies, and all of us have children. None of us have any money. If those babies don't get their milk tonight, some of them will die. They'll all die in a week or two. Will you give us milk?"

"*Give* it to you? How can I give it to you, Jim Wardell? You're crazy!"

"You've got to give it to us."

"How can I give it to you? To *all* of you?"

"You've got to give it to us. We know how to milk cows just as well as you do. If you don't give it to us, we'll go down to the barn and take it."

She screamed. "I won't."

"In other words, you want us to take it. All right, we'll take it!"

"Wait, wait a minute, wait!" She flew into the house.

All three men sat stiff and terrified as the phone rang in the bank.

"Well then, I'll answer it," said Purcell.

"They want you to *give* it to them?" he shouted. "*Guns?* Oh, I see," he said, "Wardell! I see. Well, give it to them! Give it to them! *Give it to them!*" He missed the hook as he slammed the receiver against the case.

"There's only enough here to last two days at most," said Wardell as they broke up.

"We'll make it last five," they said, laughing.

The night the bank failed, Frank's baby died.

He had not been out of the house for three days. He knew nothing of the milk seizure at Purcell's. The wailing of the baby and his own hunger kept him awake, but at last exhaustion stretched him out. He awoke with a start to see Hilda bending over the drawer where they kept the child in some dirty blankets. It seemed to him as if someone had screamed.

"What is it, Hil?" She had a blanket in her hand.

"I think baby's dead."

"No." He leaped up. He looked at it and listened for breathing.

"I'll get the doctor."

"Oh, what's the use of the doctor, he won't come now."

"He will!"

"You can't get him in time, you know there's no gas in the Ford."

"I'll go. I'll run. I'll get him. I'll get him."

He did not tie his shoes. He stumbled where he broke through the snow. He felt the ice-crust under his hands as he fell, and its edges cut his ankles. But he kept running.

"How can I get two miles through this snow?" asked old Dr. Jesperson, the bank president, who for some reason was up alone at that hour, with a bottle of whiskey on the table.

"You can make it in the car. You must try to save her, Doctor, you must."

"Oh, don't plead, don't plead, I know I've got to go! God damned Hippo-cratic oath!"

"Of course, it's dead," said the old man, standing well back from the drawer which smelt of wet as he of whiskey. "Been dead a couple of hours! What do you mean bringing a baby into this world when you can't take care of it! What do you get married for? I don't suppose there's a crumb of bread in the house," he said, looking at the walls. "Damndest profession in the world! Damndest profession in the world! Now there'll be an epidemic of dying. There ought to be."

Hilda watched him drive away.

Frank was sobbing with his head on the table. Suddenly he straightened up. "Wardell killed her," he shouted. "He stopped the milk on her, I know he did. The dirty lousy Red. He did it. He killed her, God curse him!"

"Don't be a fool," said Hilda quietly, "I killed her myself. Do you think I wanted to see her tortured to death by inches? I killed her with the blanket.—God?"

He sprang at her, but she ran away from him and out the door, slamming it. She ran farther, thinking he would follow, but he stopped beside the baby.

She saw the big square outlines of Purcell's house and barns against the white snow. Milk! She had barely passed it when it seemed to her as if an army were pursuing her, crunching through the snow, with bells and sounds like faint horns, snorting. She was overwrought. Vengeance is mine, saith the Lord. Might He find pleasure in taking vengeance on a mother who had smothered her baby? Was He after her? She ran, wilder and wilder, mad with a desire to scream, but terrified to silence. Finally she just began to laugh. It was much simpler, and it was all funny, and she just laughed and laughed and laughed.

What she had taken for God was Purcell's blooded Holsteins. He was removing the whole herd, in the dead of night, to the livery stable in Paris where there was law and order. There would be no more free milk.

When the snow fell, they moved the Mexicans into the upstairs room. The Wardell boys slept in the remnants of hay in the barn loft. It was bitter cold, and they were grateful for the meetings that postponed till late the necessity of trying to sleep.

Wardell and his wife, Davis, and the two boys would sit around the table, with the five sheets of paper and pens before them, and the bottle of ink in the middle. Carrillo, the Mexican sat to one side. He spoke only broken English, but his black eyes gazed fixedly from either side of his nose, with its coarse pores, in an undefeated effort to grasp by chance word and gesture what the others were discussing.

There was no hectograph, no mimeograph, no typewriter. Everything had to be written by hand. There were five right hands. At the top of their first handbill they printed:

"YOUR MILK GIVES OUT TODAY!
WHAT ARE YOU GOING TO DO NOW?"

The bills were tacked to the front porches of houses on each of the four roads into Paris, east and west, north and south. Drdla had one, and Doscher, Davis and Wardell. One the boys took to Ryder's, a farmer who lived ten miles farther to the south where the men seldom came to town.

"Are you going to the meeting at Wardell's?" Doscher asked Shays, who was reading the tacked up bill.

"Of course, I'm going. Who got us milk?"

"He got it for us all right last time, it might not be so easy now. Jim's a queer bird. He's a Socialist."

"Well, what of it? Anyway, I hear he ain't a Socialist."

"Ain't a Socialist?"

"No, they've got some other name for it. They call it a Comm*un*eist."

"What's that make him?"

"It makes him for us, I guess. That's all I know about it. I'll see you at Wardell's."

"Why should I go to Wardell's?" Frances answered Davis. "Don't you think I know what Wardell's up to? He'll be running for something next. Anyway, the Red Cross is going to help us, ain't it? The paper says so."

"You'll find out what a whole lot of good the Red Cross is going to do you, when they get here—if they get here."

"I guess I'll be there," Wiggens, a heavy-set farmer, who had just began to feel the pinch, told Drdla. Drdla objected to tacking up the handbill, so the men simply came to his house and read it. Wiggens stood reading it with his wife, a tall spare woman whose black eyes looked in a perfectly level line out of the bones of her face.

"I'll be there," she said. "Look at them!" The five children sat in the back of the Ford. They made no effort to get out.

"But I see the Red Cross is going to help us," her husband objected. "They won't like this." He rapped the handbill with the back of his hand.

"We may need them both," said his wife.

* * *

Purcell's frantic wires to the Governor, and Senator Bagheot in Washington, described the seizure of milk at a local farm by one hundred armed farmers, led by loafers. A supplementary wire described the leader, one Wardell, a chronic trouble-maker.

The Senator was handed both wires at breakfast by his young wife, who continued to act as his secretary.

"I did not want to disturb you with them last night, Senator," she said.

Bagheot read them through with a concentration that was partly the difficulty that he had in seeing; at seventy he would not hear of glasses.

"A cheap demogogue!" the old man exploded when he had finished the characterization of Wardell. "A cheap demagogue! Trading on the sufferings of those poor farmers! They always come to the front in times like these."

He acted with promptness and efficiency. Talking over long distance with the Governor of the State, he made sure that the Red Cross would be operating in Paris the next day.

"Even a very little relief . . ."

"I can't hear you," said the Governor.

"Well, why the Devil can't you hear me! What's the matter with your connection? I said even a very little relief will quiet the mob. Unless you take some such measures, the merchants must either put their stocks in the streets, or machine-guns in their windows."

"Yes, yes. Everything of that sort will be seen to. How is it in Washington, as cold as it is here?"

"Well, we've had a little snow," the voice quavered.

Senator Bagheot then dictated to his wife his statement to the press. "Conditions in my State, brought to my attention today by the newspapers, show extreme suffering in the country districts. I shall move for Federal aid tomorrow. Congress has not treated the suffering resulting from this winter sympathetically, but I believe that when the members of Congress return, after facing their constituents, their action will be a little different."

"That's good, eh, huh?" he chuckled to his wife. "I guess that will show them who lives in a glass house, politically speaking!"

"Remember, Dr. Styres said you were to have no undue excitement."

The State organization of the Red Cross proved itself equal to the situation which it was called upon by the Governor to control. Over night, it completed plans for immediate relief for all who could furnish evidence of bona fide suffering.

In this work it was planned to cooperate with local community leaders, since they were assumed to be better informed as to local persons, cases and needs, rather than to "foist an alien organization on the town from without."

They simply sent a supervisor, who sat beside Lily Purcell, the local head of the Red Cross, in the little relief station they had rented in her brother's empty store.

Back of the counter, at which they sat, were cans of milk, bags of flour, sugar, etc.

"We ought to spread some bags of flour on the counter. There's nothing like it for psychological effect, for raising the spirits of hungry people," said the Red Cross supervisor, who, like Miss Purcell, wore glasses. "It's unfortunate, though, that you had this thaw last night. It's opened the roads, and of course it would have been better if we had had a few days to get things firmly in hand. It will probably let more of them through to that meeting at Wardell's, too. But I calculate that our opening at the same hour as the meeting will also have its psychological effect. I guess they'll be here, rather than there."

That morning the Mexicans left Wardell. He heard them talking all night, Carrillo urging, his wife opposing, but at last her opposition growing fainter, perhaps tired out.

In the morning they all came down into the lower room. The children stood in a ragged line, mute, and stared. The wife, looking much like the children, but with a twin on either arm, also stared.

"Companero Ooardell," said Carrillo, "we are going away. You have no food for yourselves. The roads opened last night. Companero Ooardell, you are a good man. Your wife, she is a good woman. Your sons, they are good young men. If I go east or if I go west, if I go north or if I go south, I will always come back here. Sometimes I will come to take, sometimes to bring. But I will always remember that you saved our lives. I thank you, my wife thanks you, and my children thank you. Goodbye, companeros."

His wife smiled and nodded, and they all went away, having somehow gotten their Ford to start.

"So the Carrillos have left you?" said Davis. "I guess that Mex figured there was going to be shooting, and a fight's a poor place for a greaser."

"Think so? I wouldn't be too hopeful about the shooting, Mort. In the first place, what are we going to get by shooting—yet? In the second place, though that crowd learned some kind of a lesson when they took the milk from Purcell, they've had time to think it over. You'll see, those that come here today are a little scared of themselves."

"You forget their kids are still crying."

"I don't forget it at all."

Before noon the little house was so packed with men and women's bodies, you couldn't walk a foot. The heat rose perceptibly and with it the smell of cow and horse manure and humans.

"We can't talk in here," Wardell called out. "Everybody outside!"

"Line up those cars in a half dozen rows," he said, "and sit in them." His own car was standing in front of the house. It was open and the top was down. His wife got in, and Davis. Wardell stood on the front seat and talked.

"I'm glad to see that there are so few of us here," he said. "It means that only the most reliable and the most needy are here. It means we can move together easier, and have more confidence in each other. And we need that.

"I'm glad to see, too, that you women have brought your babies with you. It's another sign that you're not afraid, and it means that we'll never lose sight of why we're going to Paris.

"And we're going down to Paris. We're starving, and we're going to Paris to get food. I hear that the Red Cross is going to give it to us. Now I want to tell you *how* they're going to give to us.

"First of all, before they give us anything, we've got to prove that we're not 'imposters'. That's what they're calling some of us now. In other words, we've got to prove that we really are starving to death. Can you prove it?"

Growls.

"Then, when we've proved that we're starving, I want to tell you *what* they'll give us."

"How do you know what they're going to do?" asked a voice. Other voices: "Ssh! Ssh!"

"Never mind, Ar Crocker, just remember that we *did* tell you, when the time comes," Davis bawled back.

"They're going to give us *one* loaf of bread! Not one apiece, but one to each family! One bag of flour—the same! Maybe some bacon!"

"How much milk?" called a woman.

"Enough for two days."

"What good does two days do? We had a day's before, and we made it last three. Now if they give us two day's, and we make it last five, what'll we do when it's gone?"

"It's the same with all the rest of the relief. It will last two days. What are you going to do when it's gone? There's food enough in the stores of Paris to last us for weeks. But they won't give it to us, because the Red Cross will only give a little money for a place like Paris, and most of that went to buying Purcell's milk for today's relief. Never mind how I know!

"The thing for us to do now, is to force them to give some food today. And to do that, we've got to all go down together. If we go in one by one, they'll cheat us, or they'll say we're not starving, and we won't get any relief at all.

"Now before we go, I want to ask you something. How many of you have guns in your cars? Nine, ten, eleven. You, too, Doscher? Good! Every man who brought his gun today, was with us when we forced Purcell to give us milk. Those men learned something. But you've got to be doubly careful today not to use your guns unless somebody starts shooting at you first. I'll tell you why. We're starving. But they don't want to give us food. They give us food only to keep us quiet. You men with guns are the leaders in forcing them to give us food. Because they're afraid of guns. These babies and these children and some of you keep on fighting. They'll kill you, because you're out-numbered. And when you're dead, Purcell and the rest will be boss here, and your babies will go just as hungry, but there'll be nobody to get them food. The time is not quite ripe for shooting. Do you understand?"

"Yes."

"We can threaten them today, we can force them, we may even *have to* shoot, but don't fire a gun if you can help it. Not today!

"Now, the cars with guns in the lead! Let's go!"

The grating of thirty gears, slipping from first to second, to high.

"I don't see how he can possibly claim to be starving," said Lily Purcell to the Red Cross supervisor. (The milk Frances did not buy!) "His baby died two days ago, and nobody knows where his wife is!"

"Well, at least he can't have any milk. That settles that right off!"

Frank Frances had gone to the meeting. He was one of the first outside the relief store doors when they opened. For fifteen minutes he had been attempt-ing to establish his status as a starving man. Meanwhile the line grew behind him, at first grumbling, then shouting, "Give him something!"

"This is no way to begin!" The supervisor scanned their heads disap-provingly. "Too many eye sockets!" he thought. He was unwilling to cede ground at once, and would not give Lily Purcell the order, "Let him have some bread."

Suddenly there was a shout from the edge of the crowd. "They're coming! They're coming!"

From the west the line of thirty cars swept into the town, two abreast. They stopped in the middle of the street. The men and women got out, the men with their guns, the women with their babies.

The crowd opened for thirteen men with guns. "Now we'll get some food!"

Wardell and Davis stopped where Frances stood suspended in an act of appeal. Lily Purcell and her supervisor stared.

Shays, Doscher, Drdla, staring back over the ends of their guns, which they rested on the floor.

Mrs. Wiggens with a baby in her arms had pressed to the front.

"What are you going to give us?" said Davis.

"Yes, what are you going to give us?" asked Mrs. Wiggens.

"I don't know that we're going to give you anything. At least until you put those guns down," he said, tonguing his lips that were like earthworms that have been out too long in the rain.

"Give that man some bread," said Wardell.

"I don't think he deserves any. And I'm not taking orders here, I'm giving them!"

Several men laughed.

"And you, Lily, give Mrs. Wiggens some flour."

"She *certainly* don't need any. I know her well. She's a regular trouble-maker." She appealed to the Red Cross knight.

"Give her some flour!"

"Don't give her flour!" said the supervisor. "These people are not ready for relief. They don't know how to take it. *This place is closed!* Get out!"

"Take it, men," said Wardell. "Don't hurt anybody. See that everybody gets a bag, Mrs. Wiggens."

"Oh! Oh! They're stealing our flour! They're stealing our flour!" Lily continued to scream until the store was stripped and empty. Mrs. Wiggens, who had been passing out the bags, was the last to leave. As she took up her own bag, Lily tried to stop her.

"You can't have that, you *can't* steal it!" She hung on to the bag with the grip of a kind of death she felt freezing her. Finally Mrs. Wiggens wrenched it loose. The girl's nails had torn the bag.

"Sow!" cried Mrs. Wiggens, seeing the waste. She struck Lily Purcell across the lower face with the bag. The flour whited her face like a clown's. Her glasses fell off and smashed. She screamed.

"She's killing me! She's killing me! She's stealing! She's killing me! She's stealing!" She was sobbing, a gulping blubber that shook her breasts.

"Shut up!" Mrs. Wiggens herself screamed. "Shut up! I'm sorry I hurt you!"

Picking up the baby, she ran out of the store.

"Into the stores, men!" cried Davis and Wardell at opposite ends of the street. Some of the storekeepers tried locking up.

"If you don't open that door, we'll come in through the window," shouted Drdla.

The doors opened.

It was dark before all the milk had been taken from Purcell's cows, and the food apportioned and piled in the cars.

They started on a signal from Wardell, moving more consciously together as a mass than ever before. As they left the village, they were grim, still. Once outside it they began to laugh. They felt strong. They also felt afraid.

By then it had begun to snow again, fat, heavy flakes.

"How long do you think this lot will last?" asked Davis in the head car with Wardell.

"The food about two weeks, the milk, of course, only a few days."

"Then?" asked Davis.

"Well, they'll never *let* us do this again."

"You mean—shooting?"

"I suppose so. Everything depends on quick organization now, Mort. Shays and Doscher and Drdla and Mrs. Wiggens, and Frances, and any others we're sure about. You can be sure Purcell sent the SOS over the wires by now. Tomorrow or the day after, they'll have the troops here."

"I've been wondering about Purcell's old mine shafts in the hills."

"Oh, you have?"

Later Davis said, "I think you're wrong about Frances, Jim. I don't trust him."

"Of course, you may be right. It's true he's weak. It takes a lot to bring him over, and a lot to keep him going. But he's been through a lot by now. We've got to make the most of what we've got."

The cars moved slowly, so close together that the lights, many of them dim or missing, cast a blurred glare from the rear-ends on the snow.

A car appeared, moving in the other direction. It stopped. They came abreast and stopped also.

"Mister Ooardel?"

"It's your Mex," said Davis. Wardell got out.

"I hear in the town ten miles away, there is fighting in Paris. Everybody is much excited." He was excited himself. "Everybody say he will take food, too. So I came back, Companero, I thought you need men."

"Them greasers have a long nose for food," said Shays. "They can smell a jumping bean no matter where it hops."

"Go get your own, Mex," said Drdla, "there ain't any here for you."

"He ain't asking you for food!" Drdla's eyes blinked before Davis turned away. "He's asking you if you'll allow him to shoot a gun shoulder to shoulder with you. I suppose you know you may be needing him. You come up to my place, Carrillo. You and your reti*noo*." He looked at the battered Ford.

It stopped the laughter. The cars dropped away one by one.

"I'm sending my boys away tomorrow, Mort," said Wardell.

"Where to?"

"East, to the comrades. I want them to be gone before the troops come. I'm driving them to the main road, at Tyrone, in the morning."

"I hope so. Anyway, out there they'll be learning something. What is there for them here—shooting, lynching? That's our business yet. Theirs is to learn more about Communism first."

Silence.

"Tell the comrades what we are doing," Wardell said as he stopped the car at the cross-roads the next morning. "Tell them we're organizing. Tell them that already there are many of us. Tell them we've got the dirt farmers here in motion. And make them understand that what we need above everything else, what we must have, is a hectograph.

"Try to get jobs and stick together.

"Now go along. I think you can hitch; if you can't, be careful on the freights.

We've got no use for dead men or cripples. Come back alive in the spring, there's nothing here for you now but hunger."

The snow was fine and dry, and blew in little lifting spirals on the asphalt of the highway, which was comparatively open.

The boys got out and walked off together toward the east. The road followed the roll of the prairie. Coming to the top of the first rise, they turned and, standing together, waved.

They shouted. The cold wind preserved the ring of their voice that the snow might have muffled, blowing their words to the silent man and woman beside the Ford.

"We'll be back in the spring!"

"Could you make out both their voices?" she asked.

YOU HAVE SEEN THE HEADS

(*New Masses*, APRIL 1931)

*(To Lu ko tung, and the terrorist, Li kiang jo) "Lu ko tung was
courageous: Li kiang jo fearless."*

—Sun Yat Sen

OUR PEOPLE—poor people, and the land bare.
We live between mountains.

The pine on the lower slopes of the North Hills is green, that on the
summits black. The three dark pines, standing together in the center of our
village, were brought by the wind from the summits of the North Hills. In our
village it took them centuries to bloom.

But you have seen the heads!

The slow river that watered our rice fields is called the Peace River. In my
childhood I knew why. Now I do not.

Similarly, the friend of my boyhood was Wan gan chi, that of my manhood,
Tai i kai. The green pine and the black. At different stages, on the hills of our
life, our friends have different reasons.

When I was seventeen I was strong, but that year the harvest was bad. The
collectors left us nothing.

"What are we going to eat?" my father cried.

The official smiled. "I do not know," he said.

"You are tigers," screamed my father as they left our house and entered our
neighbor's. Their leader paused in the door and glanced back.

But Fu fu ma plucked my father's sleeve. "Actions," he said, "are difficult,
but understanding is easy." He quieted my father and led him into our house.
I could not offer Fu fu ma a little wine, for he was the elder of our village, a
wise man, and drank only water. Otherwise he fasted and meditated. My
father told me, early in my boyhood, that we owed it to his wise gentleness
that so seldom were our people killed when the tax collectors came among us. I
reverenced Fu fu ma.

That year the collections were heavier than ever because the governor of our
province was fighting and needed rice. Between the yellow and the green, the

old harvest and the new, our village was starving. I, too, starved. Though I was strong, I became sick and weak. First there was hunger, then cold and a deep snow.

At night we lay on straw on the floor, but did not sleep. As if light and darkness were one, we seldom rose during the day, but lay silent. After his father died, Wan gan chi, who was my friend, often lay among us.

Despite the cold, Fu fu ma went from house to house, and comforted our people, or talked to those who were dying.

Sitting at our feet, he once said: "Snow and floods, great heat and hunger are evils. We sow and reap, water our fields and build houses, to keep them from us. But still they are stronger. Only spirit is stronger than snow or flood or hunger. Spirit is stronger than our bodies. Spirit is stronger than death."

"Go away," said Wan gan chi.

I was shocked, first because of his disrespect, and second, because he had not uttered a sound for three nights and days.

"He is sick," said Fu fu ma, and rose and went away.

At this time, Tai i kai, a boy of our village, was attacked, on the outskirts, by a flock of ravens. He was of the poorest peasants. He screamed while he fought the birds, and many men hurried, partly to help him, partly to kill food. Frightened by our people, the ravens flew away.

Tai i kai was lying on the snow. His left eye had been picked out by the birds, and their talons had torn gashes in his cheeks. But he caught one bird and held it by its leg while he fought. It was found under him when he was lifted, for he fainted from weakness and pain.

Our people snapped the bird's neck, and each sought to tear off and eat something. The food was eaten before Tai i kai revived.

The hole where his left eye had been did not heal quickly. Though his house was near my father's, I never heard him groan.

When the snow began to thaw, it was decided to send a group of our people to beg rice from the landowner beyond the first hills to the east. This was Tseng hsi chow.

All our strongest people, about twenty, set out. At the entreaty of my father, who was very weak, I was allowed to go with them, and Wan gan chi. Each of us carried a wooden bowl on a thong.

The snow in the hills was wet and very deep, so that sometimes I disappeared up to my shoulders.

Our people moved along slowly, humped over, like plague rats.

With us was Lu chao bo, an old man who was quite weak from hunger. When he lagged behind, from time to time our people urged him forward; keeping close watch on him.

We reached the house of Tseng hsi chow about mid-day.

"Have pity on us and give us rice," said our people. "We are hungry."

"The *de-sheng* has no rice," said his steward, who spoke to us in front of the house. "The *de-sheng* is not here. The countryside is full of beggars. All the *de-sheng*'s rice has been given away."

"Rice," droned our people. "We are hungry."

"The *de-sheng* is not here," he repeated. "There is no rice. Go away before I have you driven away."

Our people slunk away, and no one said a word to anyone.

But Wan gan chi glanced behind and saw the steward staring after us.

"Perhaps he will give us something," he whispered, "because we are boys."

He began to loiter and at length pulled me into a clump of tall dry grasses. Then we went back.

"Rice for a beggar," called the steward. Wan gan chi raised his bowl, and the servant filled it. There was no more.

The sight of the brown rice made me frantic. "Where is my rice?" I shouted.

The steward laughed. "You take your rice from him." I was hungry. I obeyed. Like a wolf, I sprang at Wan gan chi. His bowl fell to the ground, and the rice was spilled. The steward laughed again as he re-entered the house.

I had always been stronger than Wan gan chi, but, though surprised, he was angry and held me off. In struggling I slipped on ice, and he fell upon me as my head struck the earth, and I became unconscious.

When I came to, we were alone in front of the house. Wan gan chi was standing with a bowl in either hand. Into each he had scooped up the spilled rice and some snow.

"This is your share," he said. "We will take some to your father."

I was ashamed, and walked behind him, and did not speak.

As we were crossing the hills, it began to grow dark. Then we came upon a place where the snow had been trampled. There was blood on the snow, and a body lying naked. It was Lu chao bo's, and pieces of flesh had been cut from the legs and thighs.

A few days later, my father died, leaving me his leased field, and many harvests owed to the money lenders.

Yet the next harvest was good. All our people worked daily in the fields, except Tai i kai, who went to join the army, and Wan gan chi, who went no one knew where.

Though the collectors took three years' taxes from our harvest, as always in good years, I married Ah jui, whom I had loved from childhood, and who loved me. In this Fu fu ma was of help to me with her parents.

Ah jui worked beside me in the field until our first born. That harvest, however, was poor, and the next, and the next. This time the money lenders took nearly all.

Another son was born to us, and another.

Yet we lived between harvests.

The day was hot. Ah jui was again with child, and I was weeding in the field when the soldiers reached our village.

A corporal ran a little way along the top of the dike, but stopped at the edge of the water.

"Come here," he said. "Come with me."

"Where to?" I asked.

"To the village."

I was suspicious but I accompanied him. At a distance I heard shouting.

Ten young men of our village were standing in a row beneath the black pine trees, soldiers before and behind them. I saw Ah jui, my children, Fu fu ma.

"Eleven!" said the officer, and, with a push, tried to add me to the line.

"What is it for?" I asked and resisted. I am strong.

"Coolie for the army."

A woman screamed.

"I won't go," I said. I struggled to break free, but a soldier twisted my arm in a strange grip while the officer pushed me.

"No," I screamed. "No! No! No!"

But Fu fu ma plucked my jacket. "Actions," he said, "are difficult, but understanding is easy."

There passed through my memory a picture of my father's face as Fu fu ma led him into our house, away from quarreling with the tax collectors. Honoring my father, I resigned myself and allowed them to push me into my place at the end of the line.

Ah jui was kneeling with one arm around our eldest son, so that her face was on a level with his head. Her eyes were fastened on me, but she did not utter a sound.

I saw Fu fu ma talking with the officer.

Because of the heat of the day, the pines smelt of resin, and, as I glanced up, for the first time in my life, I noticed how, from the rigid dark branches, short dead limbs stuck down, like blades, at us. Had I been happy, this thought would not have occurred to me.

As soon as we rejoined the main army, they separated the people from our village. I was among men from other provinces with whom it was difficult to speak. But though we were principally silent, I could understand the expression of their faces, for we carried similar burdens, day by day, for great distances.

The first night I thought of Ah jui, but I made no attempt to escape, for I knew that others would, and that our guards would then be most watchful. Five men were killed and wounded, escaping, that night.

It was the same the nights following. Before morning some of us were always killed. There are men who prefer death.

When fighting began, the sound of the machine guns terrified me. I saw hundreds die, but our troops were victorious, and we marched on.

I had been absent from our village a month the night I tried to escape. But a guard, hearing me, wounded me through the hand. When I rolled back, I lay still among the others. I could not sleep.

In the night a man crept beside me.

"You tried to escape," he said.

I recognized his voice.

"It is very foolish," he continued, "we cannot escape one by one. We must form a big union of all the coolies, then everybody will escape."

"Wan gan chi!" I cried.

His hand held my mouth shut.

"Shsh! You!" He was greatly excited. "Listen," he said, "the Communists formed a Peasant League in our village. They crushed the landlords, the moneylenders. But Tseng hsi chow came with the *ming-tuan*, and burned our village."

"Ah jui!" I sat erect. "My sons!"

"I do not know," said Wan gan chi quietly. "It is useless to fear and useless to hope. There are no more wives and sons until we can crush such as Tseng hsi chow."

"Ah jui," I said, and put my arms over my head. My wounded hand burned.

"Tai i kai returned," Wan gan chi continued more gently. "He took many of our people into the mountains. They attacked the house of Tseng hsi chow, and burned it. They also found guns. Tai i kai is leading our people in the mountains."

"Do not despair," said Wan gan chi after a silence. He took my hand, but, as it hurt, I winced.

"You are wounded!" Quickly he tore his shirt and bandaged my hand. Then he left me.

During the night, I saw him go from man to man, talking to those who could not sleep.

Because Wan gan chi said nothing certain, I knew that Ah jui was dead.

From that time I was hopeless. My hand did not heal quickly: it drew together, like a talon, and became rigid. I carried my burden and thought no more of escaping.

Shortly afterwards, our troops were defeated. I fled with others. As we ran, an officer tried to stop us. I was blind with anger. The others fled past. Then I saw that I was holding his knife and that he was dead. I kept his knife and a flask of water.

Two months later, I again looked from the east hills upon our village.

Around the three dark pines some houses were still standing or had been re-
built. There were also burned walls.

From Fu fu ma I learned that the *ming-tuan* had killed Ah jui and my sons.

All winter we lived like wolves. Only those who went into the hills, to Tai i kai,
sometimes brought back a little food.

I did not go to Tai i kai. I wished to sow my field again in the spring, and Fu
fu ma, the friend of my father, urged me to remain.

"The soldier's trade is the lowest," he said. "The *ming-tuan* are tigers. But
the Communists and Tai i kai are devils. That is why Ah jui was killed; she
became a Communist. It is bad."

As it was night I left Fu fu ma, and walked along the top of the dike, to the
middle of my field. Here Ah jui had worked beside me, I stopped. For this
reason, too, I did not go to Tai i kai.

But with spring, the soldiers came to crush Tai i kai in the hills. They filled our
village. The officers sat at a little table, under the black pines, and called each
of our people to be questioned. Even those unfriendly to Tai i kai said they
knew nothing, out of fear that the soldiers would go away and leave them at the
peasants' mercy.

But I was afraid.

"You have nothing to fear," Fu fu ma comforted me. "They know you are not
a Communist."

"How can they know?" I asked.

Among our people was a young man named Lu yin tin. He had been with
Tai i kai in the hills, and, on his return, had once brought us food.

They asked him if he had been with Tai i kai.

"No," he said.

"You never brought back food from the hills?" asked the officer with a smile.

"No," said Lu yin tin.

"You are a Communist," said the officer. He clapped his hands. Behind Lu
yin tin, a soldier with a sword stepped out. Another assisted him. Lu yin tin
did not see them.

"Kneel," said the officer.

Lu yin tin knelt.

Smiling, the officer nodded. The soldier forced Lu yin tin's wrists behind
his back. The sword flashed.

The soldier picked up the head of Lu yin tin, holding it by the hair.

"Up there," The officer pointed as he rose from the table.

By stretching, the soldier forced one of the short dead pine limbs into the
neck of Lu yin tin. His head was impaled upon the overhanging branch.

The soldier removed the table from the falling drops.

*   *   *

At dusk two days later, Wan gan chi walked into my house. Fu fu ma was with me. I was terrified.

"As boys we were always friends, let me stay with you tonight," said Wan gan chi. "If you do not, I will be killed."

"If you stay, we shall all be killed. Wolves run in the mountains. Why do you not go back to that one-eyed wolf in the hills? I will not stay where you are." Fu fu ma left us.

"Listen," said Wan gan chi, "he has gone to betray me. He betrayed Lu yin tin."

"No," I said.

"Yes! He did! Now I will not ask you to hide me. I do not want you to be killed. I came to win the soldiers to Tai i kai. I will now go about my work." He went out.

I was afraid and waited. Then, I, too, ran out.

Wan gan chi was already talking to the first soldier on guard.

"No," the soldier was saying, "No! No!" Then he began to tremble. I trembled, too, for I, too, saw the officer coming. Behind him, at a little distance, was Fu fu ma.

They seized Wan gan chi at our end of the village. They marched him through the street with his wrists tied behind his back. All our men and their wives and children ran out in the twilight and followed. There was talking and questioning.

"Land and rice for the peasants!" Wan gan chi suddenly shouted. Everything grew silent.

"Land and rice for the peasants!" he shouted again with all his might as he marched along.

They led him among the dark pines. We all gathered around, at a distance. They told him to kneel. But he stood erect.

"Listen, people," he shouted, "I am dying for Communism!"

They forced him to the ground. A soldier pressed his knee into Wan gan chi's back.

"People, I am dying for Commun—" It was darkening, but I saw the sword flash, and heard the click and the thud.

They stuck the head of Wan gan chi beside that of Lu yin tin upon the bough.

I did not make a light in the dark house. I knew in what corner I had buried the officer's knife. I dug it up with my fingers.

The lamps in the other houses were put out one by one as I lay in the darkness with the weapon in my hand. Fu fu ma's was one of the first to go out, but I waited until all were extinguished before I crept to his door.

He breathed more quietly than many old men, yet, as I crept, I could guide myself to his position on the floor, by his breathing.

The sound he made in dying was no more than a sigh.

With the same stealth, I left the house, and crept toward the black pines. I stood rigid beneath them, and warm drops fell slowly into my hair.

At that moment, a sentry passed. It had not been my intention to kill a soldier. But I sprang upon his back. My deformed hand I thrust into his mouth. With the knife in the other I stabbed his neck four times. We fell softly together.

I seized his gun. I ran in the dark toward the north.

Along the edge of the rice field that had been my father's. Toward the hills. I reached the uneven ground.

"Tai i kai!" I cried. "Tai i kai! Tai i kai! Tai i kai!"

I knew I tripped, but nothing more until I saw men's faces looking down at me. With his right eye Tai i kai stared at me.

"They executed Wan gan chi," I said. "Fu fu ma betrayed him. They stuck his head on the pine beside Lu yin tin's. His blood is in my hair. I have killed Fu fu ma and a soldier. Here is his gun."

"Keep it—among us," said Tai i kai.

We were defeated at Chun hua, we were defeated at Chen chow. The last was our eleventh defeat without a victory.

Fu fu ma was right: the spirit is stronger than the body. But not the spirit of Fu fu ma. The spirit of Tai i kai. Not the blood of Fu fu ma upon his floor. The blood of Wan gan chi, falling from the pine in darkness. A pool—and a cataract.

We are harried among mountains. The march to victory is up the sharp sides of mountains.

OUR COMRADE MUNN

(*New Masses*, OCTOBER 1931)

O UR COMRADE MUNN may not have been a "big man," and that may be the final judgment of the entire Party on his record, too. He was really too shy and unassuming, and so never reached that position in the leadership which our locality and the entire district demanded, and which we all thought him capable of. If anything, he avoided leadership, as he did all personal prominence, always passing the credit for successes which he planned, and partly executed himself, to those who helped him, and always bearing more than his share of blame.

"Little dogs have big barks," he used to say in his way. Which is probably a wrong attitude in our Party, since we are not interested in modesty, but in accomplishment, and if any comrade thinks he has done something, he ought to speak up and say so, so that he can be used again.

But I believe Comrade Munn had a much better, a real reason, and knew it, though this same modesty kept him from mentioning it. He said once to me, "There's too much skipping around. Of course, the Party is weak in forces, but no sooner does a comrade win the confidence of the local comrades, or what's harder, the local workers, and starts local organization and campaigns, than the district gets wind of him. He's too good for where he is, so they decide to put him in more important work. And they send him somewhere else, and he starts all over again. And then they put him in still more important work. It's like the turkey on the tree. You shake the tree and the turkey is there. You shake the tree again and the turkey is still there. And you shake the tree again and the turkey is gone. I want to dig in and finish one job."

That's just how he used to talk, and when I write these things, I seem to be able to hear his voice as he said them, and I see that it's going to be hard to write about Comrade Munn. We always knew he had shortcomings, but we liked him anyway, and when he was dead, we found out how much more we thought of him, more than just liking him, more than admiring him, much more. We found out we depended on him.

And if it's bad for comrades to depend on a leading comrade, what else is leadership? And that, in my opinion, is why our section is recognized today as almost a model to our Party, and why the district could study its methods of getting into the shops, at the last plenum.

And when you take into account the size of Comrade Munn's funeral, which was a real mass funeral, and consider that a number of workers threw down their tools and walked out of the shops against the bosses' orders, to march in the procession, then I say, that's a demonstration!

And I say, too, it proves Comrade Munn was at least on the right track. We didn't always think so.

It sounds impossible now and bad, but it may help comrades elsewhere— there was a time when we were very suspicious of Comrade Munn. I remember the first meeting he attended. We used to meet in a small loft. It was dirty, cold and the light was very poor. Once in a while we would have a dance there, and the red crepe paper festoons were never taken down till the next dance, but got faded and dusty unless they fell down in the meantime.

I saw the comrade, sitting to one side, the moment I came in. He seemed to be a tall man, with a long white face and heavy brown hair. I was a little late and the chairman was speaking, but Comrade Hammer, who was sitting in front, jumped up and took me into a corner. "Who is that?" he wanted to know in a worried voice. How should I know who it was? But I thought from the way he spoke it must be a Department of Justice agent.

Our branch was in a city of twenty-five thousand, with five big shoe factories, two textile mills, a gun factory, and a lot of light industry. A city of at least ten thousand workers and their families, mostly Americans.

Our branch was in existence for four years at this time. We had twenty-seven comrades, and used to be pointed out for the large proportion of workers we had, "proletarian elements" as they were called. Four of them were carpenters, two plasterers, two were plumbers, one was a laborer, and one a cutter in a shoe factory. But only one of these comrades, a Norwegian carpenter, spoke English well. Of the others, three were Russians, two Jewish, three Italians, and one a Finn. I never saw one of them talking to an American worker before Comrade Munn came. One of the Jewish comrades, Celensky, the shoe cutter, was always studying English in private, but nobody knew that then, and he spoke very badly.

But the secretary of our branch was an American. His name was Comrade Archie Pollard, and as he could write more clearly and express himself better than most of the comrades, he was made secretary. His father was a lawyer for one of the shoe companies, but Comrade Archie used to say he would never "go into bourgeois business," though he continued to live at his father's house, and never had a job. The last I heard of him he was writing for a shoe trade journal. He got the position by posing as an expert on Reds, and he is still an "expert."

The leading comrades of our branch were both Jewish. One, named Hammer, kept a small candy and newspaper store, the other, Finestone, had a dry-goods store. Behind their backs some of the comrades used to call them Finestone, Hammer & Co., but they knew how to run our section. Pollard used to go to their houses, and another American comrade, a woman whose name was Cartwright. She wrote a sonnet on Sacco and Vanzetti, beginning, "How like the Nazarene's their Calvary," which Comrade Munn called, "Puke," when someone showed it to him once. Altogether they had what you might call a "social set."

But we never increased our membership after we reached twenty-seven, and the largest number of comrades we ever got to a meeting was twenty. That was to re-elect Pollard after Comrade Celensky had called him a bourgeois, in a meeting. Generally, there were ten or so.

What I have said about Finestone and Hammer does not prove that I am an anti-Semite. The movement in this country was certainly kept alive in places at one time by the devotion of sincere Jewish comrades. I will now turn to them, for one such was Comrade Celensky.

He was a short, thin, irritable, little man, who never missed a meeting, apparently in order to attack Finestone, Hammer and Pollard. Whenever Pollard had finished reading the district letter, Celensky would demand the floor, leap up and offer a resolution to accept it, especially those parts demanding definite action, "before Finestone, Hammer & Co. have a chance to kill it." He was the only one that called them Finestone, Hammer & Co. to their faces.

Finally, it settled into a farce, in which either Comrade Finestone or Comrade Hammer took to seconding Comrade Celensky's motion, and then filling the committee with their own friends. But those committees seldom functioned, and there were always a thousand good reasons why. When they did, however, as in the Sacco and Vanzetti campaign, the leading comrades took full credit in reporting to the district.

Comrade Celensky was generally called a "leftist". So when it was discovered that the stranger at the meeting was an American named Munn, a shoe worker like Celensky, the comrades were still more suspicious, and it looked as if Comrade Celensky was the only person who would endorse his card, and he would not be admitted. Especially when Hammer said, with a smile, "What do you want? To have two Celenskys? One isn't enough?"

The stranger just sat there while everybody shouted about him, and Celensky shouted loudest while the sweat ran down his face. "But he's a worker anyway, isn't he, Comrade Hammer?" I shouted myself, "and this *is* a working class party, isn't it?"I was in the back of the loft, and I saw the stranger turn his whole body, and without moving a muscle of his face, look at me. Hammer's remark made me so mad that I endorsed the card.

And that is how I came to help bring Comrade Munn into our Party. At that time I wasn't any better, though maybe no worse, than the others, for the trouble with an atmosphere like that in our branch is that it is contagious, all the comrades finally get the same disease, and every new one is either stifled, or disgusted before he ever gets in; in any case, made useless.

At first it looked as if that had happened to Comrade Munn. For two months he never said a word, never even voted.

Then he asked for the floor one night. Hammer stopped whispering to Pollard long enough to give it to him, and Finestone was smiling. Everybody wanted to hear what the big, shambling man, who was still a stranger to the comrades, had to tell us. And Comrade Celensky broke into a sweat, as usual when he is excited, as if he were making a speech himself.

"Comrades," Comrade Munn hesitated and smiled over their heads while he slowly rubbed his chin, below one corner of his mouth, with his long little finger. "Comrades, I'm a working man myself. And when I came into this Party, it was because I thought it was a workingman's Party. You know, if not all working people, anyway people who wanted to agitate and organize workingmen. Now, of course, I may be wrong, but in two months that I've been watching, I haven't seen anybody organize as much as a dog yet!" And his voice from being quiet, suddenly became very harsh. "But I've heard a lot of *talk*."

"Comrades, there's going to be a walkout in my department Monday. I see you comrades knew all about it—from the blank looks on your faces!" Everybody felt a kind of guilt we had never felt before: how should we know about every walkout, and yet it seemed wrong.

"I want you comrades to choose a committee of three to advise the strikers. I nominate myself to head the committee, and Comrade Celensky, also a shoe worker, and . . . "

"Celensky is a Jew," Finestone objected, "and most of the shoeworkers are gentiles!"

"What difference does that make? They want to be led, they won't ask much if he's a Jew or not if they're satisfied with how he's leading them. If you knew more about workingmen, you'd know they divide Jews into good Jews and bad Jews according as they're for or against you. Besides, it's one way to overcome race prejudice in practice. So I ask for Comrade Celensky, and . . ."

"Then I nominate Hammer," shouted Finestone. They had long ago dropped the Comrade "among friends," even for official business.

"I think Comrade Hammer is the worst possible choice for the committee," said Munn. He spoke directly to the comrades. "Comrades, Comrade Hammer is not a workingman. I don't think he understands workingmen. I don't believe our committee could work well together if he was on it. The success of the strike will depend partly on the smooth running of our committee. And on the success of the strike depends the bringing nearer to our Party of all those contacts in the factory that Comrade Celensky and I have made. That is a big thing for our Party. Instead of Hammer, I nominate and wish the comrades would choose—*him*." He did not know my name.

"Him! He's an intellectual!" screamed Finestone.

"Will you call him unreliable?" asked Munn.

"Unreliable? An intellectual?"

"Would *you* call *him* unreliable?"

Finestone hesitated.

"Then I wish the comrades would put him on the committee. It's time he had strike experience."

Perhaps nothing ever surprised Finestone, Hammer & Co. in all their lives as much as that ballot in which they were the only three votes against us. Of course, next time they were prepared. But I did not set out to tell the story of the long fight before they were stopped from hampering Party work.

Though that fight was bitter, it was the external fights by which our Comrade taught us to build our Party while we were in the very act of fighting. "Like this Greek wrestler, Antaeus," he said, "Hercules killed him by holding him up in thin air, off the earth, just like Finestone & Co. have been killing our section by holding it away from the factory workers—up in the air."

"You've got to make a new contact every day, no matter where," he told a group of comrades another time. And he told me afterwards, "If I haven't made one, I go to the coffee-pot at night. You're always sure to find somebody there."

He was forever hammering away at new contacts. Two months after the strike he brought eleven workers into the section. "Don't get over-optimistic," he warned us. "We're simply reaping the crop that Comrade Celensky and I have been watering for months before this. The work of bringing in real men from the factory proletariat is the slowest, most heart-breaking business—as a rule. Of course, in time of strike it goes much faster."

It was part of his drive for contacts "with the factory proletariat" that made him insist that "we must have our own press, right here, for our own use." Finestone & Co. laughed loud and began to call him Comrade "Money."

"We've got all we can do subscribing to the Party press."

"Yes, we ought to discuss the situation here in regards to the Party press sometime," said Comrade Munn, and by then that had the sound of a threat. "But what we need now is a weekly mimeographed sheet, edited by three different comrades every week, so that everybody will learn how, and distributed by the Pioneers. That will give them something to do at last. The paper will be our local organizer. It will contain local news about the shops, worker correspondence, instructions for organization, the Party's line on local events. The first distribution at any shop will be free. From then on, a cent a copy. The act of buying links the worker to the movement. It establishes that here's something he's willing to pay for. That's worth a hundred free distributions. And where one buys, others will.

"But first we have to buy a mimeograph ourselves. It will cost money, Finestone says, and he is beginning to call me 'Comrade Money.' Behind my back, of course, so as not to hurt my feelings. Comrade Finestone's natural instinct is right: it will mean a sacrifice. But whether you've been in the Party all your life, or since the last meeting, you know that everything is accomplished in the revolutionary movement by sacrifice, nothing without it. You boycott something, you go without something, you strike while you're hungry. All sacrifice. But such sacrifice is training, it has nothing to do with Christian sacrifice, which is to glorify the ego. Our sacrifices are training of our class for the war when we, the weaker, have to overthrow the stronger class. Necessary training. Where we're so soft we have forgotten, or don't know how to sacrifice, it is necessary to learn. Comrades, I ask you to raise the money for a mimeograph."

Later, we voted the machine.

That mimeograph was the wedge with which our local Party split open the doors of the bosses' factories. In the early days, when Finestone and Hammer were still hampering such work, I have seen Comrade Munn himself selling our mimeograph papers in the snow, at a factory gate where the Pioneers had been arrested. That he was not blacklisted was because he was one of the best workers in his line. And he was always harping on the theme that Communist workers must win the regard of their shop mates by being the best in the shop.

He was criticized by Finestone for distributing papers in person, and though Finestone was looking for a talking point, there was some truth in his charges. It was a kind of rank and file-ism on Comrade Munn's part, and if he had not similarly exposed himself later, he might never have been killed.

Comrade Munn answered the attack by saying that there were occasions when a leading comrade has to expose himself for the sake of setting an example, something, he added, which Finestone would not know much about. And he began that discussion of our work with the Party press that he had threatened.

"The circulation of the Party papers," he said, "is one of the simplest and most effective ways of drawing rank and file comrades into active work. The circulation of the press in this section ought to be so well organized, (because it is a very simple matter that Pioneers could handle if necessary), that every week a different group of comrades could circulate our papers without a hitch. We are not always going to be a legal Party. We cannot always depend upon the United States post-office to deliver our papers for us. Circulation by comrades ought to be one of the most important and efficient means of organizing our underground apparatus. And hand in hand with circulation by comrades, goes the getting of new subscriptions. It is one of the best methods for developing Communist responsibility. We do each of these things separately, or we don't do them at all. But they all dovetail, they are all part of one process, and when one lags they all lag. That explains why we fail to pull ourselves out of a slump on such work—because we pay attention now to one, now to another, and never to the interlocking parts of the whole process."

We began, not all at once, but little by little, to put in practice the circulation of our Party press by our comrades, which is now so successful throughout our section, that comrades have long forgotten that it ever was anything else, and take such work as a matter of course. Of course, there are very severe penalties for failure to get the papers to our readers.

The correctness of Comrade Munn's position about the press was verified two years later, during the big shoe strike, when the post-office, police and newsdealers did everything to suppress our papers.

Five factories went out, and after two months the strikers showed no signs of weakening, though it was winter. "Relief is the backbone of any strike," Comrade Munn had said at the beginning, and he was still insisting on relief at the time he was killed. He had another variation, though,—that "the factory proletariat is the backbone of our Party," and it is only in relation to his effort to draw in that stratum that his work can really be understood.

Inevitably, as the strike struggle deepened, it began to attract the sympathies and interest of larger and larger numbers of workers, not only those who were on strike, for we had begun to have contacts in all the shops.

Meanwhile the shoe bosses began to utilize every means in their power to re-open the mills.

They bet on the religious issue as one of their best cards. Day after day for two months, the entire mill owners' press of our city wept and gnashed its teeth at the "Red atheists" and the "atheistic Reds." While the editorials warned, and the cartoons showed the horrors of irreligion in leading children into crime, prostitution, drug addiction, etc.

Of course, this was not an accidental issue. Many of the workers were Irish, Italian or Polish. And, furthermore, the largest shareholder in the Atlas Mills, and member of the city council, F. X. Queeley, was the brother of Father Patrick Queeley, one of the best known Irish priests.

He was a man of medium height, stocky and strong, with the build of a bull and a bulldog jaw, and a long straight mouth with lips so thin that he seemed to be sucking them in. "He won't stop at anything, watch out," Comrade Munn warned us.

Using the pulpit as a rostrum he was constantly calling on the workers to submit, reminding them, via the parable of Mary and Martha, that "the Marthas of this world are not the less dignified, the less noble, the less free because it is their privilege to serve." And then he would attack the idleness of the rich, drawing a comparison in favor of the life of the poor, but happy, which has been the method in his church for several thousand years.

Father Maccara, a thin, olive-faced Italian priest, with a mouth that was always smiling, ably seconded the Irish father.

By the end of three months his brother's affairs looked so dark that Father Queeley entered the arena in person. It was a cold, dark morning, and the pickets in the long lines were keeping up their spirits with "Solidarity," and the coffee which our relief handed out to every man and woman. Police were all over.

Comrade Munn was leading one line, Celensky another. Suddenly Father Queeley strode up with a police captain for escort.

"I command all Christians to leave this line," said the priest.

The men did not move.

"I command all Christians to leave this line," Father Queeley repeated.

There was some huddled consultation, and three women and an embarrassed man stepped out.

"Will the rest of you crucify Him again?" asked the Father.

More men broke the line.

"These people are fighting for their bread," Comrade Munn shouted loud enough to be heard all over the street. "You are trying to stop them because your brother, F. X. Queeley, owns this mill. The only God you serve is Money!"

The Father's jaw set like a prize fighter's.

"That man," pointing to Celensky, "is a Christ-killer! A Jew! And as for that man," pointing to Comrade Munn, "if God were not merciful, He would strike him dead where he stands for leading you into violence and sin."

It was critical. The whole long line was wavering. One of the women had begun to weep. Comrade Munn's face was pale.

He took out his watch. "I repeat," he said, "you want to break this strike because your brother owns this mill. You talk about God! Well, many of these men and women also worship God. You say He is merciful. If He is, and I am as bad as you say, He *ought* to strike me dead where I stand!" He held up his watch. "In fact, I give God just ten minutes to strike me dead and prove you're right. In the meantime the picketing will go on. Lead yourselves and don't be afraid."

They began hesitantly to march again. But the eyes of everybody remained fixed on the tall body of Comrade Munn, standing in one spot on the street, with his watch in his hand, daring God to strike him dead—and timing Him!

"Ten minutes is up," he called at last after the line had shuffled back and forth several times. "I'm still alive, Father Queeley."

The Father's face was white and distorted with rage as he whispered a word to the captain of police, who blew his whistle. It began the bloodiest charge to date, but Comrade Munn had saved the strike that day.

"It's an old trick," he told us afterwards, "every atheist soapboxer knows it. But don't think they'll stop there. I wonder what they'll do next, probably arrest us all again." And anybody who thinks Father Queeley was through reckons without the bosses or the clergy.

Queeley was on hand again the next day, and again he ordered all Christians to leave the line. For a long time no one stirred, but at the first sign of wavering, Comrade Munn took out his watch. Again he stood with it open. Again all eyes were fixed on him, but his own eyes kept wandering around the street as if he were looking for what else they had up their sleeves: he couldn't believe they were going through with this same comedy again. He was right.

Suddenly there were three thin *pings*, and Comrade Munn's tall body fell, like a gate-post going over, in a heap on the paving. The thugs had come to the aid of God. The women shrieked and men groaned. Everybody was frightened and started to run.

Celensky was the first to come to his senses. "He's shot," he kept shouting in his sick English. "Shot. Shot! Shot! Not God! Shot!" But he failed to make them understand. Everything was confusion.

"Tell them, tell them," he begged me. He forced Munn's watch into my hand. I held it up where everybody could see.

"A gunman shot Munn! Gunmen," I cried. "If it wasn't, let God strike me dead, too!"

It helped rally the Communist workers, those new comrades whom Munn had brought into the section in the last year. They formed a group to cover the confusion of the line and started to shout "Solidarity" as the police charge swept down.

It was with great difficulty that I got into the hospital to see Comrade Munn. Celensky they would not let through at all. Our Comrade was dying, and I sat beside him for three hours while he suffered with the racking pain in his stomach where one of the bullets had hit. At first he did not seem to know me, but toward the end, I saw his eyes fixed on me, and on his face was that same humorous smile I saw the first time he addressed our Communist branch.

He wanted to speak, but the thick words came with difficulty. I bent my head to his mouth.

"Celensky," I made out.

"Yes, yes," I said, "Celensky!"

"Celensky," he repeated as if he couldn't think of the rest, "Celensky—must learn . . . "

"Celensky must learn what?" I said.

"English."

Then he relapsed and it was not long before the doctor said he was dead.

I have tried to put down those things that were useful to us in the life of Comrade Munn, which Comrade Celensky omitted from his report to the district plenum. Things which I believe he would want us to analyze and discuss for present and for future work.

It is no accident that this fall, one year after the death of Comrade Munn, Comrade Celensky addressed the plenum of the district on the accomplishments of our section—in English. Celensky spoke with an accent, it is true, but you could understand every word he said. And this is not to be taken in a narrow sense of a subjective victory for Comrade Celensky, it is part of a general victory of our section on the objective field: it is part of the work of Comrade Munn. In this connection, I heard him say once, "If you drop a good sized stone in a well, it will raise the level of all the water."

THE DEATH OF THE COMMUNISTS

(*New Masses*, DECEMBER 1931)

THE COMMUNISTS were introduced into the jail shortly after Thanksgiving, in the evening. Naturally, gentlemen, the clang of a metallic door, closing behind our backs (it reverberates, no matter how deadened) cannot be expected to have the same value to your ears as the even more guarded sound of the door someone throws open for you. But while, in prison, our aural discriminations are also effected for, and not by, us, we become more than commonly acute to the selected sounds that mark the wastes of silence. Therefore, I hastened to peer through the bars.

Perhaps I should interrupt myself at once and ask indulgence if I offend by the nature of what I am recounting. But I recall the wasps that used to build under my high window in summer, and how they drew their sustenance even from the bodies of base and unformed larva, which they know to numb, but do not kill until they are quite drained of life, and which contrasted with the irresistible and attenuated beauty of the banqueters, seem designed to no higher end than to perpetuate its pitilessness. May I ask you gentlemen to go to the wasp? To hold in abeyance your natural repugnance to the subject until we have drained it of its last possible drop of interest. Then—the coup de grace. But for the moment let your minds enter, like those fierce and efficient insects, into the cell of which they were the voluntary, as I the involuntary, inmates.

That is how I came to see the Communists. Not distinctly, to be sure, since the cell I occupied was in the upper tier, and they were marched too close to the cages below for me to distinguish more than that they were five, a woman and four men.

If the presence of the woman surprised me, it aroused the inmates who began to shout obscenities, and apparently to reach out to touch her, for I heard a blow delivered by a guard, and a howl of pain as an arm was retracted. Then, gentlemen, the outbreak was terminated by what I believed, and what doubtless you, too, will agree was the absurdest spectacle I had, until then, been called upon to witness. Spontaneously, as if a button had been pressed by the striking of the blow the five began to sing a, to my ears (though I make no pretense to musical appreciation) atrociously rattle-trap tune, in voices, with the exception of one man's, as painful as the song. The words, repeated to me later by a convict, were:

Arise, ye prisoners of starvation,
Arise, ye wretched of the earth,
For justice thunders condemnation;
A better world's in birth.

And so on to the end. Laughable, though I would not in any case have laughed (for the brutality of the guards was extreme, for a less justifiable reason I am afraid, than an injured esthetic), had not one of the most uncouthly villainous of the convicts, in the cell opposite, a face from which one might have expected any atrocity, observed with the utmost awe in the silence following the song—"Political prisoners!" The quasi-technical term, pronounced in that strained tone by that unspeakably debased mouth, enabled me, as you gentlemen will readily understand, to do what I did for the first time, I believe, since entering the jail—laugh out loud. But becoming instantly aware that my laughter was the sole sound among the cells, I suffered a twinge of my old fear of lunacy, always a companion with me there.

It was not until the guards had left the newcomers alone that the silence was broken by a series of questions and answers, which I will try to repeat, but for whose sequence and accuracy I cannot vouch.

Who are you?

Communists.

Why are you here?

For organizing soldiers in the fort.

Why do you want to organize soldiers?

The soldiers are workingmen in uniform. We are trying to organize them to better their conditions, and to oppose the coming war, which the capitalist class, from which come the officers, is planning to wage to destroy the Soviet Union where the working class rules. Millions more men will be killed in that war than in 1914.

Yes, another Communist voice resumed, in their terror the capitalists will even take you out of the jails, will put a new kind of uniform on you, will drill you, will give you guns and promise you that when you have destroyed the power of the working class for them they will set you free. But you have learned from your lives, or you would not be here, what they will do for you. You will know which way to turn your guns.

I am quite certain that I am not misquoting, gentlemen, for I remember that a considerable silence followed.

Then they were asked why the military authorities had not put them in the military prison.

They answered that at first they had, but later transferred them to this civil prison. They did not understand why, but thought it peculiar that the woman was left with them in a men's jail, and they were afraid for her.

At this point the woman joined the conversation, saying that their fears, like

all fear (the comparison, gentlemen is hers), were foolish, and that the explanation was quite simple. The authorities, not knowing the extent of the Communists' activities, and connections, were terrified into believing that, even
incommunicado, they would find means of corrupting the soldiers, for a
democratic government lives in fear of nothing so much as that its soldiers may
begin to think. No woman's prison was at hand, so they had put her here
pending a decision.

It took just a week, gentlemen, for us to learn how totally inadequate are
such minds in the apprehension of motive.

During those seven alternations of light, signifying so little to me, and
hardly more to them, perhaps, I had occasion to make further, though slight,
observations upon these persons from a world so different from ours, which,
momentarily, nevertheless, had impinged upon my own. And yet not by
chance, it seems to me Peter Thompson would maintain but as the result of a
chain of causation implicit in the nature of society itself—if you will pardon
the divagation.

I learned that the woman's name was Anna Lot, that the man who seemed to
enjoy the most authority among them was the Peter Thompson I alluded to,
and that there was one named Kubelik. The names of the other two I did not
learn: they never spoke.

Gentlemen, I found astounding the directness with which, without any
preliminaries, Mr. Thompson, as their spokesman, went to work to expound
their doctrine to the prisoners, entirely oblivious, apparently, of any misgiving
that he might not be understood. Amazing, too, was the rote of this mind,
obviously untutored in any academic sense, whereby it was enabled to deliver
itself of quotation after quotation from their most unquestioned pundits. But
if I was nauseated at first, it was only to be astounded again by the simplicity
with which the speaker, suddenly, in his own words, made tangible, made
plausible, to those convicts the steps in an analysis of larceny, not as a
consequence of individual viciousness, but as the result of the structure and
pressure of a society in which some possess, but most do not. He made the
convicts understand (I tell you gentlemen, they understood) their position,
not only as individuals, but as part of a social whole, of a social process, in the
light of a universal philosophic theory. You will pardon me, gentlemen, if I,
too, join in your smile, for so plausible indeed did he become that I had to take
myself in hand and recall that I was listening to an experienced agitator, whose
substance I might dismiss, the better to free my mind for the enjoyment of an
art so unfamiliar to me.

But it was from the uncommon persuasiveness the convincing speciousness of
the Communist, Kubelik, apparently a little man, much less fluent than
Thompson, that I became conscious of a feeling which has little to do with

reason, gentlemen, and which I cite only because, to the convicts, his labored phrases seemed to strike like blows against their bars. I recall but one instance. He spoke once of his doctrine's having been invited by no one, but as a method, disclosing the reality of things. You have seen gravestones, he told their listening ears (their eyes could not see him) on which the words have been obscured by moss and dirt so that you could not read them. Well you are caged in by stones whose meaning you cannot read, though you feel its injustice. Communism is the emery that clears away the dirt and moss and lets you see the meaning of the stone imprisoning you, a meaning that is underlined with bars of steel. It was not, of course, delivered as I tell you, gentlemen, but, perhaps, even more simply, if haltingly.

I said that Kubelik was *apparently* a little man, for during the week that the Communists were among us, we never caught more than a glimpse of them: they were segregated, permitted, as far as I know, no recreation, and fed in their cells.

But on that seventh day, noticing a visible agitation among the prisoners, I inquired during the recreation period, and discovered a story going the rounds that our Communists had been held in jail only until the soldiers could be roused to violence against them. That was why the woman had been kept with them, since they wished to dispatch all together as a warning. The officers had by now succeeded in inciting the soldiers, the Communists were to be taken from their cells that night and shot under the walls.

The best-intentioned of us cannot always, as you gentlemen know, repress a smile at the obviously ingenuous, but I merely mentioned the thickness of the walls and the stoutness of steel and stones. My informants replied that the prison authorities would take care of that. Then, gentlemen, I *did* smile. I asked, however, what the Communists thought about it, and was informed that they had not been told, no one in the prison possessing the requisite cruelty to warn them. Again, gentlemen, it was hard to restrain a smile: the jail harbored some of the most vicious eliminations of the social body.

But toward nightfall, the convicts must, after long cogitation, have concluded cruelty to be the better part of valor, for I suddenly heard Peter Thompson say aloud, "Comrade Lot, they are going to take us out tonight and shoot us. That is why they kept us together." From the completeness of the silence, it seemed to me that two hundred listening ears had closed upon his words, and it was in the same silence that she answered, "I knew it from the first."

It is difficult for me, at this distance, to convey to you gentlemen, or to explain, the force impelling me to break that silence of listening men, to join for the first time in a conversation in that jail, surprising myself by an interest, which must necessarily seem curious to you in these, after all, most remote people.

"Perhaps it is not true," I ventured.

The growl that issued from that murderous beast in the cell opposite, called my attention to the fist he was shaking at me for silence.

"It is true," the Communist answered. "Democracy is the most perfect form of government for capitalism because it offers the most perfect illusion of freedom. The democratic guarantees, freedom of the ballot, freedom of speech, freedom of the press and of assembly, are guarantees to nobody but the capitalist and his followers. Freedom to bargain for his job has never meant anything to the workingman but freedom to starve. But democracy is not something that cannot be overstepped. Democracy is a stage in the course of the development from capitalism to Communism. Now Democracy is going to kill us. That means it is afraid of us. That is good."

Of course, of course, you are right—obsession. But those are the only words we had occasion to exchange.

I do not believe, gentlemen, that all the men, who lay silent in their bunks, were asleep, nor can anyone longer tell how the Communists passed the remaining hours. But toward midnight, we heard a disturbance in the outer corridor. The soldiers, with two officers, passed between the cells in an entirely orderly fashion. They carried the keys, and there was no difficulty in removing the Communists, for though the latter attempted briefly to reason with the soldiers against their officers, the futility of the procedure seemed, from certain sounds, to be brought home rather urgently to them.

Then, gentlemen, will you believe it, they began again that absurd song. If I thought it ridiculous before, it seemed doubly so now, for they were in evident pain, and must have realized as vividly as did we that they were being marched to their deaths.

> *Arise, ye prisoners of starvation,*
> *Arise, ye wretched of the earth,*
> *For justice thunders condemnation;*
> *A better world's in birth.*

My fellow prisoners cowered in their bunks, feeling, I am sure, as did I, that our citadel invaded, we ourselves were none too safe. But I, having the least to fear, stepped to the bars, and was rewarded by my only glimpse of the five. Thompson, a lean, lined face, sallow, singing, head up. The one I took to be Kubelik, short, swart and stocky. The others nondescript. Except the woman. I am most partial, as you gentlemen know, to attractive women, and she was, unfortunately, positively hideous. But, mercifully, she walked with her head bent, for the soldier holding her arm behind her back, had drawn it up between her shoulder blades. And, mercifully, too, they shut off the lights at that moment, an oversight or an afterthought in the excitement.

The prisoners continued to lie, if anything, more quietly in their bunks.

But presently the howling assailed them from another side, this time from below the windows, grew louder, for the effectiveness of this execution as a threat, was postulated, you may remember, upon its performance against the very walls of the jail. "The law's delay" for once strikingly amended by civistic promptitude. It did not, however, take place under my window, but one a little farther down, so that my ears were spared the full force of their incongruous and ceaseless singing whenever, for a moment, the shouting of the others abated.

The sudden crackle of shots I thought would end it. But, no. One voice hesitated and went on. I think it was Peter Thompson's, although because of the shattering effect of that first volley on the nerves, the dark, the tenseness of the silence in the cells, and an unnatural whining tone, which suggests that he may have been wounded, I am unable to substantiate the fact.

> 'Tis the final conflict, let each stand in his place:
> The international soviet shall be the human rrrrrrrrr

The initial r of the word "race," which, I am given to understand, is the word that the single rifle shot checked in our Communist's throat, was prolonged appropriately into a death rattle.

That is how they died, gentlemen. And to tell the truth, I had a feeling, singularly light and unsorrowful, that their deaths made no essential difference to themselves, to what they were effecting, or to that for which they stood. Indeed, I felt as I have felt only once before in my life, when I was lying on my back in a small boat, with a cool wind, but a hot sun, playing on my body, and a swell and a strong tide carrying me along with no effort on my part.

Their deaths were not horrifying. What horrified, what appalled me was, that after a brief interregnum of silence, following the end of the song, it was suddenly taken up by a lone voice in the cells which, when it had sung a bar or two, was joined by others. Ignorant alike of the words and tune, the men, who may have heard the *International* twice in all their lives, since the Communists were in the jail, began in a moaning monotone, and with voices whose rusty huskiness suggested that they could not have sung for years, barbarously to mutilate what, as I have already said, is, at best, not a good song.

> Arise ye prisoners of starvation,
> Arise, ye wretched of the earth . . .

And, of course, reacting blindly, and unfamiliar with what they were attempting to sing, broke off, unfinished. After which a really deep and appropriate silence ensued.

No, gentlemen, I could not feel sorrowful at the death of the Communists.

It was not the shooting, it was the outburst in the cells that was hideous. The Communists were obviously men of courage, single-minded no doubt, but capable of a kind of fanatical calm in the face of death, on the basis, however difficult for one of us to comprehend, of certain convictions arrived at by means of an intelligence no matter how limited. Were possessed, I mean to say, of intelligence, conviction, courage. Were, therefore, men, gentlemen, men. Men! Men, do you hear me, you beasts, men!

TWO

Night
Thoughts

INTELLIGENCE REPORT
(*Time*, MAY 1, 1939)

THE MENACING SUN—*Mona Gardner—Harcourt, Brace* ($2.50).

ONE BOMBY SUNDAY afternoon, Mona Gardner sat in a Shanghai park talking Chinese poetry during a Japanese air raid. Outside, Soochow Lane was jampacked with coolies toting vegetables to Shanghai's International Settlement, and fugitives toting babies, bedding, household goods to safety. Neither vegetables nor babies arrived. Suddenly a light bomber roared a hundred feet overhead, its machine gun working—then two more. Because the simplest horror is the most stunning—automatically "our feet take us" to look at heaped bodies on the road, on the barbed-wire barricades, or those still trying to crawl through.

The shadow of Japanese planes stayed over Mona Gardner on her eleventh-hour reconnaissance of three menaced Eastern empires (French, Dutch and British). Everywhere she found distrust of the Japanese, little evidence of their effective penetration except the inevitable Japanese photographic shop in every strategic railway junction, harbor, mining town.

Unlike most travel books this one really travels, loiters nowhere, observes brightly on the fly, dwells most approvingly on the efforts of Siam's progressive Government to turn that still independent country into a democracy despite Japanese example and proximity. Fly in the ointment: the Government's mechanization program is causing serious technological unemployment among elephants.

Britain's Singapore base looked impregnable, but rangy, Bible-brandishing Major General Dobbie, its commander, refused to say it was, thought it "probably the most peaceful spot on earth." Almost as open a secret as the 18-inch naval guns dismounted to form land batteries, blabs Traveler Gardner, is the fact that nearly one-sixth of the funds to build the base came from the British sale of opium to addicts, a Government monopoly.

Traveler's tale: in a Tonkinese sweatshop swollen-eyed children were making "real French lace." On the wall hung a picture of Rockefeller Center. Much puzzled was the factory owner to learn that Mr. Rockefeller did not live alone in the Center, that there were other inmates. At last he comprehended: "Oh, you mean Monsieur Rockefeller's concubines."

NIGHT THOUGHTS

(*Time*, MAY 8, 1939)

FINNEGANS WAKE—*James Joyce*—*Viking* ($5).

A LL CHILDREN are afraid of the night; when they grow up, they are still afraid, but more afraid of admitting it. In this frightening darkness men lie down to sleep and dream. Generations of diviners, black magicians, fortune tellers and poets have made night and dreams their province, interpreting the troubled images that float through men's sleeping minds as omens of good & evil. Only of late have psychologists asserted that dreams tell nothing about men's future, much about their hidden or forgotten past. In dreams, this past floats, usually uncensored and distorted, to the surface of their slumbering consciousness.

This week, for the first time, a writer had attempted to make articulate this wordless world of sleep. The writer is James Joyce; the book, *Finnegans Wake*—final title of his long-heralded *Work in Progress*. In his 57 years this erudite and fanciful Irishman, from homes in exile all over Europe, has written two books that have influenced the work of his contemporaries more than any others of his time: *A Portrait of the Artist as a Young Man*, the best of innumerable novels picturing an artist's struggle with his environment; *Ulysses*, considered baffling and obscure 15 years ago, now accepted as a modern masterpiece.

Finnegans Wake is a difficult book—too difficult for most people to read. In fact, it cannot be "read" in the ordinary sense. It is perhaps the most consciously obscure work that a man of acknowledged genius has produced. Its four sections run to 628 pages, and from its first line:

riverrun, past Eve and Adam's, from swerve of shore to bend of bay

to its last:

A way a lone a last a loved a long the

there is not a sentence to guide the reader in interpreting it; there is not a single direct statement of what it is about, where its action takes place, what, in the simplest sense, it means.

It is packed with jokes, plays on words; it contains nonsensical diagrams, ridiculous footnotes, obscure allusions. Sometimes it seems to be retelling, in a chattering, stammering, incoherent way, the legends of Tristan and Isolde, of

Wellington and Napoleon, Cain and Abel. Sometimes it seems to be a description, written with torrential eloquence, of the flow of a river to the sea.

As a gigantic laboratory experiment with language, *Finnegans Wake* is bound to exert an influence far beyond the circle of its immediate readers. Whether Joyce is eventually convicted of assaulting the King's English with intent to kill or whether he has really added a cubit to her stature, she will never be quite the same again.

TITLE. The title of *Finnegans Wake* comes from an Irish music-hall ballad, telling how Tim Finnigan of Dublin's Sackville Street, a hod carrier and "an Irish gentleman very odd" who loved his liquor, fell from his ladder one morning and broke his skull. His friends, thinking him dead, assembled for a wake, began to fight, weep, dance:

> *Whack Huno take your partner,*
> *Well the floor your trotters shake,*
> *Isn't it the truth I tell you,*
> *Lots of fun at Finnigan's Wake.*

In the uproar, a gallon of whiskey is spilled on Tim, who comes to, saying,

> *Whirl your liquor round like blazes,*
> *Arrah gudaguddug do you think I'm dead?*

On this old song Joyce has played a characteristic trick. Besides reminding readers that they are in for an Irish evening, his title might be taken as a simple declarative sentence meaning that Finnegans wake up. Hence the implication: ordinary people (such as his hero) do not; the nightmare existence of Everyman ends merely in a deeper sleep.

STORY. As readers hack their way through the thorny pages of *Finnegans Wake*, they become aware of certain figures and phrases that recur frequently—H. C. Earwicker, Anna Livia, Maggie, Guinness, Phoenix Park, the River Liffey that curves through Dublin. Tracing these characters and places as they bob in and out of apparently unrelated words and sentences, Critic Edmund Wilson has worked out the most intelligible interpretation of the book, supported by Joyce's own statement that, as *Ulysses* is a Dublin day, *Finnegans Wake* is a Dublin night. The long confused passages in which people change shape, the speeches that sound matter-of-fact but turn out to be gibberish, the flights, pursuits, embarrassing situations which are oddly taken for granted—all these are not mere plays on words or literary jokes; they are dreams.

Central figure appears to be a middle-aged Dubliner of Norwegian descent named H. C. Earwicker, once a postman, a shopkeeper, a hotelkeeper, an employe of Guinness' Brewery. He is married to a woman named Maggie, and father of several children, but involved in some way with a girl named Anna. Earwicker has been mixed up in some drunken misdemeanor, his dreams are filled with fears of being caught by the police. He dreams that he is coming out of a pub with his pals; a crowd gathers; one of the revelers sings a song, but it turns into a recital of Earwicker's sins and folly. He dreams that he is called upon to explain the fable of "the Mookse and the Gripes"; as he begins, the Mookse comes swaggering up and attacks the Gripes, and suddenly Earwicker himself is going over one of his encounters with the police.

He changes shape in his dream: sometimes he is H. C. Earwicker, but sometimes he is Here Comes Everybody, or Haveth Childers Everywhere. Sometimes he is an old man, worried, half-sick, mixed up in vulgar and unpleasant affairs, sometimes his dreams spring back to his youth when he was, in Critic Wilson's words, "carefree, attractive, well-liked . . . as dawn approaches, as he becomes dimly aware of the first light, the dream begins to brighten and to rise unencumbered."

Earwicker's dreams, like most people's, are troubled by hints of depravity, but they remain hints. Even suggestive words are disguised. Is the book dirty? Censors will probably never be able to tell. Melting and merging in Earwicker's dream-state, like smoke in a fog, readers sense Anna, the girl with whom he is in love: Anna on the riverbank, Anna Livia, Anna Livia Plurabelle. Through the menacing or ridiculous distortions of his dreams, the thought of Anna Livia breaks with singular lyric beauty.

There is no plot in the novel, no story in the usual sense of the word. What happens to Earwicker or what has happened to him—whether, indeed, he is as central a figure as he appears to be—is open to question: readers can construct a dozen theories to explain the form of the book, and find plausible evidence for each. Thus, it sometimes seems that sane speeches are not part of the dream, but voices from the waking world which dimly reach the sleeper. Sometimes it seems that he is hearing confused sounds of some turbulent life going on around him, which he dimly apprehends but in which he takes no part—as Finnigan might semi-consciously register the fighting and weeping over his bier. And there is a suggestion that as the dream ends, life itself ends, in the utter and profound sleep of death.

But however they interpret it, readers are not likely to miss the development in the rhythm and mood of the writing: the bobbing facetious note in the first passages; the clogged, heavy, stupefied quality that marks the middle section; the mood, half-exultation, half-sadness, on which it ends: "A hundred cares, a tithe of troubles and is there one who understands me? One in a thousand of years of the nights?"

METHOD. Joyce's idea in *Finnegans Wake* is not new. More than a hundred years ago, when Nathaniel Hawthorne was living in Salem, he jotted in his notebook an idea for a story: "To write a dream which shall resemble the real course of a dream, with all its inconsistency, its strange transformations . . . with nevertheless a leading idea running through the whole. Up to this old age of the world, no such thing has ever been written."

But Joyce's method is new. Dreams exist as sensation or impression, not as speech. Words are spoken in dreams, but they are usually not the words of waking life, may be capable of multiple meanings, or may even be understood in several different senses by the same dreamer at the same moment. Since dreams take place in a state of suspended consciousness, out of which language itself arises, Joyce creates, in *Finnegans Wake*, a dream language to communicate the dream itself.

Compounded of puns, disjointed syllables, half-words, it is closest to English, but Erse, Latin, Greek, Dutch, French, Sanskrit, even Esperanto appear, usually distorted to suggest both an alien and an English notion. The ablest punster in seven languages, Joyce sometimes combines puns and snatches of songs. Example: "ginabawdy meadabawdy!" (from a passage dealing with Earwicker's dream of a night out). Using a favorite device, he suggests that Anna Livia is the River Liffey by slyly punning on the names of other rivers: "he gave her the tigris eye," "rubbing the mouldaw stains," "And the dneepers of wet and the gangres of sin in it"—for the Tigris, Moldau, Dnieper and Ganges.*

Readers who like plain-spoken words may grow impatient, but lovers of words for themselves will find in *Finnegans Wake* some lyric passages to make them sit up:

"Can't hear with the waters of. The chittering waters of. Flittering bats, fieldmice bawk talk. Ho! Are you not gone ahome? What Thom Malone? Can't hear with bawk of bats, all thim liffeying waters of. Ho, talk save us! My foos won't moos. I feel as old as yonder elm. A tale told of Shaun or Shem? All Livia's daughter-sons. Dark hawks hear us. Night! Night! My ho head halls. I feel as heavy as yonder stone. Tell me of John or Shaun? Who were Shem and Shaun the living sons or daughters of? Night now! Tell me, tell me, tell me, elm! Night night! Telmetale of stem or stone. Beside the rivering waters of, hitherandthithering waters of. Night!"

THE AUTHOR. With the publication of *Finnegans Wake*, James Joyce has probably closed the cycle of his great works. *Ulysses* took seven years to write, *Finnegans Wake*, 17. At this rate of progression another book would take 41 years, making Joyce 98 when it was finished.

Joyce left Ireland ("the old sow that eats her farrow") 35 years ago and went to Trieste, then in Austria-Hungary, to live by "silence, exile and cunning." In Trieste his children were born. In 1915 Joyce was so busy with *Ulysses* that he

* Doodling statisticians have counted up names of 700 rivers in the 20-page Anna Livia section.

scarcely noticed that Italy and Austria were about to fight until frontiers began to close. A Greek friend (Joyce is superstitious about Greeks, believes that they bring him luck, that nuns do not) got him permission to leave through Italy. Along the frontier, each time he passed a station, it was dynamited behind him.

Resettled at Zurich, Joyce taught at the Berlitz school, as he had at Trieste. Mrs. Joyce remembers poverty and small apartments, "long on mice, short on kitchen utensils." But Joyce was happy, worked hard on *Ulysses*, enjoyed drinking white wine with English Painter Frank Budgen at the Café Pfauen. Lenin used to frequent the same café, but the literary and the proletarian revolutionists never met.

Joyce's admirers, George Moore, W. B. Yeats, Edmund Gosse, meanwhile began to worry about his perennial poverty, succeeded in getting him £100 from the Privy Purse, thought that Joyce should show his gratitude by aiding the Allied cause. Joyce, who was under oath to the Austrians not to bear arms and is resolutely unpolitical, thought he did enough by spreading British culture. He founded the English Players and put on his play *Exiles*.

The annoying War over, Joyce returned to Trieste, but the Italians had got there first. There was constant turmoil while one of Joyce's favorite authors, Commendatore Gabriele D'Annunzio, seized near-by Fiume. So in 1920 Joyce took his family to Paris, where he has lived almost continuously since.

Europe in 1920 was still a shell-shocked continent in a state of suspended war. It was impossible to travel in most directions without traveling through armies, or in northern France and Belgium through heaped wreckage and broken walls. Revolutions threatened and populations starved. Joyce in Paris was close to starving too. But help came to him from U. S. and English expatriates. American Poet Robert McAlmon lent him money, Bookshop Owner Sylvia Beach began publishing *Ulysses*. Ezra Pound, Idaho's great expatriate, introduced him to Harriet Weaver.

Owner of the Egoist Press, publisher of *The Egoist*, Harriet Weaver was a shy little wisp of a woman, terrified by the dramatic manners of the literary great she patronized. She has been called "an authentic but difficult saint." To Joyce she proved an angel. In 1922, to assure him complete peace of mind and concentration on his work, Egoist Weaver gave him a large sum of money outright. Most reliable information puts it at £40,000 (about $200,000). With this gift Joyce's biography becomes largely a bibliography.

NONO. In appearance Joyce is slight, frail but impressive. He stands five feet ten or eleven, but looks as if a strong wind might blow him down. His face is thin and fine, its profile especially delicate. He wears his greying, thinning hair brushed back without a part. Joyce reads and writes sprawling in bed or on a couch but he does not like it known. He is very formal in public, in restaurants prefers straight-back chairs in which he sits bolt upright.

He dresses with conservative elegance, never goes out without a slender walking stick, which he manipulates expertly, accenting the delicacy of his beringed hands (he has a passion for rings). His voice is soft, rich and low with a gentle, melancholy brogue. He is rather vain of his tenor, which he likes to join with his son's bass at small family celebrations.

Joyce's curious glasses give him a somewhat Martian appearance. The left lens is so thick it is almost a hemisphere, and to focus it is necessary for him to throw back his head slightly when looking at people. Ten years ago, Joyce could not see with his left eye at all, and a cataract was beginning to form on the right eye. Every operation on the left eye caused a hemorrhage. Finally Dr. Alfred Vogt of Zurich succeeded in making an artificial pupil for the left eye, set in below the position of the normal pupil. The cataract on Joyce's right eye has meanwhile developed. He has had eleven major operations on his eyes, all without anesthetics, faces another soon. But he sees far better than he did ten years ago.

The Joyce family consists of amiable Galway wife Nora, née Barnacle; a son, Giorgio, 33; a dancer-illustrator daughter, Lucia, thirtyish. Giorgio, who married American Helen Gastor, has one son, Stephen James, lives in a Paris suburb where Joyce and his wife frequently visit him. Grandson Stephen is adored by his grandfather, calls the author of *Ulysses* "Nono."

Among Joyce's closest friends are Eugene Jolas (editor of *transition*), Paul Léon, his secretary, and Stuart Gilbert, who wrote an exhaustive exegesis of *Ulysses*. With Eugene and Maria Jolas, the Joyces dine every Saturday night.

Joyce is constantly jotting down overheard phrases, is especially interested in dialects, Midwestern American, British colonial, newspaper jargon. He speaks Italian as smoothly as English, flawless French, fluent German, knows some dozen other tongues, including outlandish Lapp. At present Joyce is not writing. His wife is trying to get him started on something because when he is not working he is hard to live with.

Though he has been away from Ireland since 1904, returning only briefly in 1912 to start a motion-picture house, the *Volta*, which quickly failed, Joyce has an unrivaled knowledge of Dublin and its current life, keeps his recollections green by subscribing to Dublin newspapers, pores over their gossip and chitchat.

But no observer of his life and works can fail to note that James Joyce is a typical Irishman. Born in Dublin, he remains as Irish in Paris or Trieste as he was in the city of his birth. His friends believe that nothing short of a European war could drive him back to the "little brown bog" and the haunting Liffey.

THE NEW PICTURES: "NINOTCHKA"

(*Time*, NOVEMBER 6, 1939)

NINOTCHKA (Metro-Goldwyn-Mayer) reveals the moral, political and sartorial bankruptcy that ensues when a female Bolshevik is exposed to the bourgeois perils of running water, Melvyn Douglas and Paris. Unlike most pictures about Russian Reds, this one is neither crude clowning nor crude prejudice, but a literate and knowingly directed satire which lands many a shrewd crack about phony Five Year Plans, collective farms, Communist jargon and pseudo-scientific gab where it will do the most good—on the funny bone.

During one of those shortages of cash that seem to be chronic in the planned economy, Moscow sends Comrades Buljanoff, Iranoff and Kopalski to Paris to sell confiscated jewels. Though at first they ask, "What would Comrade Lenin say?" about stopping at a swank hotel, the answer soon comes clear: "Comrade Lenin would say, 'The prestige of the workers must be upheld.' We cannot go against Comrade Lenin." But they hastily order "the smallest, dirtiest room in the hotel" when Moscow sends Ninotchka (Greta Garbo) to check up. She is an unsmiling young Russian, with a delightful Swedish accent, who announces that love is a chemical reaction, wants to know at once how much steel the Eiffel Tower contains. At Count Leon's (Melvyn Douglas) smart bachelor apartment, Ninotchka shocks his staid old butler by asking, "Does he beat you?" and by urging that all wealth be shared equally. As the butler indignantly refuses to share his lifetime savings with his bankrupt employer, she says: "Run along to bed, little father." When the Count makes love to her while a traffic cop is tooting his whistle, grimly scientific Ninotchka asks: "What is the interval between his whistles?" Her disintegration begins when she discards her semi-military outfit, buys the most becoming hat she can find, which looks like a horse's nose bag inverted.

Though the comedy becomes somewhat chilled when the comrades return to Moscow, there are such inspirations as a parade on the Red Square with marchers stolidly carrying hundreds of identical pictures of Stalin. There are scenes in Ninotchka's small apartment whose limited *lebensraum* she shares with a girl cellist, a beefy Russian streetcar conductress of the kind Poet e. e. cummings called "non-men," and a dark, dumpy little man who plods silently in & out—"You never know whether he is going to the washroom or the secret police."

Garbo, who plays her first full-length comedy with iron, Bolshevik disregard for glamor, in a khaki uniform and middie blouse, succeeds in the difficult task of making her tight-lipped fanaticism funny without making it ridiculous. Even her change of heart is winning and plausible. But why she should change under the impact of Melvyn Douglas is one of those things even the genius of Karl Marx could not explain.

Good gag: When Ninotchka asks, "Aren't you in love with our Five Year Plan?", cracks Melvyn Douglas: "I've been in love with that Five Year Plan for the last 15 years."

THE NEW PICTURES:
"THE GRAPES OF WRATH"
(*Time*, FEBRUARY 12, 1940)

THE GRAPES OF WRATH (20th Century-Fox). It will be a red rag to bull-mad Californians who may or may not boycott it. Others, who were merely annoyed at the exaggerations, propaganda and phony pathos of John Steinbeck's best selling novel, may just stay away. Pinkos who did not bat an eye when the Soviet Government exterminated 3,000,000 peasants by famine, will go for a good cry over the hardships of the Okies. But people who go to pictures for the sake of seeing pictures will see a great one. For *The Grapes of Wrath* is possibly the best picture ever made from a so-so book. It is certainly the best picture Darryl F. Zanuck has produced or Nunnally Johnson scripted. It would be the best John Ford had directed if he had not already made *The Informer*.

Part of the credit belongs accidentally to censorship and the camera. Censorship excised John Steinbeck's well-meant excesses. Camera-craft purged the picture of the editorial rash that blotched the Steinbeck book. Cleared of excrescences, the residue is the great human story which made thousands of people, who damned the novel's phony conclusions, read it. It is the saga of an authentic U. S. farming family who lose their land. They wander, they suffer, but they endure. They are never quite defeated, and their survival is itself a triumph.

Because the picture deals with everyday U. S. types, casting was all-important. Key character was Ma Joad (Jane Darwell). If she was wrong, the picture could never be in focus. She is magnificent. Russell Simpson is owlish Pa Joad. He is also a million men who plough, seed and harvest U. S. farms. Only star used was Henry Fonda (Tom Joad). For him the part was a throwback to one of his best roles, the young lineman in *Slim*. Others like John Carradine, Charley Grapewin, Zeffie Tilbury, John Qualen, Eddie Quillan, Frank Darien have played minor roles in pictures for years and played them well. Each was as essential to *The Grapes of Wrath* as its scores of Okies, filling station men, cops, deputies. And each is right.

The Americans of this second westward trek are still fighting the desert, the mountains, hunger, thirst, death. Tame Indians stand and wonder at them. The Indians these modern pioneers fight are California deputies who resent the invasion of their State as much as earlier red men resented earlier whites. These are in a better position to show resentment.

The old people die on the march. There are great simple moments like the burial of Grandpa (Charley Grapewin). Wisely, Nunnally Johnson has retained only the bare bones of dialogue from the novel. So the burial scene is terser, more moving in picture than in book. High point is still Tom Joad's quiet rebuke when the irreligious Preacher (John Carradine) does not want to speak at the grave: "Ain't none of our folks ever been buried without a few words." There is the note Tom Joad writes to bury with the body: "This here is William James Joad, dyed of a stroke, old, old man. His fokes buried him becaws they got no money to pay for funerls. Nobody kilt him. Jus a stroke an he dyed."

John Ford's touch is everywhere. It is in Tom Joad's laboriously adding an *s* to funerl in the burial note. It is in the marvelous pantomime as Ma Joad burns her box of letters and keepsakes before starting west—a silent scene that is broken by two meaningful words: "I'm ready." It is in the three tense worried faces reflected in the windshield of the jaloppy as the family crosses the weird desert at night. Above all, it is in the ironically recurring song of the mockingbird, heard in the distance as the family first sights California's orchards.

It is no more important that California deputies kill strikers than that Tom Joad is a killer before the picture begins, kills again before it ends. It is equally unimportant that the Preacher, who has never understood religion, becomes an agitator, or that Tom Joad becomes a fugitive from justice. Ma is the important thing in *The Grapes of Wrath*, for Ma begins as one thing, ends as another. A bewildered, homeless, heartbroken woman when the picture opens, at its close she is an immovable force, holding the crumbling family together against things she does not even understand, against agitators as well as deputies.

As played by Jane Darwell, Ma is a great tragic character of the screen, even her victory is tragic. She can win it only by losing everything. But faced with hunger, homelessness, death, she sees that none of these was important. Ma is the incarnation of the dignity of human being, and the courage to assert it against odds.

THE REVOLT
OF THE INTELLECTUALS

(*Time*, JANUARY 6, 1941)

WHEN THE TRAIN OF HISTORY makes a sharp turn, said Lenin, the passengers who do not have a good grip on their seats are thrown off. Last week the Communist Limited had just about completed the dizzy turn from the Communazi Pact to the Battle of Britain, and U. S. literary liberals were spattered all over the right of way. As the Red Express hooted off into the shades of a closing decade, ex-fellow travelers rubbed their bruises, wondered how they had ever come to get aboard. Observers wondered if they had learned enough to switch to the democratic rails stretching out into the shades of the decade ahead.

The ex-fellow travelers had certainly come a long way. In the U. S. of the '20s with its humming factories and workers who were too busy raising families, buying radios and automobiles to think of striking, they had seen little to admire. Dolefully they clumped together in circles like the *New Republic* and *The Nation*. Substituting a good deal of intellectual inbreeding for organic contact with U. S. life, they developed a curious cultural provincialism. The Depression came to them as a refreshing change. Fundamentally skeptical, maladjusted, defeatist, the intellectuals felt thoroughly at home in the chaos and misery of the '30s. Fundamentally benevolent and humane, they loved their fellow countrymen in distress far more than they could ever love them in prosperity. And they particularly enjoyed life when applause began to greet their berating of the robber barons, president makers, economic royalists, malefactors of great wealth.

From this it was but a step to supporting the Communist Party, especially when Marxists pointed out that while under capitalism, a writer is either a wretched hack or a vulgar best seller, under Communism he is a privileged employe of the State.

The rise of fascism completed the intellectuals' conversion. Frightened by the fate of Germany's intelligentsia, delighted by the chance to strike at Naziism in Spain, intellectuals lent their names, prestige, money, often militant support to dozens of committees (many of which they now realize were phony) to fight fascism and aid loyalist Spain.

By 1938, U. S. Communists could count among their allies such names as

Granville Hicks, Newton Arvin, Waldo Frank, Lewis Mumford, Matthew Josephson, Kyle Crichton (Robert Forsythe), Malcolm Cowley, Donald Ogden Stewart, Erskine Caldwell, Dorothy Parker, Archibald MacLeish, Lillian Hellman, Dashiell Hammett, John Steinbeck, George Soule, many another.

With the exception of Granville Hicks, probably none of these people was a Communist. They were fellow travelers who wanted to help fight fascism. How should they know that Lenin was the first fascist and that they were cooperating with the party from which the Nazis had borrowed all their important methods and ideas?

By last week even the dullest fellow traveler had found out.

After Stalin's Purge, the Nazi-Soviet Pact, Russia's grab of half of Poland, 1940 betrayed the full nature of Stalin's hand with the attack on Finland, the seizure of part of Rumania, and all of the Baltic States. Fellow travelers began to jump off the train. Promptly Comrade V. J. Jerome the Party's Führer for the U. S. Intellectuals, wrote a pamphlet (*Intellectuals and the War*) tearing his old friends to pieces. Jerome said his erstwhile friends were just capitalist stooges anyway. They "came like arrogant slummers . . . looked upon the working class as a pedestal upon which to rise. They saw an opportunity to 'cash in' on the publicity that the movement accords to those who join with the forces of progress."

Meanwhile the intellectuals, refugees once more in their lonely remodeled farmhouses in Connecticut and the Berkshires, thought it over. Comrade Hicks, who had been closest to the Party, knew most about it, thought Communism was daily growing more like fascism. Waldo Frank, who claims that he fellow-traveled under the curious delusion that he could influence Communists toward higher things ("I knew in my heart that I couldn't"), had left the Communists so far behind that it all seemed rather funny. Lewis Mumford, whose fellow-traveling consisted largely of letting Communist-front organizations use his name on letterheads, considered this one of "the shames of my life." He also considered Communists "pernicious"—for Mumford, strong language. Malcolm Cowley, writing a book "to clarify my mind," craved only to be left in peace to lick his spiritual wounds.

Furious Communists had no intention of leaving him or any of their former allies in peace. Old hands at character assassination and the literary smear ("General Krivitsky, you are Schmelka Ginsburg!"), they vilified the deserters in cartoons and articles. But with its first-string literati gone, the *New Masses* was reduced to printing shrill invective by Ruth McKenney (*My Sister Eileen*), low growls by professional Communist Growler Mike Gold (*Jews Without Money*), venomous cartoons by William Gropper.

Lenin had warned: "The counter-revolution develops in exact proportion as the revolution develops." Better than anybody, Communists knew that the experience of the ex-fellow travelers was by no means wasted, feared that the Party had trained a group of men who would one day help to destroy it. The literary intellectuals might be slow, lazy, self-important, unpractical, fussy or funny, but they had reached their convictions, "not without years in the wilderness and days of blindness." Above all they were articulate.

In the decade beginning this year it remains to be seen whether Lenin was right, whether the U. S. literary liberals will bring their intelligence to bear effectively on the side of democracy. Already they had made a beginning. Waldo Frank had written one guide in his *Chart For Rough Water*. Mumford had written another in his simple and moving book *Faith for Living*, while in seven words he phrased what until then millions of his countrymen had felt obscurely: "The struggle is for the human soul."

SILENCE, EXILE & DEATH

(*Time*, FEBRUARY 10, 1941)

L AST WEEK a little group of people got together in Manhattan in an atmosphere of unaccustomed awe. They were friends of James Joyce—Editor
Eugene Jolas (*transition*) and his wife; Poet Padraic Colum and his wife; Robert
Nathan Kastor, brother of Joyce's daughter-in-law; others. Fortnight before, a
terse cable had announced that the author of *Ulysses* and *Finnegans Wake* was
dead in Zurich. Joyce's friends were forming a committee to aid his widow,
daughter and son.

To many a baffled reader of *Finnegans Wake*, the death of Joyce meant merely
that the "cult of unintelligibility" had lost its chief prophet. To his admirers, it
meant the loss of the greatest figure in European letters since Marcel Proust.
To his friends Joyce's death seemed like some simple lapse in nature, grandly
tragic and fitting. Joyce's writings had been the most massive, inclusive,
eloquent statement of Europe's intellectual and moral chaos, a chaos now
audible and visible in the falling walls of Europe's cities. And Joyce had died in
the midst of this downfall—perhaps because of it. There was something about
his death that suggested the great Bishop of Hippo, St. Augustine, dying at
the close of the Roman world to the echo of Vandal swords against the city
gates.

Bit by bit, Joyce's friends in Manhattan pieced together a picture of his last
months. It was a picture of monstrous ironies. Joyce, the young man who fled
from Ireland to live by "silence, exile and cunning," died a destitute refugee
from Paris. The mind that thought history "a nightmare to which I hope never
to awaken," was caught in the fall of France. The man who resented even
minor Government interference with his affairs, was caught in the wartime red
tape of three Governments. The mind that created the Miltonic rhetoric, the
subtle architecture, the poly-portmanteau language of *Ulysses* and *Finnegans
Wake*, found its last peace in talking to an eight-year-old child.

The Joyces (wife Nora, son Giorgio) lived in Paris. His daughter Lucia, who
suffered from a nervous disorder, was in a sanatorium near St. Nazaire. A
devoted father, Joyce worried much about Lucia, spent a good part of the
income left him by Admirer Harriet Weaver on Lucia's doctor and sanatorium
bills. When war broke out, he hurried to St. Nazaire to see her.

Giorgio's son Stephen was at Mrs. Jolas' school at St. Gérand-le-Puy, some
eleven miles north of Vichy. The Joyces were invited there for Christmas 1939,

had a big party. Even then Joyce was suffering a good deal of pain. For ten or twelve years he had had a mysterious intestinal ailment, which did not trouble him as long as life went smoothly, caused him agony when life did not. During the last year, friends claim, Joyce "ate practically nothing."

After Christmas the Joyces rushed back to Paris. Mrs. Joyce hated the Paris *alertes*, but Joyce could not stand the tranquillity of village life. They returned to St. Gérand-le-Puy for Joyce's birthday (Feb. 2), remained until the end of March. Joyce took long walks, read Goethe's conversations with Eckermann, occasionally went to a movie. He also read all the newspapers, though he would discuss politics only with close friends. Shortly before the time the Nazis moved to Norway, the Joyces moved to Vichy.

On June 11 Mrs. Jolas phoned Joyce that she had found a two-room flat in St. Gérand-le-Puy, urged him to move there for safety. Joyce refused. He added: "Have you heard anything about that book* that I asked you to get me from the Gotham Book Mart?" Mrs. Jolas said she hadn't. "Well," said Joyce, "it wouldn't hurt to drop a postal card into the box." The Nazis crossed the Marne.

Two days later, Mrs. Jolas phoned Joyce again to say that the Gare de Lyon in Paris was closed. Joyce said that couldn't possibly be true because his friend, Irish Poet Samuel Beckett, had just come from Paris. He added: "Have you heard anything about that book that I asked you to get me from the Gotham Book Mart?" Next day Paris fell. Day after that Mrs. Jolas ran into Giorgio Joyce on the street in St. Gérand-le-Puy, with all the Joyce luggage, looking for a place to stay. So, by then, were hundreds of others.

At 8 the following morning the James Joyces, forced out of Vichy when the army took over, arrived at St. Gérand-le-Puy. Joyce was indignant; he was not in the habit of going out before 11. Said Mrs. Joyce of the general situation: "Did you ever hear of such nonsense?" Two hours later friends found Joyce happily listening to the radio. The Joyces were not even disturbed when the Nazis occupied the village for six days. Joyce was a British subject, but they did not arrest him. Friends urged him to go to the Irish Minister in Vichy and change his citizenship. Joyce refused: "It would not be honorable."

A fellow refugee was Paul Léon who had worked with Joyce for ten years. Every afternoon at 4 sharp, Joyce and Léon reread *Finnegans Wake*. Joyce would sit with his long thin legs wrapped inextricably around each other while he held the book close to his eyes, studied it through a thick lens. Léon read aloud. They would then make corrections. When Mrs. Jolas reached the U. S. last fall, she took 30 pages of typographical corrections for a possible second edition of *Finnegans Wake*. As she was saying good-by for the last time, Joyce paused, said: "Have you heard anything about that book I asked you to get me from the Gotham Book Mart?"

* The book: Conrad Aiken's *The Coming Forth by Day of Osiris Jones*, an analogue of the Egyptian *Book of the Dead*.

Joyce made frantic efforts to get an exit visa so that he could take his family to Switzerland, scene of his World War I exile, birthplace of *Ulysses*. Thanks to influential friends (especially in the U. S. embassy), he finally procured a visa from Vichy. But the Swiss Government was fussier. At one point it refused to admit Joyce on the claim that he was a Jew. Then it demanded a $7,000 bond. The mayor of Zurich got the sum reduced to $3,500, which some Swiss friends got together. But on the day the Swiss entrance visa arrived, the French exit visa expired.

When Vichy finally granted a second visa, there was no gasoline for the drive from St. Gérand-le-Puy to Vichy. Defying police regulations, Giorgio Joyce bicycled to Vichy, begged every embassy and consulate for gasoline. Finally a bank clerk gave his last gallon of gas, which was enough to take the Joyces to the train.

In Zurich the Joyces put up at a small pension. They had almost no money. None of Joyce's cables to London for money was answered (even air mail from London to Zurich now takes a month). Moreover, the Germans had canceled the permission (obtained through the Irish Minister at Vichy) to remove Lucia from occupied France. Friends say that the thought of his daughter's spending Christmas in a bombed area intensified Joyce's intestinal pains.

He brooded over what he considered the poor reception of *Finnegans Wake*. More & more his bitter day dreams took on the prolonged, chaotic misery of the night dreams in his last great book. (*A hundred cares, a tithe of troubles and is there one who understands me? One in a thousand of years of the nights?*) And as the voices of the awakening children humanize the nightmare in *Finnegans Wake*, the voice of his eight-year-old Grandson Stephen became Joyce's chief solace. All day he would sit telling the boy (*the child we all love to place our hope in for ever*) stories from Greek and Roman mythology, the Norse sagas, Shakespeare. But when only a small sum of money arrived from the U. S., scarcely enough to pay a part of their debts, Joyce collapsed from worry.

An X-ray showed a malignant ulcer on his duodenum. Joyce at first refused an operation because it would be too expensive. After the operation, he had to have two blood transfusions. He tossed around, worrying about Lucia. Then he had a last brief talk alone with his wife. During the night he began to lose consciousness. (*My ho head halls. I feel as heavy as yonder stone. . . . Night now! Tell me, tell me, tell me, elm! Night night! Telmetale of stem or stone. Beside the rivering waters of, hitherandthithering waters of. Night!*) Unlike the Finnegans, Joyce never woke up.

PEACE & THE PAPACY

(*Time*, AUGUST 16, 1943)

Dismayed by the horrors of a war which is bringing ruin to peoples and nations, we turn, O Jesus, to Thy most loving Heart as to our last hope. O God of Mercy, with tears we invoke Thee to end this fearful scourge; O King of Peace, we humbly implore the peace for which we long. . . . Pity the countless mothers in anguish for the fate of their sons; pity the numberless families now bereaved of their fathers; pity Europe, over which broods such havoc and disaster. Do Thou inspire rulers and peoples with counsels of meekness; do Thou heal the discords that tear the nations asunder; Thou Who didst shed Thy Precious Blood that they might live as brothers, bring men together once more in loving harmony. And as once before to the cry of the Apostle Peter: "Save us, Lord, we perish. . . ."

—Benedict XV's Special Prayer for Peace

THE BEGINNING OF WISDOM about the Pope is to know that whatever else he may be doing he is always for peace. Peace rumors all over Europe last week might or might not be well founded. But there was no doubt that Pius XII was busily trying to act as grand pacificator.

Catholics would understand his position and his motives at once.

Non-Catholics might find it hard to draw the line between the Pope's diplomatic and his apostolic roles.

The world had again to take stock of this centuries-old force, the Roman Catholic Church. Who is this apostle of peace? What is Pope Pius XII as symbol, as man, as churchman, as a power for peace among nations and the more fundamental social peace?

SYMBOL OF A SYMBOL. To devout Catholics, the Catholic Church is more than an institution: it is a symbol of eternity. And the Pope, from the moment of his papal elevation, is more than a man: he is a symbol of the symbol of eternity. As symbol, Pius XII is:

• His Holiness the Pope, Bishop of Rome and Vicar of Jesus Christ, Successor of St. Peter, Prince of the Apostles, Supreme Pontiff of the Universal

66

Church, Patriarch of the West, Primate of Italy, Archbishop and Metropolitan of the Roman Province, Sovereign of Vatican City, Servant of the Servants of God.

• Representative of the Church Triumphant (which is in Heaven), of the Church Suffering (which is in Purgatory), of the Church Militant (which is on earth).

• Absolute spiritual ruler of a hierarchy which includes 47 cardinals, 13 patriarchs, some 2,000 archbishops and bishops and about 300,000 priests.

• Absolute spiritual sovereign of some 365,000,000 Roman Catholics throughout the world.

• Infallible formulator for them of dogma in faith and morals.

• Pontiff No. 262 in a prelatical line which includes the Apostle Peter (whom, Catholics believe, Christ commanded to establish the Roman Catholic Church); Leo the Great (who saved Rome from Attila's sacking Huns); Lucius III (who instigated the Inquisition); Innocent III (who exercised effective political control over all Italy and much of Europe, bringing the temporal power of the Papacy to its high-water mark); Leo X (a worldly, cultivated gentleman who excommunicated Martin Luther and proved incapable of dealing with the problems of the Reformation); Alexander VI (a Borgia, who practiced simony and nepotism and failed in his master plan to conquer and unify Italy); Pius VII (whose Concordat with Napoleon restored Catholicism to France); Leo XIII (whose encyclical, *Rerum Novarum*, first diagnosed for Catholics the sickness of contemporary society and called upon them authoritatively to cure it).

As symbol Pius XII is a spiritual autocrat of incalculable power.

THE MAN. But despite the massiveness of the symbol, the Pope is also supremely important as a man. For as Pope (when he speaks *ex cathedra*), he is infallible. But as a man, he is fallible like any other. And this fallibility determines his place among the "good" Popes or the "bad" Popes, and hence his influence upon history.

For the same reason, Popes' lives are written chiefly after their deaths. The biography of a living Pope is officially meager. Pius XII is no exception. But his biographical skeleton is important for the context of history it reveals.

Eugenio Maria Giuseppe Giovanni Pacelli, who today is one of the world's most hardheaded statesmen, was born in 1876—five years after Bismarck founded the Second Reich; six years after Italy achieved unification by Vittorio Emanuele II's seizing Rome from the Papacy, and Pope Pius IX immured himself in his last possession as "the prisoner of the Vatican"; five years after the Paris proletariat bloodily introduced Europe to a new form of the state— the commune or soviet. The consequences of these events were to mark the highlights of the career of Eugenio Pacelli and of the world.

Both Eugenio Pacelli's grandfathers were Vatican functionaries. His father was dean of the Vatican law corps. Young Pacelli practically grew up in church. As a boy he played in the piazza of Rome's Santa Maria della Pace, from whose wall he took his personal motto: *Opus justitiae pax* (The work of justice is peace).

In 1899 Pacelli was ordained a priest. Almost at once Monsignor Gasparri, later papal Secretary of State and Pius XI's grey eminence, invited Pacelli to stop teaching law at the Roman Seminary of Apollinare and to help him make history in the Congregation for Extraordinary Ecclesiastical Affairs (the Vatican's foreign relations office). Pacelli continued there and in the Secretariat of State until he became Pope in 1939. Nevertheless, he saw more of the Church Universal than any other prelate in papal history.

In 1917 (the Russian Revolution had just begun) Pacelli went as Papal Nuncio to Munich, tried (and failed) to talk the Kaiser into a peaceful frame of mind. After the Kaiser fled, Pacelli lived through the Bavarian Soviet Republic. On one occasion he faced down a band of armed revolutionaries who had broken into the Papal Embassy, intending to loot the building.

In 1925, Archbishop Pacelli* concluded a Concordat with Bavaria. Franz Ritter von Epp's forces had overthrown the Soviet, and a police spy named Adolf Hitler was snooping in revolutionary circles for the new government.

In 1929 Pacelli negotiated a Concordat with social-democratic Prussia. When Lutherans objected, Pacelli suggested calling the Concordat a "solemn convention." Everybody was pleased.

In 1929 Pacelli was called to Rome, made a Cardinal and two months later Vatican Secretary of State—the official of whom Sixtus V once wrote: "He must know everything, understand everything—but he must say nothing."

In 1936, he sailed to North America, visited Manhattan's Empire State Building, the Liberty Bell, Mount Vernon, innumerable U.S. Catholic hierarchs. He also traveled 8,000 miles by plane and lunched with the Franklin Roosevelts at Hyde Park. Said Pacelli: "I enjoyed lunching with a typical American family." This trip was an eyeopener to American travelers who saw the statesman of the church riding in a plane break out his portable typewriter and vigorously go to work in midair.

Other trips took Pacelli to Hungary, Switzerland, France, South America.

But Pacelli did not neglect Vatican City. About the time that Pius XI appointed Pacelli Prefect of the Reverend Fabric of St. Peter's (guardian of Vatican buildings), Mussolini banned the Catholic Boy Scouts and started to wipe out *Catholic Action* in Italy. The Pope wrote an encyclical (*Non abbiamo bisogno*) attacking the Fascist action, but since the Fascists controlled all the telegraph lines and cables to the outside world, Mussolini was in a position to read and reply to the encyclical before the world read it.

---

* Eight years earlier Benedict XV had made Pacelli Titular Archbishop of Sardes (an ancient See in Asia Minor).

Cardinal Pacelli got out of this dilemma by having his great friend, Monsignor (now New York's Archbishop) Francis Spellman, hustle copies of the encyclical to France by plane. But the incident made a deep impression on Pacelli. Soon he had equipped the Vatican with a short-wave radio station ("for research and propaganda"), a new electric powerhouse, a fleet of modern automobiles (gifts of the manufacturers) to replace the old carriages, electric elevators, 800 telephones (the Pope's telephone is solid gold stamped with the Papal Arms and the trade-mark of International Telephone & Telegraph Co.), a telephoto apparatus, an electric device to replace the bell ringers at St. Peter's. "The fabric of St. Peter's," said a Catholic commentator, "became as modern as the fabric of New York."

In 1939 Cardinal Pacelli came face to face with the event which was to climax his ecclesiastical career. Pope Pius XI died. From all points of the compass Cardinals rushed to Rome to elect his successor. Cardinal Pacelli personally wired the Italian Line to ask that the *Neptunia* make an extra fast trip so that the Latin American Cardinals would arrive for the voting. In his haste one Cardinal was compelled to fly from Portugal over the battle lines of the Spanish Civil War. For the first time in history U.S. Cardinals also were present at the conclave to elect a Pope.

Cardinal Pacelli was chosen Pope on the third ballot. No Pope had been chosen so quickly since 1623. Pacelli was the first Papal Secretary of State to become Pope since 1775. He was elected on his 63rd birthday. Said one Cardinal, who watched Pacelli while the votes were being counted: "I have never seen anyone look so pale and yet continue breathing."

PAPAL POLITICIAN. Cardinal Pacelli's prepontifical travels were facilitated by the fact that he talks fluently in eight languages. What he talks about in them, and whom he talks to, would constitute a key to the most sinuous and controversial politics pursued by any world power—the Church Temporal's diplomacy. It would also constitute a cryptogram of current history.

"Politics," said Cardinal Manning, "is a part of morals." It was a part of morals that has dogged Pacelli even on his most apostolic and least political missions, even when he was gently (but sure-handedly) weaving the diplomacy of the Church Militant in the reverent hush of the Secretariat of State. Whether the morals of Pacelli's diplomacy were good or bad morals is a violently debated issue.

Of those who believe them to be bad (radicals of all brands, most anti-Catholics, many non-Catholics and even some Catholics), almost none can prove his point because none but the Vatican knows all the facts and circumstances. In general the most serious charges against the Church concern the skill with which the Vatican and its hierarchs have fished and swum in the Fascist sea surrounding them. Vatican critics of various sorts point to various specific chapters of Pacelli diplomacy:

• The Vatican's support of General Franco during and after the Spanish Civil War.

• The pro-Fascist sentiments of some Catholic prelates.

• The Lateran pacts and Concordat with Mussolini whereby the Italian Government agreed to pay the Vatican $39,200,000 in cash; to give it $52,300,000 worth of Italian Government bonds; to recognize Vatican City as a sovereign state; and to make Catholicism the state religion of Italy.

• The 1933 Concordat with Hitler "in spite of many serious misgivings."

• The Vatican's haste to embrace Marshal Pétain and Vichy.

• The Vatican policy toward Russia, which pleases scarcely anybody. The papacy's unflagging crusade against Communism in & out of Russia has long infuriated Leftists. Its recent broadcasts to Russia in Russian have worried: 1) radicals, who fear Catholic propaganda; 2) conservatives, who wonder what the Vatican is up to now.

People who believe that Vatican politics are good morals (and these include most Catholics and a scattering of non-Catholics) defend papal diplomacy with pleas of necessity, adaptability, the ancient wisdom of the Church, and the long view, which in the case of Catholicism embraces eternity—a perspective so vast that differences between democracy and dictatorship sometimes blur to the ecclesiastical eye.

Vatican apologists also like to point to the fact that if Catholic-Fascist relations have been warm in the case of Spain, tolerable in the case of Italy, bearable in the case of Germany, Vatican relations with the democracies have been downright friendly.

But no matter what critics might say, it is scarcely deniable that the Church Apostolic, through the encyclicals and other papal pronouncements, has been fighting against totalitarianism more knowingly, devoutly and authoritatively, and for a longer time, than any other organized power.

THE WORK OF JUSTICE. As a power for peace, Pius XII is less a man than the continuation of a policy. But what the Catholic peace policy is, non-Catholics sometimes find it difficult to discover. And even Catholics find it hard to put the Church's peace program in a nut shell.

Enunciation of the Catholic peace policy is chiefly the work of the last five Popes (Leo XIII, Pius X, Benedict XV, Pius XI, Pius XII). It is at once the most diffuse and most fundamental of peace programs because it is based on the belief that wars between nations can never be prevented until class conflicts within nations have been adjusted. Therefore it talks less about peace than about the causes of social war—Capital and Labor, the relations between the individual and the State, Communism, the position of the family, regimentation, materialism, etc.

Men often glibly say that World War II is a social revolution. But the Catholic Church is the only Christian power that has systematically studied the problem from this viewpoint, or taken steps to end class war by compromising the struggle between Capital and Labor. What the papacy demands is social justice within nations. It believes that if this can be accomplished, wars will largely cease: the work of justice is peace. Instead of Karl Marx's violent "revolutionary reconstitution of society as a whole," the Catholic Church wants a conservative reconstitution of society in the name of God, justice, peace. Moreover, it insists on the dignity of the individual whom God created in his own image and for a decade has vigorously protested against the cruel persecution of the Jews as a violation of God's Tabernacle.

The Church's great human hope is embodied in a series of papal encyclicals of which the two most fundamental are *Rerum Novarum* (May 15, 1891) and *Quadragesimo Anno* (May 15, 1931). Not long after Eugenio Pacelli was born, Leo XIII looked beyond the Vatican and saw European civilization sick in body from social septicemia and sick at heart from the standing threat of war. In *Rerum Novarum* Leo put a fearless finger on the morbid core of Europe's social sickness. He attacked the misery of Europe's impoverished masses and those responsible for their condition.

Forty years later (the Church moves deliberately under the aspect of eternity) Pius XI affirmed his predecessor's policy in the encyclical *Quadragesimo Anno*. He pointed to the growing danger of "atheistic Communism" and Socialism. He also criticized capitalism for its religious and human indifference to the conditions of the workers and for the way in which more & more power was concentrated in the hands of fewer & fewer capitalists. Liberalism* the Pope called "the father of Socialism" and declared that its "heir" is Bolshevism; for, like Communists, most Catholics regard liberals as people who would be Communists if they had the courage or the understanding to see the implications of the liberal position.

THE BASIS OF PEACE. These encyclicals laid the basis for the Church's peace program. But no Pope has summarized more forcefully than Pius XII the Church's position on the social issues upon which peace depends. In a 50th anniversary broadcast of *Rerum Novarum* (June 1, 1941), Pius XII brought that position up to date in a series of powerful assertions:
• On the Role of the Church: "It is . . . the indisputable competence of the Church to decide whether the bases of a given social system are in accord with the unchangeable order" of God.
• On the Rights of the Individual: The power of the State "does not imply a power so extensive over the members of the community that in virtue of it the public authority can interfere with the evolution of that individual . . . decide on the beginning or . . . the ending of human life, determine . . . his

* Walter Lippmann and a pious churchman might agree that Leo XIII was attacking not liberalism as defined by Lippmann in *The Good Society*, but the common perversion of liberalism.

physical, spiritual, religious and moral movements." This would mean "falling into the error that the proper scope of man on earth is society, that society is an end in itself."

• On Labor: "The duty and right to organize the labor of the people belongs above all to the people immediately interested: the employers and the workers. . . . Every legitimate and beneficial interference of the State in the field of labor should be such as to safeguard and respect its personal character."

• On the Distribution of Goods: "The goods which were created by God for all men should flow equally to all according to the principles of justice and charity."

• On the Family: "In the family the nation finds the natural and fecund roots of its greatness and power. . . . A so-called civil progress would . . . be unnatural which—either through the excessive burdens imposed, or through exaggerated direct interference—were to render private property void of significance, practically taking from the family and its head the freedom to follow the scope set by God for the perfection of family life."

• On the Land: "As a rule, only that stability which is rooted in one's own holding, makes of the family the most vital and most perfect and fecund cell of society."

Equally emphatic was Pius XII in his 1942 Christmas broadcast:

• Against Regimentation: A Christian "should cooperate . . . in giving back to the human person the dignity given to it by God . . . should oppose the excessive herding of men, as if they were a mass without a soul. . . ."

• On the Dignity of Work: A Christian "should give to work the place assigned to it by God from the beginning. As an indispensable means toward gaining over the world that mastery which God wishes for His glory, all work has an inherent dignity and at the same time a close connection with the perfection of the person. The Church does not hesitate to draw the practical conclusions which are derived from the moral nobility of work. . . ."

• Against Legal Instability: A Christian "should collaborate toward a complete rehabilitation of the juridical order. The juridic sense of today is often altered and overturned. . . . The cure for this situation becomes feasible when we awaken again the consciousness of a juridical order resting on the supreme dominion of God, and safeguard from all human whims. . . ."

• On the State: A Christian "should help to restore the State and its power to the service of human society, to the full recognition of the respect due to the human person and his efforts to attain his eternal destiny."

Nobody knows yet whether Pius XII will be invited to the peace conference that follows World War II or whether he would accept if he were invited. Benedict XV was expressly barred from Versailles by a clause in the secret treaty of London. But whether or not the Pope is present, the influence of the Catholic Church's peace policy will be tremendous. Most Catholics and non-Catholics alike would agree that a peace that does not embody, at least roughly, the papal position on fundamental social issues will bring not social peace but a sword. For when traditional justice fails, retributive justice supervenes. Failure to grasp this fact means failure to understand the words that Dante read above the gates of Hell:

> *Giustizia mosse il mio alto Fattore;*
> *fecemi la divina Potestate,*
> *la somma Sapienza e il primo Amore. . . .*
> *Lasciate ogni speranza qui voi ch'entrate.**

---

* Justice moved my great Maker; Divine Power made me, and supreme Wisdom and primal Love. . . . All hope abandon, ye who enter here.

HISTORIAN AND HISTORY MAKER

(*The American Mercury*, JANUARY 1944)

I SUPPOSE IT IS NOT TOO SWEEPING a statement to say that many thinking men feel we are on the verge of a new Dark Ages, if not already in it. There is a lot of cold certainty in the air that republicanism has been outlived even before socialism has congealed man's spirit into authoritarian relationships. This chilling presentiment gives a curious unreality to everything honest that is written about any aspect of the basic problems of the time—the social revolution of which the war is a current, and the peace a coming, calamity. Some minds creep into the caves of history and warm themselves as best they can by stirring the embers of the great past. Others stare hard at the current world, saying in effect: "Yes, it's quite as bad as it looks. But there is a way out. All we have to do is the exact opposite of all we have been doing."

Prof. Charles Austin Beard represents the first of these attitudes, Count Richard N. Coudenhove-Kalergi the second. Their two new books, Beard's *The Republic* and Coudenhove-Kalergi's *Crusade for Pan-Europe*, are easily the most important historical volumes published in the last few months. Prof. Beard blows hotly on his historical fingers and pokes the fires of interest in the Constitution of the United States, its history and operation. Coudenhove-Kalergi flutes his oaten pipe toward the green pastures of European peace and unity hitherto desired by practically everybody but the Europeans.

"If the modern Europeans," says Prof. Beard, "had devoted to the study of *The Federalist* half the attention they give to Plato's *Republic*, they would have been better off in every way." In the gray light of 1943, *The Republic* carries on the task bequeathed by Hamilton, Madison and John Jay in their great argument for constitutional government and a republic. It is a seminar in book form. It consists of a series of pseudo-Socratic dialogues (one of the implications of Beard's title) between the author and Dr. Smyth and his wife, two mythical neighbors who apply to Beard for enlightenment. The Smyths are pretty fuddled, and ask Beard to "let us drop in one evening a week for a kind of elementary course on current issues in government and democracy. We don't mean formal lectures."

The lectures are not formal. Neither are they elementary. They begin with "We, the People," and they end with "The Fate and Fortunes of Our Republic." In between the seminarists discuss problems like "Democracy and Rights under the Constitution," "Power and the Control of Power," "Political Parties as Agencies and Motors," "The Republic in the World of Nations." Each of the twenty-one chapters gives Prof. Beard a chance to have his say about some aspect of the Constitution as it is affected by current economic and political problems. As he is the outstanding scholar in the field (he prefers to be called a "student"), what he has to say is worth listening to. It is also inclusive. For Beard's shrewd choice of the Socratic method lets him get all over his field without getting out of bounds. Dr. Beard's interlocutors do not docilely accept his views. Dr. Smyth, a rather typical Beardian, is often truculent. But the Professor does not stand for much back talk from his stooges. He sets them up and he slaps them down. Most of *The Republic* is kept moving by this informal air of vigorous intellectual give and take.

"Oh! You are beginning with that," Dr. Smyth breaks in when Dr. Beard starts out with "We, the People." "That is nothing but rhetoric from the Preamble of the Constitution . . . It means nothing in my young life. It's for politicians, and statesmen, if we have any . . . "

Prof. Beard explains that in the eighteenth century, the words, We, the People, "were revolutionary as any modern phrase which makes timid citizens look under their beds at night for bogies." He adds that they were written by the Committee on Style which included Alexander Hamilton, William S. Johnson, Rufus King, Gouveneur Morris and James Madison.

"Wait a minute," the incautious Dr. Smyth breaks in again, "I know something about those men. Nobody can say that Hamilton had anything but contempt for the people. He is the fellow who said, 'Your people are a great beast.' "

Prof. Beard agrees, but he points out in due time that when a scheme was set afoot to make Washington a dictator, Hamilton called it "a mad project" and helped scotch it. And when the Federalists, alarmed by the fellow-travelling of Jeffersonian Democrats with the French revolutionists, passed the Sedition Act, Hamilton opposed it. "Let us not establish a tyranny," he said. "Energy is a very different thing from violence." "To Hamilton," adds Beard, "justice meant more than Federalist party justice."

Dr. Smyth gets into trouble, too, when he calls Washington an aristocrat, and by doing so he brings out one of the important things about *The Republic*— the distance that Prof. Beard has travelled since his *An Economic Interpretation of the Constitution of the United States*. Beard retorts:

You say that Washington was an aristocrat. The word is vague, but, however interpreted, what has the charge to do with constitutional government? Many of the features of . . . constitutional government were brought into being by persons you would call aristocrats. Magna Charta was forced on King John by members of the English aristocracy . . . Parliamentary government, freedom of press and speech, a high degree of religious toleration, the writ of habeas corpus—many leading doctrines incorporated in the American Constitution and Bill of Rights— were developed in England by members of the upper classes and forced on Crown

and Church. There was nothing democratic about those rights in their origins . . .
consider [Washington's] performances entirely apart from his so-called aristocratic
sympathies. He did not sell out a nation in the bud. Twice Congress granted him
dictatorial powers during the war. Twice he returned those powers unsullied . . .
His firm resistance to every proposal for the seizure of power showed his unfailing
devotion to constitutional methods, even in a revolutionary war. And when
victory in arms came, Washington went before the Congress sitting at Annapolis,
surrendered to it the great powers that had been entrusted to him, and returned to
his plantation as a private citizen once more . . . If there is a more striking or
important event than this in all the toilsome struggle of humanity for civil government, for self-government, I do not know where to find it.

In 1913, Beard published his *Economic Interpretation*. In it he attempted
to prove, by a break-down of the membership of the Constitutional Convention into economic groups, that the Founding Fathers represented not the
American people, but "money, public securities, manufactures and trade and
shipping." "The Constitution," wrote Beard, "was essentially an economic
document based upon the concept that the fundamental private rights of
private property are anterior to government and morally beyond the reach of
popular majorities." There is scarcely a New Dealer who did not cut his eye
teeth on that sentence. Though its naïve economic determinism might have
made Marx shudder, there is scarcely a leftist who did not find *An Economic
Interpretation* congenial reading. Conservatives damned it, and with reason: it
is possible that no single American book has had such influence in condition-
ing a whole generation to the belief that only selfish and materialist motives
guided the Founding Fathers, or ever guide any statesman. It did not so much
lay an axe to a view of history as it laid an axe to a view of morality.

The Republic measures the degree to which Beard's purpose in the *Interpretation* has been misinterpreted. It insists that even the most conservative of the
Founding Fathers did not habitually act from selfish or materialist motives,
and that in acting constitutionally they acted in the interests of all classes. This
in itself makes *The Republic* an event.

In his last chapter with the rather portentous title—"The Fate and Fortunes
of Our Republic"—Beard asks the questions which underlie his whole book:
Will there always be an America? What will Americans make of America? For
unless America is destroyed from within, it will not be destroyed from without. And he affirms his belief that there always *will* be an America: "I believe
that, but I do not know any way by which anybody can *demonstrate* the
proposition." Prof. Beard knows his Oswald Spengler, and nothing he says
rings quite so true as the quotation from Spengler's *Man and Technics*, which he
reads aloud to the Smyths:

We are born into this time and must bravely follow the path to the destined end.
There is no other way. Our duty is to hold on to the lost position, without hope,

without rescue, like that Roman soldier whose bones were found in front of a door at Pompeii, who, during the eruption of Vesuvius, died at his post because they forgot to relieve him. That is greatness. That is what it means to be a thoroughbred. The honorable end is the one thing that can *not* be taken from a man.

II

One day in 1923, while Eastern Europe writhed with wars and revolution threatened Germany where the bottom had dropped out of the mark and the French had entered the Rhineland, several thousand European statesmen, educators, editors, industrialists, bankers and leaders of opinion received an unlooked-for gift. It was a free copy of a book called *Pan-Europe*. With every copy came a membership postcard with a pledge: "I join the Pan-European Union." Joiners were assured that there were no financial obligations. The purpose behind the pledge was explained by the book:

> This book intends to bring to life a great political idea which has long been dormant in the nations of Europe. Many dream of a united Europe but few are resolved to create it. As an object of nostalgia it remains barren; as an object of will it becomes effective. The only force that can achieve Pan-Europe is the will of Europeans. Every European holds in his hand a share of the destiny of the world.

The author of this appeal and originator of Pan-Europe was Count Richard Coudenhove-Kalergi. The Count is practically a Pan-European organization himself. His father was an Austrian and his mother a Japanese. The Coudenhoves were a wealthy Flemish family that fled to Austria during the French Revolution. The Kalergis were a wealthy Cretan family. The line has been further crossed with Poles, Norwegians, Balts, French and Germans, but since the families were selective as well as cosmopolite, the hybridization has been consistently successful.

Count Coudenhove's father was an enlightened conservative who fought pre-Hitler anti-Semitism and the idea of Aryan superiority. A diplomat, he married a Japanese with the full knowledge that the marriage would end his career. After that he devoted himself to managing his estates and supervising his children's education. At his Austrian castle of Ronsperg, the old count toughened his two sons by taking them on long walks in all weathers, insisting that they sleep on straw mattresses, take cold showers, learn to be such crack shots and fencers that no one would ever dare challenge them. He personally taught them Russian and Hungarian. He also took them to mass every Sunday.

The Good Friday service was the occasion for an unfailing ceremony on the part of the elder Count Coudenhove. After everybody had bowed his head in prayer for all heathens and heretics the priest would say: "Let us also pray for the perfidious Jews." This time, nobody was supposed to bow his head. At that point, on every Good Friday, Count Coudenhove got up and walked out of the church in protest against this perpetuation of religious anti-Semitism.

The young Coudenhoves always had one French and one English governess (who was always a Protestant) and an Austrian tutor. The countess had a Hungarian companion. The count had a Bavarian secretary and a Czech manager of his estates. An Armenian waited on the table. Among the exotic guests who came and went were various Hindus, Turks and local rabbis who taught the old count Asiatic tongues, including Hebrew. It was from one of these house guests that Count Richard Coudenhove first heard of Pan-Islam, the germ of his Pan-European idea.

The first part of the autobiographical *Crusade for Pan-Europe* describes Count Coudenhove's youth in Austria, the rest of the book is devoted to his efforts to put over Pan-Europe. The first head of a European government to support Pan-Europe was Dr. Ignaz Seipel, priest, head of Austria's Catholic party, and, in 1923, "undisputed leader of Austria." "When I asked him to back Pan-Europe publicly, he promised to do so. I offered him the presidency of the Austrian branch of the Pan-European Union, and he accepted without hesitation." Dr. Seipel gave Count Coudenhove an office in the old imperial palace in Vienna, which remained the headquarters for Pan-Europe until Hitler invaded Austria.

Next Count Coudenhove called on President Masaryk of Czechoslovakia who was friendly, but sent him on to Prime Minister Beneš. Beneš was "certainly in agreement with Pan-Europe but did not consider it an object of immediate practical policy. He favored it as a beautiful idea which would and should one day be realized."

Others were more sympathetic. At one time Pan-Europe enlisted the support of Europeans as diverse as Count Carlo Sforza and Hjalmar Horace Greeley Schacht. Count Coudenhove had a talk with Benito Mussolini but nothing came of it. But the intellectuals supported the movement. Pan-Europe held a regular congress, adopted a European flag, and caused dissensions in the Communist International which had some Pan-European ideas of its own. The high point was reached in 1929, when Aristide Briand proposed a European Union in a great speech at the League of Nations. Gustav Streseman and Beneš also spoke for union. In the 'twenties Pan-Europe seemed to be going places—but the Nazis got there first.

For a while Count Coudenhove was busy keeping a jump ahead of the German armies. First he fled from occupied Austria to Czechoslovakia, then from Czechoslovakia to France, from France to Switzerland, from Switzerland to Portugal. Now he is in the United States, conducting a seminar at New York University on a postwar European federation. The book in which he describes his life is absorbing as autobiography, direct and clear as a presentation of his Pan-European ideas. At present, these ideas include: A federation of the world (which the count does not believe feasible at present); a federation of Europe as soon as the war is over. His Pan-Europe will be united on a Bill of Rights and governed by a House of Representatives elected on a population basis, and a Senate consisting of the prime ministers and foreign ministers of the component countries. The two houses of parliament would elect an executive of seven members, each in charge of a special ministry.

For Count Coudenhove feels that the time is again ripe for a resurgence of Pan-Europeanism. He shares the common curious view that Europe, is somehow at last ready for the peace and unity it has never been able to achieve. He may be right, though not necessarily in the way he thinks.

LITERARY AUTOLYSIS

(*The American Mercury*, FEBRUARY 1944)

THREE BOOKS could scarcely look less alike than Arthur Koestler's *Arrival and Departure*, G. A. Borgese's *Common Cause*, and *Roots in the Earth*, by P. Alston Waring and Walter Magnes Teller.

Koestler's novel deals with refugees in Neutralia, a country that strangely resembles Portugal. Borgese's book is an unstanchable verbal effusion on the war, the future and the Common Man. *Roots in the Earth* is a little book about farming. Nevertheless, these three have a common cause—social revolution. The social symbol of our age is autolysis, a medical term for the process whereby the stomach, for example, by a subtle derangement of its normal functions, destroys itself by devouring its own tissues. These three books are by-products of autolysis.

Thomas Mann's voluble son-in-law, G. A. Borgese, did not leave Italy until 1931, when he refused to take the fascist oath. Until then he had been a professor of aesthetics and the history of criticism at the University of Milan. Since then he has come to the United States ("on one of the later *Mayflowers*"), become an American citizen, learned English and written *Goliath: The March of Fascism* and *Common Cause*. Both books are written in an unusual rhetoric which Borgese admirers commonly call Carlylean. Readers who struggle to find out what Borgese is driving at sometimes complain that his prose too often sounds like Carlyle translated into Italian and retranslated into English at an old actors' boarding house.

What Borgese is driving at in *Common Cause* is stated in the beginning:

> The explanation of our defeats is that we have not yet begun to fight. . . . Of late we have lifted the common man to supreme heights and discovered in him the measure and meaning of history. He, however, has not requited our tributes of adulation or faith—and remains aloof. The resistance of Russia is a mystery to many: but otherwise, in Europe and in the West, the slaves have not risen, the free have not attacked. That we have not yet begun to fight, means that the common man has not entered the fight. The common man, in plainest words, has not found the common cause.

Unfortunately, the Common Man is not likely to find the common cause in *Common Cause*—certainly not in "plainest words." For if Borgese's rush of language is sometimes suggestive of Respighi's *Fountains of Rome*, the plan of his book is just about as fluid, spurting and elusive. There is a startling chapter (which may come as a surprise to the Britishers) on "Why the British Empire Failed." There is a chapter on the "Germans" who promised the tired world peace and night:

> To everything there is a season, and a time to every purpose under the heaven. The seasons of man change, as do change the seasons of the sky. There is a time for the long proud days; and there is a time for the deeper nights. The Solstice of Man is over. We herald the Night.

There is a chapter on "Russia" with one of the strangest tributes ever penned to Stalin by an admirer:

> This Czar's hands are bloody, and yet one cannot help wondering at some traits of his face, by no means gruesome or ludicrous. . . . Earnestness, with some benevolence, seems to arch those handsome Georgian brows.

There is a tribute to the United States, in which Borgese notes with a newcomer's fresh discernment that the fondest name that Americans have for the United States is "this country."

And however much he may dash around the world—philosophically, historically, politically—it is "this country" that he is primarily interested in. For he believes that One World, the brotherhood of man and the paternalism of the State, cannot be established until the United States and Russia come to a fundamental social agreement. For this purpose, Professor Borgese would like to see Russia become a little more democratic, and America a lot more democratic. For he is one of those thinkers who believe that the Republic is dated, and that the future lies with wider and wider democracy, which always involves, by some strange paradox, more and more control of economic, political and individual life by the State.

This is a dilemma of which Professor Borgese, an intelligent man and not a Marxist, is uneasily aware. It takes him close to 400 pages to reach chapters like "Lands of Promise," "Trumpets of Jericho," and "Man, Common and Uncommon." But he is intellectually acrobatic, and though he has dragged the Common Man (in the name of greater democracy) to the brink of communism, Professor Borgese in the end pins his hopes to "the Imperator (which means commander-in-chief) who will call himself Liberator," and to "the meteoric course of some superhuman personality—whose presence among us is yet undisclosed." If this is not exactly crystal clear, don't blame the reviewer.

II

The first love of the average working revolutionist is still the working man. The working man and the revolutionist are brothers under the elevated; they are city manifestations. The discontented working man is the revolutionist's political meal ticket. The revolutionist is the discontented worker's second brain. Only in exceptional circumstances do farmers or peasants, on one hand, and revolutionists, on the other, ever understand each other. And they never have spoken the same language.

But among circles interested in social change, the word has got around that basic, nationwide social change cannot succeed without the active support of the men who work the land. Hence the great intelligence and energy with which the New Deal has tried to establish Federal controls in agriculture. Hence the great passive resistance of the farmers, who know perfectly well what is up, and who detest statism with every acre of land they own or ever hope to own. The Leftists have been busy killing the hope that the farmer can ever own and work the land profitably in this age. People like Carey McWilliams (as 'twere with one auspicious and one drooping eye), have busily broadcast the sad-glad news that the big farms are getting bigger, and the small farms smaller and poorer. Land monopoly, they claim, is just around the corner; and after that comes socialization of agriculture.

The importance of *Roots in the Earth* lies in the practical intelligence with which it denies that this trend is inevitable. The family-sized farm, say Waring and Teller, can be made to yield a living. Some of the things that can make it pay include greater use of farm machinery, cooperative buying and selling, diversification of crops, soil conservation and strip farming and very low interest rates for the small (forty acre) and middle sized (100 acre) farmer.

Waring and Teller are by no means conservative. They urge, for example, a much greater interference by the Department of Agriculture in farmers' affairs, and they look cross-eyed at big farmers. They do not want socialization of the land. If they urge a bigger cooperative movement and low interest government loans for farmers, it is to keep the farmer land-owning. And the land-owning farmer, big and little, is the conservative base of every healthy society, no matter how many miles of factories may be required to keep the average city dweller in a state of civilized neurosis.

III

Those of us who are conservatives by force of conviction differ from those who are conservatives by force of inertia chiefly in the fact that we take the social revolution seriously. I remember that, when I was scarcely grown, Ernst Toller's custom of dating his earlier plays "from the Fortress-Prison of

Niederschönenfeld, in the century of the Great Social Wars," struck me as better than almost anything else he wrote. That heading seemed to date and locate for me the destiny of my generation.

Few other generations, I suppose, have ever been so unequal to so great a destiny. It was nothing less than to end, one way or another, the Great Social Wars. One or two earlier generations had worked at it. Sensitive men and women, they chilled themselves to a semblance of metallic hardness, went "with bomb or revolver against this or that individual monster." The Terrorist, Kalyaev, was the symbol of that generation—the youth who, in a Siberian prison camp, covered himself with kerosene, set himself on fire and burnt to death. But those deeds, compared to what we did, are like the ferocities of fairy stories, far away and long ago.

We were the realists. We recognized that men are inherently lazy, that as long as they had a hope of future bliss, they would never really struggle for present happiness. So we liquidated God. We developed the total state, the monolithic party, the political police organized as uniformed praetorian armies (Gestapo and GPU), the concentration and forced labor camps (a slower but more profitable form of execution), the shooting of indiscriminate batches of hostages. We secured the safety of the total state by turning whole nations into informers and police spies. We discovered the science of destroying the dignity of an individual so that he would confess to anything we commanded. We are the first generation in history that ever killed and robbed one section of a nation to enrich another section. We destroyed the ghetto of Warsaw and we liquidated the kulaks as a class.

Yet no generation has ever brought such moral fervor to the denial of all morality in the name of Reason. For we acted from the intense conviction that the world of Great Social Wars was so debased, evil and socially cancerous that only a monstrous surgical operation could save it, if it could be saved at all. It was the pride of our generation that we alone had the cold-blooded realistic courage for whatever monstrous acts the salvation of society required. Our courage and our Reason gave us our license to practice social surgery. But suppose that after we had doomed thousands, or only one or two, to die— suppose that then we decided that we had been wrong?

Arthur Koestler's novel *Darkness at Noon* dealt in general with the moral problem of revolution. In particular, it dealt with the moral dilemma of Comrade Rubashov, a composite of a number of Old Bolshevik leaders, liquidated by Stalin. Jailed, forced to sign a false confession, and ultimately shot in the back of the neck by the revolutionary government he had helped create, Comrade Rubashov lost his moral license to practice surgery. He began to think he had been wrong. The GPU inquisitor reminded him:

> There are only two conceptions of ethics, and they are at opposite poles. One of them is Christian and humane, declares the individual to be sacrosanct, and

asserts that the rules of arithmetic are not to be applied to human units. The other starts from the basic principle that a collective aim justifies all means, and not only allows, but demands, that the individual should in every way be subordinated and sacrificed to the community—which may dispose of it as experimentation rabbit or a sacrificial lamb. The first conception could be called anti-vivisection morality, the second vivisection morality. Humbugs and dilettantes have always tried to mix the two conceptions; in practice it is impossible.

But Comrade Rubashov was ripe for shooting, for he no longer believed absolutely in his own infallibility and in the infallibility of Reason.

Old Rubashov reappears in Arthur Koestler's new novel *Arrival and Departure*. Now he is only a thought that passes through the mind of Koestler's new hero whose name is Peter Slavik. Slavik has been an intellectual and a revolutionist in a country resembling Germany. He has been captured by the political police and tortured, but he never confesses. Later he escapes to Neutralia and tries to enlist in the British Army. While he is waiting for the red tape to be untangled, he goes to live in the comfortable rooms of a refugee woman psychiatrist from his home town. She seems to him like "a carnivorous flower." He has an affair with a French refugee girl; but she sails for America, and he discovers that she and the carnivorous flower have been more than friends.

Peter has a nervous collapse. The psychiatrist restores him by making him lay bare his childhood fears and misdeeds that caused him to become a revolutionist. Cured, Peter is on the point of sailing for America. He has even boarded the ship. Then he sees the refugees coming aboard, the communists and ex-communists, the social riff-raff of the revolution which he has repudiated. He rushes off the boat. He is last seen on his way in a plane to be dropped by parachute within the fascist state to join the underground.

Arrival and Departure is only incidentally a novel of psychoanalysis. The sessions with the woman psychologist are little more than a device for telling the story of Slavik's life and revealing his purposes and their neural history. The problem of *Arrival and Departure* is again the moral problem of the revolutionist, though this time it is a much more special case, and on a much smaller scale than in *Darkness at Noon*. The problem for Rubashov was: what shall the revolutionist do when he loses his faith inside Russia? The problem for Peter Slavik is: what shall the revolutionist do who loses his faith in a free country where choices are many? But for the revolutionist who has participated in the central historical experiences of his time, there is no place in the workaday world. Having no faith in God when his life aborts, he turns to action in which he also has no faith, but which is all he knows. Koestler suggests, when Slavik returns to the fascist country, that by returning to underground activity, Peter is somehow doing as much as the army fliers to find a solution for the Great Social War. What he has really found a solution for is despair—if he has found a solution.

There is superb writing in this novel. But more interesting than the book itself, is what it suggests about the struggles in the mind of Arthur Koestler— ex-revolutionist and perhaps the best mind now writing fiction in Europe.

SANTAYANA, POET OF DISSOLUTION
(*The American Mercury*, MARCH 1944)

I FIRST HEARD the name of George Santayana when I was a very baffled student at a big eastern university. Our campus, for youths like me, represented less a concentration than a suspension of the mind's forces. There was one little tow-headed philosophy instructor with pale blue eyes. We called him *Il Porvello*, the Poor Little One, like St. Francis; or more often, the Poor Little White Thing. Now I know him as a bachelor of certified charm and intelligence, the author of some carefully contrived verse and criticism. But then, to my cruelly youthful mind, he seemed an epitome of all that was wrong with higher education. He was co-author of a textbook which was required reading for all freshmen, and which was supposed to purge young minds of the dross of the real world and initiate the pliant into the mystique of culture.

This pale instructor was also the priest of Santayana, whose cult included occasional afternoon teas for those who shared the enthusiasm. As I strove against the flatulent liberalism around me, resenting its ability to undermine my conservative values which it had nothing to replace but which I was too immature to know how to defend, George Santayana became to me, in the persons of his disciples, the symbol of the characterless American intellectual—arrogant, parochial and ineffectual.

Of course, I did not bother to read Santayana. Later, when I found the strength to repudiate the university and strike out for myself, I felt a certain kinship for Santayana because I heard that he had given up teaching as soon as he was able and that he took a rather dim view of American colleges and curricula. Much later, when I began to read Santayana, I was puzzled that a mind whose basic tensile strength was unmistakable should express itself in a prose lightly sprinkled with sugar. Even *The Last Puritan* failed to win me as completely as it won many others.

Therefore it was in a very personal way, tied in with all I have meanwhile felt, experienced and feared about our times, that I realized after reading a few chapters of his new book, *Persons and Places*, that this first volume of Santayana's reminiscences is one of the great expressions of integrity of mind and purpose in recent American letters.

The best writing of our age has everything about it but a passionate integrity. That is its characteristic, incurable failing. But in Santayana's case, there

86

is an integrity of Catholic suppleness and irrefragability, enriched by the deep experience of two cultures (one rock-bound, Protestant and New England, the other Catholic and Mediterranean), international yet intensely local (for most of Santayana's life has been passed in the Spanish provincial city of Avila and the American provincial capitol of Boston). It has been lent fluency by his necessity of thinking in two languages, Spanish and English, and tempered by the age's ultimate test of individualism, the discipline of preserving the classic mind, smiling and ascetic, in a world of technological uniformity. It is an integrity in which there is room for humor, for it has traveled in the world and looked upon the Woolworth Building as well as the Dome of St. Peter's. And it has been matured by overcoming a duality of experience that was both geographic and psychic—a divided family, the alternating influences of a Spanish father and a Spanish boyhood, and a Spanish mother and a New England boyhood.

George Santayana's maternal grandfather came of a Catalan family of Reus. His forebears were not wealthy, but "dignity to the classic mind does not involve great wealth or much territory." The classic mind, however, was in for an experience from which it has never wholly recovered. "Those were unsettled and unsettling times, the repercussions of the French Revolution had not spent themselves, and emancipation of mind was sure to follow, if it had not preceded, being cast loose upon the world." Unlike most younger sons, Santayana's grandfather did not become a monk. He became a Deist. When liberal reverses forced him to flee from Spain, he drifted to "rural, republican, distinguished, Jeffersonian Virginia," where he participated in the "pure life of reason and virtue" to such effect that President Andrew Jackson presently appointed him American consul in Barcelona.

There he arrived with Santayana's mother, then a little girl. He might have remained there humbly and contentedly enough, but again the French Revolution took a hand. "The Arab," says Santayana, "is not ashamed of his desert where he is alone with Allah; but the pupil of the French Revolution, dreaming of multitudes all possessing a multitude of things, and of the same material things, cannot rest in a few old customs and a few simple goods." He set out with his daughter to seek his fortune in the Philippine Islands, then a Spanish possession. There he died, leaving his orphaned daughter alone on a small tropical island with a handful of Indians. She chartered a boat and was making a living at the hemp trade when her plans were upset by the arrival on her island of the man who was later to be George Santayana's father. There are proprieties even in a Rousseauesque Eden. A young white man and woman could not remain together alone in the tropics without scandal. So Santayana's mother gave up hemp and retired to Manila.

There she met and married a young American, George Sturgis, of a great Boston commercial family. She was a Catholic. He was a Unitarian. Their marriage was not, Santayana thinks, eugenically blessed. Their first and second boys died in infancy. Santayana's mother never recovered from the loss of her first-born.

Then George Sturgis died, and on a rebound to Spain, and for reasons which her son finds it hard to recapture, she again met the Santayana who had driven her from her tropical island, and though they were both middle-aged, married him. When their only child was born, he was named George, in honor of his mother's first husband, with his father's consent. Then Señora Santayana returned to Boston with her Sturgis children, leaving George with his father. When George was about eight he joined his mother in America.

"Unhappy compulsion!" the elder Santayana wrote to his distant wife. "Yet it was better for him to be with you than with me, and I prefer his good to my pleasure."

II

Let no one suppose that George Santayana is so wilfully blind to the forces that are disrupting the world as were his disciples, my preceptors at college.

> Not [he says at the beginning of his book] that I would nail the flag of fatalism to the mast at the beginning of this retrospective voyage, What we call the laws of nature are hasty generalizations. . . . Yet in the turbid stream of nature there are clear stretches, and traceable currents; and it is interesting to follow the beginnings and the developments of a run here and a whirlpool there, and to watch the silent glassy volume of water slip faster and faster towards the edge of some precipice. Now my little cockle-shell and the cockle-shells of the rest of my family, and of the whole middle and upper class (except the unsinkable politicians) were being borne along more or less merrily on the surface currents of a treacherous social revolution; and the things that happened to us, and the things we did, with their pleasant and their hopeless sides, all belong to that general moral migration.

This disintegration of the most civilized classes by history is the underlying theme of *Persons and Places,* or rather it is a kind of dark chord struck occasionally to remind the reader of the flux against which the individual is building with doomed success (since the end, in any case, is death) his temporal serenity. Boston and the merchant family of the Sturgises keep turning up on the surface of that flux like bits of slag and ore in a melting cauldron.

Santayana knew Lowell "in his last phase," once shook hands with Longfellow at a garden party, and saw Dr. Holmes who was a neighbor. Otherwise, he had little contact with the Brahmanic spirit. What Santayana knew of Boston was a story of mean streets, a pinched mean house and the decaying

Sturgis family, of which the Santayanas were poor relations. Santayana "had the melancholy pleasure of watching them in their early glory and in their gradual obscuration, dispersion and decline." The most prosperous and forceful of them lost his mind. And there was Aunt Lizzie, "a tall, strong woman of fifty or more, with black hair and bushy eyebrows that met over her nose, and a bass voice, in which it was impressive to hear her tell how her brother, an unemployed clergyman with whom she had had a lawsuit, had attempted to poison her, all for the sake of the wretched pittance that remained to her." There was also Uncle Samuel, but he called only once or twice because "the dear old gentleman was not often let out from Somerville, where he resided in private apartments at the Insane Asylum." In his lucid moments, Uncle Samuel was

> amiable, dignified, and even happy. Indeed, why should he not have been secretly a philosopher, saner than any of us, like Hamlet laughing at all the world and pretending to be mad in order to be free to laugh at it unmolested? But no: such complexities . . . were far from the Sturgis mind. It was straightforward, believed in what it saw, and in what sounded right. It had just enough rope to go once round the intelligible world; to go round it twice, like a philosopher, was beyond the Sturgises.

Among the Sturgises, too, must be numbered Santayana's half-brother and his two half-sisters—especially Susana, "the greatest power, and certainly the strongest affection, in my life." It was Susana, the mixer, who took Santayana, for whom Protestant Boston was a frozen marsh, into one or two foreign Catholic households that were practically the only social contacts the children had. For their mother was sternly ungregarious. When the President of the Roxbury Plato Club invited her to join, she thanked her and excused herself. But the President of the Plato Club persisted: "Might not my mother *develop* an interest in Plato? Would she not be interested in *meeting* all those superior ladies? In what then *was* she interested?" "In winter," said Mrs. Santayana, "I try to keep warm, and in summer I try to keep cool." "Diogenes," her son adds, "could not have sent the President of the Plato Club more curtly about her business."

To Santayana's years from eight to sixteen belong also his picture of the Boston schools. His evocation of their physical and intellectual dinginess, bleakness and public poverty has the quality of clammy breath rising in wet air on a cold day. And yet the wonder grows that out of their confines came Santayana, even though they chiefly induce in him the thought that "In solitude it is possible to love mankind; in the world, for one who knows the world, there can be nothing but secret or open war." "Perhaps," he notes in another connection, "the universe is nothing but an equilibrium of idiocies."

III

Later Santayana escaped from New England with his Sturgis sisters into "the genuine, human, Mediterranean, non-hypocritical world," to the town of Avila, the birthplace of St. Teresa, where there was neither capitalist nor proletarian, where "the fundamental realities are still in evidence," where, from the city one could see at night "in the not too distant mountains, the shepherds' fires twinkle like nether stars." Santayana was nearly seventy before Avila "ceased to be the center of my deepest legal and affectionate ties." There, among its austere, barren mountains, battlemented walls and dark churches, he could feel that "everything profound, everything beautiful had not yet vanished from the world."

But before the great peace of Avila, Santayana had passed eleven quiet years in the Harvard Yard, as undergraduate, instructor and proctor. It is surprising to find the future philosopher of Essences a staff member of the Harvard *Lampoon* and a colleague of William Randolph Hearst. Of one of his Sturgis uncles, Santayana writes: "The world is rather sharply divided for me into the people I like and the people I don't like. Philosophy and charity counsel me to correct this caprice, and I don't theoretically build on it; but it persists in my inner feeling." It is nowhere more persistent than in Santayana's descriptions of the Harvard atmosphere.

Perhaps the essence of what Santayana really has to say about New England, Harvard and his generation is compressed into the last paragraph of his description of his fellow-freshman, Sanborn. Sanborn was a

> poet of lyric and modest flights, but genuine feeling, not naturally in harmony with the over-intellectualized transcendentalism of Concord, Massachusetts, where his father was a conspicuous member of the Emersonian circle. He was a misfit, shy, ungainly, and a poor conversationalist. He was unhappy, poor, helpless. He began to drink.
>
> The sparkle of a glass, the glitter of a smile, the magic of a touch could suddenly transport him out of this world, with all its stubborn hindrances and dreary conventions, into the *Auberge Verte*, the green paradise of his dreams . . . His discouragement became melancholia and began to breed hallucinations. He knew only too much about madness, as everybody did in old New England, and he feared it. He cut his throat in his bath with a razor, and we buried him in Concord, in sight of the optimistic Emerson's grave, after a parlor funeral, with the corpse visible, at which his father read a few not very pertinent passages from the Upanishads and the Psalms.

Much of *Persons and Places* was written in Rome where his "cockle-shell" has finally borne George Santayana as an old man to witness the physical destruction of the Mediterranean culture he loved in the military meeting of the German and United Nations' armies. This dramatic fact heightens the special quality of *Persons and Places*—the sense of the enormous calm of a consciously humble and disciplined mind describing, before its own dissolution, and in terms of its own life, the dissolution of a world which daily proves itself unworthy of being described with so much grace and sympathetic concern. For whatever he may be as a philosopher, Santayana is supremely the poet of the passing of a world that was pious, credulous, well-intentioned and childishly hopeful into a world that is technological, atheistic and hopeless.

THE ANATOMY OF FASCISM

(*The American Mercury*, APRIL 1944)

I F FASCISM comes to America, we shall not even have the excuse of being the first fooled. The third volume of Theodor Mommsen's *History of Rome* describes the collapse of the Roman Republic and the rise of Caesarism in exhaustive detail. But as nobody is going to read Mommsen, John T. Flynn's *As We Go Marching* must serve instead.

It is Mr. Flynn's thesis that the United States has gone quite a piece along the road to fascism in the last eleven years, but that most Americans do not know what road they are on, what fascism is or what a real fascist looks like. Americans have been told, and most of them in their simple way believe, that a fascist is a man in a brown, black or silver shirt who hates Jews. These shirted hoodlums, says Mr. Flynn, certainly exist. But their numbers are comparatively small and their activities are a matter chiefly for the police. The real fascists in the United States do not dress like color charts. Neither do they invariably hate Jews. Nor is fascism primarily a revolt against civilization. "It is, alas," says Mr. Flynn, "not a revolt against Western culture but a fruit— bitter and poisonous—of that culture."

As We Go Marching is an important book because its author skips the common notions about fascism and studies how fascism developed in the two countries where it became the government: Italy and Germany. Of course, there is no such thing as a classic fascism, just as there is no classic democracy. German fascism (Nazism) differs from Italian fascism, just as the democracy of Virginia differs from the democracy of Pennsylvania. But Italian fascism is the thing at its least complicated, and Mr. Flynn's study of it is the best part of his book. It is a historical paradigm worth examining with him.

Italy, which some sixty-two years after its birth became the world's first fascist state, was the child of two of Europe's few authentic democrats— Giuseppe Mazzini and Giuseppe Garibaldi. Until Mussolini, it was "part of that adventure in representative government that characterized the continental scene after 1848." Italy was a constitutional monarchy with an aristocratic Senate and a Premier responsible to the king but dependent for funds on the popularly elected Chamber of Deputies. There was traditional freedom of speech, and, after 1896, complete freedom of the press. Even before that, restraints on the press were almost never invoked:

The liberal parties grew continuously in numbers and power. And generally Italy must be accepted as an authentic section of the whole experiment in representative government. . . . Thus we behold the body into which the fatal germ of fascism will insert itself—a parliamentary, constitutional monarchy conforming to the general pattern of Western civilization. In one other respect it followed that pattern. It was what is commonly called a capitalist society—a society in which the instruments of production and distribution were owned and operated by private persons or groups for profit and within the framework of the money economy. That is, it was like the other countries of western Europe.

Civilized countries, like civilized individuals, like to keep their budgets balanced. For years old-fashioned Italian leaders tried to make income and outgo jibe. But in 1876 there came to power a modern politician for whom red entries had no terror, but even a certain charm. Agostino Depretis, Italy's first Liberal prime minister, started Italy on the road to fascism. He was a journalist who discovered that the key to modern power politics is the masses and their mouthpieces, the Left politicians. With their help, he managed to stay in power for eleven years. He owed this achievement to a technique that seemed inspired then, but is familiar enough now: he had no program. He simply promised every sort of reform regardless of whether or not his promises were contradictory. Thus he promised to reduce taxation but increase public works, to restore prosperity but introduce social security. This catholicity attracted men from all schools of thought. Oppressed tenants and underpaid workers, reactionary landlords and big employers all sought to collect on the promissory notes which he had issued on his way to power.

Depretis, says Mr. Flynn, was a shallow statesman, "with only the most rudimentary knowledge of the grave problems of economics and social reform. But as a politician, he was a craftsman of the first order." When "the inevitable depression" came along, Depretis switched from promises of the more abundant life to "the oldest and most reactionary device—public works financed by government spending." "He adopted," says Mr. Flynn, "the policy which in our own time has been called 'tax and tax, borrow and borrow, spend and spend.'" Depretis unbalanced the budget and it remained unbalanced for thirteen years. He planned it that way. For Depretis had made another important political discovery, which later was to be joyfully rediscovered elsewhere: an unbalanced budget is a political big stick. Political life in Italy, like political life everywhere else on earth, was notoriously corrupt. That is to say, the premier kept his job by buying up the deputies. Depretis discovered that this was horse-and-buggy tactics; he discovered that by spending increased taxes for public works, he could bypass the deputies and buy up their constituents. Then, to get their public works, the constituents would keep the deputies in line for him. "The philanthropic state," says Mr. Flynn, "was now erected in Italy and it was never to be dismantled."

His admirers called Premier Depretis "the incorruptible." Critics called him "the incorruptible corrupter of all." The contribution of Italy's first Liberal government was a spending program so huge that Italy had to finance the immense expenditures of the first World War "on top of the already staggering public debt" on which the interest alone, by 1913, made up one fourth of the public revenues.

A state is as sound as its thriftiest citizens. A social order is sick when it has to tax its thrifty citizens heavily to provide for its poor. When a social order has no other choice but to do so, that social order is doomed. There are two possible delaying stages on the way to the mortuary. Depretis discovered the first one: militarism. His successor, Francesco Crispi, discovered the second: imperialism. For taxpayers may fuss and fret, and even refuse to pay tax tribute to support the impoverished masses, but they cannot refuse to pay even astronomical taxes for the army and navy.

By 1895 Italy was spending five times as much on the army and navy as on public works. Says Mr. Flynn, "To ask an Italian statesman to agree to disarmament before the Great War would have been to ask him to liquidate the largest industry in Italy." Labor and the liberals always supported this make-work program. So did the conservatives, the great enemies of freewheeling finance.

But the hard-headed Italian politicians knew that they could not keep their people piling up taxes even for the army and navy if these were not to be used against somebody. After the Liberal Depretis came the Liberal Francesco Crispi. Crispi perceived that the people must be provided "with an arsenal of fears." "Powerful and greedy neighbors became a national necessity." Crispi, who had been one of Mazzini's favorite lieutenants, plumped for imperialism. "And of course, as the apprehensions of the people grow, the army grows with them, and so too the unbalanced budget. . . ."

In a chapter called *The Incredible Synthesis*, Mr. Flynn explores the strange paradox whereby the Left and the Right got together to create fascism:

We come now to a fact of central importance. What I have been trying to say thus far is that out of the condition of Italian society sprang certain streams of opinion and of desire that governments acted on, and that people accepted or at least surrendered to with little resistance, even though they may not have approved or understood them. Bewildered statesmen turned to government debt as a device for creating purchasing power. No one approved it in principle. But there was no effective resistance because people demanded the fruits it brought. Another was the ever-growing reliance on social-welfare measures to mitigate the privations of the indigent, the unemployed, the sick, the aged. The instruments of debt and spending became standard equipment of politicians. And this need for spending opened the door to an easy surrender to the elements most interested in militarism and . . . imperialism.

II

But the most desperate pump-priming produced not prosperity but a trickle of doubt that pump-priming ever could work. The idea got round that the trouble was in the economic structure itself. Freedom perhaps was too free and had better be regulated.

> One of the most baffling phenomena of fascism [says Mr. Flynn] is the almost incredible collaboration between men of the extreme Right and the extreme Left in its creation. The explanation lies at this point. Both Right and Left joined in this urge for regulation. The motives, the arguments, and the forms of expression were different, but all drove in the same direction. *And this was that the economic system must be controlled in its essential functions and this control must be exercised by the producing groups.*

Fascism began with the first trade union and the first cartel. "At bottom each cartel is an attempt by businessmen to subject a sector of the economic system to government by themselves. The movement marked a turning point in capitalist society. It is an attempt to get rid of the risks inherent in business by planning and direction." Meanwhile, the Left developed its own form of cartelization—syndicalism, chiefly under the theoretical inspiration of the French engineer, Georges Sorel, whose hardboiled *Reflections on Violence* was so much more appealing to our youth than the ponderosities of *Das Kapital*. For Sorel not only had the knife between his teeth; he accepted the more sweeping Marxist ideas too—class war, seizure of the instruments of production by the workers, the expropriation of anybody who owns anything:

> Here in syndicalist-socialism was the catalytic agent that was bringing together a number of hostile elements in society and gradually uniting them, however little they perceived it, in agreement upon the following set of principles:
>   1. The renunciation of the old principle of liberalism in fact, though of course the language of liberalism continued to be used. The unions were as far from liberalism as the nationalists.
>   2. The economic system must be subjected to planning.
>   3. This planning must be done outside the political state.
>   4. It must be committed to the hands of the producing groups.
>   All—employers through their trade associations and cartels, workers through their unions, socialists through their gradual indoctrination with syndicalism— were approaching a common ground by different routes. . . .

For men had lost faith in freedom, justice, religion, their traditional institutions and their leaders. What G. A. Borgese calls the Black Age had begun in Italy. The country came out of the first World War a winner—

But once more peace—dreadful and realistic peace—peace the bill collector, heavy with all her old problems was back in Rome. The deficits were larger. The debt was greater . . . The various economic planners were more relentless than ever in their determination to subject the capitalist system to control . . . Italy's Old Man of the Sea—the debt—was now a monster. The prewar debt which had frightened the conservatives and menaced the state with bankruptcy, looked trivial in the presence of the mountainous load after the war.

Meanwhile "the soldiers streamed back to the cities to find the factories discharging, not hiring men." Out of this paralyzing unemployment, the armed sit-down strikes in north Italy, the general fear and unrest, came Mussolini. How he seized power is fairly recent history. What he made of that power, the new political form which under the force of necessity Mussolini improvised is summarized by Mr. Flynn in eight points. Fascism, he says, "is a form of social organization

1. In which the government acknowledges no restraint upon its powers—totalitarianism.
2. In which this unrestrained government is managed by a dictator—the leadership principle.
3. In which the government is organized to operate the capitalist system and enable it to function under an immense bureaucracy.
4. In which the economic society is organized on the syndicalist model, that is by producing groups formed into craft and professional categories under supervision of the state.
5. In which the government and the syndicalist organizations operate the capitalist society on the planned, autarchial principle.
6. In which the government holds itself responsible to provide the nation with adequate purchasing power by public spending and borrowing.
7. In which militarism is used as a conscious mechanism of government spending, and
8. In which imperialism is included as a policy inevitably flowing from militarism as well as other elements of fascism.

"Wherever," concludes Mr. Flynn, "you find a nation using all these devices you will know that this is a fascist nation. In proportion as any nation uses most of them you may assume it is tending in the direction of fascism . . . "

Toward the end of his Italian section Mr. Flynn has a paragraph that will come as a shock to Henry Agard Wallace:

The commonly accepted theory that fascism originated in the conspiracy of the great industrialists to capture the state will not hold. It originated on the Left. Primarily it gets its first impulses in the decadent or corrupt forms of socialism— from among those erstwhile socialists who, wearying of that struggle, have turned first to syndicalism and then to becoming the saviors of capitalism by adapting the devices of socialism and syndicalism to the capitalist state. The industrialists and nationalists joined up only when the fascist squadrons had produced that disorder and confusion in which they found themselves lost. Then they supposed they perceived dimly at first, and then more clearly, in the preachments of the fascists, the germs of an economic corporativism that they could control, or they saw in the fascist squadrons the only effective enemy for the time being against communism. Fascism is a leftist product—a corrupt and diseased offshoot of leftist agitation.

As We Go Marching is a useful and effective book. It might have been even more effective if Mr. Flynn had closed it with his excellent section on the genesis of German Nazism. Instead of drawing obvious conclusions about current American history, he might have omitted Section Three, "Fascism in the United States," and taken his stand on his foreword: "Actually the book from beginning to end is about the United States." For the last section of a short book is not enough adequately to explore the totalitarian trends which Mr. Flynn believes he sees in America. An investigating committee with plenary powers might hesitate to tackle that job. They would need many books many times the size of *As We Go Marching* to contain their findings.

The last section may be the least satisfactory part of this book for other reasons too. I believe I detect evidences of haste, as if Mr. Flynn had worked on it under the crowding pressures of political events. There is reason to believe that the book was intended to give aid and comfort to conservatives, Democratic and Republican, in an election year. If so, that is a sad commentary on those political conservatives. There is no comfort for conservatives in Mr. Flynn's book. He has admirably analyzed the process by which fascism arrives. But neither he nor anybody else knows any way to stop the process. For nobody knows how to solve the chief political problem of the age—how to pacify the masses before they seize political control of the State. And Wendell Willkie is not a New Deal stooge. He is merely living proof that in this period even the least flexible political party cannot long resist the pressures of the masses which, according to Mr. Flynn, lead inevitably down the road he has ably charted. Conservatives may take a certain bleak pleasure in knowing what the score is. They can hardly be happy about it. For they now stand in one of history's darker valleys, threatened on either hand by landslides of totalitarian fascism or totalitarian communism.

AREA OF DECISION

(*Time*, OCTOBER 9, 1944)

R USSIA'S RED ARMY lunged last week across the Danube into Yugoslavia. British forces landed on the coasts of Albania, on the islands of Dalmatia, inched into Greece. From two sides of the Balkan *massif*, Europe's two greatest powers were approaching a junction in the Balkans. Waiting at this mountainous meeting place of empires was a man who had newly risen into political history after a cryptic lifetime in the political underground: Yugoslavia's Marshal Josip Broz Tito. Tossed up suddenly in the slipstream of military and political movements, he was as little familiar to most of the western world as the lands he defended. But his two years of constant guerrilla warfare with the Germans had made one fact clear: in an area of decision, he was a man of decision.

THE MAN. The details of Tito's life history were obscure, but the results were plowed deep in Tito's gullied face. But before the plowing began, before he was even Tito, he was plain Josip Broz. His father was a Croat blacksmith in the village of Klanjec, near Zagreb. He had scarcely begun to learn his father's trade when the shot with which the Serbian nationalist, Govirlo Princip, killed the Austrian Archduke Franz Ferdinand at Sarajevo, shot young Josip Broz into the Austrian Army.

He was sent to the Eastern Front. Then, like Bela Kun, the future head of Soviet Hungary, and Tibor Szamuely, the future head of Hungary's Red Terror, Josip Broz was captured by the Russians, or deserted to them. It was 1915. He was 19. The Russians packed him off to Omsk, in Siberia.

Two years later, Russia's war front collapsed like a dynamited wall. Most Russian soldiers were peasants and they had heard that inland the peasants were dividing the land. They surged homewards. In Petrograd and Moscow, the Bolsheviks were preparing to seize power. The greatest revolution in history had begun.

In Omsk Josip Broz saw the mass execution of 1,600 striking railroad workers by Tsarist Admiral Kolchak. When the Red Army reached Omsk, Josip Broz joined up. The young Croat who didn't want to fight for the Habsburgs fought through the hard, bitter years of Russia's civil wars.

When they were over, Broz entered a school in Moscow. It was probably the West School, where foreign Communists were trained for ticklish work in foreign countries. For in Moscow the blacksmith's son from Klanjec had acquired a philosophy of life and action (Marxism), a party (the Communists) for which to work, conspire,* live and if necessary die, a Russian wife and son Zharko, who was decorated last year by Marshal Stalin for heroic service in the Red Army. Like most Russian-trained Communists, Broz soon acquired a dangerous mission also.

MISSION FROM MOSCOW. Just a decade after he marched away from the smithy, Josip Broz returned to Croatia, but not to blacksmithing. His job was to organize a metal-trades union. He had left Austria. He returned to the crazy-quilt kingdom of the South Slavs whose Serbs, Croats, Slovenes, Montenegrins and Macedonians would presently be held together in uneasy union by a tight little dictatorship headed by King Alexander II. Under the dictatorship only the Serbs supported the dynasty. Only tractable parties were legal. Trade unions were outlawed. As a Croat, a Communist and a trade-union organizer, Josip Broz soon found himself in jail. He stayed there five years. He was tortured. But to Communists, jail is a commonplace, torture an annealing experience.

Marx had written: the philosophers have explained the world: it is necessary to change the world. What busy Comrade Broz was doing to change the world between his release from jail circa 1930 and his sudden emergence in Yugoslavia in 1941 is mostly his secret.

Tito emerged from underground obscurity for a brief moment during Spain's Civil War. One fall day in 1936 a group of German International Brigaders drove a band of Moors through the village of Palacete near Madrid. In the village was a unit of Yugoslavs, nearly dead from exhaustion. For days they had been holding a gorge in rain, mud, under enemy fire. But when they were ordered to retire for rest, one protested bitterly. That one was Josip Broz. Soon afterward, he was among a hand-picked group of Communists withdrawn by the Red Army's Military Intelligence to join some anti-Franco *guerrilleros* behind Franco's lines. He was next heard of in France, working in the section of the underground whose function was to dispatch men from all over Europe and the U.S. to fight in Spain. He did not reappear again until the fascism he had fought in Franco Spain had overrun Yugoslavia in the form of Naziism.

THE MARSHAL. Yugoslavia got into the war on the Allied side with no premeditation and almost no preparation. The pro-Axis Regency of Prince Paul had been tolerated until March 1941. When it knuckled under to Hitler's demands that Yugoslavia become a German satellite, the Yugoslavs rebelled.

---

* In his *Condition of the Working Classes in England*, Communist Founding Father Friedrich Engels lamented that the English workers were so backward that they had never learned to conspire.

In a bloodless *coup d'état* they tossed out Regent Paul, installed King Peter II, 17. It took the *Wehrmacht* ten days to overrun the unprepared country. The British, who are believed to have inspired the coup against him, hauled Prince Paul away to South Africa, where they are still paying his Johannesburg nightclub chits. King Peter fled first to Athens, then London. But a Yugoslav colonel, Draja Mihailovich, retired to the hills with a handful of soldiers and kept on fighting. He may or may not have heard about the hard-faced Croat named Tito, who, a month before the German armies invaded Russia, had reappeared in Zagreb and Belgrade.

Tito paid a round of quiet visits to Yugoslav leaders, asked them to forget their political differences and unite against the Germans.

For a time Tito, the Croat, and Colonel Mihailovich, the Serb, worked together. Then the followers of Draja Mihailovich clashed with Tito's Partisans. Tito accused Mihailovich of collaboration with the Germans. What had caused the rift? Was it traditional Yugoslav nationalist differences, subtly played on by the Germans? Had Moscow decided to crowd out the Communists' only important competitor for control of the Yugoslav resistance? Whatever the cause, though *Chetniks* and Partisans both continued to fight the Germans, they also began to fight each other.

Tito's movement attracted the most followers. He struck the Germans at every chance, captured their supplies and arms. His Partisans, dispersed through the hills, ate when they could, which was not often, fought when they could, which was often enough. The Partisan emblem was a red, five-pointed star. For a time a yellow hammer & sickle was used by one brigade, soon was discreetly dropped. Word spread through the hills, towns and cities: a remarkable Croat named Tito was fighting the Germans. Yugoslavs from all classes and political parties joined him, including, last week, a son of Mihailovich. Young, strong women like Stana Tomashevich marched and fought like men. Their favorite weapon was the German *Schmeisser* machine pistol. Their favorite song was a haunting old air sung to these words:

> *Hey, Slavs, in vain the depths of hell threaten,*
> *O Slavs, you still are free.*

The blacksmith's boy from Klanjec had become leader of a resistance movement that at one time or another pinned down as many as 18 German divisions in fruitless, fraying warfare in the wild Croatian and Bosnian mountains. But even in the darkest days, when it seemed as if the outside world would never hear the thunder of war reverberating among the beleaguered hills, Tito seldom grew irritable or despondent.

MISSION FROM BRITAIN. At first the outside world heard chiefly the reverberations of the Tito-Mihailovich clashes. In London and Washington the facts of the Yugoslav resistance were obscured in a game of propaganda hide-and-seek. King Peter's men, through ignorance or fear, or both, would not acknowledge the existence of the Communist leader of the Partisans. They controlled the channels of news coming out of Yugoslavia to the Allied side. For two years the Allied public did not even hear of Tito. Often the deeds of Tito were ascribed to Mihailovich, whose loyalty to King Peter was unquestioned.

Then Russia took a hand. In Tiflis (Stalin's old home town), a Free Yugoslavia radio station was set up. From it the news about Tito's Partisans was broadcast to the world. But Tiflis was three weeks by courier from Yugoslavia. News from Tito was always late.

Inside Yugoslavia, the growing Partisan movement more & more took matters into its own hands. If King Peter was not interested in the Partisans, for their part they saw little reason to be interested in their absentee monarch. This feeling increased when the King made Mihailovich a General and Minister of War. Slowly but surely the Partisan movement became also a resistance movement against the old Government.

There was another factor. For several months a British Brigadier, Fitzroy Hew Royle Maclean, had lived with the Partisans as head of an Allied military mission. Brigadier Maclean understood the relationship of politics and warfare. He put down what he had observed about Tito in a report that landed, fat, thick, crammed with a story that even yet waits to be published, on the desk of Prime Minister Winston Churchill. That report, and Britain's need for any fighting ally, convinced Downing Street that its warm smile for Peter's exiled Government, and its cold shoulder toward Tito, would have to be reversed.

Churchill acted. A shake-up occurred in the Yugoslav Government in Exile. The new Premier was Dr. Ivan Subasich, a Croat, who was in Manhattan when the summons came. In Bari, on the Italian coast, he sat down with Tito, roughed out a working agreement. The exiled Government recognized Tito as head of his provisional administration inside Yugoslavia. Tito agreed that at war's end Yugoslavs would get a chance to vote for whatever kind of government they wanted. Meanwhile, the King might continue to call himself King.

FEDERATED YUGOSLAVIA. But he was King of a new Yugoslavia he had never known. Its shadow government, which had never known him, flitted from town to town to avoid the Germans. But while it ran, it also ran a big part of Yugoslavia. And the Allies were doing business with it. It was dominated by a Communist, but it was no Communist government.

It had been brought into existence in 1943 at Jajce, with a program that provided for: 1) the creation of a federated Yugoslavia composed of the six states of Croatia, Slovenia, Serbia, Bosnia and Herzegovina, Montenegro and

Macedonia; 2) establishment of "truly democratic" rights and liberties; 3) inviolability of private property; 4) no revolutionary, economic, or social changes.

This was a program that could rally most Yugoslavs. The federated states, six small countries with equal rights within one country, could remove the traditional frictions that had divided the Yugoslavs. It was the solution a generation of Yugoslavs had dreamed of. It promised 7 million members of the Greek Orthodox Church, 5 million Roman Catholics, 1,500,000 Mohammedans more, rather than less, freedom. It held out to foreign capital, which Yugoslavia would sorely need when reconstruction came, the promise that Yugoslavia would be one place in the world where a man could turn a profit. This year the blacksmith's boy of Klanjec became Marshal and Provisional President of Yugoslavia.

The new Government, called the National Committee of Liberation, was scarcely more Communist than its program. Out of 17 Cabinet officers, five were Communists. Among the non-Communists: Foreign Minister Josip Smodlaka, friend of Czechoslovakia's late, great Thomas Masaryk, onetime Yugoslav Minister to the Vatican; the Rev. Vlado Zecevic, Minister of the Interior (and hence in charge of the police). Minister Zecevic was an Orthodox priest who commanded a detachment of *Chetniks* until late 1941, when he switched from Mihailovich to Tito.

FEDERATED BALKANS. Beyond the hope of a federated Yugoslavia loomed the larger hope of a federated Balkans. If Yugoslavia had been a crazy quilt of related national stocks in precarious cohesion, the Balkans were Europe's craziest quilt of all. Seas and islands of nationalities as different as Serbs, Rumanians, Germans, Greeks and Turks washed around each other in a confusion that defied the drawing of political frontiers. Through the centuries bigger nations, practicing the policy of divide and rule, had kept the Balkans divided and conquered. But a new spirit was abroad. At last federation seemed feasible. Russia was reported to favor the idea—for it promised peace and security in one of Europe's most troubled areas.

But what would Britain say? Britain had supported Tito as an expediency of Empire politics. But Tito's loyalty was to Moscow, not to London. It was sound policy for the Russians to refrain from setting up Communist governments in the Balkan states now occupied by the Red Army. In fact, the Russians were acting with ostentatious correctness. They had even asked Marshal Tito's permission before sending the Red Army across the Danube. But Britons would be less than empire builders if they were not aware that, in the cold-blooded language of politics, the Balkans had become a Russian sphere of influence. As such, it undid the work of a hundred years of British statecraft, and made Russia a Mediterranean power—poised massively above the artery of Empire at Suez. The area of decision for the eastern Mediterranean had been snatched from the British lion by the blacksmith's boy from Klanjec.

Britain could not fail to be aware of this development, but she showed no undue concern. Nor was she likely to, so long as she kept her imperial health and Russia kept her political head.

CRISIS
(*Time*, NOVEMBER 13, 1944)

FRANKLIN ROOSEVELT stuffed another cigaret in his long ivory holder. The White House reporters asked: " . . . Anything you can tell us in the way of background on why it was necessary to call General Stilwell home?" The President flicked ashes from his chalk-striped suit, answered:

It's a simple fact. General Stilwell has done extremely well. I'm very fond of him personally. . . . You all have your likes and dislikes because you're all extremely human. Generalissimo Chiang Kai-shek and General Stilwell had had certain fallings out, oh, quite a while ago; and finally the other day, the Generalissimo asked that somebody be sent to replace General Stilwell. And we did it. . . . It's just one of them things. . . .

The President announced that the resignation of his Ambassador to China, Clarence E. Gauss, had no connection with Stilwell's recall.

In Chungking, T. V. Soong, Chiang Kai-shek's brother-in-law and Foreign Minister, issued a written statement: "The recall of General Stilwell was entirely a matter of personality. . . ."

In Minneapolis, Minnesota's Republican Congressman Walter H. Judd, who had been in China, gave his version of what had happened: one day General Stilwell received orders to deliver an ultimatum from the White House to Chiang Kai-shek. The ultimatum demanded that General Stilwell be made commander of all China's armies or the U.S. would withdraw its military support from China. No self-respecting head of state could countenance such an ultimatum. The Generalissimo's patience snapped. Angrily he retorted: Then the U.S. will have to withdraw its support. Said Congressman Judd: It was a diplomatic mistake by the U.S. "Stilwell did not make the mistake. He was merely the goat of personal government in Washington. We had to back down from an impossible position into which we should never have put ourselves."

Last week tart, taciturn Joseph W. Stilwell arrived in Washington from the Far East. He said nothing. His silence was eloquent. For few Americans knew China so well as General Joseph Stilwell. Few understood so well as he the gravity of the crisis dramatized by his recall—its implications for the future fate of China, the U.S., the world.

CHINA'S FRIEND. Of all Americans, Joe Stilwell should apparently be *persona gratissima* to the Chinese. He is a staunch admirer of China, a close friend of her big & little people, a champion of her causes, a student of her culture. He is a rare "old China hand" who knows the language so well that he can think in Chinese—one of that surprisingly large number of Americans who have overcome the barrier of an Asiatic language to become unofficial legates in the high tradition of U.S.-Chinese friendship.

And as Chiang Kai-shek's first foreign Chief of Staff, Stilwell was the symbol of China's hope in the abiding aid and friendship of the U.S.

CHINA STUDENT. The career that was to take him to Asia began in 1883. Florida-born, Yonkers-bred Joe Stilwell, at 18, was sent by his doctor-lawyer father to West Point because he was something of an adolescent hellion. Young Stilwell would have chosen Yale. During World War I Lieut. Colonel Stilwell served in France. Back in the U.S. at war's end, he felt a cold wave of pacifism welling up over the country, asked the Army to send him abroad, far away, anywhere that he might sometimes enjoy an occasional martial mix-up. One day in 1920 he turned up in Peiping as a military language student.

Joe Stilwell developed an insatiable curiosity about China and her way of life. As military attaché at the U.S. legation in Peiping, his reports were concise, but packed with information. Soon he won the reputation of being an authority on Chinese affairs. He studied in books and at first hand. His lean, leathery figure, bedroll and knapsack slung over his shoulder, became a familiar one, tramping across China's flat, dusty, northern countryside. He liked to mingle with the *chiupa*, the rugged riflemen who, since the Manchu dynasty was overthrown (1911), have borne the burden of their nation's endless civil wars.

Between service stretches in China, Joe Stilwell taught infantry tactics back in the U.S. He also raised a family—three daughters, two sons. But Joe Stilwell, honest, good-humored scholar, teacher and family man, was also known as an acidulous observer of the world of men. For his avuncular benignity, he was called "Uncle Joe." For his biting comments on dopes and humbugs, he was nicknamed "Vinegar."

In China, Stilwell developed one deep conviction that was also a deep compliment to the Chinese nation: he believed that the straw-sandaled, under-fed Chinese soldier, properly equipped, trained and led, was the fighting equal of any other nation's soldier. He was sure that he could create a striking force with Chinese manpower and U.S. weapons that would drive the Japanese from China. After Pearl Harbor, he got the beginning of a slim chance to test this belief.

CHINA'S SOLDIER. In March 1942, General Stilwell went back to China, plunged immediately into the hopeless task of holding Burma against the Japs. His famed retreat across Burma ("I say we took a hell of a beating") did not shake his faith in the Chinese soldier. Generalissimo Chiang Kai-shek supported Stilwell at first. So did his great & good friend, U.S. Army Chief of Staff General George C. Marshall.

But on all sides, frustrations presently piled up. All of Joe Stilwell's vinegar personality could not bite a way through the conflicting confusions of U.S. foreign policy, Chinese domestic policy and Britain's Asiatic aims.

In his campaign to reopen a road to China through northern Burma, "Vinegar Joe," at 59, proved himself a crack field commander, a masterly tactician—and also a driving, red-tape-be-damned anti-diplomat. His men, Chinese and American, saw him frequently from their jungle foxholes. He jeeped across the tortuous terrain indefatigably, injected his high-octane personality into every advance.

But Joe Stilwell could not win the kind of cooperation he needed in high places. He did not get along well with the British: Churchill's policy in the Far East was consistently at variance with U.S. policy. He could not get enough supplies for the Chinese. The trickle of supplies that used to be hauled agonizingly over the Burma Road became a dribble when it had to be flown over the Himalayan "hump." It is still a dribble. The Chinese, exhausted by seven years of almost singlehanded war against Japan, were reluctant to give General Stilwell the troops he wanted for the Burma offensive; the Japs might suddenly crack down on them in earnest. When the Japs began the drive that last week seemed on the verge of cutting China in two, Chiang Kai-shek's Government might well have felt that its go-slow policy was justified.

CHINA'S PUZZLES. And there was the further complication of Washington's peripatetic global emissaries whose powers, purposes and accreditation were often more baffling than any Chinese puzzle. There was Vice President Henry Wallace. He cocked a nutritional eye at China's permanently underfed people, bent an eager ear to gossip of Chungking's and Chiang's political instability, buzzed back to Washington to pour his frightening reports into the Presidential ear. Then there were President Roosevelt's personal representatives, Donald Nelson, all new to China and China to him, and Major General Patrick Hurley. Worldly, well-tailored Pat Hurley stopped off in Moscow to garner Premier Molotov's assurances that Russian has no designs on China, stopped off in Chungking to lecture Chiang Kai-shek on the urgent need to cooperate with Russia and the Chinese Communists. The Generalissimo, however, believed that his Government's most urgent need was more supplies.

Instead of sending supplies, Washington proposed that General Stilwell be given command of all Chinese forces. The White House believed that the Nationalist Government could do a lot more in the fight against Japan by pressing domestic reforms and by coming to terms with the Chinese Communist Government at Yenan. Nobody ever urged the Chinese Communists to come to terms with Chungking.

CHINA'S PATIENCE. But, patiently, the Generalissimo continued to listen. He had learned patience in a stern school—33 years of bloody civil and foreign wars, the pangs of a nation that had not yet forged its unity, won its independence or completed a revolution from feudalism. He had swallowed his pride in dealings with the Americans before. He had agreed to let General Stilwell supervise the distribution of U.S. Lend-Lease in China. Such a condition had been imposed on no other head of a foreign state. The implication was that Chiang Kai-shek could not be trusted with Lend-Lease. But only once is he known to have complained bitterly to a colleague: "The Americans want me to be a slave. I don't mind being a slave for the sake of victory, but"—and his voice broke with anger and injury—"they treat me as if I were a thief!"

With most of the Washington suggestions, the Generalissimo, however, reluctantly agreed. He had already accepted the proposal that General Stilwell be given tactical command of China's armies. Then, seemingly in the discussion over the exact scope of Stilwell's command, he was pushed too far. Perhaps, as some reports maintained, Washington at last insisted on bringing the Chinese Communist armies into the new setup. Allegedly, the Chinese Communists, who have adamantly held out against Chiang's control, were willing to serve under an American general and thereby acquire American arms. Chiang might well have felt that Washington did not understand the danger to Nationalist China in such an arrangement. But, like Washington, General Stilwell had long believed that China's war effort would be mightily reinforced by bringing the Chinese Communist armies into the war against Japan. Did he urge it with too much vinegar?

Be that as it may, on Oct. 19 Joe Stilwell received his recall from Washington. Next day, over a formal cup of tea, he bade farewell to the Generalissimo. He declined the offer of a high Chinese decoration. He attended a final cocktail party with his staff, packed his dumbbells, captured samurai sword and traveling gear. Then he emplaned for the U.S. in the silver-painted transport known as "Uncle Joe's Chariot." Few men had been stouter friends of China.

General Stilwell's recall clumsily terminated an embarrassing episode—but not the basic situation from which it resulted. Stripped to the bare facts, that situation was that Chungking, a dictatorship ruling high-handedly in order to safeguard the last vestiges of democratic principles in China, was engaged in an undeclared civil war with Yenan, a dictatorship whose purpose was the spread of totalitarian Communism in China. At the same time Chungking was locked in a life & death struggle with Japan.

CHINA'S CRITICS. As usual Chungking, not the U.S. or Yenan, was criticized for the Stilwell incident. Typical of the tone long taken by leftists and echoed by liberals was a dispatch cleared by Washington military censors and written by New York *Times*man Brooks Atkinson, just back from Chungking:

"The decision to relieve General Stilwell represents the political triumph of a moribund, anti-democratic regime that is more concerned with maintaining its political supremacy than in driving the Japanese out of China. America is now committed . . . to support a regime that has become increasingly unpopular and distrusted in China, that maintains three secret police services and concentration camps for political prisoners, that stifles free speech and resists democratic forces. . . .

"The Chinese Communists . . . have good armies that are now fighting guerrilla warfare against the Japanese in North China. . . . The Generalissimo regards these armies as the chief threat to his supremacy . . . has made no sincere attempt to arrange at least a truce with them for the duration of the war. . . . No diplomatic genius could have overcome the Generalissimo's basic unwillingness to risk his armies in battle with the Japanese. . . ."

What kind of a government was the Communist Government of Yenan, which the White House and General Stilwell had insisted that Generalissimo Chiang must cooperate with?

Chinese Communists and their sympathizers—notably Edgar Snow (*Red Star Over China, The Battle for Asia*) and Agnes Smedley, daughter of a U.S. coal miner and author of *China's Red Army Marches* and *Battle Hymn of China*, were eloquent about Yenan. Other touring U.S. correspondents have lauded Yenan's agrarian reforms, labor unions, well-fed troops, efficient guerrilla organization. They have never reported Yenan's rigorous press censorship (much stricter than Chungking's), its iron party discipline, "traitors' [concentration] camps," secret police, other totalitarian features.

THE WILD ARTICHOKE. But a new glimpse of Yenan was revealed in four articles entitled *Wild Artichoke*. Written by Wang Shih-wei, the articles appeared in Yenan's *Emancipation Daily*. The author was the Chinese translator of Eugene O'Neill, a scholar of the Yenan Central Research Institute, for 16 years a member of the Communist Party. *Wild Artichoke*, recently smuggled out of Communist China, was written for a campaign of Communist self-criticism, initiated by the head of the Chinese Communist Government, Mao Tse-tung.

Wrote Wang of life in Yenan:

Party bosses showed neither "love nor warmth" for the rank & file; in fact, they ignored the people's welfare, neglected even the sick "who cannot obtain a mouthful of soup." The people voiced their dissatisfaction in "hushed murmurs in the dark of night." There were "three classes of uniform and five classes of food. . . . As for those who advance the fact that distinction of rank exists in the Soviet Union as a legitimate reason for our present practice, well, excuse my bluntness, but I would advise those 'high priests' to shut their mouths."

Among the youths, once burning with zeal for the revolution, there was disillusionment. "Young students are given two meals of rice gruel a day. When asked whether they have eaten enough, they are required to reply with a prescribed model phrase: 'We are well-fed!' " Said Wang: "Such conditions cause uneasiness. . . . I await comments."

They were not long in coming. Shortly after writing *Wild Artichoke*, Wang Shihwei was expelled from the Anti-Japanese Writers League, was branded a Trotskyite, charged with undermining the Communist Party. Then he disappeared.

CHINA'S SORROW. In the first year (1937–38) of the common resistance against Japan, there was an uneasy truce between Yenan and Chungking. But for the past six years an undeclared civil war has raged across North China. Each side has sought to conceal the full details of the bloody fratricide, for it does not make good reading in the chronicle of China's war effort. It has involved 15-day battles, upwards of 40,000 troops in a single action, systematic campaigns of extermination, terror and counter-terror.

In this struggle, the Communists have won a notable victory, not only because of their aggressive policies, but because the Nationalist Government has refrained from throwing its full strength against them during the war against Japan. The Communists now claim control over 80,000,000 Chinese, domination of much of occupied China (Hopei, Shantung, Kiang-su, Anhwei, Chekiang). Their infiltration of these areas has been achieved by driving out not Japs but Chungking's guerrillas and entire administration.

Chungking's military intelligence claims to have captured many Communist High Command directives to its military and political workers. One was Yenan's plan for the capture of political power in northern Kiangsu—a Chungking area: "First, create unrest in the region and unite the small local Communist bands into large units. Through local unrest, we can go forward with our regional work, start opposition to the Nationalist Government, store up grain and accumulate cash by taxation. Second, . . . sudden attacks . . . selecting the lightly defended areas held by the Nationalist troops as our targets. . . . Third, . . . encirclement and *coup d'état*. We shall occupy the whole of northern Kiangsu with all forces at our command."

Certainly it is true, as General Stilwell and others have complained, that Chiang Kai-shek has kept Chungking armies blockading Yenan. But blockading is better than open civil war. For Yenan is also a war front. If Chiang relaxed the blockade, perhaps all of China would ultimately be lost to the democratic cause.

CATASTROPHE. In *U.S. Foreign Policy: Shield of the Republic*, Walter Lippmann has pointed out that there are two powers for which the U.S. must always go to war when their existence is threatened. One is Britain. The other is China. For 100 years the chief object of U.S. Far Eastern policy has been to keep aggressors from taking over China. It is still the chief object of U.S. Far Eastern policy.

No one would deny that Franklin Roosevelt, following the traditional path of U.S. policy in the Far East, has consistently wanted, if not consistently worked for, a strong, independent, democratic China. But the Stilwell incident was a blunder of the first magnitude.

If the rift in U.S.-Chinese relations were not quickly repaired, both China and the U.S. would be the losers. For China, the loss might be great. For the U.S. it might be catastrophic. For if Chiang Kai-shek were compelled to collaborate with Yenan on Yenan's terms, or if he were forced to lift his military blockade of the Chinese Communist area, a Communist China might soon replace Chungking. And unlike Chungking, a Communist China (with its 450 million people) would turn to Russia (with its 200 million people) rather than to the U.S. (with its 130 million) as an international collaborator.

THE GHOSTS ON THE ROOF
(*Time*, MARCH 5, 1945)

The Big Three Conferees dispersed under cover of an all but news-less fog of military security. But here & there was vouchsafed a glimpse—such as Franklin Roosevelt's afterdeck chats with Near Eastern potentates; here & there a sound, like the short snort from Socialism's old warhorse, George Bernard Shaw. Snorted Shaw: "[The Yalta Conference is] an impudently incredible fairy tale. . . . Will Stalin declare war on Japan as the price of surrender of the other two over Lublin? Not a word about it. Fairy tales, fairy tales, fairy tales. I for one should like to know what really passed at Yalta. This will all come out 20 years hence, when Stalin writes his war memoirs. . . . But I shall not then be alive—I shall never know."

Taking Mr. Shaw's lead, one of TIME's *editors has written the following political fairy tale. Since fairy tales, like more solemn reports, have their implications and their moral,* TIME *wishes to make it clear that it admires and respects our heroic ally, recognizes great mutuality of interests between the U.S. and the U.S.S.R.— but that in any argument between Communism and Democracy,* TIME *is on the side of Democracy.*

WITH THE SOFTNESS of bats, seven ghosts settled down on the flat roof of the Livadia Palace at Yalta. They found someone else already there: a statuesque female figure, crouching, with her eye glued to one of the holes in the roof (it had been through the Russian revolution, three years of civil war, 21 years of Socialist reconstruction, the German invasion and the Russian reoccupation).

"Madam," said the foremost ghost, an imperious woman with a bullet hole in her head, "what are you doing on our roof?"

Clio, the Muse of History (for it was she), looked up, her finger on her lips. "Shh!" she said, "the Big Three Conference is just ending down there. What with security regulations, censorship and personal secretiveness, the only way I can find out anything these days is by peeping. And who are you?" she asked, squinting slightly (history is sometimes a little shortsighted). "I've seen you somewhere before."

"Madam," said a male ghost, rising on tiptoe to speak over his wife's shoulder (he also had a bullet hole in his forehead), "I am Nicholas II, Emperor and Autocrat of All the Russias, Tsar of Moscow, Kiev, Novgorod, Kazan, Astrakhan, of Poland, Siberia and Georgia, Grand Duke of Smolensk, Lithuania, Podolia and Finland, Prince of Estonia, Livonia and Bialystok, Lord of Pskov, Riazan, Yaroslavl, Vitebsk and All the Region of the North, Lord. . . . "

"Nicholas—how nice to see you again!" cried History. "Wherever have you been? And the Tsarina Alix! Your four charming daughters, I presume—gracious, but those bullet holes are disfiguring. And the little hemophiliac—Tsarevich Alexei! Ah, yes, I understand—doomed for a certain term to walk the night. . . . Why, I've scarcely given you a thought since that time when the Communists threw your bodies down the mine shaft in Ekaterinburg [now Sverdlovsk]. Whatever brings you here?"

"This, Madam," said the imperial ghost, "is no strange place to me. It is our former estate of Livadia. Allow me to cite the Intourist's *Pocket Guide to the Soviet Union:* 'This estate occupies 350 hectares of land, and includes a large park, two palaces and many vineyards. The newer palace [you are standing on its roof], built in 1911 by Krasnov in the style of the Italian Renaissance, is of white Inkerman stone, and contains nearly a hundred rooms. It has now been changed into a sanatorium for sick peasants, although certain of the rooms have been reserved as a museum. . . .

" 'From the alleyways of the Livadian Park. . . .' " Here the Tsarina cut her husband short with a stamp of her ghostly foot.

"Don't hedge, Nicky," she cried. "He never could come to the point. He's trying to cover up the fact that he wanted to eavesdrop on the Big Three Conference. He doesn't like to admit it in front of the Tsarevich," she added in a stage whisper, "but His Imperial Majesty is simply fascinated by Stalin—*mais tout' à fait épris?*"

"Stalin! You?" gasped the Muse of History.

"Yes, yes, oh yes," said the Tsar eagerly, elbowing his wife's ghost out of the way. "What statesmanship! What vision! What power! We have known nothing like it since my ancestor, Peter the Great, broke a window into Europe by overrunning the Baltic states in the 18th century. Stalin has made Russia great again!"

"It all began," said the Tsarina wearily, "with the German-Russian partition of Poland. . . ."

"I always wanted to take those Poles down a peg," the Tsar broke in, "but something was always tying my hands."

"Until then," the Tsarina went on, "we enjoyed a pleasant, if rather insubstantial, life. We used to haunt the Casino at Monte Carlo. But after the partition of Poland, Nicky insisted on returning to Russia. He began to attend the meetings of the Politburo. The Politburo! Oh, those interminable speeches. . . . *Ah, Katorga!*"*

"Couldn't you stay home?" asked the Muse of History.

"And leave Nicky alone with those sharpers! He never could do anything without me. Besides, I doubt if you know what it's like to be a ghost: *le silence éternel de ces espaces infinis m'effraie*—The eternal silence of these infinite spaces terrifies me. Pascal said that, you know. Not bad for a man who had never been liquidated. And then," the Tsarina added, "Stalin overran Estonia, Latvia, Lithuania."

"Bessarabia," cried the Tsar, "was recovered from Rumania."

"And Northern Bukovina," cried the Tsarina, "which had never been Russian before."

"Foreign Minister Saracoglu of Turkey was summoned to Moscow," said the Tsar, "and taken over the jumps. For a moment I thought we had the Straits."

"Constantinople," breathed the Tsarina, "the goal of 200 years of Russian diplomacy."

"After that," said the Tsar, "it could not be put off any longer."

"What?" asked the Muse of History.

"Why, my conversion," said the Tsar. "I—I became a Marxist."

"He means a Leninist-Stalinist," said the Tsarina. "By official definition Leninism-Stalinism is the Marxism of this historical period."

"Stalinists!" cried the Muse of History.

"I don't see any reason why *you* should be so surprised, Madam," said the Tsarina. "After the way you have favored Communism for the last 27 years, you are little better than a fellow traveler yourself!"

"Of course, we could not formally enter the Party," the Tsar explained. "There was the question of our former status as exploiters in Russia. Even worse was our present status as ghosts. It violates a basic tenet of Marxism which, of course, does not recognize the supernatural."

"One might suppose, though," said the Tsarina, "that since the Party was, so to speak, responsible for making us what we are, the Central Control Commission would stretch a point in our case."

"And now," said the Tsar, peering through the chink in the roof, "the greatest statesmen in the world have come to Stalin. Who but he would have had the sense of historical fitness to entertain them in my expropriated palace! There he sits, so small, so sure. He is magnificent. Greater than Rurik, greater than Peter! For Peter conquered only in the name of a limited class. But Stalin embodies the international social revolution. That is the mighty, new device of power politics which he has developed for blowing up other countries from within."

*Meaning: Hard Labor—An expletive used by Old Bolsheviks instead of Oh, Hell!

"With it he is conquering Rumania and Bulgaria!" cried the Tsarina.

"Yugoslavia and Hungary!" cried the Tsar.

"Poland and Finland," cried the Tsarina.

"His party comrades are high in the Governments of Italy and France."

"A fortnight ago they re-entered the Government of Belgium."

"Soon they will control most of Germany."

"They already control a vast region of China."

"When Russia enters the war against Japan, we shall take Manchuria, Inner Mongolia, Korea, and settle the old score with Chiang Kai-shek."

"Through the meddling of the imperialist, Churchill, we have suffered a temporary setback in Greece. But when the proper time comes, we shall sweep through Iran and reach the soft underbelly of Turkey from the south. Turkey and Greece are Britain's bastions to defend the Middle East. . . ."

" 'You have a world to win,' " cried the Tsarina, " 'You have nothing to lose but your chains.' "

"I must ask you, Madam," said the Muse of History, "to stop dancing up & down on this roof. These old palaces are scarcely more substantial than you ghosts. I am glad to see that Marxism has had the same psychotherapeutic effect on you as on so many neurotics who join the Communist Party. But your notions about Russia and Stalin are highly abnormal. All right-thinking people now agree that Russia is a mighty friend of democracy. Stalin has become a conservative. In a few hours the whole civilized world will hail the historic decisions just reached beneath your feet as proof that the Soviet Union is prepared to collaborate with her allies in making the world safe for democracy and capitalism. The revolution is over."

"*Grazhdanka!* (citizeness)," cried the Tsarina, "you have been reading banned books. Those are the views of the renegade Leon Trotsky."

"The Muse cannot help being an intellectual," said the Tsar generously, "but I do not think that we should charge her with Trotskyism. I must say, though, that for a Muse of History, you seem to have a very slight grasp of the historical dialectic. It is difficult for me to understand how a contemporary of the dialectician, Heraclitus of Ephesus, can still think in the static concepts of 19th-Century liberalism. History, Madam, is not a suburban trolley line which stops to accommodate every housewife with bundles in her arms."

"I think I liked you better, Nicholas," said the Muse of History, "when you were only a weakling Tsar. You are becoming a realist."

"Death," said the Tsarina, "is a somewhat maturing experience. What Nicky means is that between two systems of society, which embody diametrically opposed moral and political principles, even peace may be only a tactic of struggle."

"But have not the gentlemen downstairs," asked History, "just agreed to solve the Polish and Yugoslav questions in a friendly fashion?"

"What makes Stalin great," said the Tsar, "is that he understands how to adapt revolutionary tactics to the whirling spirals of history as it emerges onto new planes. He has discarded the classical type of proletarian revolution. Nevertheless, he is carrying through basic social revolutions in Rumania, Bulgaria, Yugoslavia, Hungary and Poland. Furthermore, we Marxists believe that in the years of peace Britain and the U.S. will fall apart, due, as we Marxists say, to the inability of capitalism to solve its basic contradiction—that is, its inability to provide continuous work for the masses so that they can buy the goods whose production would provide continuous work for the masses. Britain and America can solve this problem only by becoming Communist states."

"If that were true, Stalin would be wrong," said History, "because America and Britain, though they may undergo great changes, will not become Communist states. More is at stake than economic and political systems. Two faiths are at issue. It is just that problem which these gentlemen below are trying to work out in practical terms. But if they fail, I foresee more wars, more revolutions, greater proscriptions, bloodshed and human misery."

"Well," said the Tsarina, "if you can foresee all that, why don't you do something to prevent it?"

The Muse of History drew the Tsarevich to her, for he had become restless. "Poor little bleeder," she said, stroking his hair, "different only in the organic nature of your disease from so many others who have bled and died. In answer to your question, Madam," she said, glancing at the Tsarina, "I never permit my fore-knowledge to interfere with human folly, if only because I never expect human folly to learn much from history. Besides, I must leave something for my sister, Melpomene, to work on."*

*In the Greek pantheon, Melpomene was the Muse of Tragedy.

THE OLD DEAL

(*Time*, OCTOBER 22, 1945)

THE AGE OF JACKSON—*Arthur Schlesinger Jr.*—*Little, Brown* ($5).

ONCE UPON A TIME, when the Yewnited States was just a little shaver among the nations, but already very spoiled along the literate Eastern fringes, there lived younder in Tennessee a lovable old man with a tongue like a rat-tailed file and a face so hard they called him Old Hickory. He was a great hero. In the War of 1812, he licked the British in the Battle of Noo Orleens (some time after peace had been made). Everybody loved him because he had come up the hard way from nothing to a plantation and owning slaves, but he never forgot the COMMON MAN. Sitting on his plantation porch of an evening, he would say: "I still love the COMMON MAN," and, with a jet of tobacco juice slanchwise between the Ionic columns, would drown a doodlebug at five yards. So they called him the SAGE of The Hermitage (his plantation).

Now, in the big city of Philadelphia, across the mountains, lived a very wicked man. His name was Nicholas Biddle. He was president of the Yewnited States Bank, which was a wily scheme to get hard money away from the COMMON MAN and give him scraps of paper in exchange. This Biddle was a bad actor. He did not eat with his knife and he foregathered with cronies who drank soup in silence so they could hear each other plot against the COMMON MAN. They were called Federalists. They held that some of the COMMON MEN could be hoodwinked all of the time, and that that was enough. They plotted to keep the COMMON MAN from being hoodwinked by anybody else.

One day Old Hickory got so mad he roared: "My name is Andrew Jackson, fresh from the backwoods, half-horse, half-alligator, a little touched with snapping turtle. I can wade the Mississippi, leap the Ohio, ride a streak of lightning, slip without a scratch down the honey locust, whip my weight in wildcats, hug a bear too close for comfort and eat anybody opposed to the COMMON MAN! Come on, boys, let's get Nicholas Biddle."

So all the peckerwoods and rednecks and the big planters from the South (who did not like the tariff) and the farmers from the West (who did not like the Bank), they voted Old Hickory to be the seventh President of the Yewnited States. Then they all marched to Washington. Old Hickory kicked Nicholas Biddle higher than the day before yesterday and the Yewnited States Bank higher than the day before next. Then they all went to the White House for free grog and climbed over the fancy chairs with muddy boots. Everybody got jobs with the Government because, as Old Hickory said: "To the victors belong the spoils!" And everybody agreed that it was democracy at work.

Everybody, that is, except the Federalists, who were right pokey about it and thought that democracy could be made to work quite well without the cowhide boots, and that the great thing about democracy was that it gave the COMMON MAN the chance not to be common.

ENERGETIC EMBRYO. So runs the Jackson legend. Now Arthur M. Schlesinger Jr., son of the professor of American History at Harvard University, in a brilliant justification of the New Deal disguised as a history of the age of Jackson, says that the legend and the facts do not jibe at all. In 577 pages, he implies that the "Jacksonian Revolution," which finally drove the Federalists out, and brought entirely new social forces into political power in the U.S., was just the Roosevelt revolution in embryo. The social forces that broke the Federalists and the power of the "mercantile classes" and made Old Hickory President were the same kind of forces that made the New Deal powerful. (The COMMON MAN reversed his field when Old Hickory bequeathed him an executive successor in the form of Martin Van Buren, the Harry S. Truman of the time.)

Mr. Schlesinger's purpose in the *Age of Jackson* is to re-examine the political ideas and motives that animated the Jacksonian leaders of the masses, and to establish these ideas as the missing link between the somewhat contradictory body of theory and practice known as Jeffersonianism and the somewhat contradictory body of theory and practice called the New Deal. The result is an unusually readable history about one of the most opaque episodes in the American past.

In a series of crisp biographical sketches, Schlesinger resuscitates the men around Jackson, some of them members of his official family, some of them members of the unofficial "Kitchen Cabinet" which sometimes played a more effective role in governing the country than the cabinet officers. Many of these men have been forgotten. There was Thomas Hart Benton ("He had a giant conviction that he and the people were one. 'Nobody opposes Benton,' he would roar, pronouncing it 'Bane-ton,' 'but a few blackjack prairie lawyers; these are the only opponents of Benton. Benton and the people are one and the same, sir; synonymous terms, sir; synonymous terms, sir.' ").

There was C. C. Cambreleng, "the crony of Van Buren"; Roger B. ("Dred Scott") Taney, "the spearhead of radicalism in the new cabinet" ("a tall sharp-faced man, with irregular yellow teeth, generally clamped on a long black cigar, he made a bad first impression," but his reasoning and his conviction won him friends). There was Amos Kendall, the Harry Hopkins of the age ("his chronic bad health may have created a special bond with the President,

and Jackson soon began to rely on Kendall for aid in writing his messages. . . .
Gradually, Kendall's supreme skill in interpreting, verbalizing and document-
ing Jackson's intuitions made him indispensable").

There was John Taylor of Caroline, farmer, Jeffersonian theorist and author
of *An Enquiry into the Principles and Policy of the Government of the United States*,
which John Randolph considered "a monument of the force and weakness of
the human mind," and Mr. Schlesinger considers great political writing.

CHRONIC INFLAMMATION. It is Author Schlesinger's novel contention that
the orthodox schoolmen have been wrong about Jackson's popular support.
Says Schlesinger: The enduring basis of Jackson's strength was not the intermittent radicalism of the West and South, but the chronic radicalism of the
Eastern working classes. It was alliance with them which enabled Jacksonism
to advance beyond Jeffersonism, to the Jeffersonian insistence on political
freedom, Jacksonism added the insistence on economic freedom—the catch-
word of the New Deal.

Says Schlesinger: "The Jacksonians believed that there was a deep-rooted
conflict in society between the 'producing' and 'non-producing' classes—the
farmers and laborers on the one hand, and the business community on the
other. The business community was considered to hold high cards in this
conflict through its network of banks and corporations, its control of education
and the press, above all, its power over the state. . . ."

Democracy, Schlesinger holds, is a condition of tension, in which neither
side has a permanent advantage. This theory of tension distinguishes Historian Schlesinger's from Revolutionist Karl Marx's theory of class struggle,
which ends each bout in a sullen victory for one side or the other, or "in the
common ruin of the contending classes."

The history of the next few decades will tell which theorist is right.

CHRISTMAS 1945
(*Time*, DECEMBER 24, 1945)

PEACE AND HOMECOMING, peace and homecoming rang like the clangor of Christmas bells in the heart of nearly every American last week.

For most Americans, on the first Christmas without war since 1938, these two facts transcended all others: peace (at least, the cessation of major war) had come back to earth; millions of U.S. fighting men, now a peaceful army of longed-for occupation, were streaming back to their homes. As families were reunited, often after years of separation, it was small wonder if the Christmas desire to give turned, as a result of the famine of goods, into a frenzy to buy, if Christmas as a domestic holiday and a public manifestation was sometimes of staggering inconsequence.

As a religious holiday, Christmas 1945 had, at least in the secret mind of those who shared the Christian vision, a new solemnity. Well might they read with a new anguish of hope, a new resoluteness of faith, a new temper of charity, the age-old words—perhaps the most perfect ever uttered:

And there were in the same country shepherds abiding in the field, keeping watch over their flock by night.

And, lo, the angel of the Lord came upon them, and the glory of the Lord shone round about them, and they were sore afraid.

And the angel said unto them, fear not: for, behold, I bring you good tidings of great joy, which shall be to all people.

For unto you is born this day, in the city of David, a Saviour, which is Christ the Lord.

And this shall be a sign unto you: ye shall find the babe wrapped in swaddling clothes lying in a manger.

And suddenly there was with the angel a multitude of the heavenly host, praising God, and saying,

Glory to God in the highest, and on earth peace, good will toward men.

Christmas 1945 lay deep in the long shadow of eternity. Beside every U.S. celebrant of Christmas, there watched, like the shepherds, three presences: the war's dead, the wretched and The Bomb.

The war's dead included not only those who died that Christians might celebrate Christmas in peace and freedom. They also included the millions who died in concentration camps, the children who perished from exhaustion, cold and fear, in flight from battling armies or in air raids, the children who have died by thousands from hunger and cold in Europe and Asia this year.

The wretched included not only war's fugitives, the millions of displaced persons drifting in hunger, cold and anxiety over the hard face of the world; and those others, allies and enemies, who had been shattered in life and soul by defeat in war—and some by victory. They also included the wretched who by reason of man's nature and destiny are always among us. The hollow eyes of the dead, who cannot speak, asked a question: What have you done? The beseeching eyes of the wretched, who cannot be heard, asked a question: What will you do?

The Bomb was itself a question. It was little to his credit that it stirred man's ultimate despair more than all the rest of his calamitous handiwork because it seemed to transfer responsibility for his fate from God to man. Presumptuous man, who in all his pryings into matter below vision and into space beyond sight had never been able to answer the first question which the Voice from the Whirlwind put to Job: *Where wast thou when I laid the foundations of the earth?*

The practical aspects of these questions would be settled in time, in the world's way, by able men, purposeful men, shrewd men, perhaps ruthless men, and always confused men. There would be Babels of planning and organization, pyramids of policy. But these would come to no more than all those that had gone before unless, as on this day of Nativity, 1945, man felt within himself a rebirth of what some have called "the Inner Light," others "the Christ within." They would fail like all the rest unless man achieved the ultimate humility and the power implied in one of the Bible's most peremptory commandments:

Be still, and know that I am God.

THREE

A
Lenten
Age

PROBLEM OF THE CENTURY
(*Time*, FEBRUARY 25, 1946)

REVEILLE FOR RADICALS—*Saul D. Alinsky—University of Chicago Press* ($2.50).
SOVIET POLITICS—*Frederick L. Schuman—Knopf* ($4).

THE DOMINANT PROBLEM of the 20th Century is the reconciliation of economic security with political liberty. All other problems are secondary—even The Bomb. At the present time, the divergent attitudes of Russia and the Anglo-U.S. community toward the age's No. 1 problem confront each other in nearly every area of the world, and in almost every thinking mind.

Reveille for Radicals and *Soviet Politics* are U.S. contributions to this great discussion. Both are in dead earnest. Both gain importance from the magnitude of the subject they deal with. *Reveille for Radicals* is a plea to reintegrate along the lines of a "People's Organization" the fragments of the U.S. community. In part it is an organizer's handbook for the same purpose. To some it may sound like a new name for an old enterprise—social revolution. To others it may sound like a glad shout of: everybody join the daisy chain!

Professor Frederick L. Schuman's book is probably the ablest apology for Russia ever written by an American. It is like a brilliant brief by a very clever lawyer who is fortified rather than handicapped by knowing that his client did commit the murder, and even where the body is buried.

RADICALS, AWAKE! In 1939 Saul D. Alinsky turned his back on a brilliant criminological career in favor of a life in the Jungle—the slums that lie back of Chicago's stockyards. It was his simple faith that if leaders of the fragmented sections of any U.S. community could be got to sit down together and talk or participate in common action, democracy would be reborn.

Said he: "As I looked into the vast chasm that divides the mass of the people and our middle class attempts at charity, I realized that the only way out is a democratically informed, active, participating people who have confidence in themselves and their fellow-men, a People's Organization, whose program is limited only by the horizon of humanity itself."

Neither Conservatives nor Liberals, he felt, were suitable messengers of the new evangel. ("Time need not be wasted on Conservatives, since time itself will take care of them." "A Liberal is [a person] who puts his foot down firmly on thin air.") Society's crisis called for Radicals. The first part of *Reveille for Radicals* is a paean to the Tom Paine type of U.S. Radical. But even Radicals must first be awakened: "Deep in the cradle of organized labor America's Radicals restlessly toss in their sleep—but they sleep."

Reveille for Radicals is written with burning honesty. The author has glimpsed a vision which is greater than his ability to put it in practical terms. But this vision, which is no less than the revitalization of democracy, explains why Chicago's Auxiliary Bishop Bernard J. Sheil calls *Reveille for Radicals* "a life-saving handbook for the salvation of democracy," and why Philosopher Jacques Maritain calls it "epoch-making."

RUSSIA REVISITED. The Soviet Union has solved the problem of economic security *v.* political liberty—by liquidating political liberty. Hence few things are so important to the future of the U.S. as an understanding of the Soviet Union, the functioning of its single party, the character and purposes of its leaders, the meaning and purposes of Marxism, its guiding philosophy, and what the sum of these things mean in the daily life of the Soviet nationalities. Few subjects are so controversial, or more confused by the unqualified adulation of the Russia-lovers and the almost equally unqualified abhorrence of those who see in the Soviet system the complete negation of democracy.

Professor Frederick L. Schuman, Woodrow Wilson professor of government at Williams College, has been looking at Russia steadily for some 20 years, and each time that he looked he liked better what he saw. His purpose in *Soviet Politics* is to show, with a disarming air of objectivity, how the Soviet Union got that way and what that way really is. He brings to his task the methods of a trained historian, great learning, unflagging industry and a firm belief that, if Russia and the western democracies cannot get together, civilization is doomed.

Soviet Politics is, first, a great historical recapitulation from the twilight of Russian history through the expulsion of the Mongols (twelve years before Columbus discovered the New World) to the end of World War II. From this historical background, and from the meddling stupidities of the western democracies, Author Schuman argues, have resulted those terrorist and tyrannical aspects of Russian Communism that have shocked or baffled many Americans. For it is Schuman's basic premise that Marxism is merely a contemporary and inevitable development of the libertarian and humanitarian ideals of the French and American revolutions.

Unlike most apologists for Russia, Author Schuman is much too intelligent to blink the facts about Russia. He does not hesitate to say that Russia is "the first of the totalitarian states." But "Soviet 'totalitarianism' was not inevitable nor necessarily implicit in the Bolshevism of 1917-18 but was forced upon it, with death as the alternative, by the decisions of Russian democrats and of the Western Democracies."

This premise once granted, it is possible to construct a plausible exoneration of Russian Communism for almost everything that it has ever done. The result is this book, which, in the guise of objective appraisal, is 689 pages of special pleading so adroit that many readers will not realize the nature of the device.

Prof. Schuman's indictment of the western democracies is clever, but it is unlikely that many western democrats will find themselves seriously indicted. They are more likely to find Schuman's reasoning, in this case, of a piece with his justification of the Purge: because "in my considered opinion the portrait of conspiracy spread on the Soviet court record appears . . . to be closer to reality than any alternative explanation." In the presence of equally cogent alternative explanations, that merely raises the question of the value of Schuman's opinion.

More importantly, it raises the question of the value of all justification, however eloquent or authoritative. For justification is not truth. And only through the rigorous search for truth can come a solid basis for U.S. understanding of Russia's success or failure in solving the critical question of the 20th Century.

CROSSROADS
(*Time*, July 1, 1946)

FOR AGES LOST in the drifts of time, some of the most mysterious eyes on earth have stared cryptically toward tiny Bikini Atoll. On Easter Island, outrigger of the fleets of archipelagoes that ride the Pacific Ocean, a long file of stone colossi rear cold, immortal faces. No one knows what men carved these gigantic symbols, what hands, what primitive technology raised them, with what devotion or what fears. Whether they are gods or images of human greatness, they are menacing; they are monuments to the fact that man's history can perish utterly from the earth.

Of all strange things that the Easter Island idols have looked out upon through the ages, the strangest was preparing last week. A world, with the power of universal suicide at last within its grasp, was about to make its first scientific test of that power. During the earliest favorable weather after July 1, two atom bombs would be exploded at Bikini Island. The first bomb (and the fourth ever to be detonated anywhere) would be dropped on 75 obsolete warcraft anchored in the Bikini lagoon. About three weeks later, a second atom bomb would be exploded under the surface of the lagoon.

TREMOR OF FINALITY. "Operation Crossroads" (the irony of the name is intentional) had been ordered by the Combined Chiefs of Staff in Washington, would be carried out under the command of Vice Admiral W.H.P. Blandy, Commander of the joint Army-Navy task force. Against the peaceful backdrop of palm frond and pandanus, on this most "backward" of islands, the most progressive of centuries would write in one blinding stroke of disintegration the inner meaning of technological civilization: all matter is speed and flame. Well might the stone giants embedded in the solid earth of Easter Island feel, in the far ripple of fission brought them by the waves, a tremor of finality.

On A-day the *Enola Gay*, the B-29 that dropped the atom bomb on Hiroshima, will take off from Kwajalein, 250 miles from Bikini. As it makes three trial runs over the orange-colored U.S.S. *Nevada*, takes readings of wind drift and adjusts the bomb sights, a loudspeaker will alert the whole area. Ten or more miles from the target, the operational ships will keep up steam in case the wind shifts. Aboard, some 40,000 men will lie down on the decks with their feet toward the blast and their eyes covered against blinding.

Then the *Enola Gay* will take off on its fourth and final run. The bomb bay will open. The bombardier, Major Harold Wood, before World War II a grocery clerk of Bordentown, N.J., will release the bomb.

THE GENIUS. Through the incomparable blast and flame that will follow, there will be dimly discernible, to those who are interested in cause & effect in history, the features of a shy, almost saintly, childlike little man with the soft brown eyes, the drooping facial lines of a world-weary hound, and hair like an aurora borealis. He is Professor Albert Einstein, author of the Theory of Special Relativity, the Unified Field Theory, and a decisive expansion of Max Planck's Quantum Theory, onetime director of Berlin's Kaiser Wilhelm Institute, Professor Emeritus at Princeton's Institute for Advanced Study, onetime Swiss citizen, onetime Enemy No. 1 of Hitler's Third Reich, now a U.S. citizen.

Albert Einstein did not work directly on the atom bomb. When the serpent of necessity hissed, the men and the woman who bit into the apple of scientific good & evil bore different names: Dr. Arthur Holly Compton, Dr. Enrico Fermi, Dr. Leo Szilard, Dr. H. C. Urey, Dr. Niels Bohr, Dr. J. R. Oppenheimer, *et al*. The woman was Dr. Lise Meitner, a German refugee.

But Einstein was the father of the bomb in two important ways: 1) it was his initiative which started U.S. bomb research; 2) it was his equation (E = mc²) which made the atomic bomb theoretically possible.

Late in 1939, after the German *Panzers* had driven through Poland, and the citizens of Hiroshima were still going quietly about their daily tasks, the little man who hates to write letters wrote a letter to Franklin Roosevelt. In it he stated his conviction that a controlled chain reaction of atomic fission (and hence the atom bomb) was now feasible, that the German Government was working on an atomic bomb, that the U.S. must begin research on the bomb at once or civilization would perish. Einstein enclosed a report by his friend, Dr. Leo Szilard, describing in more technical language how & why the bomb was possible. Franklin Roosevelt acted. Result: the Manhattan Project, the bomb, the 125,000 dead of Hiroshima and Nagasaki, and the biggest boost humanity has yet been given toward terminating its brief history of misery and grandeur.

If any future civilizations should be left to con the records of the modern world, they will probably declare Albert Einstein the 20th Century's greatest mind. Among 20th-Century men, he blends to an extraordinary degree those highly distilled powers of intellect, intuition and imagination which are rarely combined in one mind, but which, when they do occur together, men call genius. It was all but inevitable that this genius should appear in the field of science, for 20th-Century civilization is first & foremost technological.

PATHETIC PARADOX. It is typical of the dilemma of this civilization that masses of men humbly accept the fact of Einstein's genius, but only a handful understand in what it consists. They have heard that, in his Special and his

General Theories of Relativity, Einstein finally explained the form and the nature of the physical universe and the laws governing it. They cannot understand his explanation. To a small elite of mathematicians and physicists, the score of equations in which Einstein embodied his picture of the universe and its functioning are as concrete as a kitchen table. To the layman they are as staggering as to be told, when he is straining to make out the smudge which is all he can see of the great cluster in the constellation Hercules, that the faint light that strikes his eye left its source 34,000 years ago.

Hence the pathetic paradox that Einstein's discoveries, the greatest triumph of reasoning mind on record, are accepted by most people on faith. Hence the fact that most people never expect to understand more about Relativity than is told by the limerick:

> *There was a young lady called Bright,*
> *Who could travel much faster than light;*
> *She went out one day,*
> *In a relative way,*
> *And came back the previous night.*

NEWTON'S SIMPLE WORLD. For 200 years before Einstein, physicists had faithfully followed a set of basic laws published by the great Sir Isaac Newton in 1687. Their faithfulness had paid off. Sir Isaac led them to many triumphs and promised them many more.

Newton's laws were high-school simple. He assumed the existence of two independent entities—mass and force, which interacted as follows:

1) Every body (mass) continues in its state of rest, or of uniform motion in a straight line, except so far as it may be compelled by force to change that state.

2) Any two bodies attract one another with a force (gravitation) which is proportional to the product of their masses divided by the square of the distance between them.

Upon these basic rules (and others closely related), physicists built an imposing structure of knowledge. They predicted the motions of the earth, the moon, the planets. They derived a maze of useful mechanical sub-laws. They explained the behavior of gases, and discovered the nature of heat. Newton's laws did not account for everything, but the physicists felt that this was due to their own ignorance. Eventually, they were sure, all phenomena could be explained in Newton's terms.

When conflicting facts were discovered by increasingly sensitive instruments, physicists tended to ignore them, or to explain them away by highly artificial creations. Most famous of these was the ether—a tenuous material supposed to fill all space. Ether was necessary (in Newtonian physics) for carrying light waves.

END OF THE ETHER. The ether had another valuable property: it was at rest—"the calm ether-sea"—while everything else in the universe was in motion. Thus it provided the only stable "frame of reference." The earth, for instance, was thought to have "absolute motion" through the motionless ether.

In 1887 came that dreadful day when the ether was done to death. Two U.S. physicists, Albert A. Michelson and E. W. Morley, measured the speed of light simultaneously in two directions at right angles to one another. The speeds were expected to differ slightly because of "ether drift" past the earth. They turned out to be exactly the same, proving conclusively that ether did not exist.

Loss of the ether left the physicists inconsolable. Without it, light waves had no medium to carry them. The vital "frame of reference" was gone. No motion was "absolute" now. The motion of every moving body could be measured only "relative" to some other moving body.

For nearly 20 years, the physicists worked hard to "save" the ether. But the ether could not be saved, and with it went the authority of Newton's scientific decalogue, which depended upon it. Science, the guiding mind of technological civilization, was in crisis.

Albert Einstein, then an unknown clerk in a Swiss patent office, rescued science. In his Theory of Special Relativity (1905) he abandoned Newton's assumption of independent mass and force. In its place he put the assumption, well supported by observation, that the speed of light in a vacuum is constant, no matter what the speed of its source.

This assumption was the heart of Relativity. When properly developed, mathematically, it led to astonishing conclusions, some of them (like many scientific facts) "contrary to common sense." Suppose, for instance, that the earth is moving at many feet per second toward a star. This approaching motion does not increase the arrival speed of the star's light, which strikes the earth at exactly the same speed (186,000 miles per second) as if the earth were at rest. Expressed in an equation, it looks like this:

186,000 m p s + velocity of earth = 186,000 m p s

Even if the earth speeds toward the star at 100,000 m p s, it makes no difference:

186,000 m p s + 100,000 m p s = 186,000 m p s

SLOW CLOCKS, HEAVY MATTER. Obviously, something is wrong, for even Relativity does not abolish simple arithmetic. Einstein's daring conclusion was that only the speed of light is invariable. When the speed of a body changes, its dimensions and its mass and its time also change. As it speeds up, it shrinks (in the direction of the motion); its clocks slow down; its matter grows heavier. If the earth were to reach a speed of 161,000 m p s, every pound of matter in it would double in weight.

Observers on the speeded-up earth would not know that anything had changed. But with their slowed-down clocks and their shrunken yardsticks, they would measure the arriving starlight in such a way that its speed would come out 186,000 m p s. Under Relativity, the "absurd" equations above are not absurd.

Shrunken yardsticks are hard to measure, but the increase of mass which Einstein predicted in 1905 has been observed accurately. Certain material particles shot out by radium move at 185,000 m p s, almost the speed of light. When they are weighed in flight (by a magnetic device), their mass is shown to have increased according to his prediction.

What makes the mass increase? A fast-moving body, Einstein proved mathematically, has more energy, and energy has mass. Thus the mass of a moving body is its "rest-mass" plus the mass of the energy it contains.

This was a revolutionary concept. If energy can turn into mass by speeding up a moving body, then mass, perhaps, can turn into energy. "Certainly," said Einstein. "Mass, including the mass of all matter, is merely another form of energy." In his famous equation, he gave their equivalent values: $E = mc^2$.* This meant that every pound of any kind of matter contained as much energy as is given off by the explosion of 14 million tons of TNT. It took the world 40 years (until Hiroshima) to appreciate this shocker.

PHOTONS AND QUANTA. In that same year, 1905, Einstein advanced another theory which many historians of science consider even more important than Relativity. The ether was gone, and although Relativity established the velocity of light as the firmest figure in the universe, it did not supply any medium to carry the waves of light.

At that time nearly all physicists agreed that light consisted of waves whose properties had been observed in great detail. The old theory (favored by Newton) that light was speeding corpuscles had been abandoned. But the theory had one great advantage: corpuscles can move through space by themselves. Unlike waves, they need no medium to carry them.

Einstein's solution of this dilemma was characteristically bold. "Light," he said, "is both corpuscles and waves." A light ray is a shower of energy particles called "photons" whose energy increases with the wave frequency of the light.

Out of this simple but daring idea developed the supremely important knowledge that energy comes in small, discontinuous "quanta" analogous to the atoms of matter and the electrons of electricity.

GRAVITATION AND STARLIGHT. "Special Relativity," though it stood many rigorous tests, was not accepted at once. For ten years Einstein worked,

---

* $E = mc^2$, with E standing for energy expressed in ergs, m the mass in grams, and c the speed of light in centimeters per second.

extending his theory to cover more varied "frames of reference." In 1915, he published his "General Relativity." It explained the force of gravitation itself, which Newton had merely pointed out.

Here was a chance for a final, convincing test. According to Einstein, light carried energy. Therefore it had mass. Therefore rays of light from a star should be bent by a definite amount when they passed through the strong gravitational field near the sun. A convenient solar eclipse provided the opportunity to test the theory. Star images near the rim of the blacked-out sun were displaced by almost exactly the amount which Einstein predicted, proving that their rays had been bent.

From that day, Relativity was the basic law of the universe. Einstein's photons, too, grew into the head-splitting Quantum Mechanics, which teaches that all matter is nothing but waves, crossing and interacting. Little by little, both theories have worked their way into nearly all branches of science.

The end of the physical revolution which Einstein started is not yet in sight. Perhaps it will stop itself—suddenly—in mid-development under the impact of that equation, $E = mc^2$, which inspired the nuclear physicists to turn small bits of matter into world-shaking energy.

If the atom bomb blasted the last popular skepticism about Einstein's genius it also blasted man's complacent pride in the power of unaided intellect. At the very moment that it was finally mastered, matter was most elusive and most menacing.

The fateful mind behind the bomb was born into the world it was to change so greatly, at Ulm, Germany, in 1879.

Einstein's father was an unsuccessful merchant turned unsuccessful electrical engineer.

The boy was painfully shy, introspective, and so slow in learning to speak that his parents feared he was subnormal. At school he was a poor student. But he learned to improvise on the piano, and used to make up religious songs which he would hum in his own room where no one could hear him.

At 13, Albert was reading Kant's *Critique of Pure Reason*. Soon he discovered Schopenhauer and Nietzsche.

In 1895, Einstein took the entrance examinations for the Polytechnicum in Zurich, Switzerland. He failed, but got in a year later. At Zurich he completed his formal scientific education, became fast friends with the Austrian Socialist leader, political assassin and physicist, Friedrich Adler.

After graduation Einstein became a Swiss citizen, later married the Serbian mathematician, Mileva Marech, by whom he had two sons.

PATENT APPLIED FOR. For two years Einstein earned a wretched living by tutoring. Then he got an obscure job as patent examiner in the Bern patent office. He worked there for seven years. They were among his most productive, theoretically. Scribbling his ideas on scraps of paper, which he thrust out of sight whenever a supervisor approached. Einstein developed his Theory of Special Relativity, which he published without fanfare under the modest title: *On the Electrodynamics of Moving Bodies.*

Relativity had been born, and among scientists the patent clerk was already famous. Soon he became a lecturer at Bern University, then extraordinary professor of physics at the University of Zurich. He taught for a year at the University of Prague, and in the most medieval city in Europe continued his development of the General Theory of Relativity (published in 1915).

One year before World War I, Max Planck (Quantum Theory) used his influence to have Einstein appointed professor at Berlin's Academy of Sciences. One of his duties was managing the Kaiser Wilhelm Institute for Physical Research. Since Einstein would not relinquish his Swiss citizenship, the Prussian Government gave him honorary citizenship.

THE AMERICAN. After Hitler came to power, Einstein went first to Belgium and England, then to the U.S. In 1940 he became a U.S. citizen. In the U.S. he has continued to work on his Unified Field Theory, which he hopes will bridge the gap between his Relativity Theory and the Quantum Theory, thus producing a universal law of nature. There is a story that as he was crossing the Princeton campus one day with Dr. Abraham Flexner, head of the Institute for Advanced Study, Einstein said: "I think I am on the verge of my greatest discovery." A few weeks later he asked Flexner: "Do you remember that I told you that I was about to make my greatest discovery?" "Yes," said Flexner, "I wonder how I restrained myself from asking you what it was." "Well," said Einstein, "it didn't pan out."

In Princeton, Einstein lives with simplicity in a prim, box-shaped frame house, with a wistaria vine shrouding the front porch. Until her death in 1936, his second wife (and cousin), Elsa, was the female Fafnir who guarded his peace, seclusion and his household accounts. It was Elsa who managed his swelling correspondence (20 letters on dull days, hundreds in season), kept off nosy newshawks and curious neighbors. The Einsteins loved music but did not approve of jazz. One neighbor, a friendly woman who was a great chess enthusiast and had heard that Einstein was too, dropped in to offer to play. "Chezz!" cried Elsa Einstein, who spoke English with a pronounced accent— "There shall be no chezz in this house."

Einstein works in an austerely simple room with no instrument but a pencil. He has never made a laboratory experiment, though he likes to pad around the Institute's laboratory, and make suggestions for improving the apparatus. When people explain to him why the improvement will not improve, he says sadly: "*Ja, Ja,* I see that it will not work."

THE NAVIGATOR. He likes to play the fiddle (favorite composers: Bach, Mozart), and to sail a boat. In sailing, his system is to set the sail, make it fast, and with no thought of velocity or energy, loll back while the boat drifts. He smokes a pipe, but never drinks.

Einstein is probably happiest among children, with whom he loses all his shyness and whom he keeps in gales of laughter. His kindness to children is proverbial. One little Princeton girl used this to good advantage: she got him to do her arithmetic homework for her. When suspected, she confessed simply: "Einstein did it for me."

Einstein was once violently pacifist. In 1930 he wrote: ". . . That vilest offspring of the herd mind—the odious militia. . . ." After Hitler, his thoughts became somewhat more martial. He is also a Zionist ("The Jew is most happy if he remains a Jew"), an internationalist ("Nationalism is the measles of mankind"). Einstein claims that he is a religious man ("Every really deep scientist must necessarily have religious feeling"). But he does not believe in the immortality of the soul.

BLAST SHOCK. Last week Professor Einstein seemed suffering from blast shock from the bomb he had fathered. In the New York *Times* he warned Americans that "There is no foreseeable defense against atomic bombs. . . . Scientists do not even know of any field which promises us any hope of adequate defense." The Emergency Committee of Atomic Scientists, of which Einstein is chairman, frantically appealed for $200,000 to educate people to "a new type of thinking . . . if mankind is to survive and move toward a higher level."

Mankind, in general less apocalyptic, scarcely knew what to think or do. Most of them were inclined to accept the bomb stolidly—like an earthquake, an act of God. Few were even yet willing to accept Oswald Spengler's bracing pessimism about the age: "There is no question of prudent retreat or wise renunciation. Only dreamers believe that there is a way out. Optimism is cowardice." But there was a growing sense that the Brothers de Goncourt had been grimly farsighted when they wrote in their *Journal* (in 1870):

"They were saying that Berthelot had predicted that a hundred years from now, thanks to physical and chemical science, men would know of what the atom is constituted. . . . To all this we raised no objection, but we have the feeling that when this time comes in science, God with His white beard will come down to earth, swinging a bunch of keys, and will say to humanity, the way they say at 5 o'clock at the Salon, 'Closing time, gentlemen.' "

IN EGYPT LAND
(*Time*, DECEMBER 30, 1946)

Go tell it on the mountain,
Over the hills and everywheah;
Go tell it on the mountain,
That Jesus Christ is aborn.

AT SALZBURG, backdropped by magical mountains, where Austria's great musical festivals were held before the war, and where he first heard Marian Anderson sing, Arturo Toscanini cried: "Yours is a voice such as one hears once in a hundred years."

Toscanini was hailing a great artist, but that voice was more than a magnificent personal talent. It was the religious voice of a whole religious people—probably the most God-obsessed (and man-despised) people since the ancient Hebrews.

White Americans had withheld from Negro Americans practically everything but God. In return the Negroes had enriched American culture with an incomparable religious poetry and music, and its only truly great religious art—the spiritual.

This religious and esthetic achievement of Negro Americans has found profound expression in Marian Anderson. She is not only the world's greatest contralto and one of the very great voices of all time, she is also a dedicated character, devoutly simple, calm, religious. Manifest in the tranquil architecture of her face is her constant submission to the "Spirit, that dost prefer before all temples the upright heart and pure."

UP FROM PHILADELPHIA. Thanks to the ostracism into which they are born, Negro Americans live very deeply to themselves. They look out upon, and shrewdly observe, the life around them, are rarely observed by it. They are not evasive about their lives; many are simply incapable of discussing them.

The known facts about Marian Anderson's personal life are few. She was born (in Philadelphia) some 40 years ago (she will not tell her age). Her mother had been a schoolteacher in Virginia. Her father was a coal & ice dealer. There were two younger sisters.

When she was twelve, her father died. To keep the home together, Mrs.

Anderson went to work. Miss Anderson says that the happiest moment of her life came the day that she was able to tell her mother to stop working. Later she bought her mother a two-story brick house on Philadelphia's South Martin Street. She bought the house next door for one of her sisters.

Miss Anderson's childhood seems to have been as untroubled as is possible to Negro Americans. In part, this was due to the circumstances of her birth, family, and natural gift. In part, it was due to the calm with which she surmounts all unpleasantness. If there were shadows, she never mentions them. Perhaps the most characteristic fact about her childhood is that Marian disliked bright colors and gay dresses as much as her sisters loved them.

Shortly after her father's death, Marian Anderson was "converted." Her mother is a Methodist. But Marian was converted in her father's Union Baptist Church, largely because the late Rev. Wesley G. Parks was deeply interested in music, loved his choirs and encouraged any outstanding singer in them. At 13, Marian was singing in the church's adult choir. She took home the scores, and sang all the parts (soprano, alto, tenor, bass) over & over to her family until she had learned them. Since work is also a religion to her, Miss Anderson considers this one of the most important experiences of her life. She could then sing high C like a soprano.

At 15, she took her first formal music lesson. At 16, she gave her first important concert, at a Negro school in Atlanta. From then on, her life almost ceases to be personal. It is an individual achievement, but, as with every Negro, it is inseparable from the general achievement of her people. It was the congregation of the Union Baptist Church that gave Miss Anderson her start. Then a group of interested music lovers gave a concert at her church, collected about $500 to pay for training her voice under the late Philadelphia singing teacher, Giuseppe Boghetti.

In 1924, she won the New York Stadium contest (prize: the right to appear with the New York Symphony Orchestra). In 1930, she decided that she must study in Germany. When she had perfected her lieder, songs by Schubert, Brahms, Wolf, she gave her first concert on the Continent. It cost her $500 (the Germans explained that it was customary for Americans to pay for their own concerts). She never paid again.

Applause followed her through Norway and Sweden. In Finland, Composer Jean Sibelius offered her coffee, but after hearing her sing, cried: "Champagne!" In Paris, her first house was "papered." From her second concert, enthusiasts were turned away in droves. She swept through South America.

THE TROUBLE I'VE SEEN. In the U.S. the ovation continued. Only one notably ugly incident marred her triumph. In Washington, the management of Constitution Hall, owned by the Daughters of the American Revolution, announced that it would be unable to lease the hall on the date which Sol

Hurok, Miss Anderson's manager, had asked for. The refusal resulted in Eleanor Roosevelt's resignation from the D.A.R. and an enormous ground swell of sympathy for Miss Anderson and her people. Miss Anderson, who has carefully kept herself and her art from being used for political purposes, said nothing.

But Washington heard her. She sang, first in the open air in front of the Lincoln Memorial. Later the D.A.R. leased her Constitution Hall, and she sang to a brilliant white and Negro audience. She had insisted only that there should be no segregation in the seating. Nobody knows the trouble that an incident like this one causes to a spirit like Marian Anderson's. No doubt such things are in her mind when she says, with typical understatement: "Religion, the treasure of religion helps one, I think, to face the difficulties one sometimes meets."

For this greatly gifted American, pouring out the riches of her art to houses that are sold out weeks in advance, could not for a long time travel about her country like her fellow citizens. She has given concerts in the South, where her voice is greatly admired (and where she avoids Jim Crow by traveling in drawing rooms on night trains). Even in the North, she could not until fairly recently stay at most good hotels. In the South, she must still stay with friends. In New York City, she used to leave frantically applauding audiences to sleep at the Harlem Y.W.C.A. Then Manhattan's Hotel Algonquin, long-time rendezvous of U.S. literati, received her. Now most other Northern hotels have also opened their doors.

Usually, Miss Anderson travels with six pieces of luggage, one of which contains her electric iron (she presses her own gowns before a concert), and cooking utensils (she likes to prepare snacks for herself and she has had some unpleasant experiences with hotel dining rooms).

AGRARIAN PROBLEMS. In 1943 Miss Anderson married Orpheus Fisher, an architect who works in Danbury, Conn. Now they live, not far from Danbury, on a beautiful, 105-acre farm. "Marianna." Inside, the handsome, white frame, hillside house has been remodeled by Architect Fisher. He also designed the big, good-looking studio in which Miss Anderson practices.

When not on tour or practicing, Miss Anderson dabbles in farming. She sells grade-A vegetables to the local market, regrets that Marianna, like many farms run by hired help, costs more than it brings in. And there are other problems in the agrarian life. This year, Miss Anderson was much puzzled when the big (but unbred) daughter of her registered Guernsey cow did not give milk. "Heifers have to be freshened before you can milk them," she explains with some astonishment. "Did you know that?"

The question measures the very real distance she has traveled from the peasant roots of her people. But, as she has traveled, she has taken to new heights the best that Negro Americans are. For the Deep River of her life and theirs runs in the same religious channel. In her life, as in the spiritual, the Big Wheel moves by faith. With a naturalness impossible to most people, she says: "I do a good deal of praying."

GIFT FROM GOD. For to her, her voice is directly a gift from God, her singing a religious experience. This is true of all her singing (she is preeminently a singer of classical music). It is especially true of her singing of Negro spirituals. She does not sing many, and only those which she feels are suited to her voice or which, like *Crucifixion*, her favorite, move her deeply.

There are lovers of spirituals who do not care for the highly arranged versions that Miss Anderson sings, or the finished artistry with which she sings them. But if something has been lost in freshness and authenticity, much has been gained by the assimilation of these great religious songs to the body of great music. For they are the soul of the Negro people, and she has taken that soul as far as art can take it.

As the thousands who have heard her can testify, Miss Anderson's singing of spirituals is unforgettable. She stands simply, but with impressive presence, beside the piano. She closes her eyes (she always sings with her eyes closed). Her voice pours out, soft, vast, enveloping:

> *They crucified my Lord,*
> *An' He never said a mumblin' word;*
> *They crucified my Lord,*
> *An' He never said a mumblin' word.*
> *Not a word, not a word, not a word.*
>
> *They pierced Him in the side,*
> *An' He never said a mumblin' word;*
> *They pierced Him in the side,*
> *An' He never said a mumblin' word.*
> *Not a word, not a word, not a word.*
> *He bowed His head an' died,*
>
> *An' He never said a mumblin' word;*
> *He bowed His head an' died,*
> *An' He never said a mumblin' word.*
> *Not a word, not a word, not a word.*

Audiences who have heard Miss Anderson sing *Crucifixion* have sometimes been too awed to applaud. They have sensed that they are participants in an act of creation—the moment at which religion informs art, and makes it greater than itself.

BIRTH OF THE SOUL. The theme of the greatest music is always the birth of the soul. Words can describe, painting can suggest, but music alone enables the listener to participate, beyond conscious thought, in this act. Beethoven's

Violin Concerto is a work secular beyond question. But when, in the first movement, the simple theme subtly changes, the mind is lifted and rent—not because the strings have zipped to another key, but by a tone of divinity conveyed through the composer's growing deafness by an inspiration inexplicable to the mind. The spirituals are perhaps the greatest single burst of such inspiration, communicated, not through deafness, but through the darkness of minds which knew nothing of formal music and very little of the language they were singing.

Professional musicians and musicologists are still locked in hot debate about the musical origins of the spirituals and the manner of their creation. One simple fact is clear—they were created in direct answer to the Psalmist's question: *How shall we sing the Lord's song in a strange land?* For the land in which the slaves found themselves was strange beyond the fact that it was foreign. It was a nocturnal land of vast, shadowy pine woods, vast fields of cotton whose endless rows converged sometimes on a solitary cabin, vast swamps reptilian and furtive—a land alive with all the elements of lonely beauty, except compassion. In this deep night of land and man, the singers saw visions; grief, like a tuning fork, gave the tone, and the Sorrow Songs were uttered.

Perhaps, in little unpainted churches or in turpentine clearings, the preacher, who soon became the pastor and social leader of his wretched people, gave the lead:

> *Way over yonder in the harvest fiel'*—

The flock caught the vision too:

> *Way up in the middle of the air,*
> *The angel shovin' at the chariot wheel,*
> *Way up in the middle of the air.*
> *O, yes, Ezekiel saw the wheel,*
> *Way up in the middle of the air,*
> *Ezekiel saw the wheel.*
> *Up in the middle of the air.*
> *The Big Wheel moved by faith,*
> *The Little Wheel moved by the grace of God,*
> *A wheel in a wheel,*
> *Up in the middle of the air.*

SOUGHING WIND. It was a theological image splendid beyond any ever conceived on this continent. For a great wind of the spirit soughed through the night of slavery and, as in Ezekiel's vision, on the field of dead hope the dry bones stirred with life.

They kept stirring as, through the dismal years, the great hymnal testimonies moaned forth. Sometimes they were lyric visions of deliverance:

> *Swing low, sweet chariot,*
> *Comin' for to carry me home;*
> *I look'd over Jordan,*
> *And what did I see,*
> *Comin' for to carry me home,*
> *A band of angels comin' after me,*
> *Comin' for to carry me home.*

Sometimes they were statements of bottomless sorrow:

> *Nobody knows de trouble I've seen,*
> *Nobody knows but Jesus.*

Sometimes they were rumbling adjurations:

> *Go down, Moses,*
> *Way down in Egypt land,*
> *Tell ol' Pharaoh*
> *To let my people go.*

Sometimes they were simple longings:

> *Deep River, my home is over Jordan,*
> *Deep River, Lord,*
> *I want to cross over into camp ground.*

Sometimes they were unsurpassed paeans of death:

> *Ezekiel weep, Ezekiel moan,*
> *Flesh come acreepin' off ol' Ezekiel's bones,*
> *Church, I know you goin' to miss me when I'm gone.*
> *When I'm gone, gone, gone.*
> *When I'm gone to come no more,*
> *Church, I know you goin' to miss me when I'm gone.*

Always they were ringing assertions of faith:

> *I got a home in dat Rock, don't you see?*
> *I got a home in dat Rock, don't you see?*
> *Between de earth an' Sky,*
> *Thought I heard my Saviour cry,*
> *You got a home in dat Rock, don't you see?*

The Magnificat of their music has sometimes obscured the poetry of the spirituals. There are few religious poems of any people that can equal this one:

I know moon-rise, I know star-rise,
   I lay dis body down.
I walk in de moonlight, I walk in de starlight,
   To lay dis body, heah, down. . . .

I lie in de grave an' stretch out my arms,
   I lay dis body, heah, down.
I go to judgment in de evenin' of de day,
   When I lay dis body down.

The problem of the white American and the Negro American has rarely been more simply evoked than in those last lines. The problem could be explained (and must in part be solved) in political, social and economic terms. But it is deeper than that, and so must its eventual solution be.

Well might all Americans, at Christmas, 1946, ponder upon the fact that it is, like all the great problems of mankind, at bottom a religious problem, and that the religious solution must be made before any other solutions could be effective. It will, in fact, never be solved exclusively in human terms.

Of the possible meaning of Negro Americans to all white Christians. Historian Arnold J. Toynbee wrote (in his monumental work-in-progress, *A Study of History*): "The Negro appears to be answering our tremendous challenge with a religious response which may prove in the event, when it can be seen in retrospect, to bear comparison with the ancient Oriental's response to the challenge from his Roman masters. . . . Opening a simple and impressionable mind to the Gospels, he has divined the true nature of Jesus' mission. He has understood that this was a prophet who came into the world not to confirm the mighty in their seat but to exalt the meek and the humble. . . . The Syrian slave-immigrants who once brought Christianity into Roman Italy performed the miracle of establishing a new religion which was alive in the place of an old religion which was already dead. It is possible that the Negro slave-immigrants who have found Christianity in America may perform the greater miracle of raising the dead to life. With their childlike intuition and their genius for giving spontaneous esthetic expression to emotional religious experience, they may perhaps be capable of rekindling the cold grey ashes of Christianity which have been transmitted to them by us, until in their hearts the divine fire glows again. It is thus, perhaps, if at all, that Christianity may conceivably become the living faith of a dying civilization for the second time. If this miracle were indeed to be performed by an American Negro Church, that would be the most dynamic response to the challenge of social penalization that had yet been made by Man."

Go tell it on the mountain,
Over the hills and everywheah;
Go tell it on the mountain,
That Jesus Christ is aborn.

THE CHALLENGE

(*Time*, MARCH 17, 1947)

THAT IMPLACABLE EDUCATOR, History, at last assigned a lesson that even the duller members of the class could grasp. Britain, its Government had announced, no longer possessed the resources to continue its comparatively puny military aid to Greece. India had all but left the Empire. Burma and Malaya were going. South Africa was tugging at the tether. In the citadel itself were hunger, cold and socialism.

History was moving with 20th Century acceleration. Americans, who between boyhood and manhood had seen the collapse of four mighty states (the Russian and Austrian empires, Germany and France), heard the news almost with awe. For they grasped the fact that this was no merely political or military crisis; it was a crisis in Western civilization itself. It meant that the U.S. must take over from Britain the job of trying to solve the problem of contemporary history. The U.S. must, in Britain's place, consciously become what she had been, in reluctant fact, since the beginning of World War II: the champion of the remnant of Christian civilization against the forces that threatened it.

But most Americans had no more idea that there is a problem of history than that there is a problem of evil. And they had been so busy creating the world's first great technology that they had little more notion than the Indians they had supplanted what a civilization is or what to do with one.

THE HISTORIAN. The one man in the world probably best equipped to tell them was in the U.S. last week. Professor Arnold Joseph Toynbee, cultural legate from a Britain in crisis to a U.S. at the crossroads, was delivering six lectures ("Encounters between Civilizations") to the history-haunted young women of Bryn Mawr College. So many students and visitors (one woman drove from Minneapolis to hear Toynbee) crammed the 1,000-seat lecture hall that people had to be turned away.

But outside of intellectual circles, Professor Toynbee's name was known to few Americans. Even fewer had read his monumental work in progress, modestly titled *A Study of History*, of which six volumes (with a possible three more to come) have appeared at intervals since 1934. Yet *A Study of History* was the most provocative work of historical theory written in England since Karl Marx's *Capital*.

For Professor Toynbee, while avoiding the sins that beset Oswald Spengler's *Decline of the West*—"baffling immensity and enigmatic gloom"—had met the German philosopher's requirement for the writing of 20th Century history: Toynbee had found history Ptolemaic and left it Copernican. He had found historical thinking nation-centered, as before Copernicus astronomical thinking had been geocentric. The nation (Greece, Rome, Japan, the U.S.) was the common unit of history. Toynbee believed that not nations but civilizations were the "intelligible fields of study."

If Toynbee's repudiation of the nation as history's central fact was Copernican, it also had an Einsteinian effect. For the relations of civilizations could not be investigated without introducing a new space-time factor into the study of history. Where, before, there had been nations, dramatizing their buzzing brevity upon the linear scale of history, there were, from Toynbee's vantage point, vertical progressions of human effort. Where there had been a plane, there was now chasmic depth, the all but unimaginable tract of time.

Toynbee had introduced into the theory of history two other ideas of far-reaching consequence:

1) To the theory of Spengler (whom Toynbee, nevertheless, calls "a man of genius") that civilizations are tragic organisms, growing inexorably toward predetermined dooms, Toynbee advanced a dryly lucid counter-proposition: civilizations are not things-in-themselves, but simply the relations that exist between men living in a given society at a given moment of history.

2) He shattered the frozen patterns of historical determinism and materialism by again asserting God as an active force in history. His assertion, implicit throughout the 3,488 pages of *A Study of History*, implied another: the goal of history, however dimly sensed in human terms, is the Kingdom of God. That aspiration redeems history from being a futile tragedy of blood.

Hence the saying of Toynbee admirers that the writing of history must be dated B.T. and A.T.—Before Toynbee and After Toynbee.

THE MAN. Arnold Toynbee was born (1889) in London toward the end of one of the world's rare Golden Ages (the Victorian).

His family tree was an exfoliation of the eager 19th Century British mind. His uncle, Arnold Toynbee, economist, author of *The Industrial Revolution*, and possessor of a restless social conscience, died when he was only 31. But he so impressed his contemporaries that they named Toynbee Hall, first of London's East End social settlements, in his honor. Toynbee's father was a social worker. Toynbee's mother was one of the first British women to receive a college degree.* The Golden Age shed its westering light over young Toynbee in the guise of a thorough classical training at Balliol, the most intellectual of Oxford's colleges.

But all men, including the historian, are a part of history. Europe's Iron Age, closing over Toynbee while he was studying at the American School of Classical Studies in Athens, taught him that history is also the present. It was the eve of the Balkan wars. In dingy Greek cafés, Toynbee heard something he had never heard at Balliol—discussion of the foreign policy of Sir Edward Grey.

In Greece, he had been in the grave of one dead civilization—the Hellenic. Then he went on a walking trip in Crete (walking is still Toynbee's chief recreation) through an even more cryptic graveyard. Minoan civilization is vivacious and inscrutable, and, with its underground vaults, its Minotaur legend, its statues of snake goddesses and bull-fighting maidens, slightly sinister. What disaster overwhelmed by fire some 1,400 years B.C. the mighty palace of Cnossos? No one knows, for the traces of the flames, still visible upon the stones, are like the Cretan inscriptions—indecipherable. But the doom of this first great thalassocracy (sea power) haunts men's minds like a shriek arrested through the centuries. It haunted Toynbee. Then one day he came upon the ruins of another thalassocracy—a Venetian doge's palace. For Venice had once held the gorgeous East in fee largely through its military occupation of the island of Crete.

THE THALASSOCRAT. There dawned upon the history-sensitive mind of young Toynbee that, as a citizen of the world's No. 1 naval power, he too was a thalassocrat. There was borne in upon him, if not the outlines of his grand design, a presentiment that, in historic time, these three thalassocracies (Crete, Venice, Britain) had more in common than the members of the Triple Entente, were more contemporary than King and Kaiser. And he felt a foreboding of their common fate.

But politics is the present tense of history. The future theoretician of civilizations served his apprenticeship to practical politics by editing a Government pamphlet for Lord Bryce and (during World War I) by working in various intelligence sections of the Foreign Office. (Toynbee speaks five languages; thinks almost as readily in classic Greek as in English.) Then, in 1918, Hindenburg's dinosauric war machine threatened to crush the British drive in

* In 1913, Toynbee allied himself with another British scholarly dynasty by marrying the daughter of Professor Gilbert Murray, famous classical scholar and the Swinburnian translator of Euripides and other Greek dramatists. They had three sons, of whom the best known is Philip Toynbee, novelist (*School in Private*, *The Barricades*) and reviewer for British magazines like *Horizon*, *Contact* and others. Shortly after World War II, Toynbee and Rosalind Murray were divorced. Toynbee then married Veronica Boulter, for many years his secretary and researcher.

France. The Field Marshal failed to break through, but he gave the genesis of
A Study of History a new turn. Feverishly in those days Toynbee read and reread
Thucydides, finding, as others have found since, that the history of *The
Peloponnesian War* threw more light than any contemporary commentary on the
struggles of our times.

At close range, Toynbee had watched the waging of war. As an adviser to
the British delegation at the Versailles peace conference,* he finished his
education in the history of his own time by watching the powers wage peace.
He had seen a war, which cost 8½ million dead and settled almost nothing,
end in a peace which settled little but the inevitability of another war. Toynbee
rounded out his knowledge of the modern world by serving as a newspaper
correspondent in the Turko-Greek War and by making a trip to India, Japan
and China, returning through Siberia and Russia. He also made several trips
to the U.S.

In 1922, Toynbee jotted down, on half a sheet of writing paper, his plan for
A Study of History. He estimated calmly that the project would run to some two
million words and that he might, the vicissitudes of civilization permitting,
finish it in his old age. Meanwhile, he earned a living as director of studies at
the Royal Institute of International Affairs and research professor of international history at the University of London.

THE CLIFFHANGERS. *A Study of History* is dominated by an image of genius.
The view is of the chasm of precipitous time. On its sheer rock walls, as the eye
of the spectator adjusts itself to the somber light of human history, are seen the
bodies of climbers. Some, prone and inert, lie on the ledges to which they have
hurtled to death. Some dangle, arrested, over the void as they cling by their
fingernails to cliffs too steep for their exhausted strength to scale. Above these,
a few still strain upward in a convulsive effort to attain a height hidden from
them as well as from the spectator.

These agonists are the personifications of the human societies we call civilizations, in their upward impulse from the pit of primitive times. Downward,
beyond the extreme range of vision, plunges a depth measured by 300,000
unenlightened years—the time required for the lowest climber to reach, from
primitive to civilized man, the lowest visible ledge. The others have been
climbing, at one stage or another, for the 6,000 years of discernible history.

Of the myriads who may have attempted the ascent, Professor Toynbee
distinguishes 26 civilizations. Of these there are only five active survivors: 1)
Western civilization (Western Europe, the British Commonwealth, the U.S.,
Latin America); 2) Orthodox Christian civilization (Russia and the Orthodox
sections of southeastern Europe); 3) Islamic civilization; 4) Hindu civilization;
5) Far Eastern civilization (China, Korea, Japan). Of these five, four show signs

---

* He served in a similar capacity at the recent Foreign Ministers conference in Paris.

of imminent exhaustion, and the fifth, Western civilization, is breathing heavily.

Those dangling, immobile, from the cliffs are the Eskimos, the Polynesians, the Nomads—the arrested civilizations. Among the debris on the ledges are the bodies of the Sumeric, Babylonic, Egyptiac, Hellenic, Mexic and eleven other extinct societies. This is the image; and its evocation of the "infinitely multiple ordeal of man" is made bearable by Professor Toynbee's unifying insistence: history is not predetermined. Man may still choose to climb or not to climb.

How, then, did these climbers come to be upon the cliffs at all? Why do these men suffer this millennial death by inches? Toynbee's answer to the problem of causation is illumined by a daring dialectic. "The play," he says, "opens with a perfect state of Yin [the Sinic term for the state of perfect passivity opposed to which is Yang, the state of ordeal and creativity]."

God, in short, is bound to passivity by the perfection of what He has created. Further progress is impossible. Says Toynbee: ". . . The impulse or motive which makes a perfect Yin-state pass over into a new Yang-activity comes from an intrusion of the Devil into the universe of God. . . .

"In the language of mythology, when one of God's creatures is tempted by the Devil, God Himself is thereby given the opportunity to recreate the World. By the stroke of the Adversary's trident, all the fountains of the great deep are broken up. The Devil's intervention has accomplished that transition from Yin [passivity] to Yang [creativity] . . . for which God has been yearning ever since His Yin-state became complete, but which it was impossible for God to accomplish by Himself, out of His own perfection. And the Devil has done more for God than this; for, when once Yin has passed over into Yang, not the Devil himself can prevent God from completing His fresh act of creation by passing over again from Yang to Yin on a higher level. . . . Thus the Devil is bound to lose the wager, not because he has been cheated by God, but because he has overreached himself."

In this sense, the answer to the problem of history is the answer to the problem of evil. This is the philosophic crux of that act of creation which in the birth of civilizations Toynbee calls Challenge and Response.

THE THEORY. Toynbee's theory of history is a dialectic. That is, it reports the challenge of something (in this case, communities of men) by an exterior force. If the response to the initial challenge is successful, the success involves new challenges, new responses. If the new responses are not successful, the community breaks down, thereby liberating new creative forces—but on a higher plane, which has been reached by the society during the long developmental ordeal of responding to its challenges.

No attempt to simplify Toynbee's theory can communicate the scope of his historic purpose, the flexibility (amounting to wariness) of his cautious, scholarly mind, the grasp of his erudition, the profusion of historical comparison, contrast, allusion and quiet humor with which he weaves and vivifies his argument. Nevertheless, even grossly simplified, his main design, as on the reverse of a great tapestry, comes through.

Toynbee begins his investigation far down in the pit of history, when the Ice Age ground Europe beneath a creeping glacier. The plains of North Africa and the Middle East (now deserts) were then fertile, supporting a thick population of hunters and their prey—aurochs, oryx, etc. Among these hunters lived the progenitors of one of those broken bodies on the rock ledges of time—the Egyptiac civilization. Later, the ice retreated. The plains turned into deserts. The game fled. The hunters, too, had to retreat.

Some of them, says Toynbee, migrated to the moist Sudan, where their descendants probably survive as the primitive tribes of Shilluk and Dinka. But others, responding to the challenge of desiccation, resolved to change their lives completely. The valley of the Nile was then an all but inaccessible jungle of rank reeds, the lair of hippopotamuses and crocodiles. To live at all under such conditions required an effort beyond any that such men had ever made. Through the centuries, they drained the swamps, felled the reeds, diked the Nile, laid out fields. This response, Toynbee believes, was the genesis of Egyptian civilization—a response so powerful that its career, some 4,000 years, outlasted that of any civilization known to man.

Sumeric civilization was a similar response to a similar challenge. But not all challenges are the same. Minoan and Hellenic civilizations were responses to the challenge of the sea. Mayan civilization was a response to the challenge of the exuberant tropical forests.

Toynbee's title for one of his chapters on challenge and response is three Greek words which mean: "The beautiful is difficult." But some challenges are too difficult. That is the meaning of those bodies dangling over space from the rock wall. For the Eskimos, the challenge of Arctic life left no energy for further change. The Polynesians failed because they responded to the challenge of the sea with no instrument better than a canoe. The energy of the Nomads was consumed in providing pasture for their herds.

Two ideas have dominated historical thinking in our time: Environment and Race. Race is not the decisive factor, says Toynbee, for men of many races have successfully met their challenges in different ways. It is not environment that makes societies of men what they are. It is the response men make to challenges that determines what they may be.

THE CREATIVE MINORITY. For not all challenges are environmental. There are human challenges. These occur when a civilization is faced with death and a section of the old society secedes from the morbid body to help form a new civilization. Young civilizations emerge vigorous from the old. But, like men, their very energy bears within itself the seeds of its decay. This pathological progress is the drama of A *Study of History*.

Toynbee finds that the pathology repeats itself in somewhat similar forms in nearly all civilizations. At first, the civilization is led by "a creative minority." The masses, stimulated by the common challenge that has called the society into being, and by the creative leadership that has guided its response, follow without undue questioning. But response to a challenge calls forth a further challenge. Thus the challenge of overpopulation on a thin soil, to which the Athenians responded by taking to the sea as a commercial empire, called forth a new challenge resulting from Athens' new relations with its vassals and with Sparta.

Nor does successful response to one challenge presuppose success in response to the next. On the contrary, one success tends to make the responder self-satisfied. He comes to believe that the successful response to Challenge I is inevitably the successful response to Challenge II. (Usually it is not.) The elasticity of thought and effort, which is essential to successful response, is lost. The forms (government, culture, habit) in which the successful response has been made tend to freeze and impose themselves on the solution of the new challenge, for which they are wholly unsuited. The creative minority ceases to be creative.

THE UNIVERSAL STATE. At that point the internal proletariat ("a social element which is *in* but not *of* any given society") no longer follows the lead of the no longer creative minority which, threatened by the internal proletariat, becomes a dominant minority, ruling by force. A "time of troubles" ensues—a time of internal struggle and foreign wars, which more & more take the form of world wars. This period is terminated only when one nation, among its distracted fellows, delivers a knockout blow to all its rivals and becomes a "universal state." Rome, having knocked out Carthage and Macedonia, thus became the universal state of Hellenic civilization.

THE UNIVERSAL CHURCH. Universal states, which look strong, are one of history's great illusions. In the past, Toynbee finds, a universal state is almost invariably a symptom that the civilization it represents is far gone in decline. This symptom is almost always accompanied by another: the emergence among the internal proletariat of a "universal church." Christianity was the universal church of Hellenic civilization, Islam of Syriac civilization, Mahayanian Buddhism of Sinic civilization.

The downfall of the universal state is characterized by "schism in the body social," which in turn reflects a "schism in the soul" of the mortally sick society. "The schism in the body social . . . is an experience which is collective and therefore superficial. Its significance lies in its being the outward and visible sign of an inward and spiritual rift."

In this disintegrative process, the manners of the external proletariat become freer, those of the dominant minority more vulgar. But, as in Western civilization today, the equivalents of chewing gum and jazz become the common cultural bond of all classes. The division between proletariat and dominant minority tends to disappear as both are lapped and welded in one indiscriminate vulgarity.

Then the saviors appear. For the creative spark, though it has died out of the dominant minority, still exists in other men. "Such saviors will be of diverse types. . . . There will be would-be saviors *of* a disintegrating society who . . . will lead forlorn hopes in an endeavor to convert the rout into a fresh advance. These would-be saviors will be men of the dominant minority, and their common characteristic will be their ultimate failure to save. But there will be also saviors *from* a disintegrating society. . . . The savior-archaist [Gandhi and his spinning wheel] will try to reconstruct an imaginary past; the savior-futurist [Lenin] will attempt a leap into an imagined future. The savior who points the way to detachment will present himself as a philosopher taking cover behind the mask of a king; the savior who points the way to transfiguration will appear as a god incarnate in a man."

Only one transfiguring Savior has ever appeared in human history: Christ—the highest symbol of man's triumph through ordeal and death.

WESTERN CIVILIZATION. If the topmost climber from the pit of the past could take time from his desperate effort to save himself by climbing higher, he would see below a paralyzing panorama of desolation. Must he join it too? How much longer can he keep going? What is the state of Western civilization? How firm is its grip upon the rocks which can kill more easily than they can help his ascent?

Our civilization, says Toynbee, is in its time of troubles (he dates them from the wars of the Reformation), perhaps toward the end of them. He finds bleak comfort in the thought that as yet no universal state has been imposed despite Napoleon's attempt, and two attempts by the Germans. But from the vast design and complex achievement of *A Study of History* one hopeful meaning stands out: not materialist but psychic factors are the decisive forces of history. The action takes place within the amphitheater of the world and the flux of time; the real drama unfolds within the mind of man. It is determined by his responses to the challenges of life; and since his capacity for response is infinitely varied, no civilization, including our own, is inexorably doomed. Under God, man, being the equal of his fate, is the measure of his own aspiration.

Says Toynbee (near the end of the one-volume edition): "This chapter itself was written on the eve of the outbreak of the General War of 1939–45 for readers who had already lived through the General War of 1914–18, and it was recast for re-publication on the morrow of the ending of the second of these two world wars within one lifetime by the invention and employment of a bomb in which a newly contrived release of atomic energy has been directed by man to the destruction of human life and works on an unprecedented scale.

"This swift succession of catastrophic events on a steeply mounting gradient inevitably inspires a dark doubt about our future, and this doubt threatens to undermine our faith and hope at a critical eleventh hour which calls for the utmost exertion of these saving spiritual faculties. Here is a challenge which we cannot evade, and our destiny depends on our response."

THE TRAGIC SENSE OF LIFE

(*Time*, APRIL 28, 1947)

FRANZ KAFKA (236 pp.)—*Max Brod*—*Schocken* ($3).

THE ROUGE APPLIED by an undertaker to the lips of a 20th Century corpse is one measure of 20th Century civilization. But modern man's effort to deny or minimize death is part of a much more important necessity—the need to deny or minimize God.

Hence the paradox that the more civilization calls itself civilized, the more imperturbably it shrugs at the death of men by millions. Hence, too, the surprising fact that the name of one of the century's three or four most remarkable writers is still practically unknown in the U.S. For Franz Kafka's unrelenting theme, told and retold in some of the greatest horror stories ever written (*The Castle, The Trial, Metamorphosis*, the stories in *The Great Wall of China*), was the nature of God and man's relationship to God.

The moonlight chilliness of his mood, his refusal to soften the deepening ambiguities of truth (as he saw it), the pitiless obsession of his God-seeking, and the scary symbolism in which he embodied his God-seeking, have kept Kafka from becoming a popular writer. Yet readers with the requisite staying power will find that in the scope of the problem to which he dedicated himself, in the depth and integrity of his discernments and in the variety of means by which he dramatized his vision in terms of everyday life (thereby giving to everyday life new implications and new dimensions), Franz Kafka is a major artist.

MODERN *PILGRIM'S PROGRESS*. This is exemplified in *The Castle*. *The Castle* is an inverted *Pilgrim's Progress*. Its subject is a man's obsessive struggle to achieve God (the Castle)—who does not recognize man's vocation—while trying to integrate himself in the community of men (the village at the foot of the Castle)—who do not want him. K., a land surveyor, believes that he has been ordered to take a job at the Castle. But when he arrives, at night, in winter, he is rudely ordered off the premises. The Castle authorities (a vast, apparently shiftless bureaucracy) first deny that K. has a job there at all, then grudgingly concede that he may have one. K. tries desperately to reach the Castle by telephone. "The receiver gave out a buzz of a kind that K. had never heard on a telephone. It was like the hum of countless children's voices—but yet not a hum, the echo rather of voices singing at an infinite distance—blended by sheer impossibility into one high but resonant sound which vibrated on the ear as if it were trying to penetrate beyond mere hearing." K. asks when he can come to the Castle. " 'Never,' was the answer."

The rest of *The Castle* describes K.'s efforts to force himself upon God by frontal attack, by subterfuge, by lies. His intrusions are always repulsed. His subterfuges are loftily analyzed for him with merciless logic. His lies are always found out. He is humiliated daily, degraded from his post as land surveyor to school janitor. He submits, so that he may stay on in the village. But the villagers, if less urbane than the Castle, are just as hostile. They have achieved grace through simple living and because they do not try to force themselves upon God. K. never does reach the Castle. But in the end he is permitted to stay on in the village, not because he has any right to, not because he is a good or devout man, but because he happens to be there and might as well remain—who cares? *The Castle* is unfinished, perhaps because there is no possible conclusion.

THE AUTHOR. The practically unknown author of this practically unread book is the subject of a recently published biography, the first (it was translated from German) in English. The biographer was Kafka's close friend and literary executor, German Novelist Max Brod (*The Redemption of Tycho Brahe*, *The Kingdom of Love*, etc.). Readers will find in it a muster of biographical facts, possessed by no one else but Brod, arranged with discerning intelligence and affectionate understanding. The biography also includes one of the soundest and most moderate critical appraisals of Kafka's intellectual purpose and achievement.

Franz Kafka was born (in Prague) of a Czechish Jewish family. He was born at the moment (1883) when, like a somber, accelerating drumbeat, the theme of Europe's downfall was insistently prefigured, and at the spot (the old Austro-Hungarian empire) at which the collapse of the part was to be most premonitory for the whole.

His father was a prosperous dry-goods wholesaler, whom Kafka respected and feared, but who, like the world, found his son baffling and enigmatic. At Prague University, Kafka studied law. He never practiced. But his legal training is implicit in the tortuous dialectics of his writings. The most abiding result of his university career was his friendship with Biographer Brod.

As long as his health permitted, Kafka worked as a minor official in Prague's Arbeiter-Unfall-Versicherungs-Anstalt (workmen's accident insurance company), where his reports of dingy claims, written in some of the century's most lucid prose, won the discreet approval of his superiors. For several years, Kafka suffered an off-again-on-again engagement with a German girl, the manager of a Berlin firm. In part from reasons of health, in part, perhaps, from

a morbid sense of a sexual inadequacy, Franz Kafka could never bring himself
to marry her. Toward the end of his life, Kafka enjoyed a brief, happy love
affair with Dora Dymant, a Polish Jewish girl who was a Hebrew scholar.

In 1917, Kafka began to cough blood. He bore for years his premature death
within him. In 1924, tuberculosis killed him. Three years before he died,
Kafka requested Max Brod to destroy all his unpublished manuscripts, including the two novels, *The Trial* and *The Castle*, and most of the stories in *The Great
Wall of China*. That he did not destroy them himself betrays an ambiguity
characteristic of Kafka. In any case, Brod disobeyed.

By ordinary standards, Kafka's was a life in which practically nothing
happened, a life as short and simple as a single day—and as terrible, not
because its vicissitudes were overwhelming, but because, as in most life, they
were endurable.

THRESHOLD OF SILENCE. All the great creators are lonely travelers. For their
vocation and their plight, one of the loneliest frontiers of modern science—jet
propulsion—has found an accurate metaphor. They are commissioned (but at
their own risk) to cross the supersonic thresholds of the mind—the point at
which the familiar sound-lengths of human life dissolve into inhuman silence.
If they pass the barrier of dissolution, they may investigate in uncompetitive
privacy the mysteries inaudible to the other minds. If they can recross the
sonic sill, alive and sane, they may report what they have experienced to men
who, never having known the experience, will never quite understand the
report. Franz Kafka ventured across the barrier, reported with an apparent
lucidity the cryptographs of silence, and was little understood. "Franz Kafka,"
wrote Franz Werfel, "was a messenger from above, a great chosen one. . . ."

For the area of silence which Kafka sought to decode, and which he succeeded at least in marvelously dramatizing, was that bleak void in which man,
like a rat in a laboratory maze, strives frantically (and often ludicrously) to
approach God, while God (with the detachment of the scientific mind) observes the data of the frenzy and the fun. Milton, in his blindness, sought "to
justify the ways of God to men." The sum of Kafka's report was that the ways
of God and man are irreconcilable.

Thus Grace (for no reason discoverable by human standards) may be con-
ferred on a man who hardly cares, and may be denied to another who strives
most desperately for it. Guilt may overthrow a man who (by human standards)
is unconscious that he has incurred any guilt. Chance, the irrational number
by which man confesses the failure of his intellectual algebra, may throw a
man off course for a whole lifetime, and even beyond the grave. "When you
have once been misled by bells tolling in the night," wrote Kafka, "you can
never find the right path again."

Nor is there any by-passing God. For, while men may try to forget or deny
God, they cannot forget what Philosopher Miguel de Unamuno called "the

God-ache." Implicit or explicit in all Kafka's work, the source of his religious rage, his drama, irony, despair and compassion, is this incompatibility, this eternal misunderstanding of God by man—the inability of man to grasp, by limited human standards, the standards of divine Justice or divine Grace.

Says Biographer Brod: "Of all believers [Kafka] was the freest from illusions, and among all those who see the world as it is, without illusions, he was the most unshakable believer."

RELIGIOUS HUMORIST. The mood in which Kafka energizes his perception of the incompatibility of God and man is unequivocal, masculine and as glitteringly clear as winter air. He is the least sentimental or feminine of modern writers. But truth and derangement are galleymates, since the horror that tugs at the same oar is the perception that man and his fate by human standards are monstrous. Kafka retains his sanity by his realization that man's fate is also divine comedy. This is the hinge of his unearthly irony.

Kafka has been called a gloomy writer, a follower of bleak Danish Philosopher Sören Kierkegaard. He was, in fact, one of the rarest types in literature— a religious humorist.

Max Brod recalls that when Kafka read to friends the opening chapters of *The Trial* (the story of a man crucified by inches), they laughed till the tears ran down their cheeks, and Kafka himself laughed so hard he could not go on reading. It is, says Novelist Thomas Mann solemnly, "very deep-rooted and involved" humor. Kafka's cosmic comedy of man's foredoomed failure in his quest for God is brought down to earth and up to the minute by the use (in *The Trial* and *The Castle*) of all the adventitious paraphernalia of 20th Century living—telephones, railroad trains, banks, boardinghouses, taxicabs.

Kafka has also been called a theological writer, a philosophical writer, a Zionist, a Freudian, a bitter social critic, a Kafkaist. Plain readers may brush aside the tags. For them two facts are important: 1) to express the manifold, intangible anguish of life, Kafka told his greatest stories in the condition of dreams (he understood that dreams, despite their infinite fluidity of merging forms, have great narrative economy); 2) as a symbolist (Kafka's long books are called novels chiefly by reason of their length), he found for his two greatest stories, *The Trial* and *The Castle*, two of the most dramatically powerful images in literature.*

MODERN BOOK OF JOB. If *The Castle* is a modern *Pilgrim's Progress*, *The Trial* is a 20th Century *Book of Job*. Like Job, Joseph K. is a good and upright man, one

---

* For his minor nightmares, too, Kafka invented a variety of dramatic images. Sometimes (*Investigations of a Dog*), the victim of murder by mortality is a dog. Sometimes (*Metamorphosis*), he is a man who has been bestialized into a gigantic beetle. Sometimes (*The Burrow*), he is a little, nameless, furred animal, burrowing or scuttling in terror under the earth.

who fears God and eschews evil. *The Trial* reports his oncreeping sense of guilt as a human being and the slow progress of that divine, intangible, but inexorable Justice to which he therefore feels that he must submit ("You may object that it is not a trial at all; you are quite right, for it is only a trial if I recognize it as such").

The story begins with a sentence as direct as a news lead: "Someone must have been telling lies about Joseph K., for without having done anything wrong, he was arrested one fine morning."

Divine Justice is as preposterous (to human understanding) as divine Grace. The divine detectives who arrest Joseph K. are brassy louts who eat his breakfast, try to get a rake-off by sending out for his food, try to make off with his shirt and underwear. "Much better give these things to us than hand them over to the depot . . . for in the depot there's lots of thieving, and besides they sell everything there after a certain length of time, no matter whether your case is settled or not. And you never know how long these cases will last, especially these days. Of course you would get the money out of the depot in the long run, but in the first place the prices they pay you are always wretched, for they sell your things to the best briber, not the best bidder, and anyhow it's well known that money dwindles a lot if it passes from hand to hand from one year to another."

THE EXECUTIONERS WAIT. Though Joseph K. is "arrested," he is permitted to go on working in the bank where he is a minor official. Sometimes he is summoned to the "Court." It is held in a filthy room in a tenement in a slum district. The spectators are all petty police agents of the Court. The attorneys, judge, and law students misbehave in public with the wives of the Court attendants. The law books, when Joseph K. finally peeks into them, are filled with obscene pictures. He never can find out the nature of the charge against him. He never can find out what Justice is, except that it is utterly inhuman.

He never finds the High Court or sees the Supreme Judge except as a vague figure waving its arms from a window. He never comes to trial. His reputation is ruined. His work at the bank falls off. His health fails. When his executioners arrive at last, without any sentence's ever having been passed on K., he is relieved to go along with them.

The night before K.'s 31st birthday, two big men in frock coats come for him. "They kept their shoulders close behind his and instead of crooking their elbows, wound their arms around his at full length, holding his hands in a methodical, practised, irresistible grip. K. walked rigidly between them. . . . 'Perhaps they are tenors,' he thought, as he studied their fat, double chins."

Thus they walked beyond the town. "A small stone quarry, deserted and bleak, lay quite near to a still completely urban house. . . . Now they loosened their hold of K., who stood waiting dumbly, took off their top hats and wiped the sweat from their brows with pocket handkerchiefs, meanwhile surveying the quarry. The moon shone down with that simplicity and serenity which no other light possesses."

They made K. lie down against a rock. Then one of them drew out "a long, thin, double-edged butcher's knife, held it up and tested the cutting edge in the moonlight. . . . With a flicker as of a light going up, the casements of a window [in the house] suddenly flew open; a human figure, faint and insubstantial, at that distance and at that height, leaned abruptly far forward and stretched both arms still farther. Who was it? A friend? A good man? Someone who sympathized? Someone who wanted to help? . . . Was help at hand? . . . Where was the Judge whom he had never seen? Where was the High Court to which he had never penetrated? He raised his hands and spread out all his fingers.

"But the hands of one of the partners were already at K.'s throat, while the other thrust the knife into his heart and turned it there twice. With failing eyes K. could still see the two of them, cheek leaning against cheek, immediately before his face, watching the final act. 'Like a dog!' he said. . . ."

Beside that scene, against the cumulative background of that terrible story, most that has been written in our time about man's lot seems rather childlike. And beside Kafka's insatiable posing of the infinite question, most of his contemporaries' answers seem rather childish.

CIRCLES OF PERDITION

(*Time*, DECEMBER 8, 1947)

THE MEANING OF TREASON (307 pp.)—*Rebecca West*—*Viking* ($3.50).

When, in 1936, General Emilio Mola announced that he would capture Madrid because he had four columns outside the city and a fifth column of sympathizers within, the world pounced on the phrase with the eagerness of a man who has been groping for an important word. The world might better have been stunned as by a tocsin of calamity. For what Mola had done was to indicate the dimension of treason in our time.

Other ages have had their individual traitors—men who from faint-heartedness or hope of gain sold out their causes. But in the 20th Century, for the first time, men banded together by millions, in movements like fascism and communism, dedicated to the purpose of betraying the institutions they lived under. In the 20th Century, treason became a vocation whose modern form was specifically the treason of ideas.

Modern man was challenged to choose between the traditions of a 2,000-year-old Christian civilization and the new totalitarian systems which, in the name of social progress, contended for the allegiance of man's secular mind. The promise of the new ideas was as old as that serpentine whisper heard in the dawn of the Creation: "You shall become as gods"—for the first traitor was the first man.

And yet, though the new ideas had been violently avowed, and the hallmark of their advocates was a fanaticism unknown since the first flush of Islam, wherever the fanatics were brought to trial, almost without exception they failed to defend their beliefs. Why?

A book published in the U.S. this week, *The Meaning of Treason*, is a clue to this clouded question.

THE BOOK. *The Meaning of Treason* is a collection of Rebecca West's reports of the trials of a number of British World War II traitors. She covered the trials on assignment for the *New Yorker*, where her articles (now expanded and revised) were first published. But the idea was her own, and she could scarcely have chosen a better person for the job.

Rebecca West is a novelist of note (*The Thinking Reed*), a distinguished literary critic (*The Strange Necessity*). But, above all, as she proved in *Black Lamb and Grey Falcon*, she is one of the greatest of living journalists.

Most reporters report in one dimension, achieving at best the dramatic surface of a mural or a movie. Rebecca West reports in depth—a depth whose winding recesses of character, situation and context she divines by the play of unusually acute instincts and intuitions guided by an eye for significant detail. And she floods the planes of her perception with the generous human warmth of a womanly nature and a culture-crowded brain that gives to the meanest fact a new perspective.

The treason trials, as she records them, were not just the raw pulp of daily news, tatters of irrelevant wretchedness or cold inquests of justice upon a succession of dingy destinies. They become three-dimensional—as events in a process of history, which Miss West views as organic and continuously alive; as ordeals of a common humanity, which the men on trial shared with the men who tried them; as glimpses of a common hell, which all men know (since all men betray themselves continually), but know less terribly than those traitors who in addition had betrayed their fellows.

DARK DESCENT. Miss West's book is a descent into the circles of a drab inferno. It was reached through several pit heads—the bomb-battered building of London's Central Criminal Court, the House of Lords, a court martial near the blitzed waterfront at Portsmouth. Above all, it was reached through the collapsing corridors of many ruined minds.

There were about 20 traitors. In the first circle were those whom Miss West calls the children of treason—"The ones who thought like children, and felt like children, and were treacherous as children are, without malice, only because someone was giving away sweetmeats or because the whole gang was chasing the dog."

There was Kenneth Edward. When World War II began, Kenneth Edward was 13. In 1940 he went to sea in an ammunition ship. At 15, he transferred to the *Cymbeline*, which was sunk by a German raider. The raider landed him in France and he was sent to an internment camp, then to another and another and another. He did not know where these camps were or how long he stayed in them. At last Kenneth came to the attention of John Amery, another British traitor, who was organizing a British Free Corps to fight the Russians. In time the boy enjoyed the distinction of being the only private in the British Free Corps (all the others were officers). Then he was forgotten.

He spoke little German and so was often arrested—perhaps 23 times. The collapse of Germany came. Kenneth surrendered to the Russians, who turned him over to the Americans, who turned him over to the British. He was almost 18, and a traitor.

THE REPENTANT. There were other children of treason. Says Author West: "The children who go from their homes with strangers because they have been given cakes and sweets are unsustained by pride when the unkindness falls on them. They know well that they have done wrong. A person should be loyal to his father and mother, to his brothers and sisters, to his friends, to his town or village, to his province, to his country; and a person should do nothing for a bribe, even if it takes the form of a promise that he should live instead of die."

All the children repented: "This attitude was clearly distinguishable from regret at having been on the losing side, and it was not feigned; the rush of blood from the cheek after the shameful admission, the greenish swaying sickness of repentance are inimitable. It is not an attitude which has been taught them by an exploiting class. They were born into a tongue-tied age, and neither their school teachers or the culture within their reach had given them such positive instruction. The judgment they passed on their own disloyalty and the loyalty of others was a spontaneous reaction to experience."

CIRCLE NO. 2. The second circle of Miss West's inferno is that of the grotesques—those who were more developed but scarcely older than the children. Some were, like Kenneth Edward, merchant seamen. Some were British prisoners of war who went over to the Germans. Some had been members of Sir Oswald Mosley's British Union of Fascists. Almost all became members of the British Free Corps.

"There was poor Herbert George, who, though of medium height, had the look of a Disney dwarf. His deeply lined skin was puckered into thin folds in the apprehensive expression of a chimpanzee, and his features so far departed from the normal that those who met him found themselves looking back again and again to see if they could be as they were remembered, though the total impression was by no means monstrous, merely animal and odd."

During the Spanish Civil War Herbert George had joined the International Brigade. Later he deserted. During World War II his ship was torpedoed off Narvik, and he went from one German camp to another. Then he got a letter saying that his wife in England had a baby. He thought it over for a long time and decided the baby could not be his. So one day when recruiters for the British Free Corps came around, he joined up, "just as a sad little dog, finding himself far from home in streets where they throw things, with rain falling and the dusk thickening, will follow any passerby."

Thomas Haller Cooper was a different kind of grotesque. His father was an English photographer: his mother was German. Somehow his mother had instilled in him a love for Germany. "It cannot be put down in black and white how she wove the spell about him. . . . The secret does not lie in the promise of conquest. That secret is a lyricism that extends the kingdom of the nightingale, diffuses everywhere the secret perfume of the rose. The home where this man's mother lived was distinguished from all the other red-brick and stucco houses in a shabby suburban street by the wealth of flowering bulbs, jonquil packed beside narcissus, crocus beside grape hyacinth, which crammed the bow-windows of the ground floor flat. . . . When the spring came, they made a truly German window. Loving this lovely Germany, her son joined the *SS*, which bled and died that there should be camps where starved prisoners fell on the bodies of their dead comrades and, if not too disgusted by the lice, ate their kidneys and livers and the soft parts of their thighs."

These traitors and their mates were sent to jail for varying terms. They will come out, says Author West, as they went in: "Unchanged in their essential and dangerous quality. . . . They will be timber for the next international revolutionary movement."

CIRCLE NO. 3. John Amery deserved a circle of perdition to himself. He was the worthless son of a distinguished father, Leopold Amery, Secretary of State for India in the Churchill government. He had been convicted 74 times on traffic charges. He had caused a scandal by falling in love with the prostitute who nightly occupied the most conspicuous spot in Piccadilly. He was a bankrupt. He had been an aide to Francisco Franco. During the war he joined the Germans and organized the British Free Corps.

His trial lasted eight minutes, for he said, in answer to the court's question: "I plead guilty to all counts." "A murmur ran through the court which was horrified. . . . In effect, the young man was saying, 'I insist on being hanged by the neck in three weeks' time,' and the strength of his desire to die was forcing his weak voice through his shuddering lips and ignoring his pain, which was great, for he was blasted by what he did. He was like an insect that falls on a hot stove and is withered, and what he did felt like an act of cruelty to the whole court. It rejected the life that was in all of us."

THE PIT. Circle No. 4 is the pit. Here, in that ambiguous clarity which Milton called "no light but rather darkness visible," are two architects of betrayal. These men committed not the treason of the unlighted mind, like Kenneth Edward or Herbert George, nor the treason of depravity like John Amery, but the fully conscious treason of ideas. One was a Communist. One was a Fascist.

"Not guilty," pled Dr. Alan Nunn May. He could scarcely force the plea between his chattering teeth. He was glazed with sweat. ". . . His body assumed without shame the very shape of fear. In his cringing motions, however, there were indications of an extreme fineness of intellect, unfoldings of a lacework of perceptions, of associations, of interpretations, which made the Nazi-Fascists seem like hogs rooting among the simple unimproved beech-mast of the world. No matter how he stooped and wavered, out of his head proceeded mental patterns intricate and brilliant as the etchings of frost on a winter pane. Surely the others, the Nazi-Fascists, were not fully human. But neither was he."

For Dr. Alan Nunn May had been for years a member of the Communist Party. He had been a lecturer on physics at the University of London. During World War II, he volunteered for service as the senior member of the nuclear physics division of the atomic bomb project. Then he had turned over to Russia samples of uranium 235 enriched and uranium 233. Says Miss West: "If Russia ever drops an atomic bomb on Great Britain or America, the blame for the death and the blindness and the sores it scatters will rest largely on this fatuous and gifted man."

And yet: "The spectators were plainly appalled when the judge passed sentence [ten years' penal servitude] on Dr. Alan Nunn May, though none of them was his follower. . . . It was the light about the man's head which made the thought of his imprisonment intolerable: the changing and complicated intellectual patterns proceeding from his brow and spelling out a meaning which men required."

THE VOICE. There was no such light about the head of Dr. May's pit-mate. "Not guilty," pled the scar-faced prisoner on trial for his life in London's Central Criminal Court. The little man who, in his self-conscious spruceness looked like a somewhat comic gangster, was Lord Haw Haw—William Joyce—the British Fascist who, during World War II, had nightly tried to sap his countrymen's will to survive by broadcasting defeatist propaganda from Germany.

At those two words, "not guilty"—the first words he had spoken—the spectators in the courtroom started. Few of them had ever seen the man before, but in all of them the sound of his voice touched a nerve of terrible memory.

"Never before," wrote Author West, "have people known the voice of one they have never seen as well as if he had been a husband or a brother or a close friend; and if they had foreseen such a miracle, they would not have imagined the familiar unknown would speak to them only to prophesy their death and ruin. All of us in England had experienced that hideous novelty. It was difficult not to chance on Joyce's wavelength when one was tuning in to the English stations, and there was an arresting quality about his voice which made it a sacrifice not to go on listening. . . . It seemed as if one had better hearken and take warning, when he suggested that the destiny of the people he had left in England was death, and the destiny of his new masters in Germany life and conquest, and that, therefore, his listeners had better change sides and submit. This was often terrible to hear, for the news in the papers confirmed it. He was not only alarming, he was ugly; he opened a vista into a mean life. . . . He went further than that smug mockery of our plight. He sinned that sin which is the dark travesty of legitimate hatred . . . just as incest is the dark travesty of legitimate love."

BIOGRAPHY OF BETRAYAL. The facts in the life of William Joyce were neither clear nor simple, but their meaning was. He had been born in Brooklyn, N.Y. (an important part of his defense was that he was not a British subject). His parents were Irish. They were loyal to England. When Ireland became Eire, they were forced to emigrate to Britain. Joyce's father was suspected of being a British informer. William Joyce claimed that he had done intelligence work for the Black & Tans.

The Joyces did not prosper in the land to which they had remained loyal and which did not reward their loyalty. But young Joyce graduated from the University of London, where he was an excellent student. He became a highly successful tutor. His love for England was intense—"such a love as led him in afterlife habitually to make a demand—which struck many of his English acquaintances as a sign of insanity—that any quiet social evening he spent with his friends should end with the singing of the national anthem."

"It was this love," says Miss West, "slanting across time, which made him a Fascist. He had been brought up to believe in an England who held Ireland by force, and felt betrayed when Home Rule was given."

So Joyce joined Sir Oswald Mosley, the founder of the British Union of Fascists. (In time he broke away to form his own British National Socialist League.) And so just before the war he fled to Germany, to lend to the treason of ideas his vibrant voice. For this he was hanged.

Miss West lights up the darkness of this trial with fierce flashes of observation. But none is so shocking as the reaction of Joyce when he heard the word "hanging" casually mentioned in court. By an unconscious reflex, he raised his hand and with his finger touched his throat.

THE VACUUM. Why did the traitors commit double treason by failing to defend the beliefs in whose name they had committed treason first? One of the most intelligent of totalitarians has tried to give the answer in a cry from the brink of the grave. In March 1938 Nikolai Ivanovich Bukharin, once one of the most powerful figures in Russia, made his last plea to the Soviet Supreme Court. He admitted that he was a traitor, and explained why he had confessed.

He said: "For three months I refused to say anything. Then I began to testify. Why? Because while in prison I made a revaluation of my entire past. For when you ask yourself: 'If you must die, what are you dying for?'—an absolutely black vacuity suddenly rises before you. . . . There was nothing to die for, if one wanted to die unrepentant. . . . And when you ask yourself: 'Very well, suppose you do not die; suppose by some miracle you remain alive, again for what? . . .' And at once the same reply arises. And at such moments, Citizen Judges, everything personal, all the personal incrustation, all rancor, pride and a number of other things, fall away, disappear. . . . I am about to finish. I am perhaps speaking for the last time in my life. I am explaining how I came to realize the necessity of capitulating to the investigating authorities and to you, Citizen Judges."

In her own way, Miss West is saying the same thing when she writes of Dr. May: "A man with so dynamic a mind will be specially conscious of the vacuum left by the disappearance of God." For the horror of treason is its sin against the spirit. And for him who violates this truth there rises inevitably Bukharin's "absolutely black vacuity," which is in reality a circle of absolute loneliness into which neither father, wife, child nor friend, however compassionate, can bring the grace of absolution. For this loneliness is a penalty inflicted by a justice that transcends the merely summary justice of men. It is the retributive meaning of treason because it is also one of the meanings of hell.

THE IBSEN GIRL. Rebecca West is a Socialist by habit of mind, and a conservative by cell structure. She has the true genealogical instinct. "I am descended," she has written, "from one of the first governors of Madras. . . . One of my close relatives is counted as a maker of British Africa, and . . . the more I live in intellectual circles the less does this heredity displease me."

She was born Cicily Fairfield, in London, in 1892. Her father had been a Confederate stretcher-bearer at the siege of Richmond in the U.S. Civil War. After returning to England he became a newspaperman. Cicily took the pen name, Rebecca West, in her teens, when concealment became necessary after she sold her first article to the *Freewoman*, a feminist magazine which her mother had forbidden her to read. Rebecca West is the name of a character in Ibsen's play, *Rosmersholm*.

BRUSHING OFF THE WEBBS. In less time than it takes to say Emmeline Pankhurst, Rebecca West was in London writing literary criticism on the *Freewoman*'s staff. A year later she was a full-fledged political writer on the old Socialist *Clarion*, and a member of that Socialist intellectual advance guard, the Fabian Society. Its pundits, Sidney & Beatrice Webb, had her in for dinner, but "I argued with the Webbs, so I was never invited back."

Plenty of other doors flew open. Rebecca, despite a somewhat unconstructed chin, had a beauty of face which was heightened by a beauty of the mind when her dark brown eyes grew intense with the animation of ideas. Talk poured from her in a brilliant jet, and had upon her listeners the effect of an electric impulse. She has been talking ever since, for her writing is, in fact, a burst of brilliant conversation.

Rebecca also possessed two other provocative talents—an ability to put her mental finger on the key detail of a complicated situation or character, and a sharp tongue. She is still in brisk command of both assets. In Manhattan last summer, she was introduced to arch John Erskine, author of *The Private Life of Helen of Troy, The Human Life of Jesus* and some 40 other books. Said Erskine: "I've been reading your clever articles and I wonder if they're sincere."

Snapped Miss West: "I've been reading yours, and I never wonder about either of those things."

FEET FIRST. Rebecca had not been in London long before she sat at the feet (a vantage point of signal value) of practically everybody worth observing. Her great friend, Novelist G. B. Stern, with whom Rebecca shared meager quarters in those pioneer days, would be struck speechless by the arrival of successive literary lions with whom Miss West would chat, easily and informally, about the private lives and feuds of the legendary characters then dominating the British literary scene.

On high reigned the Big Four—"The Uncles," Miss West called them in *The Strange Necessity*. There was Uncle John Galsworthy, Uncle H. G. Wells, Uncle Arnold Bennett and Uncle Bernard Shaw, of whom she now observes: "The trouble with Shaw is that he was a wonderful writer with nothing important to say. It's too bad he couldn't have been a Christian."

"Uncle Wells arrived always a little out of breath, with his arms full of parcels, sometimes rather carelessly tied, but always bursting with all manner of attractive gifts that ranged from the little pot of sweet jelly that is *Mr. Polly* to the complete Meccano set for the mind that is in *The First Men on the Moon*. . . . One had, in actual fact, the luck to be young just as the most bubbling creative mind . . . since the days of Leonardo da Vinci was showing its form."

NO. 1 WOMAN WRITER. When, at the end of World War I, Rebecca West became the book critic of the *New Statesman and Nation*, she was already a minor celebrity. She wrote with an authority beyond her years or experience in a prose in which, at its best, a logic of music was magnificently mated to a logic of ideas. At its worst, it was excessive and overblown. Sometimes she took time out from her bread-winning chores to write a novel (*Harriet Hume*). Sometimes she collaborated on satirical sketches (*Lions and Lambs, The Rake's Progress*) with Cartoonist David Low. She managed to get abroad a good deal, and a shimmering list of continental hosts and hostesses were always eager to entertain her. The posh social life of Paris, the spas and resorts, which Miss West described in loving detail in *The Thinking Reed*, was first-hand reporting. When in 1937 the British Council sent Miss West to Yugoslavia and she recorded her experience in *Black Lamb and Grey Falcon*, she became indisputably the world's No. 1 woman writer.

FLOWERS & COWS. At 55, Rebecca West is greying and has put on weight which makes her look stocky rather than stout. Vestiges of her girlhood beauty now light a face that is impressive with mature intelligence. But, since she has little interest in dress, she often looks as if somebody had thrown her clothes on her as she rushed for the train.

With her devoted husband, Henry Maxwell Andrews, an investment banker with a cool, scholarly, finely whetted mind, she lives at Ibstone House, in the county of Buckinghamshire, 36 miles from London. There she prefers to be known as Mrs. Andrews. Ibstone is an 18th Century manor house whose back windows command one of the noblest vistas in southern England— broad fields falling away to a deep valley in the Chiltern Hills. Around the house lies the 85-acre farm, where the Andrewses raise fruit, vegetables, flowers, hogs, and pasture their purebred Jersey herd. Near the house is an immaculate modern dairy equipped with electric milkers. Miss West has been known to take visitors to the dairy and, in one of those transports common to cattle lovers, throw her arms around a cow's neck and murmur: "You beautiful, beautiful creature!"

Unlike most writers' farms, the Andrews project makes a profit. But not enough to support Ibstone House. Since her husband has lost most of his fortune, Rebecca West must still write for a living. The U.S. market pays her top rates for practically anything she cares to write, and she writes at top speed. Her report on Lord Haw Haw's trial, some 6,500 words, was in the *New Yorker*'s office 24 hours after the trial ended, and almost no editing had to be done on it. Says grateful *New Yorker* Editor Harold Ross: "It was the quickest piece of journalism I've seen." Says grateful Miss West of Ross: "The best editor I've ever known."

Last fortnight, her 2,500-word report on the Princess Elizabeth wedding was dashed off in time to make the London *Evening Standard*'s early afternoon edition and the New York *Herald Tribune*'s morning edition. It was a mood piece with one notable dig at the Labor government. Her jab was about a huge national savings advertisement sign opposite Westminster Abbey: "An imaginative administration would surely have blanketed it for this one day."

TWIPE, TWIPE, TWIPE. Miss West's present political temper worries her Laborite friends. "The individualist," she wrote recently, "is being looted by his own country as if it were an enemy." She has lately been raising the dust with her articles (in the *Evening Standard*) on the Fascist open-air meetings in London and the political use that the Communists are making out of them. She heard herself denounced by one little soapboxer who, unfortunately, could not pronounce the letter R. He rose to a climax with the cry: "I want to say that Miss Webecca West's articles are twipe, twipe, twipe from the gweatest twipe shop in the universe, Fleet Stweet."

Rebecca West rather enjoys it. For with all her warmth of heart and incandescence of mind, she is seldom averse to a good brawl. She listens, calmly poised for pouncing, when she is called a Fascist, a Communist, an anti-Semite, though she is none of those things. The root of the misunderstanding is that in a world racked by partisan passion, which more & more insists on viewing men in black & white, as caricatures of good or evil, she finds them blends of both. Her view asserts the faith that what distinguishes men, not so much from the brutes as from their more habitual selves, is the fact that however tirelessly they pursue evil, their inveterate aspiration, invariable even in depravity, is never for anything else but for the good.

This faith Rebecca West tries to express with a tonality equal to its meaning. Thus, in a prosy age, her style strives continually toward a condition of poetry, and comes to rest in a rhetoric that, at its best, is one of the most personal and eloquent idioms of our time.

THE DEVIL

(*Life*, FEBRUARY 2, 1948)

Throughout most of Christian history the Devil was real and personal and never far from the minds of men. But during the last several centuries he has retreated into the realm of myth. Today to most people he is only a joke. Recently, however, several perceptive philosophers have seen him roaming the world and have identified him as the same old Prince of Evil. On New Year's Eve, a favorite occasion with the Devil, he visited a New York nightclub. There his conversation was overheard by Whittaker Chambers, one of the editors of TIME.

AT A NEW YEAR'S PARTY in the Plutonium Room of Manhattan's swank Hotel Nineveh & Tyre, a pessimist was sitting in a corner trying not to look too much out of things. It was the year when, as midnight struck and the guests broke gulpingly into *Auld Lang Syne*, the drums of Sid Svoluch's orchestra punctuated the 12 strokes with solemn thuds. Chromatic lights flickered like lightning flashes and beautiful women screamed with happy hysteria. From the dance floor slowly swelled a big balloon crusted with diamond dust and labeled: I'M THE ATOM—SMASH ME. When the balloon filled the space between floor and ceiling, the guests rushed up and stuck pins into the glittering bag, which blew up with a terrific bang. Out stepped 20 girls covered only with gilt paint, silver top hats and two electric lights, like fore and aft fig leaves. The front light flashed out as the tail light flashed on and the girls danced and sang:

> *Baby, don't tell me to be calm,*
> *My heart's a plutonium bomb.*
> *In my condition,*
> *What do I care*
> *For atomic fission;*
> *I'm all up in the air.*
> *Let the world blow apart,*
> *Just like my heart,*
> *So long as you're still there.*

From the gay chaos of the room, a massive and immaculate stranger with a rich Miami tan suddenly materialized and sat down quietly at the pessimist's left. "You wanted to see me?" asked the stranger.

"I am afraid," said the pessimist, "that I do not place you. And yet I do seem to have met you somewhere. . . ."

"Millions have," said the stranger. "Perhaps you have seen me seated on some mountaintop, my gigantic pinions folded against the sunset, my chin sunk, brooding, on my clenched fists, on the evening of the day of an earthquake?"

"I beg your pardon!"

"Or leaning intently through the fires of a blitzed city, I listen, transfigured by that paralysis of pain which is half the pleasure of great music, while a child puddles in the stew of bones and shrieks, 'Father!' in a scream purged by pure terror of all gross humanity."

The pessimist half rose, clutching the arms of his chair.

"Yes," mused the stranger, "even in the 20th Century which, in the name of civilization, has popularized vulgarity by making it complicated and expensive, one can still enjoy the finer things of life. But please sit down. I see by that look of dawning recognition that you realize who I am. You are quite right: I am the Devil—Satan, the Fiend, called, and rightly so, the Prince of this World."

The pessimist stared at his visitor. He had never talked with the Devil before. But he had read descriptions of him by people who had and who remembered Satan as a goat, a bull, a dog, a cat, a big black man with horns, claws and a tail. The presence beside him looked distinguished, relaxed, urbane. Except for a face a little too characterful to be contemporary, the Devil might have been a movie magnate, an airline executive, a college president, a great surgeon or a grain speculator. "And yet," thought the pessimist, "those are certainly not the eyes of a Yale man." For the pupils of the Devil's eyes were a swampy black, and into their depths all vision sank without leaving a trace, like a toad in a pool of petroleum. They hung suspended in their sockets like orbs in a void of omnivorous vigilance, motionless, enveloping and contemplative without compassion.

"I do not wish to alarm you," said the Devil, "but if I were you, I do not think that I should stare too long into eyes which, in better times, have borne the inexpressible light of Heaven and read their doom by the flocculent night of Hell. Eyes," he went on, seeming to loom taller, as if by the action of a kind of cellular rhetoric, "which, in the dawn of the Creation, have watched with flaming envy as, at the great words, 'Fiat Lux,' primal darkness shimmered into the first day and Earth took form from seething chaos. Eyes that have seen the first sun rise and set again, and night return lit by the wonder of the first moon. Eyes that for 600,000 years have patiently probed the purulent heart of evil as a finger pushes through the walls of an ulcer. . . ."

"You certainly have a first-rate front," said the pessimist. "For a moment I took you for a gentleman."

"Did you really?" said the Devil with evident pleasure. "How do you judge?"

"Oh, the usual way," said the pessimist, "set of the shirt collar and the way the scarf is knotted."

"Yes," said Satan, "I think we can claim with a certain smugness that in the last couple of hundred years Hell has really turned the sartorial corner. In the underground," he added, dropping his voice to a confidential whisper, "we have now got together a group of experts in such things—deceased leftists from the International Tailors, Clothiers and Haberdashers Union, I believe."

"Underground?" said the pessimist.

"My dear fellow," said the Devil, "if what I hear of your background is true, it can be no secret from you that for the last 250 years all Hell has been underground. And I don't mean underground in any narrowly geographic or doctrinal sense. Hell is a conspiracy. Like all good conspiracies, its first requirement is that nobody shall believe in it. Well, we have succeeded so well that for centuries there has been no Hell, and there is scarcely a rational man in the world today who, despite the overwhelming evidence to the contrary, believes that the Devil exists."

"There is, of course, Reinhold Niebuhr at the Union Theological Seminary," said the pessimist. "In *The Nature and Destiny of Man* I believe that he found traces of your work. And C. S. Lewis has had some fun with you in *The Screwtape Letters*. Denis de Rougemont has devoted a whole book to your existence. And it seems to me that Monsignor Sheen has more than once, if I may be pardoned the expression, given your tail a shrewd twist."

The Devil exploded. "Nasty finks and informers!" he cried. "Beastly lackeys of celestial imperialism! But I know how to deal with such diversionists. I'm already making plans to turn their findings into a fad."

"I should think," said the pessimist, "that in a world which is in a state of almost total collapse, the fact that only a half-dozen men know your part in the plot is the proof of your success."

"Probably," said the Devil, rubbing his hands together lightly, "the greatest deception in history. For few facts in human experience are better documented than the fact of my existence. It is, indeed, indisputable. Not only is there the incontrovertible evidence of revealed truth in the Bible. I mention only Revelations XII: 7–9: 'And there was war in heaven: Michael and his angels fought against the dragon. . . . And the great dragon was cast out, that old serpent, called the Devil, and Satan, which deceiveth the whole world. . . .' Isaiah, in a style which, to my way of thinking, is even better suited to the subject, is just as explicit: 'How art thou fallen from heaven, O Lucifer, son of the morning! *how* art thou cut down to the ground, which didst weaken the nations!'

"There is also the unimpeachable testimony of the saints. Has it not been known for centuries that St. Anthony found no refuge from the Fiend even in the sandy seclusion of the Egyptian desert? Has it not been minutely described how the Devil dared to enter his cell and in the form of a ravishing woman sinuously distracted the holy man from his meditations?

"Has not St. Teresa of Avila reported that the Devil hurled her against the walls of her cell so fiercely that she was severely bruised? He might have done her more serious injury if, with a woman's intuition, she had not sensed that the Devil cannot stand contempt and repelled the Fiend by calling him 'goose!'

"Even in our times my existence, though discredited, has not gone unrecorded. I refer you to the work of André Pineau, crowned by the French Academy, *Marie-Thérèse Noblet, Servant of Our Lord in Papua*. Marie-Thérèse herself has written; 'The Old Boy'—meaning myself—'used to knock down everything in my room and to keep me from sleeping at night would grab me by the hair.'

"And lest you suspect me of a Roman Catholic bias," said the Devil, "let me point out that my existence is no less emphatically affirmed by the best Protestant authorities. Martin Luther himself has described how, when he was translating the Bible, the Devil often appeared and debated with him the proper interpretation of the Hebrew text. On one occasion Luther hurled an inkstand at him. It missed the Fiend but left a mark which can still be seen on the wall of Luther's cell in the Wartburg.

"Nor should we overlook," the Devil went on, "the researches of lay scholarship which have discerned behind my apparent unity that Hellish multiplicity which explains why one of my names is Legion. The ages of faith have given us very sweeping statistics on Hell. Basing its computations on Revelations XII:4, which implies that a third of the angels deserted to me in my great *coup d'état*, scholarship has calculated that I commanded 2,400 legions, or 14,400,000 devils—which will give you some idea of the forces opposed to us.

"True, Johannes Wierus, author of the learned 16th Century study, *Concerning the Artifices of Demons*, credits me with commanding only 1,111 legions, each comprising 6,666 demons or a total of 7,405,926—'without,' he adds, 'any possibility of error in calculation.' On the other hand Martinus Barrhaus, the Swiss theologian, computed the total number of demons to be exactly 2,665,866,746,664. I need scarcely tell you that the real strength of our effectives is one of the most jealously guarded secrets in Hell.

"Nor," the Devil continued, "can one write off the testimony of hundreds of eyewitnesses who have met me, talked with me, touched me and even claim to have enjoyed my more familiar attentions. And it is in the face of this overwhelming evidence that I succeeded in making mankind believe that I do not exist. Baudelaire, that old flower of evil, was right: 'The Devil's cleverest wile is to make men believe that he does not exist.' But you smile. I must confess that I deliberately arranged my evidence so that you would. Oh, how well I know the rationalist and liberal mind—the modern mind that still does not understand the nature of a commonplace like electricity but does not hesitate to question the existence of Heaven and Hell; the mind that cannot grasp the mystery of the universe in which it has lived 600,000 years, let alone those greater universes beyond the myopia of man's greatest telescopes, but does not hesitate to doubt that its Creator and the Creation are divine. Do you still doubt my existence? Then I will give you evidence that even you cannot refute: '*Si monumentum requiris, circumspice*—If you are seeking my monument, look around you.' "

The Devil had drawn the pessimist to a window which overlooked the city and the harbor. Said Satan, "Behold the world! Behold my handiwork!"

In the room behind them the band had struck up "*Bongo, bongo, bongo, I don't want to leave the Congo. . . .*" Below them the sheer walls of the buildings of Rockefeller Center, abstractly glittering with their geometry of electrically lighted windows, plunged gray and chasmic to the city at their base. "A proud architecture," said the Devil. "We have a view in Hell rather like it. And certain it is that in all human history man has never before closed such a haughty edifice above his head to fend off the wind and rain. And yet if you could see, as I can, behind the great stone face of this city, across the seas and the continents beyond, even into the humblest yurt on the Mongolian steppes, you would scarcely find one human heart which is not gripped by a fear and a sense of helplessness unknown to man in any other age. They are like animals stampeding from a forest fire, who have reached their last refuge, the brink of an abyss. On one side is a sheer drop. On the other the ring of flames is roaring closer. They do not know how they came into this plight. But *I* know. It is my work. And their panic is my peace.

"It seems but yesterday that I launched Hell's Five Hundred Year Plan. I still remember when the inspiration struck me. I still remember the disdainful laughter with which Hell and its reactionaries heard the plan—the most luminous plan, perhaps, that ever lit the darkened mind of fallen angel. I had had a look at the record—thousands and thousands of years of tempting stubborn saints and seducing all too willing mortals, pandering to the grossest vices of a breed already depraved by original sin; years of frightening dim-witted peasants with horns and hoofs and tricks that a sideshow conjuror would be ashamed of; years of making theatrical blood pacts and mixing obscene love potions for senescent scholars whose libidos had outlasted their wits; years of dancing on drafty mountaintops with bevies of bearded hags who wanted to be Rockettes for a night; years of tormenting damned souls until the mouth of Hell smelled like the open door of a cafeteria kitchen. And where had it got us? In all those years Hell had not advanced one inch. It was all just leftism, infantile leftism. A new revolutionary strategy was in order in keeping with the progressive nature of the times we were living in.

"It was the 18th Century. The Enlightenment had begun. As I read Voltaire and Diderot, Locke and Helvetius, and pored over the *Principia Mathematica* of

Sir Isaac Newton, I saw that mankind had reached one of the decisive turning points in its history. The Middle Ages were liquidated. Faith in the human mind had supplanted faith in God. I saw that Hell must write Progress on its banners and Science in its methods."

"What's wrong with Progress and Science?" asked the pessimist.

"Absolutely nothing," said the Devil. "Only the most primitive mind would suppose there was. They are, in fact, positively good. That was the nub of my inspiration. Hitherto Hell had tried to destroy man by seducing him to evil. My revolutionary thought was to destroy man by seducing him through good. Intellectual pride has always been my specific sin and, like most sinners, I have always felt secretly a little proud of my fault. Now, I perceived, all mankind had sinned the same sin. I saw that Hell had only to move with the tide and leave the rest to rationalism, liberalism and universal compulsory education, while Up There"—he pointed to the ceiling—"they lost ground daily by insisting on a positively 13th Century view of history. Only Hell must be careful not to show its hand. That is why Hell went underground. That is why for 250 years I have ceased to exist. It was even easier than I anticipated."

"And you suffered no setbacks?" asked the pessimist.

"On the whole," said the Devil, "I think we can say that progress has been steady. At first there was some opposition in Hell. Baal, Beelzebub and a handful of almost aboriginal demons who are still living in the 10th Century B.C. and have not had an idea since the Fall, naturally opposed the New Deal. But Mammon and the majority went along with me. Our slogan was the Five Hundred Year Plan in Three Hundred Years. The three hundred years are almost up. In less than a generation the ideas of the Enlightenment led directly to the French Revolution. France, the cultural focus of Europe, was split down the middle and has remained so ever since. A chain reaction was set up all over the world. Though it was not felt everywhere at once, that instability of all traditional institutions, which is part of modern man's distress, was begun. The industrial and the scientific revolutions furthered the process. Meanwhile another first-rate idea occurred to me.

"Shall I ever forget the day when the prodigious thought of Evolution popped into my head? I was lying at full length on a pleasant height watching the armies of the most civilized nations exterminate one another with a ferocity worthy of Comanches but with weapons which were, as weapons always are, at the forefront of the technology of their time. Evolution, I thought. It was but the work of a moment to transmit the idea to a human brain. Of course if I had called it adjustment or adaptation, nobody would have bought it. But Evolution—man, with his incurable, divinely inspired obsession with perfection, could not fail to snap it up—one of my sublimest strokes, for the only trouble with it is that, as far as the human race is concerned, it simply ain't so." The Devil uttered a shrill cackle.

"What price progress now?" said the pessimist. "That lines you up with dodoes like Bishop Wilberforce, who wanted to know if Thomas Huxley was descended from an ape through his grandfather or his grandmother."

"The Devil," said Satan, "likes to have it both ways. And how the little monsters snapped at the bait! In less than a century I had undone the work of more than a thousand years and knocked the studs from under the religious culture of Europe. Why? Because Evolution explained the universe without *Him*. They wanted to get rid of *Him*. Then I knew the secret longing of their nasty hearts. Then I knew I had them.

"The rest followed as a matter of course: the growth of factories to supply the huge demand for material goods which were the only values secular man could really feel; the growth of cities and slums, the corruption by the cities of the countryside which in other times had been the reservoir from which exhausted cultures replenished their faith and forces; the inhuman industrial oppression of men, women and children whose desperation found expression in the inhuman horrors of communism, socialism and anarchism; the debasement of all standards of conduct and taste as God was forgotten and with Him the only absolute standard; finally, the world wars with millions of men dying by all the horrors contrived by secular genius. Consider for a moment the miracle of the flame thrower; or the spectacle of a government physically destroying millions of the people in whose interests it was created to govern. Do you doubt my triumph when you stop to think that the mind of man conceived the concentration camps? Then came the atomic bomb—my ultimate perversion of the highest powers of the human brain and scientific good for the purpose of total destruction."

"Poor Devil," said the pessimist.

"Poor Devil?" said Satan, plainly taken aback.

"Doomed by the dialectic of creation continually to make new good out of old evil. For God, being perfect, would be incapable of further creation were it not for you who, by disturbing the equipoise of His perfection, restore to Him the necessity of new creation. In our time Arnold Toynbee has perhaps best formulated this great concept in his *Study of History:* 'In the language of Mythology, when one of God's creatures is tempted by the Devil, God Himself is thereby given the opportunity to re-create the World. By the stroke of the Adversary's trident, all the fountains of the great deep are broken up. The Devil's intervention has accomplished that transition from Yin to Yang, from static to dynamic, for which God had been yearning ever since the moment when His Yin-state became complete, but which it was impossible for God to accomplish by Himself, out of His own perfection.' "

A shade of slightly malevolent annoyance crossed the Devil's face. "I have been watching the man Toynbee and his followers for some time," he said, "and, as a trained theologian, I should like to challenge his proposition with a question: May not there be an end even to dialectics? What you and your dialectical friends may tend to overlook is the fact that I have brought man to the point of intellectual pride where self-extermination lies within his power. There is not only the bomb, of which, frankly, I am a little tired of hearing. There are the much less discussed delights of bacteriological annihilation. And it is only a question of time until whole populations can be driven ultra-sonically insane in time of war by sound which their ears cannot hear but their nerves cannot bear. It would be an amusing paradox if the babble of the cosmic argument were ended once and for all by an ultrasonic silence."

"Just what do you get out of it?" asked the pessimist.

"My friend," said Satan, "you do not understand the Devil's secret. But since shamelessness is part of my pathos, there is no reason why I should not tell you. The Devil is sterile. I possess the will to create (hence my pride), but I am incapable of creating (hence my envy). And with an envy raised to such power as immortal minds can feel, I hate the Creator and His Creation. My greatest masterpiece is never more than a perversion—an ingenious disorder-ing of Another's grand design, a perversion of order into chaos, of life into death."

"Why?" asked the pessimist.

"If I knew the answer to that one," said Satan, "perhaps I should not be the Devil. Perhaps it is simply, as every craftsman knows, that nothing enduring, great or small, can ever be created without love. But I am as incapable of love as I am of goodness. I am as insensible to either as a dead hand is to a needle thrust through it."

In the room behind them the party was in its last throes. A strikingly beautiful woman, who had somehow got a dab of mayonnaise on her chin and was bibulously unaware of the blemish, was being egged on by her friends to stand on a table and sing:

> *Baby, I don't want to be calm,*
> *My heart's a plutonium bomb.*
> *In my condition*
> *What do I care*
> *For atomic fission;*
> *I'm all up in the air. . . .*

The Devil's voice grew less harsh and he dropped his hand to his side in a gesture of weariness. "Goodness," he said, "is a perpetual benediction, the seed within the minute husk which is the promise of the summer, the un-multiplied image of the harvest. Not to know goodness is not to understand creation. In no way is my mark more clearly on the modern world than in the death of the creative imagination.

"And yet it is at this very point that man, the monstrous midget, still has the edge on the Devil: he suffers. For at the heart of all human suffering is the anguish of the chance that that creative seed of goodness, that little flash of inward light, however brief, may not perpetuate itself, that a man can leave this life, this light, without communicating that one cell of himself which is real. Not one man, however base, quite lacks the capacity for this specific suffering, which is the seal of his divine commitment—this suffering which I cannot feel because of that light which in me is dark. Intellectually I can understand it since, by my origin, I share the intellect of angels. But I cannot feel it or I would not be the Devil. That is the source of my frustration and root of my rage against the breed. That is why I shall never cease working to entangle man in evil until the world becomes one universal graveyard whose lifeless peace is broken only by my shriek of triumph as I plunge into a deeper pit than Hell. For only One knows better than I that should I succeed in making man destroy himself, I will destroy myself with him, having destroyed my function. It still lies with man to make the choice (after all, the filthy beetles have free will): a skeleton beside a broken wall on a dead planet purged of all suffering because purged of all life; or Him, with all that that entails. Personally, as I glance around this room, I have never felt my chances to be so good.

"Happy New Year, young man."

DR. CRANKLEY'S CHILDREN
(*Time*, FEBRUARY 23, 1948)

WHEN CLIO, THE MUSE OF HISTORY, gets her diary up to date, whom will she write down as the Man of the 20th Century? Barring the unlikely appearance, before 2000, of an extraordinarily effective saint or major prophet, the Man of the Century will be a German intellectual, devoted to children, caviar and Aeschylus.

He does not look the part. His scholarly forehead, his small, sparkling eyes, his massive and majestic beard set him apart from other 20th Century heroes. The black-rimmed eyeglass, which he carries on a thin ribbon around his neck, is a gentle anachronism. Above all, his dates seem wrong. For it was at the height of the Victorian era, when the atom appeared almost as indestructible as Britain's dominion of the waves, that Karl Heinrich Marx died.

But that was a technicality. In the historic sense (as distinguished from the merely biological), Karl Marx has only just begun to live.

HAPPY BIRTHDAY. This month marks an anniversary for Karl Marx. Just 100 years ago his *Communist Manifesto*, a slender pamphlet bound in green, was first presented to a deeply uninterested public. Since then, public interest has increased. Karl Marx this week is everywhere.

"Marxist" is the word that divides the world. In the lands drained by the Sava, the Bug, the Moskva, the Dnieper, the Don, the Volga, the Yenisei and the Amur, a man who wishes to express approval—of a painting, a factory production record or a military operation—is likely to call it "Marxist." In the lands drained by the St. Lawrence, the Mississippi, the Orinoco, the Amazon, the Tagus, the Thames and the Clyde, a man who wishes to express disapproval—of a painting, a production record or a military operation—is likely to call it "Marxist." In the lands drained by the Yangtze, the Yellow River, the Mekong, the Tiber, the Po, the Rhone, the Scheldt, the Rhine, men are divided—in some cases bloodily—over whether "Marxist" should express approval or disapproval.

In the lands drained by the Shannon, the Niger, the Nile, the Euphrates, the Ganges, the Indus and the Irrawaddy, Marxism is not the paramount issue. These lands are regarded by both Marxists and anti-Marxists as somewhat backward.

Marxism last week made men fight in the ragged mountains of Greece. It inspired strikes in Seoul, Korea, and San Ferdinando di Puglia, Italy. A Shanghai girl student asked a boy to write in her autograph book. Instead of an affectionate personal sentiment, he wrote: "What is the reason for the existence of people who reap wealth without laboring?" Marx, who guided the Chinese boy's hand, was also last week the most important man in the world's two great centers of power, the U.S. Congress and Moscow's Politburo.

Quite a birthday for a manifesto. Quite a ripple for an unsociable old refugee who had sat, day after day, year after year, under the high glass dome of the British Museum's reading room, his clothes untidy, a sarcastic line edging his mouth.

THE IDEA MARKET. Marx got into the center of all this commotion by making a statement about The Machine. It was not a clear statement, and every year more evidence piles up that it was wrong. In the market place of ideas, however, it did not have very effective competition. Among its competitors were:

1) The idea (still popular) that The Machine doesn't matter, that human society is not deeply affected by it.

2) The idea that The Machine is pure evil, and should be destroyed. (This idea was first expressed by a village idiot, Ned Ludd, who stalked around Nottingham, England, in the late 18th Century, smashing stocking frames.)*

3) The idea that The Machine is pure good, the center of a new evolution towards greater & greater prosperity.

In Marx's day, Europe was divided between these three attitudes towards The Machine. The old aristocracy tended to ignore The Machine, or to agree with Ned Ludd. The new aristocracy of trade committed itself to a philosophy of materialist progress. Some of the workers believed the promise; some believed Ned Ludd.

Marx accepted The Machine. He accepted and further glorified the materialism of the capitalists, but rejected the idea of progress and said that The Machine would lead the workers where Ned Ludd said it would, unless the workers took control of The Machine away from the capitalists.

The idea of class struggle was certainly not original with Marx. What he did was rewrite history with class struggle in the center. Superficially, it might seem that the abundance of goods The Machine could produce would soften the class struggle; Marx said that this very possibility of abundance would sharpen class struggle, that the capitalists would use the state's police power, its war-making power and all other means to prevent glutted markets, *i.e.,* abundance. It followed that the workers had to seize the state by revolution (they would never get it any other way) and use the state's powers to control

* A few decades later his followers were an organized force, called Luddites. They would converge on an industrial village at dusk, post guards, and smash and burn machinery while the villagers cowered in their cottages. Their counterparts existed in many continental countries.

The Machine. This would lead to the world's first classless society; its goal: unlimited material prosperity.

THE SECRET OF SUCCESS. These ideas were set forth in the 1848 *Manifesto* and developed in *Das Kapital* and other children of Karl Marx's mind. The most interesting thing about these ideas is their success in the teeth of developments proving that Marx's main assumptions were wrong. He assumed, for example, that the spectacular poverty of industrial workers of his day would spread and deepen. The capitalist philosophers, who predicted rising living standards, were right. A hundred years after the *Manifesto*, however, the class struggle is sharper in spite of the fact that the living standard of the "exploited classes" is almost everywhere higher than it has ever been.

The other day a keen U.S. observer, back from a year in Italy, was warning of the danger of a Marxist political victory there. A listener asked: "But when the Marshall Plan gets going, won't rising living standards greatly reduce the unrest?" The observer replied: "Not necessarily. The discrepancy between the rich and the poor will still be there, and that is what counts."

Why? For over 2,000 years, a deep gulf between rich and poor had existed in Italy. Why had class conflict now hardened into its present menacing aspect? The answer, for Italy and everywhere, was that before The Machine poverty was suffered as inevitable; since The Machine's promise of prosperity, poverty is regarded (with Marx's prompting) as the result of a conspiracy.

That is the secret of Marx's success. The results may not be what Marx intended. In many countries, notably Britain, the consciousness of poverty results in a drive toward leveling, rather than toward revolution. The Machine is controlled in the interest of reducing the prosperity and power of the "exploiting classes," rather than in the interest of abundance. Economic initiative, instead of being restricted by capitalist greed, is in danger of being fettered by proletarian envy.

THE SUPREMACY OF THE COP. In countries truer to Marx, where control of The Machine has actually been taken away from the capitalist, the most extraordinary growth occurred in the meaning of "control." Control of production by "the state," in place of ownership by private people, turned out to need bolstering up. It meant control of speech, thought and personal life. It was not the freed worker who replaced the capitalist; it was the cop, the spy, the bureaucrat.

Old Prince Otto von Bismarck saw what was implicit in Marx more clearly than Marx himself did. He noted the reluctance of Marxists to discuss the nature of the society for which they struggled. Said Bismarck in 1878: "If only I could find out what the future [Marxist] state . . . is like. We can only catch glimpses of it through the cracks. . . . If every man has to have his share allotted to him from above, we arrive at a kind of prison existence where everyone is at the mercy of the warders. And in our modern prisons the warder is at any rate a recognized official, against whom one can lodge a complaint. But who will be the warders in the general socialist prison? There will be no question of lodging complaints against them; they will be the most merciless tyrants ever seen, and the rest will be the slaves of these tyrants."

YEARNINGS OF A CREATOR. Despite the fear of the warders (and in Marxist countries, because of this fear), Marxism persists. It offers far more than a critique of capitalism; in addition, its converts get the only fully developed materialist religion, complete with creed, church, directions for salvation, answers to every question, saints, doctors and devils.

The ingredients in Marxism's emotional force are 1) pity, 2) hate, 3) desire for power. All three were conspicuously present in the life and character of Karl Marx.

He was born (1818) in the ancient archbishopric of Trier. From his ancestry (which included generations of rabbis and Talmudic scholars) he undoubtedly inherited his gift for subtle and untiring disputation. When Karl was six Father Hirschel Marx, a lawyer, took the family to be baptized in the Protestant Church. Karl became an evangelical atheist.

He wrote poetry for his beautiful neighbor, Fraulein Jenny von Westphalen, who, whenever she read one of his poems, "burst into tears of joy and melancholy." Sample: "If we can but weld our souls together, then with contempt I shall fling my glove in the world's face; then I, a creator, shall stride through the wreckage!"

He fell under the influence of the philosopher Georg Wilhelm Friedrich Hegel and learned from him two persistent tendencies: a respect for the state (very rare in 19th Century radicals), and the dialectical method.

The conventional way of thinking about causes and effects imagines them as a chain, one link leading to the next. Hegel's dialectic presented a more turbulent picture: every idea (thesis) has its opposite (antithesis) with which it struggles until they produce a third idea (synthesis); this in turn has its antithesis, and so on. Marx expressed history by putting class conflicts in the place of thesis and antithesis. The culminating conflict was that called forth by The Machine. The last synthesis, which would be unique because it would not contain its own negation, would be the classless society.

The Communist who imagines history as moving in a spiral toward his goal will have no compunction in allying himself first with Hitler, then with Churchill, in the belief that the struggle between them will produce a "synthesis" of benefit to Communism. When a Communist wrecks a labor union or helps a reactionary to power, he is not being cynical but "systematic."

FRONTS & PURGES. Marx did not absorb the morals of the dialectic immediately. When, at 24, he became editor of the *Rheinische Zeitung* (a paper owned by bourgeois and written by their radical sons), he promptly ordered contributors to stop smuggling socialist propaganda into casual drama reviews, he said the practice was downright "immoral."

His atheism got the *Rheinische Zeitung* into censorship trouble and King Frederick William himself ordered the "Whore on the Rhine" to cease publication. Marx married Jenny, against the opposition of her aristocratic family, and went to Paris. By the time he wrote the *Manifesto*, he had ironed out the basic tenets of his faith.

One day, Marx and his new friend Friedrich Engels (a young man of good bourgeois family) began calling themselves "The Communist Party." It soon grew to include 17 members, all of whom were bourgeois intellectuals, bearing in true dialectical fashion the seeds of the destruction of the middle class and of intellectual freedom.

Marx created the first Communist front organization. When the revolutions of 1848 swept Europe, he organized a workers' club in Paris whose agitators had instructions not to mention Communism, but to emphasize democracy. Later, Marx sent 300 agents into Germany with instructions to organize Communist cells but to appear as good, hard-working liberals. In 1848 Marx himself revived the old *Rheinische Zeitung;* its masthead now proclaimed it an "organ of democracy." Admitted Marx: "It was in reality nothing but a plan of war against democracy."

Marx also conducted the first Party purges. He denounced anyone who disagreed with him as an "unscientific socialist." The usual instrument of execution was slander, from stories that the accused had embezzled workers' funds to rumors that he had gonorrhea.

It was Mikhail Bakunin, the legendary Russian anarchist, who was the first to spot Karl Marx as a tyrant. Cried he: "I hate Communism. . . . It is the negation of liberty." Marx drove him from the First International by accusing him (falsely) of being a blackmailer and a Czarist agent. (In the process, Marx helped wreck the International).

"Baring his teeth and grinning," an acquaintance once said, "Marx will slaughter anybody who blocks his way."

Marx hated "sentimental socialism," was bitterly impatient of efforts to better the lot of the workers by gradual progress. As the years went on, he spoke more & more of the necessity of "capturing" the state (with its police power) rather than of "destroying" the state, as other socialists hoped to do. Toward the end of his life he wrote the words "dictatorship of the proletariat" to describe the post-revolutionary period which was to precede the classless society. That phrase had always been buried in Marx's thought; he had in fact used it in conversation. Written down, it was to become an extension of his own tyrannical political methods, the excuse for the most pitiless tyranny the world has ever seen.

FATHER MARX. Yet the man was certainly not without pity and warm humanity. The children of his neighborhood in London (where he spent most of his life), as well as the members of his party, called him "Father Marx." With children, he lost all the hatred and suspicion he constantly harbored toward grownups. On Sunday nights, he would read fairy tales to his children (*Bluebeard, Snow White, Rumpelstilzchen*) or build paper boats for them (which he usually set on fire like Zeus destroying a mortal fleet). He took the children for picnics on Hampstead Heath, where he rode the donkeys with them or led them to the year's first forget-me-nots in defiance of bourgeois "no trespassing" signs. Once he answered a dinner invitation for his daughter:

Dear Miss Lilliput,

  . . . Having ascertained your respectability and the high tone of your transactions with your tradespeople, I shall feel happy to seize this rather strange opportunity of getting at your eatables and drinkables. . . . Being somewhat deaf in the right ear, please put a dull fellow, of whom I daresay your company will not be in want, at my right side. . . . Having [through] former intercourse with Yankees taken to the habitude of spitting, I hope spittoons will not be missing. Being rather easy in my manners and disgusted at the hot and close English atmosphere, you must prepare for seeing me in a dress rather adamatic. I hope your female guests are somewhat in the same line.

  Addio, my dear unknown little minx,

Yours forever,
Dr. Crankley

But Dr. Crankley was unhappy even as a father. Of his seven children, one was born dead, four others died before him. When Marx's daughter Franziska died of bronchitis, there was no money to buy a coffin. "Her little lifeless body rested in the small back room," related Jenny Marx. "We all moved together into the front room and when night came we made up beds on the floor." (A fellow refugee finally lent the Marxes £2 for the coffin.)

THE ORDEAL OF A COMMUNIST. Marx's life was veined by the ordeal of his own poverty. With the egotism of genius, he refused to be turned "into a [bourgeois] money-making machine." He never had a regular job, and only once tried to get one; a railroad company turned him down as a clerk because of his bad handwriting. Once he reported to Engels: "I can no longer leave the house, because my clothes are in pawn." Another time he was arrested on suspicion of theft when he tried to pawn his wife's family silver (it bore the crest of the Dukes of Argyll, from whom she was descended through her paternal grandmother). Guiltily, he wrote to Engels: "My wife cried all night and that infuriates me."

The Prussian government, which kept a close watch on him in London, received the following report, probably unique in the literature of espionage, on Marx's apartment at 28 Dean Street, Soho:

"In the middle of the living room there is a big table covered with oilcloth. On it are piled his manuscripts, books and papers; the children's toys; his wife's sewing, chipped teacups; dirty spoons, knives and forks; lamps, an inkwell, glasses, clay pipes, tobacco ash; in a word, it is the most indescribable muddle. . . . One's eyes are so blinded by coal and tobacco smoke that it is like walking around in a cave until one becomes accustomed to it and objects begin to loom up through the fog. . . . Sitting down is a dangerous business. One of the chairs has only three legs; and the children are playing at cooking on another one which happens to be whole, and which they offer to the guest; so if you sit down it is at the risk of ruining your trousers."

THE END & THE BEGINNING. His book, *Das Kapital*, was a disappointment to Marx. When it finally appeared (after some 18 years of work), Engels was pressed into service to write reviews, both pro & con, in a vain attempt to attract some attention to it. Marx said: "*Das Kapital* will not bring in enough money to pay for the cigars I smoked while I wrote it." Marx's contemporaries scarcely knew that he was alive, much less what he stood for. He did acquire a brief notoriety during the Paris Commune of 1871, which was regarded as his handiwork. Said he: "Newspaper men and all kinds of people dog my steps for a glimpse of 'The Monster.' It does one's heart good."

Because of his intrigues and his intolerance, he lost most of his friends; the only people outside his family whose affections he kept were Lenchen Demuth, the Marxes' lifelong, devoted servant (who could handle Marx even in his blackest moods) and Friedrich Engels, whom one acquaintance described as "the little Pomeranian." Engels, first with his father's money, then with his own profits as a textile manufacturer, paid Marx's bills. (In a letter to Engels Marx wrote: "I have worked out a sure scheme for getting some money out of your Old Man.")

Marx's only lasting comforts were algebra (his favorite form of escape) and Jenny. Protectively, she used to call him "my big child." Once, when he briefly returned to Trier, he wrote: "I have been making a daily pilgrimage to the old Westphalen house . . . which used to shelter my sweetheart. And every day people ask me right and left about the quondam 'most beautiful girl' in Trier, the 'Queen of the ball.' It's damned agreeable for a man to find that his wife lives on as an 'enchanted princess' in the imagination of a whole town."

Then Jenny died. Her last words were: "Karl, my strength is broken." So was his. On March 14, 1883, death came quietly to Karl Marx as he sat in his easy chair. He was buried in Highgate Cemetery under a flat stone. At the grave, Friedrich Engels said: "The greatest of living thinkers ceased to think. . . . He discovered the simple fact . . . that mankind must first of all eat and drink, have shelter and clothing, before it can pursue politics, science, religion, art. . . ."

Marx himself had unwittingly composed an even better obituary. Once, tortured by boils as he often was, Marx wrote: "I hope as long as they live, the bourgeois will remember my carbuncles."

THE HERITAGE. It was perhaps a tragic accident—though its symbolism can scarcely escape a death-ridden world—that none of Father Marx's beloved children lived happily; the two daughters who survived him committed suicide. But he was to have other children. They came to him by the thousands. Dr. Crankley's spiritual children inherited in varying degree his three outstanding characteristics: pity, hatred and love of power.

The children of pity accepted Marx's indictment of capitalism's evils, but they did not want to substitute the greater evil of his proletarian dictatorship. They were the backbone (if backbone it had) of Social Democracy. They were perhaps best epitomized by Sidney Webb, later Lord Passfield. He and his wife Beatrice loved the bicycle, and untiringly cycled about the business of their Fabian Society; once they pedaled 40 miles to Cardiff to attend a trade union congress. They believed not in the inevitability of revolution but in the "inevitability of gradualness," *i.e.*, in a steady bicycle ride toward socialism.

One of the Webbs' best works was the *English Poor Law History*. Gradually, the semi-Marxist influence of the Webbs might make Britain the most efficiently, equitably, and humanely operated poorhouse the world had ever seen. But there was always the possibility that it would turn back from socialism. As Engels put it despairingly: "The English have all the material conditions necessary for . . . revolution. What they lack is the spirit of generalization. . . ."

Then there were the children of hate. Their archetype is Benito Mussolini. As a young Socialist, he was poor, sickly and beset by strange anguish. "I am afraid of trees, of dogs, of the sky and my own shadow." He was always hungry and he despised the rich. Once, in a Lausanne park, he saw two elderly Englishwomen on a bench, lunching on hard-boiled eggs; he pounced on the women and snatched their lunch.

Mussolini seized the state as he had grabbed the eggs, and out of hatred and hunger men followed him. He never tried seriously to control The Machine or resolve the basis of class conflict. He put the machines and the classes to work for war.

The most important and the most terrible in the Marxist brood are those who inherited the cold, disciplined logic necessary for the serious pursuit of power. Their leader is the late Vladimir Ilyich Ulyanov, better known as Lenin. When the Russian people, without his help, snatched at democracy, he snatched it away from them. Like Father Marx, he knew what was best. He organized riots that weakened and, finally, a coup that overpowered the Kerensky government. He organized, as Marx had taught, a dictatorship of the proletariat (*i.e.*, a disciplined little gang of power monopolists). In 1917, in the assembly hall of a swank girls' school in Petrograd, behind unwashed windows that excluded the sky, Lenin stood up. His ill-fitting, over-long trousers flapped about his feet. Gripping the rostrum, he said quietly: "We shall now proceed to construct the proletarian socialist order in Russia."

In the process of reconstructing humanity to fit The Machine, Lenin's followers smashed men as freely as the idiot boy of Nottingham had smashed machines.

"YOURS FOREVER." Today, the children of pity are largely ineffectual; the children of hate are at bay. The West faces the children of power who rule Russia and all Communist parties throughout the world. Against them stands capitalist democracy, which has certainly not fulfilled the shiny, steam-driven dreams of some of its early prophets. There is no need, however, for capitalism to cringe silently beneath the Marxist indictment. The *Communist Manifesto* made better reading before Marxism had been tried. Capitalism, for all the regimentation and degradation that occasionally went with it, has made a compromise with The Machine which is, on the record, superior to the Marxist compromise with human nature. Capitalism does not get all it can out of The Machine, or give men all they should have. But it has left man essentially free, while it gets more out of The Machine than Marxism does. But capitalism has failed to proclaim, so that the world can hear—and that is not to capitalism's credit—the victory it has won over the argument of the *Manifesto*.

They were telling a story in Europe this week. In a Bulgarian classroom, a Communist teacher asked her hungry pupils to recite the Lord's Prayer. When they had finished, they were still hungry. Then the teacher led them in a new prayer which began "Our Father Stalin. . . ." Suddenly, through a hole in the ceiling, straight from the Marxist heaven, tumbled loaf after loaf of bread.

That story summarized Marxism's challenge. For Marxism offered both reason and faith, both bread and miracles. Sharp ears this week could hear Karl Marx laugh quietly to himself on the *Manifesto*'s birthday. The bourgeois, forgetting their own accomplishments, were remembering his carbuncles. "Yours forever," the old man seemed to say, "Yours forever, Dr. Crankley."

FAITH FOR A LENTEN AGE
(*Time*, MARCH 8, 1948)

IT WAS LENT. On Manhattan's Fifth Avenue, a woman and a little girl were stopped by the traffic at a cross street. On the opposite curb stood a young man with an Ash Wednesday mark on his forehead. "Look," said the little girl. "Mustn't point," said the woman. "But Mother," asked the little girl, "why has he got that black mark on his forehead?" "Hush," said her mother. "It's something they do in church, I think."

With prayer, with humility of spirit tempering his temerity of mind, man has always sought to define the nature of the most important fact in his experience: God. To this unending effort to know God, man is driven by the noblest of his intuitions—the sense of his mortal incompleteness—and by hard experience. For man's occasional lapses from God-seeking inevitably result in intolerable shallowness of thought combined with incalculable mischief in action.

Modern man knows a great deal about the nature of the atom. But he knows almost nothing about the nature of God, almost never thinks about it, and is complacently unaware that there may be any reason to. Theology, the intellectual system whereby man sorts out his thoughts about faith and grace, enjoys much less popular appeal than astrology. With its "devolutionary theopantism"* and "axiological eschatology,"† theology is jaw-breakingly abstract. And its mood is widely felt to be about as bracing as an unaired vestry.

WORTHY HABIT. This is scarcely strange, since among millions of Christians religion itself is little more than a worthy mental habit, socially manifested in church attendance often more sporadic and much less disturbing than regular visits to the dentist.

To the mass of untheological Christians, God has become, at best, a rather unfairly furtive presence, a lurking luminosity, a cozy thought. At worst, He is conversationally embarrassing. There is scarcely any danger that a member

* The doctrine that God is the sole cause of the world process, the world and man having no independent reality.
† The belief that every generation is directly under God's judgment (as opposed to "teleological eschatology," which puts the judgment at some future time).

of the neighborhood church will, like Job, hear God speak out of the whirl-wind (whirlwinds are dangerous), or that he will be moved to dash down the center aisle, crying, like Isaiah: "Howl, ye ships of Tarshish!"

Under the bland influence of the idea of progress, man, supposing himself more & more to be the measure of all things, achieved a singularly easy conscience and an almost hermetically smug optimism. The idea that man is sinful and needs redemption was subtly changed into the idea that man is by nature good and hence capable of indefinite perfectibility. This perfectibility is being achieved through technology, science, politics, social reform, education. Man is essentially good, says 20th Century liberalism, because he is rational, and his rationality is (if the speaker happens to be a liberal Protestant) divine, or (if he happens to be religiously unattached) at least benign. Thus the reason-defying paradoxes of Christian faith are happily bypassed.

CATASTROPHIC PARADOXES. And yet, as 20th Century civilization reaches a climax, its own paradoxes grow catastrophic. The incomparable technological achievement is more & more dedicated to the task of destruction. Man's marvelous conquest of space has made total war a household experience and, over vast reaches of the world, the commonest of childhood memories. The more abundance increases, the more resentment becomes the characteristic new look on 20th Century faces. The more production multiplies, the more scarcities become endemic. The faster science gains on disease (which, ulti-mately, seems always to elude it), the more the human race dies at the hands of living men. Men have never been so educated, but wisdom, even as an idea, has conspicuously vanished from the world.

Yet liberal Protestants could do little more than chant with Lord Tennyson:

> *O, yet we trust that somehow good*
> *Will be the final goal of ill,*
> *To pangs of nature, sins of will,*
> *Dejects of doubt, and taints of blood . . .*

It was a good deal easier to see that Tennyson was silly than to see that the attitude itself was silly. That was the blind impasse of optimistic liberalism. At the open end of that impasse stood a forbidding and impressive figure. To Protestantism's easy conscience and easy optimism that figure was saying, with every muscle of its being: No.

His name was Reinhold Niebuhr. He was an Evangelical* pastor, a pro-fessor of applied Christianity at Manhattan's Union Theological Seminary, an editor of *Christianity and Crisis, Christianity and Society*, contributing editor of

* Dr. Niebuhr was ordained in the Evangelical Synod of North America, a German Lutheran church now a part of the Evangelical and Reformed Church.

the *Nation*, and an ex-Socialist who was still unflaggingly active in non-Communist leftist movements. He was also the author of countless magazine articles and eleven books on theology. His magnum opus, the two-volume *Nature and Destiny of Man*, was the most complete statement of his position.

Against the easy conscience, Dr. Niebuhr asserted: man is by the nature of his creation sinful; at the height of man's perfection there is always the possibility of evil. Against easy optimism, he asserted that life is inevitably tragic. Says Niebuhr: "Mankind is living in a Lenten age."

Dr. Niebuhr was one liberal Protestant who had indeed heard the Voice out of the whirlwind. It spoke the thought of three God-tormented men: Russian Novelist Fyodor Dostoevsky, Danish Theologian Sören Kierkegaard and Swiss Theologian Karl Barth.

World War I ended the age of liberalism. More than half a century before it ended, two men had felt that it was ending. They were Fyodor Dostoevsky and Sören Kierkegaard. Both men were pessimists. To Dostoevsky, the human situation was a tragic drama. To Kierkegaard, it was a tragic argument. Both men felt that the anguish of human experience, the truth of man's nature and God's nature and the relationship of God and man, could be grasped only by a new dimension of perception.

Against liberalism's social optimism (progress by reform) and the social optimism of the revolutionary left (progress by force), Dostoevsky asserted the eternal necessity of the soul to be itself. But he discerned that the moment man indulged this freedom to the point where he was also free from God, it led him into tragedy, evil, and often the exact opposite of what he had intended. In human terms there was no solution for the problem of evil. This insight Dostoevsky dramatized on a scale of titanic tragedy in *The Brothers Karamazov* and *The Idiot*, and of titanic comedy in *The Possessed*.

Kierkegaard too was obsessed with "the ultimate potentialities of the human soul." And like the great Russian, the great Dane was haunted by the tragic sense of life whose full implication only the presentiments of religious faith could grasp.

Karl Barth, too, heard the Voice from the whirlwind. But this time the Voice spoke in the tones of cannon. During World War I, Barth was a Christian Socialist and pastor of a small Swiss Reformed Church near the Alsatian frontier. As he preached, on quiet Sunday mornings, about the fulfillment of God's intentions as evidenced in human progress, the thump and slam of German and Allied artillery punctuated his periods. It caused him, said Barth, acute embarrassment.

It also caused him 1) to doubt that the will of God was being fulfilled by man's good works, or could be; 2) to re-examine the Bible, where, to his surprise (since he, too, had been an optimist), he discovered that most of the principal characters shared his new pessimism about human nature. God, Barth decided, was above and beyond all human effort. Between man's purposes in history and God's purposes in eternity was what Kierkegaard had called an "infinite qualitative difference." Man, said Barth, cannot define God by talking about man, in however loud a voice. God is *ganz anders*—wholly different.

THEOLOGY OF CRISIS. Barth's "neo-orthodoxy" was called the "theology of crisis." By crisis, Barth did not mean the present crisis of Western civilization. He meant, like Dostoevsky, that permanent crisis in which man lives.

The relationship between God and man, said Barth's neo-orthodoxy, is a one-way affair; it proceeds always from God to man, never from man to God—the desperate situation that Franz Kafka dramatized in *The Castle*. Between the ages of God's revelation in Christ and His final judgment, man must live by faith and wait upon God's will for that grace which He alone can bestow.

Barth and his theology have both undergone changes. But his importance as a prophet of the new orthodoxy and the crisis of the soul are best reported in his own disclaimer: he merely climbed the steeple to get his bearings. No one was more surprised than he when, in the darkness, his hand touched the bell rope and the great bell of prophecy began to toll.

Reinhold Niebuhr heard the bell. Though the term "neo-orthodox," applied to himself, makes him wince, Niebuhr matured in the climate of crisis. Though he charges Barth with a paralyzing pessimism and a Bible worship that amounts to obsession, Niebuhr shares Barth's view of the perpetual crisis of the soul and Kierkegaard's "infinite qualitative difference" of God.

THE LOGIC OF PARADOX. Orthodox Protestantism by & large subscribes to a body of beliefs among which are: that man is by nature inevitably evil, partaking of the original sin of Adam; that salvation is by faith alone, that good works are meritorious but not essential; that grace is God's gratuitous benevolence; that the Atonement is the redeeming power of Christ's incarnation, suffering and death; that the end of history will be the Last Judgment.

Reinhold Niebuhr's new orthodoxy is the oldtime religion put through the intellectual wringer. It is a re-examination of orthodoxy for an age dominated by such trends as rationalism, liberalism, Marxism, fascism, idealism and the idea of progress.

It is customary to say that Niebuhr's books are hard reading. But any person of average patience can find out what he is saying in *The Nature and Destiny of Man*.

Like Karl Barth's, his method is dialectic; that is, he sees in paradox not the defeat of logic but the grist of an intellectual calculus—a necessary climbing tool for attempting the higher peaks of thought. The twists & turns of his reasoning and his wary qualifications are not hedging, but the effort to clamber after truth. He knows that simplicity is often merely the misleading coherence of complexity.

Niebuhr's overarching theme is the paradox of faith—in St. Paul's words: "The substance of things hoped for, the evidence of things not seen." But Christian faith is a paradox which is the sum of paradoxes. Its passion mounts, like a surge of music, insubstantial and sustaining, between two great cries of the spirit—the paradoxic sadness of "Lord, I believe; help Thou mine unbelief," and the paradoxic triumph of Tertullian's "*Credo quia impossibile*" (I believe because it is impossible).

To the rigorously secular mind the total paradox must, like its parts, be "unto the Jews a stumbling block, and to the Greeks foolishness." It is not irrational, but it is not the logic of two & two makes four. Theologically, it is the dialectical logic of that trinitarian oneness whose triunity is as much a necessity to the understanding of Godhead as higher mathematics is to the measurement of motion. Religiously, its logic, human beyond rationality, is the expression of a need epitomized in the paradox of Solon weeping for his dead son. "Why do you weep," asked a friend, "since it cannot help?" Said Solon: "That is why I weep—because it cannot help."

THE SINGULAR ANIMAL. But basic to Niebuhr's doctrine is another paradox—the lever of his cosmic argument and that part of his teaching which is most arresting and ruffling to liberal Protestantism's cozy conscience. It is the paradox of sin. Sin arises from man's precarious position in the creation.

Man, says Dr. Niebuhr, has always been his own greatest problem child— the creature who continually asks: "What am I?" Sometimes he puts the question modestly: "Am I a child of nature who should not pretend to be different from the other brutes?" But if man asks this question sincerely, he quickly realizes that, were he like the other brutes, he would not ask the question at all.

In more exalted moods, man puts the question differently: "Am I not, indeed, the paragon of the creation, distinctive, unique, set apart and above it by my faculty of reason?" But man has only to observe himself in his dining, bath and bed rooms to feel a stabbing sense of his kinship with the animals.

This paradox is related to another. Sometimes man boasts: "I am essentially good, and all the evils of human life are due to social and historical causes (capitalism, communism, underprivilege, overprivilege)." But a closer look shows man that these things are consequences, not causes. They would not be there if man had not produced them.

If, in a chastened mood, man says, "I am essentially evil," he is baffled by another question, "Then how can I be good enough to know that I am bad?"

THE TRANSCENDENT ANIMAL. "The obvious fact," says Dr. Niebuhr, "is that man is a child of nature, subject to its vicissitudes, compelled by its necessities, driven by its impulses, and confined within the brevity of the years which nature permits its varied organic forms. . . . The other less obvious fact is that man is a spirit who stands outside of nature, life, himself, his reason and the world." Man is, in fact, the creature who continually transcends nature and reason—and in this transcendence lies man's presentiment of God.

Man's world is not evil, for God, who is good, created the world. Man is not evil, because God created man. Why, then, does man sin?

"Anxiety," says Reinhold Niebuhr, "is the internal precondition of sin"— the inevitable spiritual state of man, in the paradox of his freedom and his finiteness. Anxiety is not sin because there is always the ideal possibility that faith might purge anxiety of the tendency toward sin. The ideal possibility is that faith in God's love would overcome all immediate insecurities of nature and history. Hence Christian orthodoxy has consistently defined unbelief as the root of sin. Anxiety is the state of temptation—that anxiety which Kierkegaard called "the dizziness of freedom."

Man seeks to escape from the insecurity of freedom and finiteness by asserting his power beyond the limits of his nature. Limited by his finiteness, he pretends that he is not limited. Sensing his transcendence, man "assumes that he can gradually transcend [his finiteness] until his mind becomes identical with universal mind. All his intellectual and cultural pursuits . . . become infected with the sin of pride. . . . The religious dimension of sin," says Dr. Niebuhr, "is man's rebellion against God. . . . The moral and social dimension of sin is injustice."

But man does not always sin by denying his finiteness. Sometimes, instead, he denies his freedom. He seeks to lose himself "in some aspect of the world's vitalities." This is sensual sin.

The paradox of man's freedom and finiteness is common to all great religions. But the Christian approach to the problem is unique, for it asserts that the crux of the problem is not man's finiteness—the qualities that make him one with the brute creation—but man's sin. It is not from the paradox that Christianity seeks to redeem man; it is from the sin that arises from the paradox. It is man who seeks to redeem himself from the paradox. His efforts are the stuff of history. Hence history, despite man's goals of goodness, proliferates sin.

JUNCTURE OF NATURE & SPIRIT. For man stands at the juncture of nature and spirit. Like the animals, he is involved in the necessities and contingencies of nature. Unlike the animals, "he sees this situation and antici-pates its perils." As man tries to protect himself against the vicissitudes of na-ture, he falls into the sin of seeking security at the expense of other life. "The perils of nature are thereby transmuted into the more grievous perils of human history."

There are other perils—a dissolving perspective of paradox. Man's knowl-edge is limited, but not completely limited, since he has some sense of the limits—and, to that degree, transcends them. And, as he transcends them, he seeks to understand his immediate situation in terms of a total situation—*i.e.*, God's will. But man is unable to understand the total situation except in the finite terms of his immediate situation. "The realization of the relativity of his knowledge subjects him to the peril of skepticism. The abyss of meaningless-ness yawns on the brink of all his mighty spiritual endeavors. Therefore man is tempted to deny the limited character of his knowledge, and the finiteness of his perspectives. He pretends to have achieved a degree of knowledge which is beyond the limit of finite life. This is the 'ideological taint' in which all human knowledge is involved and which is always something more than mere human ignorance. It is always partly an effort to hide that ignorance by pretension." This is pre-eminently the sin of the 20th Century.

CREATIVE TEMPTATION. But man's sin is more than a simple sin of pride under the guise of pretension. Man's anxiety is also the source of "all human creativity." Man is anxious because his life is limited and he senses his limita-tions. But "he is also anxious because he does not know the limits of his possibilities."

He achieves, but he knows no peace, because higher possibilities are re-vealed in each achievement. In all his anxious acts man faces the temptation of illimitable possibility. "There is therefore no limit of achievement in any sphere of activity in which human history can rest with equanimity." History cannot pause. Its evil and its good are inextricably interwoven. Says Niebuhr: the creative and the destructive elements in anxiety are so mixed that to purge even moral achievement of sin is not so easy as moralists imagine.

ORIGINAL SIN. This grand but somewhat anxious survey of man's fate Dr. Niebuhr clinches with a doctrine of original sin in which he leans heavily upon an insight of Kierkegaard's: "Sin presupposes sin." That is, sin need not inevitably arise from man's anxiety if sin were not already in the world. Niebuhr finds the agent of this prehistoric sin in the Devil, a fallen angel who "fell because [like man] he sought to lift himself above his measure, and who in turn insinuates temptation into human life." Thus, "the sin of each individual is preceded by Adam's sin; but even this first sin of history is not the first sin. One may, in other words, go farther back than human history and still not escape the paradoxical conclusion that the situation of finiteness and freedom would not lead to sin if sin were not already introduced into the situation."

This original sin, infecting the paradox in which man asserts his freedom against his finiteness, and complicating with a fatality of evil a destiny which man senses to be divine, is the tissue of history. It explains why man's history, even at its highest moments, is not a success story. It yawns, like a bottomless crater, across the broad and easy avenue of optimism. It would be intolerable without faith, without hope, without love.

NO. 1 THEOLOGIAN. The intricate architecture of his thought explains why even Roman Catholic theologians respect Dr. Niebuhr. Both Catholics and Protestants may disagree with this or that aspect of his doctrine, or bypass or reject it as a whole. Few care to challenge it.

Clearly it is not a faith for the tenderminded. It is a faith for a Lenten age. Even those who fail to follow all the sinuosities of his reasoning must sense that, whatever else he has done or left undone, Niebuhr has restored to Protestantism a Christian virility. For, in the name of courage, which men have always rightly esteemed in one another as the indispensable virtue, he summons Protestants to seek truth.

Though he warns that the human implications of truth are tragic, he does not condemn the pursuit of happiness which modern civilization, more than any other, has legitimatized. But he implies that the pursuit of happiness loses measure, just as optimism loses reality, if neither is aware of what Wordsworth called "the still sad music of humanity." And he gives a discipline of mind and a structure of meaning to the tragic cry of Philosopher Miguel de Unamuno: "A *Miserere* sung in a cathedral by a multitude tormented by destiny has as much value as a philosophy."

THE MAN. The elaborator of somber paradoxes is something of a paradox himself. Hawk-nosed and saturnine, Reinhold Niebuhr is, nevertheless, a cheerful and gracious (though conversationally explosive) man. An intellectual's intellectual, he nevertheless lectures and preaches with the angular armswinging of a revivalist. An orthodox Protestant, he is one of the busiest of leftist working politicians—a member of the Liberal party. For his gloomy view of man and history does not inhibit his belief that man should act for what he holds to be the highest good (always bearing in mind that sin will dog his action).

Reinhold Niebuhr was born (1892) in Wright City, Mo., where his father, who emigrated from Germany when he was 17, was an Evangelical pastor. Young Niebuhr never intended to be anything else but a minister. Though he lacked any degree, he succeeded in 1913 in enrolling in Yale Divinity School (they were short of students, he explains). Two years later, in a burst of his usual energy, Niebuhr had his B.D. and M.A.

To help support his mother, he took his first and only parish, in a dingy district of Detroit. Niebuhr had intended to stay a couple of years. Instead, he stayed 13. His congregation on the first Sunday consisted of 18 souls. To eke out his salary ($50 a month), Niebuhr began writing, and out of necessity discovered his vocation.

"I have a horror of Ladies Aid," says Niebuhr. But he waded into the social problems of his parish and the city, presiding at labor forums, lecturing at Midwestern colleges. Sometimes he unburdened himself of remarks like: "The lowliest peasant of the Dark Ages had more opportunity for self-expression than the highest-paid employee at the Ford factory." When, in 1928, Niebuhr became an associate professor at Union Theological Seminary, Detroit's automotive tycoons breathed a sigh of relief.

At Union his reception was cool. But soon his classes were among the most crowded in the seminary. He moved from class to class surrounded by disputatious students, who soon called him "Reinie." In 1939, Niebuhr became the fifth American* to be invited to deliver the Gifford Lectures at Edinburgh University. Niebuhr drew the biggest crowds in Gifford history, later published the lectures as *The Nature and Destiny of Man*.

Now he lives strenuously at the seminary with his British-born wife, the former Ursula Keppel-Compton, and their two children, Christopher, 13, and Elizabeth, 9. Mrs. Niebuhr, a theologian in her own right, was the first woman to win a First in theology at Oxford. She has lectured on religion at Barnard College for six years. In summer, the Niebuhrs rusticate at Heath, Mass., near the Vermont line. There Niebuhr writes and rests, after his fashion, from the nervous pace at which he drives himself.

THE LIBERAL. Most U.S. liberals think of Niebuhr as a solid socialist who has some obscure connection with Union Theological Seminary that does not interfere with his political work. Unlike most clergymen in politics, Dr. Niebuhr is a pragmatist. Says James Loeb, secretary of Americans for Democratic Action: "Most so-called liberals are idealists. They let their hearts run away with their heads. Niebuhr never does. For example, he has always been the leading liberal opponent of pacifism. In that period before we got into the war when pacifism was popular, he held out against it steadfastly." He is also an opponent of Marxism.

Niebuhr's chief contribution to U.S. liberal thinking, his friends say, is keeping his fellow liberals on the path of the possible. "You don't get world government," he once said, "by drawing up a fine constitution. You get it through the process of history. You grow into it."

* The other four: Philosophers William James, Josiah Joyce, John Dewey, William Ernest Hocking.

The feelings of his fellow theologians are more mixed. Some criticize his failure to think and act in terms of the church or to generate ideas that would help to counteract modern irreligion and immorality. Others find his ideas of sin too grandiose, too remote from the common cares of mankind. Some feel that he could do with more human warmth and less intellectual incandescence.

But there are few who do not respect his questing intelligence or the spiritual inspiration which has infused old orthodoxy with the tremor of new life. Most would agree with the words of the late Dr. William Temple, Archbishop of Canterbury, when he met Reinhold Niebuhr for the first time: "At last I've met the troubler of my peace."

FOUR

The History
of
Western
Culture

THE MIDDLE AGES

(*Life*, APRIL 7, 1947)

ONE DAY IN the Dark Ages, St. Scothinus, having purged himself by severe chastisements from all molestations and imperfections of lustful desires, started to walk across the sea to England. By chance he met a ship that carried St. Barry the Bishop, who, beholding and recognizing this man of God, inquired of him wherefore he thus walked on the sea. To whom St. Scothinus answered that this was a flowery field whereon he walked, and presently, stretching his hand down to the water, he took from the midst of the ocean a handful of vermilion flowers which, in proof of his assertion, he cast into the bishop's lap. The bishop for his part, to maintain his own truth, drew a fish from the water and cast it toward St. Scothinus; whereupon, magnifying God in His marvelous works, they departed with blessings one from the other.

Such an encounter might well have startled a 20th Century American to whom the miracle of electric light is nevertheless a commonplace. It would scarcely have startled a medieval man. For, as the American knows that all things are possible to science, medieval man knew that all things are possible to faith.

Moreover he had read (or had heard, if he was one of the millions who could not read) scores of such testimonies from one of the Middle Ages' most popular anthologies, the *Golden Legend*. The spontaneity with which both saints magnified the miracle of God's works demonstrated the faith in which all Christian men, according to their degrees of understanding, were at one. And their casual parting there in mid-sea rang true to the sweetness of the medieval mind. This same sweetness would presently soften the rigors of Catholic orthodoxy with the cult of the Virgin, the loving Mother of Christ, and the rough and tumble of secular life with the cult of chivalry.

This singular sweetness, at once childlike and virile, is the unique quality of the medieval mind. It characterizes every achievement of the Middle Ages. Stern Dante, the man who, his contemporaries said, had been in hell, felt it in paradise when he once more saw Beatrice, his dead but lifelong love, and she turned to him and said, "Direct thy mind to God in gratitude who hath united us with the first star."

This sweetness is in the name which transfigures the obese and disputatious Thomas of Aquino, greatest of medieval minds—the Angelic Doctor. It humanizes the austerity of those superearthly figures that guard the west portal of Chartres Cathedral. And it rings from the Middle Ages' characteristic epic, the Song of Roland, in the sound of the paladin's horn, winding, indomitable in disaster, like medieval man himself, from the lost battlefield of Roncesvalles.

In the deepest sense, this sweetness is an aspect of that *caritas* (St. Paul's loving charity) which St. Thomas Aquinas declared to be inseparable from the right understanding of God. And it redeems from historic horror a blood-soaked, brutal, riotous, lustful and chaotic age.

For the miracle of medieval man is that he began not, for the most part, as a barbarian, but as the heir of fallen Roman civilization, debased almost to a brute in the Dark Ages following Rome's collapse. His historic task was to infuse into the total ruin a new life and spirit. In six centuries, thought by groping thought, stone by heavy stone, from the ground up, by faith and works, he created a new Christian civilization. Then, in an incomparable outburst of creative energy, he made all succeeding men his heirs in the architecture of the Gothic cathedrals, in the splendor of their stained-glass windows, in the all but flawless structure of St. Thomas' philosophy, in the *Divine Comedy* of Dante Alighieri and the scientific insights of Roger Bacon.

The Dark Ages, which were the first part of the Middle Ages, blanketed Europe for 500 years (from 400 to about 900 A.D.). Through their monumental night thudded year after year the onrushing feet of barbarian or other marauding war bands, drowning the shuffle of fugitive native populations displaced on a 20th Century scale. Like intermittent beacons of despair, burning strongholds, burning hovels, burning crops lit up the gloom. Population dwindled. Cities were in ruins. Men fled for safety to the countryside, where they clumped apart in communal distrust.

Here and there, in little communities remote from one another, the precious flames of civilization still burned. These were the houses of the monastic orders, chiefly of the Benedictines (founded at Monte Cassino, where St. Thomas was educated). These monasteries were built low, thick-walled and almost windowless for safety, in the new Romanesque style. They opposed the harshness of monastic discipline within and their stony carapaces without to the hazards of the darkened world.

Not all the hazards of the Dark Ages were human. Hell and its legions were also abroad. Incubi, succubi, sylphs, undines, witches and the hierarchies of devils, spirits of seduction and malefaction romped through the night. They would never quit the world, or the medieval mind, as long as the Middle Ages lasted.

Then as the invasions grew less frequent, in the gray dawn in which the Dark Ages blended into the early Middle Ages, the landscape of a new Europe was revealed. The bones of the dead civilization were still there, immense and mute, in the form of Roman aqueducts, baths and amphitheaters, many of which now served as lairs for local strongmen. But a new architectural feature dominated the new Christendom—the tower. It had a twofold use. Militarily it answered the need of ever vigilant defense. Religiously it symbolized the fact that the Church, which spoke to the minds and souls of its believing multitudes, was the center of men's lives; the bell tower was its convoking voice.

For Rome, in dying, had bequeathed two mighty legacies to medieval man of Christendom—a common Catholic faith and the Latin tongue, the most sonorous of prelatical languages. This common tongue would bond together literate men of all national stocks, in spite of the hodgepodge of medieval political divisions and the babble of newly emerging national languages.

Men were obsessed with salvation and, therefore, with God. For when the world had been destroyed there had been nothing left but God. And to restore the world, there was no unifying principle but God. They enshrined their obsession in a creed of majestic simplicity: *Credo in unum Deum, Patrem omnipotentem, factorem coeli et terrae, visibiliem omnium et invisibilium . . .* "I believe in one God, the Father almighty, maker of heaven and earth, and of all things visible and invisible. And in one Lord Jesus Christ, the only begotten Son of God; born of the Father before all ages; God of God, light of light, true God of true God; begotten, not made; being of one substance with the Father; by whom all things were made. Who for us men, and for our salvation, came down from heaven. . . . I confess one baptism for the remission of sins. And I look for the resurrection of the dead. And the life of the world to come."

This creed medieval man exalted in the thrusting spires of the Gothic cathedrals. He gave it elevation in the Gothic groined vault. He gave it illumination in stained glass. He gave it intonation in the *Alleluia*, the *Gloria*, the *Kyrie*, the *Agnus Dei*, the Requiem, *Te Deum*, and the great medieval hymns like the *Dies Irae*. He flooded it with the light of reason and gave it the strength of logical structure in the works of St. Thomas Aquinas.

Medieval man carried his creed into secular life. He embodied it in his political system, feudalism, in which every man held his rank and obligation in descending order from the sovereign whose right proceeds from God. Medieval man converted his creed into economic terms in the guild system. He denied himself many profitable practices (for example, usury) because his religion prohibited them. He implemented his creed in law and, in so far as erring man can, practiced it in his civic conduct. With it, he sanctified the indissoluble union of the family. And when medieval man's faith waned, the Middle Ages died.

The Emperor Charlemagne (742–814), a great patron of learning, kept a writing tablet under his pillow and practiced pothooks in bed. But he never learned to write. In the early Middle Ages men began to go to school, doggedly studying Latin grammar and the other rudiments of learning. By 1150 there were famous schools in all corners of Christendom, and the grand medieval debate on theology and philosophy had begun.

To the 20th Century mind, the problems that bedeviled medieval school-men, their obsession with allegory and symbolism, with abstruse definition and dialectic, are arid and irrelevant. The din of their theological disputations, mounting to a clamor, after the great universities were founded at Paris, Oxford, Bologna, seems a boring babble. Twentieth Century man may be absorbed in the all but mystical motions of the atom, for science is power. But he cannot feel the passionate concern of medieval man in the burning question: can angels move from one point to another without passing through the intervening space? For to medieval man, faith was power since it was the way to God, and angels were a concept as important as atoms.

The great men connected with the debate were William of Champeaux, Peter Abelard, Bernard of Clairvaux, Albertus Magnus, Duns Scotus—from whom we derive the word "dunce." Their names have lost their historical resonance and intellectual identity, as have the great issues they debated. But in the thrust and flashing snicksnack of such dialectics the medieval mind was honed to a trenchancy and rigor never since equaled.

While the struggle to know God raged in men's minds, life for the mass of medieval men was hard and often brutal. The cities were close-built and dark. Plagues ravaged the Continent. Such conditions have caused the popular impression that medieval life was universally ugly and harsh.

But medieval man was the creator of arts and master of a craftsmanship that has never since been equaled. He wove Europe's most superb tapestries. He made stained glass of a beauty that modern man has failed to imitate. His book-making excelled anything that 20th Century book designers and manu-facturers have done. His hymns, like Adam of St. Victor's hymns to the Virgin, are still unexcelled. The universities, a medieval creation that the classical world had never known, have come down to us in the same form. In countless ways modern man is the heir of the Middle Ages.

He is, romantically, the heir of the medieval idea of love. Medieval man was a great lover. He dedicated himself to love in the cult of chivalry in which a knight plighted his troth to a lady. He devoted his life to her and sometimes died for her. But, as with almost everything else, medieval man sought to transfigure love, in the cult of the Virgin, whom the Middle Ages exalted to the post of guardian of superabundant grace and intercessor for the souls of men with God.

In the last centuries of the Middle Ages medieval mind burst into creativity in its three ultimate glories: the Gothic cathedrals, the philosophy of Aquinas, the poetry of Dante.

More than any other great architecture, the Gothic cathedrals look as if they had risen from the soil beneath. Medieval men had been building modified Romanesque churches for 200 years. In the 12th Century a new surge of faith and power flowered in a new style, the Gothic. The cathedrals of Chartres, Amiens, Notre-Dame at Paris, Laon and others rose from the earth. In one century alone, the 13th, it is estimated that the equivalent of $1 billion were spent in France on the cathedrals. The nobility contributed heavily. But money came from all men, and all men came to help in the building, contributing their time to the great work of glorifying God.

The Gothic cathedral is a prayerful uprush of stone. It is as solid as the earth it stands on. At the same time it seems to float in the air. In Romanesque churches the walls had been thick. It was the inspiration of the medieval master builder to make the walls skeletal enough to achieve space and elevation but strong enough to sustain the weight of spires and roof. For the same purpose, he set the flying buttress, a bridge between earth and air, to resist the thrust of superabundant mass. The rest is an expanse of stained glass whose function was not to exclude but to enhance light.

To medieval man, the Gothic cathedral was rich in allegorical symbols. The plan of the cathedral copied the Cross and pointed east to Jerusalem, the center of the Christian world. All meanings that the medieval mind had found in life and faith were gathered here, as delicate and as unbreakable as the embodying stone. When the scaffolds were cleared away medieval man perceived that he had magnificently created his need of God in stone.

A comparable achievement was meanwhile being effected for medieval theology. Thomas Aquinas was born about 1225 in Italy near the abbey of Monte Cassino, now a 20th Century ruin. He defied his family by becoming a Dominican friar. In Paris he became the pupil and friend of Albertus Magnus, the weightiest theologian of his time. In manner St. Thomas was heavy and slow, which earned him the name of the "big dumb ox of Sicily." But in matters of thought he was an irresistible and subtle force. He composed more than 60 works, of which the most important are the *Summa Contra Gentiles* ("The Summation of Doctrine Against the Unbelievers") and the *Summa Theologica* ("The Summation of Theology"). These works are still the most complete and explicit assertion of Roman Catholic doctrine.

What man loves he seeks to possess. What the soul loves it seeks to exalt. What the mind loves it seeks to know. When 20th Century man switches on his electric light, he cares little about the nature of electricity. He does not love electricity. Medieval man loved God and sought with his whole mind, for hundreds of years, to know Him. But the more medieval man sought to know God, the less he seemed able to agree as to what God is. By the 13th Century theology had become a complicated feud among philosophies.

Into this strife of the God-seeking mind St. Thomas Aquinas brought clarity, order, harmony. The *Summa Theologica* was intended as a simple manual of Christian doctrine for the use of students. Its method is the application of reason to religious feeling. But reason and the knowledge that results from the use of reason are not enough. Revelation is also necessary, for reason unaided by revelation could not enable men to know the supernatural end—

salvation—toward which their acts of faith will lead them. It is necessary first to accept revealed truths so that the mind can explain them and draw conclusions from them. This process is called theology, which is a science because it proceeds from principles which are certain, having been revealed by God. The subject of this science is God and His relation to His creations. The function of reason is not to prove the facts of faith, which are accepted on the authority of God, but to defend, develop and explain the revealed doctrines.

The great *Summa* is divided into three parts and arranged in the form of question and answer. Part I (God in Himself and as Creator) treats of the nature of God. Part II (God as the End of all things) treats of man, the rational creature, and his advance toward God. Part III (God as Redeemer) treats of Christ, "who, as man, is the way by which we tend to God." The work is immense, the achievement incomparable, for its field is all that had existed, might have existed or ever could exist. It treated of many things—the world, science, medicine, incubi, succubi, beatitude. It answers once for all the question: can angels move from one point to another without passing through the intervening space? They can.

This vast work rested primarily on the philosophy of Aristotle, the great body of whose thought had at last reached medieval Europe in Arabic translation by way of Moslem Spain. Compared with the *Summas*, modern systems of philosophy seem complex, chaotic, self-contradictory and fragmentary. In the 20th Century neo-Thomists have gone back to the *Summas* for a more satisfying philosophy than later men have produced. It might not fully satisfy theological extremists of any school. But like the Gothic cathedral it was spacious enough to include them all. And, as the cathedral, embodying in stone man's need for God, soared above the medieval town, the *Summas*, embodying man's need to know God, soared above the invisible landscape of the mind.

These were the twin cathedral spires of medievalism. A third was to be added—Dante's *Divine Comedy*. When Dante, around 1300, started to write his poem he was a political refugee from Florence. Dante rejected Latin in favor of Italian for his poem. This first great literary use of a national language was also an expression of the new popular stirrings that were to burst out in the Renaissance.

Dante was the last great medieval mind. The *Divine Comedy* is the ordeal of medieval man's love of God. Its ending is salvation. To achieve it Dante, in the three books of his masterpiece, *Inferno, Purgatorio* and *Paradiso*, took the Middle Ages through hell, purgatory and heaven. The whole Middle Ages is in this poem. It crowns and ends them.

The *Divine Comedy* is the *Summa* in poetic form. Its theology and philosophy are St. Thomas'. But modern men do not read the *Divine Comedy* with delight simply because it dramatizes the *Summa*. They read it for its poetry, incomparable of its kind, and for its evocation of the whole medieval mind. For here is chivalry and the cult of love, expressed in terms of Dante's pure and personal love for his childhood sweetheart, Beatrice, merging in heaven into the cult of the Virgin. Here is much that was grim, cruel, vengeful and monstrous in medieval life and thought. And here is medieval sweetness, touching us even after six centuries, like winds blown across pools of melting snow.

"*Come i gru van cantando lor lai* (As the cranes fly singing their lays)," writes Dante. And we see against the medieval sky, with the simple vividness of the earliest primitive paintings, the line of birds who, in their seasonal flight from the darkness of the barbarian north to the ruins of Egypt, had crossed and recrossed for 500 years the ruins of Europe's Dark Ages.

Here is more of God than any later man has put into a secular book. And hell is here—not the hell whose devils had terrified medieval man in superstition and darkness, but a more terrible hell fixed for eternity in the terms of rational Aquinian theology. Above its gates is set its awful charter:

> *Justice moved my great Creator,*
> *Divine Power made me—*
> *The summation of Wisdom and Primal Love. . . .*
> *Abandon all hope, ye who enter.*

It might have been a legend for the Dark Ages. But there is pity too in hell. As early medieval man turned for enlightenment to classical culture, Dante turns to his guide Virgil, the pagan poet, for consolation. And in words that might have applied to the Middle Ages, Virgil replies, "Here must all distrust be left; all cowardice must here be dead."

Light had been the supreme craving of medieval man—light after historical darkness, light in ignorance, light in human despair, light as God. It was given to Dante to see this light in Heaven: "O supreme Light, Who liftest Thyself so high above mortal thought, lend me again a little of that which Thou didst seem; and give my tongue such power that it may leave even a single spark of Thy glory to all men to come."

Medieval man could do no more. And as he looked back, in the evening of the Middle Ages, at the darkness from which he had come and the heights which he had achieved, he could say with Dante, climbing out of the pit of hell:

> *E quindi uscimmo a riveder le stelle*
> (And thus we emerged again to see the stars.)

MEDIEVAL LIFE
(*Life*, MAY 26, 1947)

AS THE YEAR 999 drew to a close, many medieval men experienced a terror such as 20th Century men might feel if they knew that an atomic chain reaction was about to wipe out the world. To people who lived in constant awareness of Final Judgment the coming of the year 1000, the millennial year, portended the last judgment and the end of the world.

An ancient chronicle sets down the dramatic story of what supposedly happened in Rome, spiritual center of medieval Europe. Many peasants neglected to sow their fields. Few men were so hardy as to steal or cheat. Bakers distributed their bread free. There was an endless round of confessions, absolutions, Masses and Communions.

On the last day of the year, as midnight neared, masters and servants embraced, weeping. In the old basilica of St. Peter's, Pope Sylvester II performed Midnight Mass in silence. The church was jammed. The door of the sacristy was open, and inside a huge clock ticked once each second.

The Pope prayed in silence. The worshipers lay face down, afraid to look up. Suddenly the clock stopped ticking. Hundreds shrieked. Others died of fright. Then the clock struck midnight. As Pope Sylvester raised his hands all the bells rang out at once. From the choir loft came: *Te deum laudamus!* And when the hymn was over, people fell into each other's arms and laughed like lunatics.

Today historians regard this chronicle as an overimaginative version of events. But the year 1000 does take on a real historic significance. For more than anything else, perhaps, the millennium marks the invisible sill over which the Dark Ages passed into the Middle Ages. After that medieval man could buckle down to the business of living, for, whatever human bestiality might achieve, there would be no other occasion for divine interference on such a scale in the workaday world.

Contrary to general belief it was a world of fresh hope and surging vitality. Medieval men were the survivors of a universal disaster—the fall of Rome—and their sense that, having known the worst, nothing would ever again be so bad goes far to explain their patience amid conditions that to later ages seem unbearable. Hope flashed from the bright banners snapping in the wind on the watch towers of the new castles that studded medieval Europe. Hope gleamed from the armor of the new warrior, the knight, guardian and symbol of the new social system, feudalism. Hope echoed from the cries of ladies and squires gaily pursuing the medieval sport of hunting with hawks. It rang from the songs of the strolling minstrels and shone in the bright costumes of parties swarming the wretched roads in pilgrimage to holy shrines. It clashed from the shock of jousting squires practicing to be knights.

Even the peasant had his hopes. The collapse of Rome, terrible for all classes, had been most terrible for the poor. But feudalism gave even the serf a new security and the hope that by tireless effort he might better his lot.

Nobody planned feudalism. It grew. It possessed the vigor and the haphazard proliferation of organic growths. It did not take exactly the same forms in all parts of Europe. Even in the same region it did not remain the same from century to century. Feudalism's main features were simple. Its practice was complex. Its chief idea was to offer something that almost anybody could give—loyalty and service—in exchange for something that only a powerful few could give—protection and land. There were two kinds of feudalism— political and economic. Economic feudalism was the relationship between a lord and his free peasants, serfs and slaves. In return for his protection and the right to work his lands, the peasants performed specified services and paid specified fees. The lord became their sole lawgiver and judge.

Political feudalism was the relationship of the nobles among themselves and to the king. Every medieval man was another man's vassal. The king was God's vassal. The moral sanction of feudalism was the belief that the king received his right divinely from God. Thus all other men in descending order received their rights from God through the king. To the medieval mind vassalage was not humiliating. A man became a vassal by placing his hands between those of his superior and swearing fealty to him as long as either lived. In return the vassal received a grant of land but sometimes the right to levy a toll on a road or bridge. Vassalage obliged a man to pay his lord a regular fee, to follow his lord in war. A man might be the vassal of more than one lord. In that case he owed first allegiance to his liege (first) lord. Kings, great lords and even bishops and abbots might be one another's vassals. Bishops and abbots, usually the sons of great lords, often led their retainers into battle.

Feudalism's touchstones were loyalty and service. Thus it spun a vertical web of direct human relationships from the king through the secular and Church lords to the lowest serf. It was ideally organized to further the Middle Ages' three chief activities—fighting, farming and praying. (Trading did not reach its full development until the late Middle Ages.)

The fighter was the lord in his military aspect as a knight. His function was to defend peace, order, justice. Actually the rivalries of the knightly lords kept society in constant commotion. The farmers were the peasants. The Church was responsible for the salvation of souls. For the fact that distinguished medieval society from the Roman civilization that it replaced, the spring of its vitality and its capacity for progress toward justice and freedom, was its belief that every man—king, saint, robber-knight and unwashed serf—had an inviolable, immortal soul.

The castle and the serf-worked manor lands around it were the hub on which medieval life turned. The first fact of medieval life was brute force, and the castle was the stony answer.

The castle was the seat of an autonomous government pursuing its own affairs of state. The castle's lord was a knight. In the castle, surrounded by a garrison always in arms, the lord and his lady lived the courtly life of the medieval manor.

When not incased in iron clothing a well-dressed lord or knight wore linen underdrawers and undershirt. Fashion decreed staid stockings though dashing dressers sometimes affected black hose with red stripes. The chief outer garment was a fur-trimmed pelisse, a long woolen tunic. Over the pelisse went another pull-on tunic. For outdoor wear a tasseled cape, fur-lined even in summer, was in vogue. Men's hair was done in bangs and fetching curls. The Church had long inveighed against beards, which it associated with the devil. By the 13th Century lords endured the ordeal of shaving at least twice a week. Women wore long linen shifts, then the fur-trimmed pelisse and blouse, snug-fitting and tightly laced to set off the female figure, and with flowing sleeves for casual elegance.

Medieval woman's main business was marriage. Elaborate specifications governed her appearance and conduct. Blondes were preferred. They should be tall and slender. They should not trot or run, scold, overeat or drink too much in public. Aniseed was recommended for bad breath. And ladies were advised to wipe their greasy fingers (knives were used but not forks) on a napkin rather than on the tablecloth.

Because a castle was a military encampment, medieval women were accustomed to coarse talk and jokes and could take (and give) broad banter. They talked to men on the most intimate subjects with a freedom that might make even modern women blush.

The splendor of the feudal achievement and the vivid hurly-burly of medieval noble life were only a merry din or a martial menace on the daily horizon of the peasant. Peasants might be freemen, serfs or slaves. A serf had no political rights. He could own no property. His earnings belonged to his lord. He could save for himself only by his lord's consent. He was bound by law to the soil. But he was free of it if he could escape for a year and a day (hence the modern expression). He and his heirs could be bought and sold or given with the land they lived on. He could not leave the soil but the soil could be taken from him; he could be sold as a chattel. When the peasant's wife baked, she had to bake in the lord's oven and pay a fee in loaves. If the peasant built his own oven, there was a fee for that. There was a fee if a peasant's daughter married off the manor and even a fee if a peasant died.

Peasants had to give a certain number of days to working on the lord's lands.

They cleaned the castle moat and kept the walls in repair. In war they defended the castle or marched off to battle with the lord.

Much of the peasants' time was spent not in working but in walking, for peasants' fields were scattered all over the lord's manor. They were constantly being subdivided among the peasants' children. The farming was extremely primitive. There were ox-drawn plows, but they had wooden shares. A crude crop rotation was practiced. One field was sown with wheat, a second with another grain, a third was left fallow. Thus a third of the land was always idle. The soil was often impoverished and a famine every four years was considered normal.

The peasant wore a cloth or sheepskin blouse and trousers, a knee-length mantle. He usually went barefoot or wore wooden clogs. Women's clothes were much the same, but with skirts instead of trousers. Clothes were seldom changed. Few peasants had ever been out of sight of their native village. Through wandering peddlers, beggars and friars word of doings in the great world spread with surprising speed, especially news of peasant revolts. Throughout the Middle Ages the peasants' desperate conditions led to desperate outbreaks. They always ended the same way—in defeat and fierce vengeance.

And yet medieval men in peasants' smocks—these illiterate boors whose social standing is suggested by the fact that their medieval name (villein) has become our word villain—are no strangers to modern man. The knights were making history. But the peasants were history itself, for they were the forebears of most of the freemen in Europe and America. By infinite patience, by incomparable thrift, by clinching a demand here and taking advantage of a lapsed baronial right there they achieved over the long centuries the status of freemen. Sometimes on his deathbed a lord freed his serfs in order to better his chances of salvation. More often the serfs bought their freedom. As the Middle Ages wore on, the most intelligent and ambitious peasants became the burghers—merchants, traders, craftsmen—of the first towns.

The battle trumpet sounded the theme of the secular Middle Ages. War was a normal condition, peace an unnatural pause between battles. Knight made private war against knight, coalitions of lords fought coalitions of lords, lords fought kings, and embattled churchmen fought on all sides. Most of the time these wars, governed by the code of Christian chivalry, were conducted in a spirit that would seem inefficient to modern man. Often medieval wars ended in the victor's marrying the defeated lord's sister, daughter or widow. But war kept medieval society distracted.

In the 11th Century, Pope Urban II decided to direct the martial energy and pervading piety of the Middle Ages against the Seljuk Turks by preaching an armed crusade for the redemption of the Holy Land. For all who went on the crusades the Church promised remission of sins.

There were eight major crusades. They occupied 200 years and much of the energy of Western Europe. Involved in them were the great and colorful figures of the Middle Ages, who led armies of nobles and adventurers going to the Holy Land, not just from piety but to see new places, find new opportunities and renew fading fortunes.

The first crusades set up a series of shaky feudal states in Syria and Palestine. Later crusades were sent to save them. Politically the crusades proved a costly failure. They ended with Mohammedanism's conquering the Near East and pushing into Europe. By the end of the 13th Century nothing was left of the crusading kingdoms except vast ruins of their feudal fortresses and a surprising number of fair-haired children among the dark natives of the Holy Land.

But the influence of the crusades on Western Europe was immense. Before the crusades Europe had been shut off from the rest of the world as by the walls of a medieval castle. The crusades brought Europe and Asia face to face again. New goods, new ways and views of life, new knowledge seeped back. Part of this new knowledge was a rediscovery of Asia brought about by attempts of the crusaders and the Church to form alliances with the Mongols against the Turks and Arabs. Church emissaries to Asia, along with the 13th Century travels of Marco Polo, resulted in a rediscovery of Asia comparable in importance to the voyages of Vasco da Gama and Columbus.

From the East the crusaders brought back sugar, melons, lemons, muslin and damask cloth, lilac and purple dyes, the use of powder, glass mirrors and even the rosary.

The crusades changed Europe in more important ways. They contributed to the end of feudalism by putting masses of property on the market (crusading was an expensive business) and disturbing the validity of titles. They introduced medieval man to the beginnings of modern taxation. In 1147 Louis VII of France levied the first general tax to promote the crusades.

Even more important was the impulse given by the crusades to the growth of medieval trading towns. Not only was there the profitable business involved in equipping and financing the crusaders. With the rise of the crusading kingdoms a brisk new trade developed between East and West.

With its geographic position, its fleet, its trading and financial resources no town profited more from this new commerce than Venice. Medieval man did not know it, but in accepting Venetian financial and naval aid he was helping to make the city of the lagoons the heir of the Middle Ages and the most opulent republic of the Renaissance.

THE GLORY OF VENICE
(*Life*, AUGUST 4, 1947)

ONE DAY DURING the Renaissance—that cultural convulsion by which the modern world was born from the Middle Ages—the rulers of Venice met to debate an offer of murder. For a consideration the Archbishop of Trebizond had volunteered to poison Marsiglio da Carrara, the ruler of Padua. The minutes of the meeting survive. For the Republic of Venice, the first modern state and the most stable and efficient government in Europe between the fall of Rome and the rise of Britain, left the most massive and detailed secret files in history.

"Inasmuch," say the official minutes, "as the said archbishop offers to poison Marsiglio da Carrara by means of Francesco Pierlamberti of Lucca, and wishes to travel in person with the said Francesco that he may assure himself of the actual execution of the deed; but for this purpose he requires a poison, which he charges himself to have made by a capable poison master if the money be supplied him. . . . Be it resolved, that for making the poison, for necessary expenses, and for buying a horse for the said archbishop—for his own is dead—the sum of 50 ducats out of our treasury be given to the archbishop and his companion, Francesco Pierlamberti. Ayes 10; noes 5; doubtful 1."

Twentieth Century readers to whom the weapons of Renaissance politics are unfamiliar may be shocked to learn that for more than 500 years Venice employed an official poisoner; that at various times Venice attempted to poison the Holy Roman Emperor, the King of Hungary, two despots of Milan, the Sultan of Turkey, Charles VIII of France, Pope Pius IV and the Czar of Russia. They may be further surprised to know that Venice invented bacterial warfare. In 1649 she sent a physician with a flask containing buboes to spread bubonic plague among the Turkish army in Crete. "*Venenossissima ac resurgens vipera*," a French ambassador once called her, "a very venomous and indestructible viper."

In part this passion for poison as an instrument of policy was a custom of the times (insanity from poisoning was so common that the Renaissance had a name for it—*erberia*). In part it was due to the republic's peculiar position—a cluster of sea islands at the head of the Adriatic, through the ages threatened by Franks, Lombards, the Papacy, Milan, Genoa (Venice's great naval rival), France, Spain, Hungary, the Byzantine empire and the furious lunges of the

Ottoman Turks. In part it was a heritage of that gorgeous East for whose commerce and culture Venice, during the centuries of her greatness, was the golden gate to Europe.

For Venice was almost as much an Eastern as a Western city. The aura of Asia was over her as the fragrance of spice is said to envelop the Spice Islands, spreading far out to sea. It gleamed in the brilliant tesselation of her piazzas and the Byzantine mosaics of her church walls. It glowed in gold, jewels and marble from that cathedral—St. Mark's, ornate like a Byzantine crown—in which the unmatable styles of Gothic and Byzantine meet, and, as in a baffling marriage, blend.

Eastern violence and despotism were implicit in her government, a closed oligarchy of patrician merchants run by the Council of Ten, whose motto was *"Secretezza et Iterum Secretezza"* ("Secrecy, and Then More Secrecy"). The council's life-and-death decisions were usually without appeal and beyond review. Its nocturnal police were the sinister *Signori di Notte* (Lords of the Night). Its agents, the dread *Sbirri*, commonly made arrests by muffling their victims' heads in their cloaks before whisking them into prison. The Orient was incarnate, too, in the doges, the dukes of the Venetian Republic, whose dignity was imperial but who more and more tended to be resplendent figureheads and presiding ornaments of the state's sumptuous pageantry.

In the 15th and 16th Centuries the long latent esthetic genius of Venice ignited from the Italian Renaissance an Oriental sunburst of color and an Oriental voluptuousness, fleshly and fluent. These combined with a vigor born of seafaring and a sense of space and tumultuous motion born of wind and waves. This whirled Venetian painting to heights rarely attained in the history of art.

The sumptuousness of the forms which was so much a part of the glory of Venice had flowered from 12 mud banks. Venice was born in the agonies of Rome's death. (It died, 14 centuries later, the oldest state on earth, in the birth pangs of modern Europe at the hands of the French Revolution and Napoleon Bonaparte.) Her founders were displaced persons, Roman fugitives from the Huns. About 450 they fled, in the shipwreck of their world, to the marshy Venetian islands and joined the handful of original settlers, simple fishermen, saltmakers and perhaps a few patricians who hoped to ride out the collapse of civilization near what, in quieter times, had been their seaside villas. On clear days the refugees could see across the Lagoon the source from which the land of their refuge had come—the blue line of the Alps. The 12 mud banks had been washed down through ages from these mountains by the rivers of north Italy's fertile plain.

The key to Venice's greatness was her destitution. Everything had to be brought to the islands—vegetables, fruit, grain, cloth, wood (and later stone) for building. While the rest of Europe shattered into a thousand quarreling feudal castles, concerned chiefly with fighting and farming, Venice looked seaward and lived by the only means she had—trade. Unlike the mass of medieval men, the Venetians were never tied to the soil. Venice knew no serfs. She scarcely knew the Middle Ages, remaining throughout those battlemented times Europe's one great city which never built a wall. So her people, despite the paternalistic despotism of their government, felt the freedom of seafarers who can never be regimented because they are always on the move. They kept for 1,000 years the independence of mind of those who daily mix with men of other nations and creeds. They kept, in form at least, the government of a republic. Other Italian city-states came under the power of individual despots and fell, after the Renaissance, in the rising surge of European nationalism. But Venice kept the flexibility of a government in which many of the people retained the right, if not the real power, to govern themselves.

At first the Venetians traded with the mainland in light, shallow boats which, with the addition of the slender beak and stern post, graceful as the curve of lifting waves, would one day become gondolas. But the open sea was the buoyant highway. Beyond its tossing horizon lay the rich bazaars of Antioch and Alexandria and the golden domes of Constantinople, opulent capital of the Byzantine Empire, of which Venice at first was a nominal dependency. In time her galleys, powered by wind or banks of rowing slaves and grouped in convoys for protection, drove down the Dalmatian coast, into the mouth of the Nile, through the Bosphorus and her merchants planted a trading post in the Crimea.

She has been called "a joint stock company for the exploitation of the East." For 500 years Venice lived for little else. Trade was the pulse of policy and trade tempered for Venice the crusading enthusiasms of medieval Europe. Moslems and Christians alike were her customers. Trade made Venice prefer peace to war, which was itself but a reflex of trade and which she waged fiercely when she had to. Trade defined her foreign policy, which consisted in supporting her weakest neighbor until he became strong enough to threaten her, at which moment she abandoned him.

Discovery was a thrust of trade, which drove her merchants to some of the most famous explorations in history. It drove the three most famous of merchants—Marco Polo and his father and uncle—to open up to the incredulous Middle Ages the wonders of Kublai Khan's China, India and unheard of Cipango (Japan). When, in the Age of Discovery, Columbus stumbled on a new world, his portentous miscalculation was largely based on the dog-eared copy of Marco Polo's travels, which he kept always by him.

Her empire came to Venice not like Britain's in what has been called "moments of absentmindedness" but as a calculated commercial risk. She acquired Istria for wood for her ships. She acquired Dalmatia to control the coastal pirates. She acquired Aegean islands, the Morea and Crete in the

shipwreck of Byzantium, which she helped the Crusaders to conquer in order
to reinforce her monopoly of Eastern trade. To secure her food supply she
eventually acquired possessions on the Italian mainland, extending from Lake
Como on the west to the mouth of the Po on the south.

All these territorial treasures, widely separated by the sea, were threaded
together by her shuttling ships, which she standardized (for Venice knew
about standardization before Henry Ford) so that her trading galleys were
quickly convertible to ships of war. Her galleys were built in the Arsenal,
which was the dynamo of Venetian sea power. Dante, seeing in a vision the
lake of burning pitch in Hell, could think of only one comparison:

> Quale nell' Arzana de' Veneziani
> Bolle l'inverno la tenace pece . . .

(As in the Arsenal at Venice, in winter they boil the sticky pitch . . .)
   During the Renaissance, in the 14th and 15th Centuries, the Arsenal was
the world's biggest industrial plant, manufacturing everything from nails to
cannon, turning out complete ships on its assembly line. "As one enters the
gate," wrote a Spanish visitor in 1436, "there is a great street on either hand
with the sea in the middle, and on one side are windows opening out of the
houses of the Arsenal, and the same on the other side. And out came a galley
towed by a boat, and from the windows they handed out to them, from one the
cordage, from another the bread, from another the arms, and from another the
ballistas and mortars, and so from all sides everything that was required. And
when the galley had reached the end of the street, all the men required were on
board, together with the complement of oars, and she was fully equipped from
end to end. In this manner there came out 10 galleys fully armed, between the
hours of 3 and 9." In 1570, during the war with the Turks, the Arsenal turned
out 100 fully outfitted galleys in 100 days. Four years later, when King Henry
III of France dropped in, he was shown a galley with only the keel and ribs in
position. Then he sat down to a two-hour feast. When he got up the galley,
now completely constructed, equipped, armed and manned, was launched in
his presence.

If this dynamo hummed with the shipbuilding that floated Venetian power,
the city hummed with the life that depended on the ships. The Rialto, the
main bridge over the Grand Canal, was the hub of commercial Venice. The
surrounding wharves, streets and piazzas teemed with the most cosmopolitan
population in the world—Turks, Byzantine Greeks, Cretans, French, Spanish, English, Russians, Germans, even a delegation of Japanese. The docks
were piled high with Venetian export goods—salt and salt fish, wooden
utensils, wrought iron, damask and cloth of gold for which the city was

famous, woolen goods, gold and silver filigree work and the wonderful Venetian glass from the little island of Murano, the most beautiful glass that Europe has ever produced.

The galleys, moored in the heart of the city, unloaded the spoils of Europe, Asia and Africa—silks, satins, cotton goods, furs, spices and sandalwood from as far away as Timor, and marble looted from the temples of Greece or Syria for the churches of Venice.

This tide of wealth rose on the docks of Renaissance Venice and flooded the lives of Venetians with an unparalleled prosperity. It was visible in the characteristic Venetian manner—the air of authority, luxury and indolent well-being, in the city's gorgeous trappings and, above all, in the magnificent panoply of the official festivities.

One of these festivities occurred whenever a new doge was installed. On that occasion the craft guilds, each in a different costume, marched past the doge, two by two, in ostentatious parade. The furriers were dressed in ermine. The clothes of the 10 master sailors were decorated with vermilion stars. The master weavers of gold cloth were dressed in cloth of gold and garlands of pearls, and the master glassmakers in fur-trimmed scarlet. The goldsmiths wore garlands and necklaces of gold and silver, pearls, sapphires, emeralds, diamonds, topazes, jacinths, rubies. The clothmakers carried trumpets, cups of silver and jars of wine, and the comb and lantern makers carried lanterns filled with live birds.

But the most impressive festival of the Venetian year was the wedding of Venice and the sea, *La Sposalizio*, held on Ascension Day—originally to commemorate the victory of Doge Pietro Orseolo II over the Dalmatians in the year 1000. The doge would appear on his official barge, the Bucentaur, rowed by young merchant princes. Thousands of gondolas and other craft would follow in his wake to the Lido, the sandy spit at the edge of the Venetian Lagoon. The Bishop of Castello rowed out to meet the doge and offered him peeled chestnuts, red wine and a bunch of red roses in a silver vase. After prayers the bishop blessed a gold ring. The doge then rose from his seat, threw the ring into the Adriatic and cried, "*Desponsamus te, mare, in signum veri perpetuique dominii Serenissimae Republicae Venetae*" (We wed thee, Sea, in sign of the true and perpetual domination of the Most Serene Venetian Republic). After Mass the doge held a great reception and official feast. The Piazza San Marco became the scene of a great fair, where the reveling went on uninterruptedly for eight days.

From all over Europe men came to see the city whose merchants in power and luxury were the peers of Europe's monarchs. Dante, on the long inferno of his exile from Florence, wandered beside her canals. Petrarch, humanist, sonneteer, sometimes called "the first modern man," visited Venice and in grateful memory bequeathed her his incomparable collection of ancient manuscripts and books, for which Venice built the world's first public library.

Benvenuto Cellini, swinging between murder and masterpieces of silverwork, was her guest. Pietro Aretino, "the scourge of kings" and prototype of today's columnist, penned from Venice the wittily scandalous personal attacks for which the great men of the Renaissance paid him to desist. In Venice he was safe from the daggers of outraged victims and the rack of the Inquisition, since Venice never permitted the Church a free hand on her soil. Manuel Chrysoloras and the other Eastern scholars who taught Italy to read Homer in the original entered the West through the water gate of Venice.

Few of them lingered long, for Venice was not, like Florence, a conflagration of the mind. But they brought to the splendid, worldly, commercial city of the sea the turmoil of the mind which we call the Renaissance. For like nearly everything else, the Renaissance too was imported into Venice.

Every great civilization is no more than the effort of the men who briefly compose it to arrest and perpetuate in art, in literature, in politics, in religion, their vision of the meaning of life. To medieval man the meaning of life had been salvation. He looked about him, and the logic of his judgment seemed to him irrefutable: the world being what it was, happiness here was difficult and transitory. Not all but much of the energies of his mind were directed to achieving life beyond this world.

Renaissance man also looked about him and his cry of exultation was epitomized by the greatest of Renaissance poets, Shakespeare, in lines that might have been uttered at the Creation: ". . . This goodly frame, the earth . . . this most excellent canopy, the air, look you, this brave o'erhanging firmament, this majestical roof fretted with golden fire! . . . What a piece of work is a man! how noble in reason! how infinite in faculty! in form and moving how express and admirable! in action how like an angel! in apprehension how like a god! . . ."

This revolutionary shift in viewpoint came slowly. There are roots of the Renaissance in the Middle Ages. Medieval traces lingered into the Renaissance. But by the 14th Century the Middle Ages had grown tired. They were exhausted by their prodigious effort to create a new civilization from the debris left by fallen Rome, exhausted by the effort of the medieval mind to capture God in abstract definitions, exhausted by their piety. Men did not forsake the Church, but they sought a new authority for their new yearnings and thought that they had found it in the half-effaced or forgotten literary, architectural and sculptural remains of Greece and Rome. In their longing they prospected as eagerly for these classical treasures as men now prospect for oil.

The Italian earth was full of buried statues. The monasteries were filled with buried works of classical greatness—Plato, Homer, Lucretius, Horace, Cicero, Tacitus, Apuleius—evidences of a lost world of light, reason and luxury. The ancient seed stirred in the ancient Italian soil and, like the harvest of the dragon's teeth, there burst forth, at this contact with the Hellenic and Roman past, Renaissance man.

Violence and individualism were the mode of the Renaissance. Often individualism took the form of a criminal passion for political power. Borgias, Medici, Carraras, Visconti and Sforzas quite literally waded through blood to make themselves masters of some city and its countryside, no bigger than an American county. But there was also violence in the consuming passion with which literary men and scholars threw themselves into the study of Latin and Greek or devoured the ancient authors, seeking to produce a new classical literature of Ciceronian elegance and a philosophy that would blend Christianity and Plato. There was violence in the effort of individual men to pack multiple careers into one lifetime. Lorenzo de' Medici was a statesman, financier, poet, musician, Hellenist, playboy. Aeneas Sylvius Piccolomini was a scholar, a poet and a politician who finally became a pope. Leonardo da Vinci was the painter of the *Mona Lisa* and the *Last Supper*, a military engineer, a scientist and aeronautical experimenter.

Renaissance man aspired to be "*l'uomo universale*" (the universal man). "Men," said Leon Alberti with the voice of modernity, "can do all things if they will." This optimism led to monstrous excesses and magnificent achievements. It also led to an unusual human equality. In the Renaissance world of uncommon men a talented peasant was rated the superior of a dull duke and was treated as such.

This violent enfranchisement of the mind and prowess of the individual man was the meaning of the Renaissance. As creative imagination, it found a supreme expression in painting. In this art the greatness of the Renaissance and the greatness of Venice flowed together.

The imagination of Venice was practical and fully occupied by the arts of governing men, seafaring and sumptuous living. To the intellectual ferment of the Renaissance she added little. But there is a genius of place, and Venice was caught by a visual music of the sea and air. The water sucked at the mooring posts, lapping the stone stairs of the docks. Over the city, air quivered like liquid glass and blazed with lights reverberated by the sea or softened into mist which deposited salt crystals on the tinted façades of the *palazzi*. Sometimes the sky was tumultuous with such storms as ships sustain on the open sea. Always, in immense contrasting silence, the clouds sailed, like fleets, out to the Adriatic. This color saturated Venice from the sky and water. And while the city went about her daily, worldly tasks of buying and selling, it entered, like the beauty born of murmuring sound, into her stony face as each *palazzo*, bridge and ship rode above its shadow in the still canals. This dreamy presence beside the waters shimmered into incomparable life in the art of seven great painters: Gentile and Giovanni Bellini, Carpaccio, Giorgione, Titian, Tintoretto and Veronese.

There is an art of irreducible simplicities: tragic, as man reviews his fate in the light of the qualities of nobility, justice and compassion that are his claim to greatness; ironic, as with courage, the quality that makes it possible for him to persist at all, he reviews the absurdity of his dilemma. This is the art of Giotto and Michelangelo. But there is another art—an art of the grace of opulence, of the fully ripened character, of the full-blown flesh, of the fruit sun-seasoned to bursting, of life without the implications of fate. Of this art, adult and autumnal, the Venetians were the masters.

This supreme art was a sunset. By the 17th Century the conquest of Byzantium by the Turks had shut off Venetian trade with the East. With the opening of the new sea route to Asia and the New World, Venice lived more and more on small change and past greatness. She did not go down at once. Anchored on her islands, she swung with the currents of history in which she no longer played a decisive role. For two more centuries she listed, settling as a doomed ship settles until, when Napoleon arrived and Wordsworth wrote his obituary sonnet, she sank.

"Men are we," Wordsworth wrote, that is to say, the only living creatures which conserve in memory the cultures that have made us what we are. The shade of Venice's greatness has merged with history's deeper shadows. The panoply, the lavish life, the teeming trade, lie with her galleys fathoms deep in time. But the memory of the Sea-born City haunts us still, like the luminous streak left by an oar at night or Dante's *tremolo del mar*—the tremulous play of light and waves at sea.

THE AGE OF ENLIGHTENMENT
(*Life*, SEPTEMBER 15, 1947)

MADEMOISELLE DE COIGNY kept a corpse in her coach. The Age of Reason was dawning in France—it was the 18th Century—and there were otherwise just not enough minutes in those days of wonderful Enlightenment for mademoiselle to pursue, like other dedicated bluestockings, the fascinating study of anatomy. But with the corpse handy and her scalpel as keen as M. de Voltaire's wickedly witty mind, she could, while rattling over the Paris cobbles, slice and eviscerate in daily officiation at the new faith whose deity was reason, whose ritual was science and whose high priests were the *philosophes*, the new order of literary skeptics. The outstanding ones, glittering with intellectuality, were Baron de Montesquieu, Denis Diderot, Jean Jacques Rousseau and M. de Voltaire, especially Voltaire, for he had given the Enlightenment its watchword, "*Ecrasez l'infame*" (Crush the infamous thing). The infamous thing was generally taken to mean the intolerance of any religious or social authority, but the censors of King Louis XV were inclined to think it meant Church and state. For with the knife-edge of his wit, Monsieur de Voltaire had been anatomizing both for half a century.

In the history of the human spirit the Enlightenment was an interlude between the stake and faggots and the guillotine. It may be dated from the close of the 17th Century, when Western Europe was exhausted by dynastic wars, to 1789 when the French Revolution opened the cycle of great social wars which, by the middle of the 20th Century, have again all but exhausted Europe and are still far from ended. The Enlightenment flowered under Louis XV, though it began in the time of Louis XIV, who reigned from 1643 to 1715 and outlived all his sons and grandsons, handing on to his great-grandson, Louis XV, a nation in which the king was absolute monarch and in which a bureaucracy ran the government by an increasingly inflexible pattern of precedent.

In the history of nations the Enlightenment—a name given the era by Philosopher Immanuel Kant—was the age when, as the result of conflicts culminating in the Seven Years' War (the 1756–63 French and Indian War of American history), the French lost much of their great colonial empire in the east and west to the British. It was the age when Prussia under Frederick the Great succeeded in dominating Central Europe, and Russia under Catherine the Great succeeded in dominating Eastern Europe.

In the history of economics it was the age when the production of wealth, which had been steadily increasing in Europe since the Middle Ages, reached a vast new volume. Maritime commerce was swelling with the development of the new world, the exploitation of new colonies, the trade with the East. Overland commerce was pulsing along the newly constructed canals and roads. In England a process for smelting iron by pit coal was revived. The fly shuttle and the spinning jenny were invented. In France the milling of silk was perfected.

In art it was the age when painters reproduced the gay upper-class life of the day with a spirit that gave grace and elegance to the frivolity of court society. In social history the Enlightenment was the age when the middle class, which controlled the new sources of wealth, began to challenge the once dominant aristocracy for overt power in the state which they as bureaucrats were already administering.

The great divide of cultures is the moment when men feel within themselves a force equal to the vicissitudes of new vision. The vision of the Enlightenment was freedom—freedom from superstition, freedom from intolerance, freedom to know (for knowledge was held to be the ultimate power), freedom from the arbitrary authority of church or state, freedom to trade or work without vestigial feudal restrictions. This vision was embodied in the American Bill of Rights (for 18th Century America was also a part of the Enlightenment) and in the French Revolution's Rights of Man.

In the name of this vision the Enlightenment finally reversed the whole trend of European culture. Before the Enlightenment culture had been essentially religious. Carrying further the work of the Renaissance, the Enlightenment made culture essentially secular. Before the Enlightenment the proper study of mankind had been the will of God. The proper study of mankind, said the Enlightenment with the voice of Alexander Pope, is man. Revelation had been held to be the highest form of truth. Looking back to Descartes, the 17th Century French philosopher who had synthesized mathematics and philosophy, and to Newton, the English physicist whose theory of gravitation had systematized all the discoveries of contemporary science, the Enlightenment sought system and reason in all things. There is no truth, said the Enlightenment, which cannot stand the test of reason. Slowly and surely the Enlightenment began that process whereby philosophy, the search for truth, was supplanted by science, the search for facts. Theology, the effort to know God's will, was replaced by history, the record of man's follies.

The Enlightenment is one great source of modern culture. In a brief 100 years, it revised the fundamental ideas of man's destiny and purpose which civilization had developed over more than 1,000 years. The Enlightenment was the intellectual chemistry whose gradual precipitate was the modern mind—secular, practical and utilitarian.

The function of the Middle Ages had been to reconstruct human civilization from the debris of fallen Rome. The function of the Renaissance had been to liberate the creative energies of the individual man and to reunite the culture of the ancient world with the culture that man had developed since. These movements had been spontaneous and organic. Their ideas were evolved, not superimposed. The Enlightenment in France began with ideas, and its immediate purpose was to reform or revolutionize French life.

It was a rather discouraging prospect. For one doubt rarely assailed the otherwise skeptical French mind of that century; few doubted that French civilization had reached a perfection unmatched in human history.

In the museum at Versailles there hangs a picture by the 18th Century painter Olivier. Behind an open clavichord sits a little boy. Above him high, delicately white-paneled walls rise to the corniced ceiling; ceiling-high windows of many panes let in the light, or, more probably, through them the light within holds off for a moment the crowding dark without. Above a tall mirror portraits of two noble women gaze down from their height at a company below. It is the salon of the Prince de Conti, one of the most distinguished salons in 18th Century France. Its presiding spirit is the prince's mistress, the Comtesse de Boufflers, who is busy with a chafing dish, for on these intimate occasions servants are excused.

The boy at the clavichord is young Wolfgang Amadeus Mozart, the most famous child prodigy of his time. The little company is quite unconscious that it is dwarfed by the noble proportions of the hall it has chosen for its setting; in stiff, knee-length, embroidered jackets, the men stand and talk or roam about. The women, like honeybees, with wide panniered skirts and tight bodices above tiny, corseted waists, sit, rove, flirt with their fans. The conversation, like an intricate, dignified dance, weaves in and out, retreats, softens, swells, as one or another joins or falls out; sometimes wit, like a grace note, flashes, sometimes laughter tinkles.

We know the names of these figures to which even recollection can now give no more duration than a note of music—the Princesse de Beauvau, the Comtesse d'Egmont, the Maréchale de Luxembourg, the Maréchale de Mirepoix. These are among the great names of the 18th Century salons and they pluck wistfully for a moment at the iron chord of history as the quills of a harpsichord pluck at its metal strings.

Conversation was the impalpable element that held the men and women of this society in a common bond. The 18th Century talked itself into the immortality of memoirs and anecdotes, for conversation was an art; indeed, in France, the age had none greater. It was talk of dry grace; common sense and clarity were its prerequisites. Earnestness was at a discount. Talk was an easy modulation of *bon mots*, gallantries, clear analysis of political and moral questions, light mockery of the question of human fate—brilliant, winged, facile talk.

Sometimes the thrusts were merely catty, as when her friends praised Mme. de Lutzelbourg for being, at 68, one of the most active women in France. "As active," snapped the Marquise de Polignac, "as fleas can make her." Sometimes a flash of wit like burning magnesium ribbon lit up character or problem. A talkative cardinal was describing to sceptical Mme. du Deffand the martyr-dom of St. Denis, who, when his head was cut off, picked it up and carried it in his hands. What was less well known, said the cardinal, was that the saint walked with his head under his arm from Montmartre to the church of St. Denis, a distance of some 6 miles. "Ah, Monseigneur," said Madame du Deffand gravely, "*dans une telle situation, il n'y a que le premier pas qui coûte*" (in a situation like that, it is only the first step that is the hardest).

This glittering, brittle, fastidious life of the salons made 18th Century France the motherland of European culture and Paris the capital of the human mind. It was a woman's world. Louis XV was the legitimate king of France, but in his time the country had had as many separate reigns as the king had had mistresses. There had been the reign of Mme. de Prie, of Madame de Mailly, of Madame de Châteauroux, of Madame de Pompadour (whom the king's daughter, Mademoiselle Adelaide, called "Mama Strumpet") and of Madame du Barry.

Coming up to Paris from Bordeaux, Montesquieu noted "the monstrous regiment of women." Wrote the political philosopher (whose own election to the Paris Academy of the Sciences was the work of Mademoiselle de Cler-mont), "There is no one holding an office at court, in Paris or in the provinces, without a woman through whose hands pass all the favors and at times all the injustices he can dispense. All these women entertain mutual relations; they form a kind of republic whose ever active members succor and serve one another reciprocally; they are a new state as it were within the state; and a man at court, in Paris or in the provinces, who observes ministers, magistrates and prelates perform their duties, unless he knows the women who govern them, is comparable to the man who sees a machine in play quite clearly but who knows nothing about its springs."

These women were terrifying in their hold on power. Mme. de Tencin was a wisp of a woman who kept Versailles in a tight mesh of her intrigue. Consider her unemotional statesmanship on the question of sending Louis XV to the Flanders front: "Between us, it is not that he is capable of commanding a company of grenadiers; but his presence will do much good. The troops will accomplish their duty better and the generals will not dare to fail in theirs so openly. . . . A king, whatever he be, is for the soldiery and the people what the Ark of the Covenant was for the Hebrews; his mere presence is a presage of success."

Here is the Maréchale de Mirepoix reassuring Madame de Pompadour, who had been badly frightened by rumors that a rival was threatening to oust her from the royal bedchamber: "The friendship the king bears you is the same as that he bears your apartment and surroundings; you have adapted yourself to his manners and stories; he is not embarrassed, he does not fear to bore you; how can you expect him to have the courage to uproot all this in one day?"

Here is Mme. de Jully, discussing her husband with his sister: "M. de Jully would be astonished indeed if someone were to tell him that he does not care for me at all. It would be a cruel trick to play on him, and me also, for he is the sort of man to be thoroughly put out if he were robbed of his hobby."

The worldliness is of a piece with the wit and explains better than definitions the only reverence 18th Century France knew—the reverence for common sense. These women were tacticians of character. Their realism was of the unclouded kind that is invulnerable to pity. Their world held for them only one terror, ennui, and only one horror, a lapse of taste. It was one of the most elegantly unreal worlds in history, a world which drained away the resources of a country and lay oppressively on an impoverished and overburdened people.

Of the four men—Montesquieu, Diderot, Voltaire and Rousseau—who chiefly meant the Enlightenment to this scintillant and foredoomed society, the least influential in France was Montesquieu. But his book, *The Spirit of the Laws*, propounded a doctrine of the separation of powers between the legislative and executive branches of government which influenced profoundly the framers of the American Constitution.

Denis Diderot had an all-embracing influence on his country for he had an omnibus talent. First of psychological novelists (*Le Neveu de Rameau*), evolutionary biologist at the dawn of the age of evolution, art critic and devout philosophical materialist, he was most famous for his editorship of the encyclopedia. This vast work, which ran through six editions and to which practically all the *philosophes* contributed, was the greatest single propaganda focus of Enlightenment in France. Voltaire wrote the article on history, Rousseau wrote the article on music. Montesquieu contributed an essay on taste. The physiocrats, Turgot and Quesnay, wrote on economic subjects advocating economic enlightenment in the form of *laissez faire*, free trade and enterprise unhampered by mercantilism, which had placed the hard hand of state regulation on business.

The plan was ambitious, the success remarkable. The editors made a brave effort to keep an enlightened, critical and scientific attitude and to free themselves from the prejudices of the past. The encyclopedia's articles on science insisted on the experimental method. The most advanced views on political economy were presented. The happiness of the working class was declared to be the chief purpose of good government. The historical and religious articles were conservative; they had to get by the censor. But free thought and attacks

on authority were slipped into casual pieces. Thus the article on Aius Locu-
tius, a Roman deity, urged freedom of thought; the article on Juno cast doubt
on the Virgin.

Although they were banded together to advance tolerance and reason, the
encyclopedists quarreled among themselves. Many of them, Diderot included, bitterly attacked Voltaire because he acknowledged the existence of a
creator, although Voltaire's God was not the God of Christianity but the
impersonal Supreme Being of the deists, a God who created man and then left
him to his own devices, having no interest in his actions or ultimate salvation.

The Enlightenment had no more complete or prolific son than Voltaire. He
was almost involuntarily witty and organically skeptical. But what he believed, he believed in fanatically. He believed in the physics of Sir Isaac
Newton, the psychology of John Locke, freedom of thought, civil rights and
personal security. In his *Age of Louis XIV* and his *Essay on the Manners and Spirit
of the Nations* Voltaire revolutionized the writing of history by discussing social
and cultural movements instead of simply chronicling the succession of kings
and wars. But his famous work, one of the few books of the Enlightenment
that is still read for pleasure, is *Candide*, which savagely satirized the complacent belief, falsely derived from orthodox philosophers, that this is the best of
all possible worlds. Unlike other *philosophes*, Voltaire had cut deep into a more
enduring subject than doctrinaire controversy or the battle of ideas—the
eternal subject of human folly.

Voltaire and Diderot had been popularizers of the scientific and philosophic
sides of the Enlightenment. Jean Jacques Rousseau was the great prophet of
the democratic revolution in every field. His *Social Contract*, with its theory of
the right to power of the sovereign people, was a powerful spur to the French
Revolution. Through Rousseau, the Enlightenment leads directly to the Revolution. He was dead before it came. So was Voltaire. This was a pity, for a very
minor confrontation of values during The Terror might have tickled the old
philosopher's ironic sense. Mme. de Gramont had possibly never had an idea
in her unenlightened head when she was called before the Revolutionary
Tribunal to stand trial for her life. "Had she ever aided the aristocrats who had
escaped abroad?" the court asked her. Mme. de Gramont knew that if she
answered yes she would be guillotined at once. For some seconds she looked at
her judges in silence, then, "I was going to answer no," she said, "but life is not
worth the lie."

THE EDWARDIANS

(*Life*, NOVEMBER 17, 1947)

"TA-RA-RA BOOM-DE-AY! Ta-ra-ra Boom-de-ay! Ta-ra-ra Boom-de-ay!" Queen Victoria was dying. In the sudden hush the larricking refrain of the decade's hit song, still framed with delight by the lips of butcher boys and duchesses, rang out like a salute to the new age that was coming to birth with the old queen's death. "Send but a song oversea to us," Swinburne had invoked America; and up from the stews of New Orleans came the obsessive syllables. They swept all classes of British society. In the person of Albert Edward Prince of Wales, they even ventured into the royal presence. For the heir apparent, shut out by maternal order from affairs of state and doomed to be Prince of Wales for 60 years, found partial compensation as king of that gay life which *Ta-ra-ra* celebrated and which, like the top hat and the diamond tiara, crowned early 20th Century society:

A sweet Tuxedo girl you see;
Queen of swell society,
Fond of fun as fond can be,
When it's on the strict Q.T.
Ta-ra-ra Boom-de-ay! Ta-ra-ra . . .

In the new century's second year on Jan. 25, 1901, the beat of *Ta-ra-ra* was drowned in the blare of trumpets. On to the balcony of St. James's Palace stepped the Garter King-of-Arms to proclaim that the queen was dead and that a new king lived:

"Whereas it has pleased Almighty God to call to His Mercy Our late Sovereign Lady Queen Victoria, of Blessed and Glorious Memory, by whose Decease the Imperial Crown of the United Kingdom of Great Britain and Ireland is solely and rightfully come to the High and Mighty Prince Albert Edward. . . ."

To the hushed crowds the queen's death, after a 64-year reign, was like a lesion in the order of life. But the language of the ancient ritual, touched with the tone of the Middle Ages, fell comfortingly from the balcony with the assurance that tradition cushions the disruptions of change; that order, personified in the succession of kings, can defy death itself; that dynasty transcends mortality. A new era—the Edwardian—had begun. The king himself set the final seal on the change. Boarding his yacht, the *Victoria and Albert*, he noticed that the royal standard was flying at half-mast and asked why. Said the commander, "The queen is dead." "But," said Edward VII, "the king is alive." The standard shot up to the top of the staff. Ta-ra-ra Boom-de-ay!

The new era was to be officially brief—less than a decade—and exuberant with a sense of culmination. Not only was it the heir of almost 2,000 years of Western civilization. Proceeding from the long, somnolent summer of Victoria's latter years, beneficiaries of the industrial and scientific revolutions which had bountifully changed the conditions of human life, rich beyond any prior heirs of history with the developing enterprise of America, the diverted treasures of India, the newly discovered gold and diamonds of South Africa and the enormous wealth of industrial and commercial Britain itself, the Edwardians set out to enjoy the world they had inherited. It was a world of confidence and security. World peace had been a fact so long (since Napoleon) that world war seemed like an aboriginal horror which civilized men had simply grown too adult to commit. Crises and rumors of war were recurrent, but the mass of men had an almost organic confidence in peace.

For confidence was everywhere. It flamed in the steel furnaces of Britain and of America and the German empire, which had risen in 20 years to challenge British goods in the world market. It was embodied in steel in the great hulls of the dreadnoughts and in the vast, perfectly equilibrated luxury liners. It pulsed through the whole world along the infinitely complex arterial system of international trade and finance. So prosaic a fact as the spread of double-entry bookkeeping, viewed in terms of world business and facilitated credit, was scarcely less a wonder than the electric light with which Edwardian cities were beginning to be illuminated. A new tempo was entering life with the abridgement of time and distance by speed and the multiplication of power by the generation of energy.

At the bottom of Edwardian confidence—of its faith in life and its faith in peace—was the idea of progress. For the Edwardian era was the fulfillment of the 18th Century's Enlightenment, and the Enlightenment's basic intuition was the idea of progress—the belief that man, by the aid of science, can achieve a perfection of living limited only by the imaginative powers of his mind. Implicitly the Enlightenment denied faith in the name of science and the Kingdom of God in the name of the kingdoms of this world. It whetted that knife-edge, dividing the world's greatest focuses of force—the power of religion and the power of science—along which the thoughtful man has teetered ever since.

But the Edwardians were too busy working and playing to think much and too confident to teeter. They thoroughly enjoyed the kingdom of this world. Their watchword was happiness—happiness for those whose means nearly everybody understood to be a rough measure of a man's worth, good works for those whom circumstances of fate or fortune had not favored. For the Edwardian era was one of those rare interludes of history where everybody who could possibly do so had a wonderful time. The means were all at hand.

Railroads (King Edward was almost the same age as the steam locomotive) were bringing the country to the city and the city to the country on a scale unprecedented in history. The late Victorian fad of cycling had improved the wretched roads which the earlier Victorian age had allowed to lapse into a condition of Wordsworthian rusticity and disrepair. The new horseless carriage, the auto car, would soon complete the revolution the bicycle had begun.

The stately houses of England, like Hatfield, Chatsworth, Wynyard and Easton, linked by the new accessibility, were the brilliant centers of the new life. By special train (which never cost more than £10), by automobile and by carriage, gay parties made the rounds of the country houses for the hunts, the shoots, horseracing and cozy social gatherings, or returned to London for gaudy routs in the great town houses. For as the pursuit of happiness turned into the pursuit of pleasure, sport became a democratic function of wealth which would be aped and shared by all classes.

There were premonitory rumblings, but who in that holiday humor could take them seriously? In England the Labor party elected its first members to Parliament and the Fabian Society, through its energizing brains, Beatrice and Sidney Webb, was tailoring the doctrines of Karl Marx to suit British fashions. In the name of social justice a galaxy of writers—H. G. Wells, Bernard Shaw, John Galsworthy, Arnold Bennett—was preaching reform or revolution. In the name of Catholic enlightenment Gilbert K. Chesterton was needling capitalism and the middle class with wit and paradox. But, like King Edward, the great majority of his subjects preferred the somewhat luridly arresting love stories of Marie Corelli. The great struggle of the Victorian age—the church versus science in the guise of Darwinian evolution—was of further interest chiefly to the professionals of both teams. Most people were no longer upset by an ape in the family tree.

In the heart of Europe, Germany kept clanking its saber and frantically building a navy whose sole purpose must be to challenge the British fleet. But then, was not the German kaiser a little theatrical, a little too much like Lohengrin in stage armor alighting from the swan boat? Hardly had the age begun when a small revolutionary sect called the Russian Social Democratic Workers' party split into a minority (Mensheviks) and a majority (Bolsheviks, under the leadership of a short, pale fanatic with the face of a Mongol and the uncouth name of Lenin). But this was of interest chiefly to the police.

Russia was the only country in Europe (except Turkey) which had internal passports. Between Britain and America people could travel as freely as from one English county to another. And everybody who could travel did. Civilization had launched its last great party.

* * *

The portly and imperious guiding spirit of the age was King Edward VII. He was not only the King of England; he was "the uncle of Europe." Kaiser Wilhelm II of Germany was his nephew. The Empress of Russia was his niece. King Leopold of Belgium was his cousin once removed. His wife, Queen Alexandra, was the daughter of the King of Denmark. The King of Greece was his brother-in-law and the King of Norway was his son-in-law. In one degree or another he was related to the wearer of nearly every crown in Europe and to a swarm of princelings, dukes and barons who, whatever their faults and foibles, embodied a standard of civilized living and the responsibilities of rank which their lapses chiefly served to emphasize. The envious kaiser might detest the king, call him "the old peacock," and, when Sir Thomas Lipton's *Shamrock II*, the British tea merchant's America's Cup challenger, lost a mast, express his imperial relief that his uncle had not lost his life while sporting with his mistress aboard his grocer's yacht. King Edward might think that his cousin of Belgium was a monstrous roué with the ethics of a shady resort keeper. But it was all in the family, and by constant correspondence and personal contacts, by genealogical intimacy, the king was the active head of an international aristocracy which gave a style and form to the Edwardian era not quite recaptured by the Comintern.

The short, stout figure with the slightly protuberant eyes, dominating a broad face which the Edwardian beard and the habit of regality just raised above the average, seemed the apotheosis of middle-class mien. But the spirit within lifted kingship to a high level. This consciousness of royal function was at the root of the king's preoccupation with punctilio (for he knew that tradition is conserved by a minute attention to forms). Thus he could say to Lord Rosebery, who appeared at court in knee breeches when the command had been given for full dress, "I presume you have come in the suite of the American ambassador?" Thus, at a private showing of some early moving pictures of himself, the royal voice was heard to mutter in the semidarkness, "Decorations on the wrong side."

The Edwardian in the street (he would have been insulted to be called the "common man") thought he understood the king well enough and called him "good, old Teddy." The royal tastes were by and large, his tastes, and more power to the man who could satisfy them. The king's love of sports and games of chance, of dancing, of parties, of money, of a rather overblown splendor, of good eating and drinking, of automobiles, of band music and Italian opera, of the theater, of the beauty of women and the legend of his prowess with them— even his outbreaks of horseplay, into which, as he matured, he introduced a discreet fastidiousness of occasion and décor—were part and parcel of the "swell-elegant" Edwardian world.

For Edward was the first Edwardian, and in his person the age was projected decades into the past and, given a rich and somewhat racy retrospect, a lore, inseparable from an understanding of the age.

There had been the great days in the Paris of the Second Empire—that strange political stage set, lamplit and unreal, over which Napoleon III brooded like a wistful gargoyle until empire and emperor were washed away in the blood of Sedan. In Paris the Prince of Wales was in the heart of Western civilization. There the Middle Ages survived in the Cathedral of Notre Dame. In France, St. Thomas Aquinas had written the great *Summas*. There the Enlightenment had heated the secular mind of man to a new incandescence until it burst into the flame of the French Revolution.

The Prince of Wales was less familiar with Notre Dame than with the maze of Bohemian Montmartre. At the Moulin Rouge, a contemporaneous synonym for cardinal sin, the prince advanced the Edwardian education by watching La Goulue ("The Glutton"), with a heart embroidered on the seat of her underthings as everybody could see despite 60 yards of lace flounces on her petticoat, dance the *chahut*, which has been described as a "quadrille in delirium."

In Paris he entertained the Duchess of Warwick. A lifelong friend, the duchess was one of the radiantly beautiful women whom, as prince and king, Edward always kept around, like living jewels. The duchess was one of the first possessors of what would be known a few decades later as a "social conscience." She tried to interest her friend in socialism but he just shrugged his shoulders. "Societies are not made," he said. "They grow."

Few aspects of the Edwardian legend were more appealing to his subjects than the king as a sportsman, the more so because in sport too he maintained the common touch and, like the mass of men, was not outstandingly good at anything. His horsemanship was more daring than masterly, but he was a mighty fox hunter and rode to hounds with a dash that sometimes earned him six falls in as many miles. He was one of the most implacable enemies pheasants have ever known. The king liked croquet, and after the tensions of a day at the races he found it sedative, especially as played on the broad lawns of Moulton Paddocks, the Newmarket estate of his great friend and banker, Sir Ernest Cassel. And in the Duchess of Sermoneta the king found the perfect partner. The duchess could seldom hit a ball, "missing the easiest hoops and therefore keeping him in the best of tempers." Then one day, in one of those flashes with which despair sometimes inspires the inveterate loser, the duchess connected. She has left a description of what followed: "It [the ball] flew right across the ground, straight through the right hoop (I didn't even know it was the right one) and, continuing its glorious career, hit the King's ball straight into the rose bushes. But by the icy stillness that prevailed, I realized that never, never was such a thing to happen again."

The king was a more formidable yachtsman, and the regatta at Cowes was one of the high points of the Edwardian social whirl. There Edwardian society was seen at its sunniest and airiest as the ladies of fashion raised their parasols and lorgnettes while the wind from the water waywardly whipped their skirts, conniving with the king, who had a sailor's urge for the cut of any jib.

But the king's great passion was horse racing, and one of the great moments for himself and his loyal subjects came in 1909 when his horse Minoru won the Derby. This passion had developed early, to the great concern of Queen Victoria, who never raced horses though she seldom missed a day's drive in her donkey cart. "Dearest Bertie," she had written, ". . . now that the Ascot races are approaching, I wish to repeat earnestly and seriously . . . confine your *visits* to the two days, Tuesday and Thursday and not go on Wednesday and Friday. . . . If you are anxious to go on the *two* great days (though I should prefer your not going *every year* to *both*) there is no *real* objection to *that*. . . ." To which Bertie had replied, "I am always most anxious to meet your wishes, dear Mama, in every respect, and always regret if we are not quite d'accord— but I am past 28 and have some considerable knowledge of the world. . . ."

It was a knowledge dearly won by a total immersion in the swirling life of his age. The king learned to know men and women in the adventitious intensities of card play and gambling, in the rugged test of the hunt course and the finesse and follies of boudoirs before he transmuted his knowledge to an art in the more hazardous play of diplomacy. Within their light-hearted limits the Edwardian swell set lived dangerously. Scandals were almost a reflex of the energy of the age. In the Tranby Croft scandal Edward had to testify in behalf of a man accused of cheating at cards. In the Mordaunt scandal Edward had to appear as a witness in court and declare, "in a very firm voice," that he was not the father of Lady Mordaunt's premature baby.

Every great age seeks to find its meaning in an ideal of beauty. The Edwardians worshiped the very tangible beauty of women, and the king was among the most devout worshipers. The era epitomized its devotion in the term "professional beauty," and the term was often, though not always, used in conjunction with the word "fast," which the Edwardians raised to a new power of sinful sibilance. The first of the professional beauties was the actress Lily Langtry, daughter of the Dean of the island of Jersey. With a face like Athene's, a Junoesque figure and one black dress, she had reversed the late Victorian standards of beauty—the Burne-Jones eyes, the rosebud mouth, the phthisic slope of the shoulders. The "Jersey Lily," the discovery of Prince Leopold, Edward's younger brother, met Edward at a supper party. She heard a deep, cheerful voice say, "I'm afraid I'm a little late," and the Prince of Wales was beside her. She sat at many suppers and spent many jolly, carefree evenings with him until, with her habitual playfulness, she is rumored to have slid a piece of ice down his neck to watch the royal reaction. It was icy. For Edward did not like indiscriminate horseplay.

It was common knowledge that Mrs. Langtry was Edward's favorite, for Edwardian fun was not always on the strict Q.T. But the Dean of Jersey spread the odor of sanctity about her tea table; Gladstone read Shakespeare to her; she was received by the Prince of Wales and Princess Alexandra at Marlborough House and even at court.

Another great beauty was Mrs. Keppel, daughter of Sir William Edmonstone and wife of George Keppel, son of the Earl of Albemarle. She was widely known to be the king's mistress, but she moved in the highest circles of London society. She was endowed with tireless vitality, vast if somewhat adenoidal beauty and perdurable tact.

The Keppels' sumptuous house in London's West End was the scene of many cozy Edwardian parties. For they had a famous chef, and the king's taste in food set a standard for his gourmandizing age. Mr. Keppel viewed his peculiar position with Edwardian discretion. He would sometimes point out a knickknack to visitors, saying, "His Majesty gave this to my wife."

Mrs. Keppel died last September. But her old age had not been without its cross: her sense of propriety was shocked by the marriage of King Edward VIII and Mrs. Wallace Warfield.

This abounding freedom, beauty, luxury and glamour found its brilliant focus in the royal receptions at Buckingham Palace. There, as the veritable light of a new age—the new electric lights—blazed on the majestic figures of the king and queen, the court in full panoply and the festive tiaras and some of the most fabulously beautiful shoulders in history, the power and surging energy of the great industrial and commercial age were transmuted into its special kind of splendor, material, worldly and cosmopolitan. For among the most glamorous women at court were American women.

The American invasion of England had begun under Queen Victoria when beautiful Jennie Jerome had married Lord Randolph Churchill and become the mother of Winston, and the lovely and wealthy Mary Victoria Leiter had married Lord Curzon. Under Edward VII the Americans came in droves. The Gibson girl as a tourist (during the Edwardian age tourism became one of Europe's most profitable businesses) or in the guise of a rich, title-hunting heiress thronged Paris, Biarritz, Monte Carlo, the great continental spas and crowded the London hotels—the Carlton, the Savoy and the Berkeley.

Edward VII welcomed Americans and admitted them to his cosmopolitan set. He liked the beauty and vitality of American women whom he considered less squeamish, better educated and better able to take care of themselves than English women. He liked the hard vigor of American men. He liked the stories they told and their passion for cards, for they came bringing poker in their hands. He shared their respect for money as a creative power, a means for organizing and enjoying life.

For the Edwardian era was one of the most expensive ages in history. Civilization's last great party cost a lot of money. The king, who had a shrewd Edwardian business head, was always in need of money. "It is necessary to have a lot in order to be able to lose it," he explained to Yvette Guilbert. But he was at one with his age in understanding how to make money work for him.

Money was a key to his circle of cosmopolitan cronies whose cluster of Jewish businessmen—the Rothschild brothers, Baron Hirsch, Sir Ernest Cassel—caused a constant buzz. "The cleverest head in England," said the king of Sir Ernest Cassel, who by the use of an imagination entirely financial had amassed a huge fortune. Said Lord Knollys on the king's accession, "Gentlemen, it is my happy duty to inform you that for the first time in English history the heir-apparent comes forward to claim his right to the throne unencumbered by a single penny of debt." The king's friends had wrought the miracle. One of them, it was reported, had advanced £100,000 against a £25,000 repayment and the promise of a knighthood.

So, under the king's expert eye the gay Edwardian carrousel whirled round with dashing horses, clinking coins and goblets and splendid sport and spectacles. If the music was a little brassy (*Champagne Charlie* and *Picadilly Johnny with a Window in His Eye* were almost as popular as *Ta-ra-ra Boom-de-ay*), it was loud, cheery and pervasive.

The flighty songs drowned out some highly important things that were going on. In science the age was one of the most portentous in history. Into the brief decade were crowded a constellation of scientific names whose discoveries were to determine the history, the mood and perhaps the fate of the 20th Century. No one country had a monopoly of the new creative outburst which manifested itself in almost all the centers of Western civilization. Scarcely had the world accustomed itself to peering into solid matter, with the help of Professor Röntgen's X-rays, than Pierre and Marie Curie tossed at it a scientific bomb in the form of radium—little knowing that the bomb was atomic. In England, Ernest Rutherford in a series of brilliant researches established the existence and nature of radioactivity and the nuclear structure of the atom. In Germany, Max Planck published the quantum theory, liberating the theoretical imagination of science with his hypothesis that energy of radiation is not continuous but exists in small, exact units, measured in terms called "quanta." In America, Charles Martin Hall achieved the electrolytic extraction of aluminum, adding an important new metal to developing technology. Through the work of Marconi and Nikola Tesla in radio, sound was made to conquer space with only the ether as a conveyor. Through the work of Daimler and others, the automobile replaced the horse. Henry Ford would soon give masses of men a new freedom by bringing the automobile within their purchasing power while developing new techniques of mass production to make this possible. Through the work of Samuel Langley and the Wright brothers, man realized the age-old dream of rising up as with the wings of eagles.

While the scientific mind was learning from nature the secret of power, other scientists were peering into the secrets of the mind itself—the greatest force in the universe. In Austria, Sigmund Freud, in the course of the study of neurology, discovered the existence of the unconscious mind and its influence on the conscious mind. In his new system of psychoanalysis, Freud fluttered the Victorian shades by asserting the importance of sex on the development of the mind and, for the discussion of his discoveries, gave the age a new idiom of which the word "repression" has become the most fashionable. In Switzerland, Freud's disciple Carl Jung later broke away from his master to replace psychoanalysis with analytical psychology, to reject the influence of sex on neurosis and to stress man's creative impress.

This worldly age had a vision equal to its sense of power and wealth—the vision of peace and progress. No era of history has invested its imagination and its money more lavishly in projects for human betterment. It was scarcely 100 years since the last serfs had been freed in Western Europe. It was scarcely 40 years since America had freed some 4 million Negro slaves and Russia had freed 20 million of its own people who had been held in human bondage. The spirit of freedom was in the air, but now technology was to be the liberating agent. The machine would free millions from the drudgeries inseparable from organizing and servicing a civilization which was growing ever more massive and complex.

The idea of leisure as one of civilization's highest boons began to grip the mind of the age. What was to be done with this leisure by masses of men whose human capacities were just about equal to the simplest tasks was a problem which the Edwardian age was not called upon to answer. But in any case part of the answer was no doubt education. For faith in education as a universal cure, a direct heritage from Jean Jacques Rousseau and the Enlightenment, was almost as deep-rooted as the Edwardian faith in science.

Good works abounded in the form of hospitals, settlement houses, social services, educational projects and foundations. The age dipped into its bulging pockets and endowed every kind of beneficent institution.

Andrew Carnegie was typical of the era's boundless goodwill and its legend of human opportunity. Starting as a poor Scottish immigrant laborer in the U.S., Carnegie had organized the great industry which gave the age its technological framework—steel. By the use of his free intelligence he had made a fortune estimated at hundreds of millions of dollars. He gave it away in countless benefactions, of which the most memorable were the free public libraries, which brought civilization's literary wealth into obscure villages, and the Carnegie Endowment for International Peace, to which he gave $10 million. In the British Empire, Cecil Rhodes used his huge fortune to endow the Rhodes Scholarships to further international goodwill and understanding. In Sweden, Alfred Nobel used his vast wealth to endow the Nobel Prizes for peace, science and literary merit.

In the Hague, a monument to the age's passion for peace, stood the Hague Tribunal, whose experts sought to codify a system of international law binding on all nations. So general was the Edwardian mood of confidence that the Czar of Russia, who was not generally considered to be an enlightened monarch, proposed to the Hague Conference that all the nations disarm. The Edwardian age sought its historic meaning and justification in the achievement of universal peace. But history, in the tone of a horn, winding from the depths of the Prussian conifer forests now planted in tidy rows by the diligence of that highly disciplined state, was sounding over the Edwardian era the theme of fate. It was history's irony that this happy age should prefigure the forces whose collision was to threaten the whole structure of Western civilization and set the foreboding mood of the rest of the 20th Century. For now the great coalitions—the Triple Alliance and the Triple Entente—which were to make World War I possible and then to fight it, began to take form, rising like savage, black, confronting rocks from a summer sea.

In the name of peace and to the degree that politics is fate, the age had done its work. Thereafter the two great coalitions rested in a poise so precarious that one mortal shot, fired by an obscure Serb student in the primitive Bosnian town of Sarajevo, tipped their balance and they rushed headlong in military avalanches on each other: chaos.

Back from 76 years of circling in ranges of space beyond vision, there swung into the night sky a pale, celestial visitor—Halley's comet. To the masses of men a comet was still a portent of war and the death of kings. Thousands of readers, terrified by sensational stories in the new popular press, chiefly the creation of Alfred Charles Harmsworth (Lord Northcliffe), believed that, as the earth passed near the comet's gaseous tail, the end of the world would come. But it was only an age that was ending.

In 1910 King Edward, who had long suffered from chronic bronchitis, suddenly became worse. He insisted on working and playing. Someone saw him let himself, unaccompanied, into his special box at Covent Garden to hear Luisa Tetrazzini sing Gilda in *Rigoletto*. A few days later he saw *Alias Jimmy Valentine*, one of the first of those un-Edwardian plays of which a thief was the hero.

"No," said the king to someone who ventured to suggest rest, "I shall go on. I shall work to the end. Of what use is it to be alive if one cannot work?" A few days later Edward VII was dying. Taking Mrs. Keppel by the hand, in a final gesture that summed up the age that was ending, Queen Alexandra led the king's mistress to his bedside for a last farewell.

AGE OF EXPLORATION

(Life, MARCH 22, 1948)

ONE DAY, four centuries after Columbus reached the new world, a Minnesota farmer grubbed up a stump on his farm and found a flat stone embedded in the roots. On the stone was an inscription in Scandinavian runes. For nine years the stone served as a step to the farmer's granary. Then it was translated. The runes read:

"8 Goths and 22 Norwegians on [an] exploration-journey from Vinland through the West. We had camp . . . one day's journey north of this stone. We were [out] and fished one day. After we came home . . . found ten men red with blood and dead. AV[e] M[aria] Save [us] from evil."

A shorter inscription on the edge of the stone bore the date: 1326.

What did this inscription mean? What had happened in the night of history? What shrieks had died away, in thinning circles of unheard horror, into the continental quiet? Who were those "8 Goths and 22 Norwegians," and what were they doing in the middle of Minnesota more than a century before the discovery of America?

The Kensington Stone (as it is called) may or may not be a peculiarly inscrutable hoax; scholars cannot make up their minds. But other discoveries in the same general region are not hoaxes—medieval Norse battle axes, a spearhead, a fire steel, a Viking's hatchet and (in Ontario) a Viking's grave and moldering arms.

In 1492 Christopher Columbus, by dramatizing the ordeal whereby he burst into the darkness of an unknown hemisphere, dramatized the fact that a new age—the Age of Discovery—had begun.

But all through the Middle Ages parts of northern Europe had been dimly aware, as a groping man is aware of obstacles in the darkness, of land far out in the western Atlantic. There were the multiple legends of St. Brendan, the Irish monk who had crossed the open sea in a curragh of stitched hides and had found a misty land far out in the west—St. Brendan's Isle—which mariners still looked for during the Age of Discovery. There were the legends of King Arthur, who had conquered Ireland and Iceland. He had voyaged beyond, the legends said, and found a blessed land to which, after his mortal wounding in the last great battle with the heathen, a barge with three mourning queens bore him away—"the island-valley of Avilion."

Even in the ancient world Iceland was known by the name of Ultima Thule, which meant the end of the earth for Pytheas of Massilia (Marseille), a contemporary of Alexander the Great, had made a voyage there. But ages which believed in hippogriffs and unicorns laughed at Pytheas' reports of seas of floating ice, winters when there was no daylight and summers when there was no night.

When the Norse sea rovers reached Iceland (around 860) they found that others besides Pytheas had been there. On the shore they discovered crosses, bells and books in Irish characters.

By 986 Greenland was colonized from Iceland by Eric the Red. By the year 1000 Eric's son Leif, making a nonstop voyage from Norway to Greenland, was blown upon the North American coast, probably Nova Scotia or Newfoundland. He had no trouble finding his way home. Because of the abundant wild grapes, Leif called the new land Vinland.

More than one attempt was made by Greenlanders to colonize Vinland, probably around Cape Cod and Martha's Vineyard. But the skraellings (savages) attacked in overwhelming numbers. In one battle the Norsemen were routed until Eric the Red's daughter exposed her breast and whetted a sword against it. This gesture so shocked the native New Englanders that they fled.

Greenlanders were so familiar with the North American coast that they had divided it into three regions—Helluland, the bleak wastes of Labrador; Markland, where Greenlanders went for masts and timbers for their boats and houses, and Vinland.

And medieval Europe was well aware of Greenland. For decades the bishopric of Greenland was part of the archbishopric of Hamburg, and the bishop of Greenland presided over 16 churches, a monastery and a nunnery. Three popes wrote of their concern for this remote Christian outpost. Greenland paid regular tithes and Greenland products were in brisk demand in Europe's markets—especially walrus thongs for ships' hawsers and white falcons for one of the Middle Ages' favorite sports. Intercourse between medieval Europe and the New World must have been considerable. But the Norsemen left few records. Men and ships shuttled to and fro as in a kind of Arctic fog. Now and then the fog parts for a tantalizing moment to show, for example, that bodies buried in late Greenland graves were dressed in the height of 15th Century fashion; or for a brief record: in 1121 "Bishop Erik Gnupsson . . . went to Vinland." Nothing more; the fog closes again.

But the Greenland traffic was not medieval Europe's only reminder that there was "something" beyond the green Sea of Darkness, the Atlantic. Sometimes off the shores of Europe and the Atlantic islands sailors found sticks carved with an intricate, savage art unknown to Europe. Sometimes the bodies of strange men floated up on the shores. These were not the bodies of Moors or Negroes with whom the late Middle Ages were increasingly familiar. They had broad faces and were probably Indians who had been carried thousands of miles by the Atlantic currents, after fates as mysterious as those of the men of the Kensington Stone. And some of those who saw them must have stared at those bodies with a wild surmise.

Thus medieval Europe strained toward America as a sail strains from a mast. But the wind that must fill it was fitful and lacked consistent force. That force was supplied by the Renaissance.

All things must be moved by spirit before they can be imagined by mind or achieved by hands. The Renaissance had begun as a spiritual ferment—in art, in literature, in learning, philosophy and science—whose energies began the shaping of the modern mind. The Age of Discovery was the energy of the Renaissance hurling itself into the conquest of space and distance to reveal the modern world. The qualities wanted for discovery were the qualities which the Renaissance nourished and which challenge calls forth in average men—alertness, audacity, durability, vigor, instant force. With the Age of Discovery the great door of opportunity for simple men began to swing back until it opened fully on the western world and became synonymous with America.

A religious and a practical challenge called forth these qualities. By the 15th Century the great Crusades were over. But the crusading temper still persisted, for the Mohammedan menace remained. The Mohammedan Turks were an aggressor nation. By 1453 they had captured Constantinople and extinguished the Byzantine Empire. In less than a hundred years they would be at the gates of Vienna. The Mohammedan Moors still ruled in southern Spain. The secular side of this situation concerned the trade with the East in textiles and spices—indispensable for the preservation of meat in those unrefrigerated days—which passed through Mohammedan hands. Turks, Arabs and Moors levied tariffs on everything that came by the overland trade routes from the East. Thus a sea route to India became a necessity and the underlying religious conflict explains why this commercial aim was constantly complicated among Spaniards and Portuguese by a crusading spirit that was always fanatical and sometimes more strongly cruel.

The Age of Discovery was made possible by certain technical developments and by the vision of two extraordinary men. The technical developments were in naval architecture, the construction of more seaworthy ships, first by the Genoese, who even in the 13th Century made voyages as far as the Canary Islands, and later by the Portuguese. Just as important were the development of the card compass, the quadrant (for rough reckoning of latitude) and the portolanos, practical navigators' charts of detailed exactitude.

The men were Henry the Navigator, a prince of Portugal, and Christopher Columbus, the wool carder of Genoa.

Prince Henry was the organizer of victory. His mother was a daughter of John of Gaunt, the English kingmaker. His cousin was Henry V of England, the victor of Agincourt. Henry established himself at Sagres (now Cape St. Vincent). On this rocky point he built a palace, a chapel (for he was an intensely religious man, ascetic and celibate), an observatory and housing for the cartographers, mathematicians and navigators who soon surrounded him. At Lagos nearby he constructed docks and shipyards. A systematic study of charts and navigators' records was begun. Soon Sagres had assembled the best geographical and nautical library in the world. Nautical instruments were developed. At Lagos the caravel, the best sailing ship of its time, was constructed.

Henry was obsessed with opening a sea route to the Guinea Coast of Africa and by a desire to find Prester John, the mythical Christian ruler whose fabulously wealthy kingdom the Middle Ages located first in Asia, then in Africa.

When Henry began his work no Portuguese navigator had been farther south than Cape Bojador. It took 12 years for a Portuguese ship to pass it. Criticism of Henry's projects as dangerous and profitless was intense. For while few navigators believed that the world was flat, many still believed that in the tropics "the sun poured down sheets of liquid flame," the ocean boiled and the searing heat turned white men black. But when Prince Henry's men passed Cape Blanco and brought back gold dust and slaves, criticism died away. Companies were quickly formed to exploit the new wealth.

Prince Henry took success with the same "virtuous obstinacy" as failure. He gave away his own share of the slaves, insisting that the captives be baptized, well-treated and taught trades. His interest in slavery was religious—"The salvation of those souls that before were lost." Religiously he belonged to the Middle Ages. But in practical matters he was a man of the Renaissance, driven by an intelligence whose mode was mathematics.

By the time Prince Henry died (1460) his captains had sailed south more than 2,000 miles and west to the Azores, almost a third of the way across the Atlantic. Portuguese projects became imperial. Negro chiefs were baptized up and down the coast of Africa. Ambassadors were dispatched to Cairo and Aden to get in touch with Prester John. They failed to find that elusive priest-king. But one of them made his way to Abyssinia and India and discovered the Arab trade routes on the Indian Ocean. It was a fateful discovery. Prince Henry's patience was paying off. In 1487 Bartolomeu Dias made the decisive voyage. His three ships pushed far toward the end of Africa. For 13 days, while the men's teeth chattered with fear and the cold, which suddenly became intense, the little ships were driven south before a storm. Then Dias turned north and found land to larboard. He had rounded the Cape of Good Hope and found the way around Africa.

Wrote Luís de Camões of his countrymen's exploits in *The Lusiad*, the epic of Portuguese discovery: "*E se mais mundo houvera, lá chegára*" ("And if there had been more of the world, they would have got there").

* * *

If Prince Henry prepared, Columbus personified the Age of Discovery. His story is one of the world's great legends, and the instinct of the world has been quite right to reject the censures of his detractors and to read between the lines of the legend the meaning of the age. Most meaning lay in the character of a man possessed of practically nothing but a great idea, which against tremendous odds he put across. The drama was merely heightened by the fact that the idea was right in theory and wrong in practice and that Columbus' failure was enormously more successful than his dream of success.

The idea, of course, was the paradox that the East could be reached most quickly by sailing west, that India, China and Japan lay not too far beyond the frightening silences and the terrifying rages of what Portuguese and Spaniards called "the Ocean Sea." The failure, due to a simple miscalculation of the earth's circumference, meant the providential disclosure of the land mass of the Americas.

One of Prince Henry's navigators had been a Portuguese nobleman named Bartolomeu Perestrello. He had been governor of the island of Porto Santo, off Africa. There his son-in-law Christopher Columbus had stayed, studying the maps and cosmographical works about which the Portuguese were so secretive. There too, it is rumored, came the Alonso Sánchez whose caravel had been blown off its course and carried to a strange western land, probably Haiti. Columbus took care of Sánchez, and when Sánchez died he left the future Admiral of the Ocean Sea instructions about how to reach the western land. Certainly in sailing west with the trade winds and east with the westerly winds, Columbus unerringly chose the best routes for coming from and returning to Spain.

The rest of the Columbian epic is familiar, evocative and satisfying. He tried to get backing from the King of Portugal and was turned down, paid court to Queen Isabella and King Ferdinand of Spain, had set out in despair to offer his services to the King of France when a royal messenger overtook him.

He had stood out for some rather stiff terms and got most of them. Columbus was to be admiral of all the seas and lands he might discover and this title was to be hereditary in his family. He was to be viceroy of his discoveries. He was to have 10% of all profits from the new lands.

The Spanish sovereigns also gave Columbus a letter with a blank space to be filled in with the name of the Grand Khan, Prester John or any other potentate he might meet with:

"To the most serene prince _____, our very dear friend, Ferdinand and Isabella, King and Queen of Castile, Aragon, Léon, etc., greeting and increase of good fortune. We have learned with joy of your esteem and high regard for us and our nation and of your great eagerness to receive information concerning our successes. Wherefore we have resolved to dispatch our noble captain Christopherus Colon to you, with letters, from which you may learn of our good health and prosperity. . . ."

On Aug. 3, 1492 Columbus' three vessels set sail from Palos. The *Niña* and the *Pinta* were smaller than many a Viking craft. The *Santa Maria* was larger. On board were 120 men, including an interpreter who spoke Hebrew, Greek, Chaldean and Arabic and might prove useful with the Grand Khan. The voyage (36 days) was exceptionally easy. But it was not so easy as moderns suppose. The crews' opinion of the Ocean Sea was much like Algernon Swinburne's,

> *Where beyond the extreme sea-wall and between the remote sea-gates,*
> *Waste water washes, and tall ships founder, and deep death waits.*

It was this grim mood that Columbus beat to his will as the three boats measured the thousands of miles of trackless sea with the sliding keels. Then, on the night of Oct. 11, Columbus saw a light. He called Pedro Gutiérrez, groom of the king's bedchamber, who also saw it. They called Rodrigo Sánchez, whom the sovereigns had sent along as their personal overseer. At first, as is the nature of such men, he did not see the light. But at last it was officially seen. "It appeared like a candle that went up and down, and Don Christopher did not doubt that it was a true light, and that it was on land; and so it proved, as it came from people passing with lights from one cottage to another."

The sovereigns had promised 10,000 *maravedis* to the man who first sighted land. At 2 o'clock in the morning Rodrigo de Triana, a sailor, cried, "Land ho!" from the *Pinta*. But the reward was given to Columbus for reasons reported by the Spanish historian Herrera: "He [Columbus] saw the light in the midst of darkness, signifying the spiritual light which was introduced amongst those barbarous people. . . ." In his disappointment Rodrigo de Triana became a Mohammedan.

The Spaniards went ashore on an island which the Indians called Guanahaní, probably Watlings Island in the Bahamas. While the natives watched in awe, Columbus unfurled the banners of Spain and renamed the island San Salvador. Falling on their knees, he and all his men uttered their "immense thanksgiving to Almighty God."

This was the moment toward which the vision had unknowingly tended. The rest was tumultuous anticlimax. Columbus was to enjoy a great triumph in Spain—soon chilled by the suspicion that his new lands were not Asia. He was to search with trifling results for gold and discover tobacco. He was to make three more voyages, discover the mainland of South America, see Central America and make his crew sign a statement that Cuba was a part of Asia. For he would not relinquish his vision of the greater reality. "*Il mondo è poco*— the world is small," he insisted, arguing to the bitter end against his glory and the facts of longitude. He was to prove himself an incompetent viceroy and be sent back to Spain in irons. There the sovereigns restored him to his dignities (but not to his authority) and there he died, an embittered and comfortably well-off man.

But the great moment had been on Guanahaní when he had turned a hemisphere from the darkness of oblivion to human knowledge and hope, as, in the subtropical light, the old world became a thing of the past and the actual world was revealed.

Before the Age of Discovery, Europe was a small but seethingly self-contained promontory, walled off from the greater part of the world by cliffs of ignorance and religious implacability. In the Age of Discovery the energy of the Renaissance, indefatigable and irresistible, hurled itself beyond those cliffs. Portugal outflanked the religious barriers of Arab, Turk and Moor by pioneering the sea route to India and the East. Five years after Columbus' first voyage, Vasco da Gama, following the route of Bartolomeu Dias, swept around the Cape of Good Hope up to Zanzibar across the Indian Ocean to Calicut on the coast of India.

The wealth of India flowed back to Europe. But the Renaissance, except for a savage commercial, military and religious energy, gave little to the East. It was too greedy, too intolerant and too busy exploiting.

Soon the Portuguese commander, Alfonso de Albuquerque, had swept the Arabs from the Eastern seas and established a Portuguese empire which controlled the Persian Gulf and the Indonesian trade. With the addition of Macao in China, this empire lasted until Dutch power rose in the 17th Century to dismember it.

But one more momentous voyage was made by a Portuguese (serving under the Spanish flag). In 1520 Fernando Magellan penetrated the strait that bears his name. He and the crews of his three ships were the first white men to burst into the ocean which he called Pacific—though a Spaniard, Vasco Núñez de Balboa, had already seen it from a peak in Darien and claimed it for the Spanish crown.

Antonio Pigafetta, one of the ships' company, has left a description of the first Pacific voyage. "We were three months and twenty days without getting any kind of fresh food. We ate biscuit, which was no longer biscuit but powder of biscuits swarming with worms, for they had eaten the food. It stank strongly of the urine of rats. We also ate some ox hides which covered the top of the mainyard . . . and which had become exceedingly hard. . . . We left them in the sea for four or five days, and then placed them for a few minutes on the top of the embers, and so ate them. Rats were sold for one-half ducat apiece, and even then we could not get them. . . ."

At last the one surviving ship limped back to Spain—without Magellan, for he had been killed in the Philippines in a fight with natives. The globe had been circumnavigated, its sphericity tragically demonstrated.

Spain's opportunity had been greater than Portugal's. For Spain dealt not with an ancient, tenacious, proliferating culture, but with vast colonizable tracts of the earth. The only aboriginal cultures that the Spaniards encountered, the splendid Inca and Aztec empires, they looted and obliterated. The conquistador Hernando Cortes with a handful of followers captured the capital of Montezuma and enslaved the Aztec nation. Francisco Pizarro, an illiterate who could not sign his own name, performed the same exploit on a greater scale in Peru, capturing the Inca king, extorting a ransom worth more than $15,500,000 and then killing him.

As Spain expended its energies on conquest and get-rich-quick plunder, new nations took to discovery. England had early sent out John Cabot, like Columbus a Genoese, who had become a naturalized Venetian. On two voyages he sighted the coast of North America. Like Columbus he thought that it was Asia. France sent off Juan Verrazano, a Florentine, and presently a galaxy of French explorers—Cartier, Champlain, La Salle, Pére Marquette—staked out the French claims to Canada, the Great Lakes country and the Mississippi Valley. The Dutch explored the Hudson River country.

It was soon pretty well understood that the New World was a continental land mass, and a frantic search began for a passage to Asia around or through the Americas. For the two continents had acquired a name. Amerigo Vespucci, a Florentine, sailing first under the Spanish, then under the Portuguese flag, had explored the coast of South America. Through a swindle or a map-making fumble, he had given his name to both continents.

From Peru and Mexico, the great treasure galleons still ferried to Spain the Inca and Aztec wealth and the gold and silver dug by those enslaved nations from the mines that had been theirs. The looted wealth and the immense proceeds of the Spanish and Portuguese import trade affected Europe in many ways. Luxuries became cheaper and more people enjoyed them. About a fifth of the new wealth was used for embellishment. Gold chains, cloth of gold and silver, gold and silver lace were widely used. Jewels from the East and the New World decked the well-to-do in new profusion. There was a fad of the new cheap fabrics—muslin, gingham, calico, chintz. Their cheapness promoted the wearing of underwear and the use of handkerchiefs. Carpets from Persia, and china, wallpaper and umbrellas introduced from China became popular.

In Spain and Portugal the wealth did very little good. The influx of bullion and the sudden increase in currency brought a weakening inflation. Neither Spain nor Portugal kept the wealth because they could not put it to work. It flowed quickly north to France, The Netherlands and England, which had what was lacking in the south: energy, efficient labor and an emerging middle class which could and did use the wealth to build up capital for their burgeoning capitalism.

Trade became the game of great powers, and the fight for it grew into wars of the 18th Century, which were fought over the resources and markets of the new worlds and which were later to sharpen in Europe the growing feeling of nationalism. The discoveries were unsettling in other ways. Travelers came back with stories of new kinds of people who worshiped different gods, lived under different forms of societies and yet seemed to get along very well in their worlds. People began to compare and question. A new sense of relative values brought with it an exciting skepticism which flowered in France's enlightenment.

But, more imposing than anything else, the explorations made Europe the base of world empire. Colonies became the support of countries who got them early and kept them. They also became the envy of those who came too late. The explorations made the world a place which more and more belonged to Europeans who, in exploiting it, also spread their culture and (what would have happened if another crusading religion, the Mohammedan, had discovered and colonized?) their Christianity.

A century after Columbus, the Age of Discovery had simmered down into the more humdrum business of colonization and an entirely new breed of discoverers appeared. Compared to the dashing Spaniards they were drab. But they too were stirred by religious motives. They were a minor group of dissenters, for the Reformation was tearing Europe apart.

In 1620 the Pilgrims set out in a leaky boat, the *Mayflower,* to plant the second successful English colony in North America. They were chiefly tradesmen and townfolk. They had come to live and worship as free men. They nearly perished of hunger and disease, for they were possibly the group most supremely unfitted to survive in a wilderness teeming with game, beside a sea crowded with fish. They learned from some of the world's worst farmers how to plant corn.

But they, too, had made a discovery which was, in its way, more important than any but Columbus'. And while not new, it was a discovery that has to be perpetually renewed before the eyes of the world so that civilization may not perish. It was: that it is better to die if that must be the price of freedom, but it is better yet to have the resolution and the strength to live that freedom may endure.

THE PROTESTANT REVOLUTION

(*Life*, JUNE 14, 1948)

ONE DISTRESSING DAY in the 16th Century a Roman Catholic bishop of Wales faced an unpleasant duty. Rawlins White, for 20 years an industrious and respectable fisherman of Cardiff had been arrested on a charge of heresy. The bishop, by nature a kindly man, might have to have the fisherman burned at the stake.

For the Protestant revolution had begun, and the titanic assertion that all men should be free to worship God according to their own consciences had resulted in the greatest spiritual crisis in Christian history. All over central and western Europe the new Protestant doctrines defied the authority of the Roman Catholic Church. They rent the seamless unity of Western Christendom and exposed the souls of those who professed them, and those they might mislead, to the dangers of an eternal hellfire so vivid to 16th Century minds that its foretaste in the flames of execution was little more than a just and merciful initiation.

Rawlins White might be let off if he would sign a simple recantation. Yet Rawlins White would not recant. The bishop tried promises and threats. White was stubborn. The bishop offered a prayer for his conversion. "You find," said White, "that your prayer is not granted, for I remain the same and God will strengthen me in support of this truth." The bishop said Mass. White would not bow down to the Host.

Three weeks later Rawlins White was led outside the city to be burned. Crowds followed. White wept when he passed his wife and children, who were also weeping. But at the stake he fell on his knees and kissed the ground. "Earth unto earth," he said, "and dust unto dust; thou art my mother, and unto thee I shall return."

Then he was chained on a heap of faggots with his back against the stake. Some of the crowd shouted, "Put fire! Set on fire!" The straw blazed up and the wood burned with a steady flame in which, after the custom of his kind, Rawlins White bathed his sinful hands until the flesh burned away and the sinews shrank. As sometimes happened the fire was too low, so that White's legs were burned completely away before his upper body was touched. As a result he fell from the supporting chains and his torso was consumed among the embers. But as long as he was able, White cried with a loud voice, "Lord, receive my spirit."

Slowly the crowd, each man with his own thoughts, turned back to the city. For few, whatever their beliefs, could fail to sense that when a fisherman, as obscure as any who fished in Galilee, chose to die in fire rather than deny his faith, there was at work in the world a force capable of transforming it. That transforming was the Reformation.

Men pay lip homage to the Middle Ages and Renaissance and are sometimes aware of their heritage. But the Reformation, one of the most decisive ages in history, is much less familiar though its results and influences are all around us and press upon even the least conscious man every time he enters a Roman Catholic or a Protestant church.

The Reformation, which split Christendom irreparably into Protestants and Catholics, was, to begin with, wholly the work of Roman Catholics. For in the early 16th Century all Europeans were Catholics. The simplified version of the story is that the Protestant revolution was a result of the moral, political and financial corruption of the Roman Catholic Church. This corruption was flagrant and undeniable and a source of shame and grief to all devout 16th Century Catholics. It was wholly and solely the intention of most of the dissident Catholics to reform those abuses. Only in the course of that reform did it become clear that the real issue was much deeper and more divisive. That issue was a difference in religious viewpoint, and perhaps of quality of soul, between those (the orthodox Catholics) who in worshiping felt the need for a "machinery of mediation"—priesthood, sacraments, ritual—between the soul of man and God, and those (the Protestants) who in worshiping preferred to leave the soul face to face with God. It was the difference between a largely objective form of religion and a more nearly subjective form of religion. It was the sundering choice between authority and freedom. This difference cut across the body of faith and only a forcible suture could heal it. The Roman Catholic Church attempted that suture and, in a struggle of unparalleled ferocity lasting some 150 years, it failed.

This ferocious struggle coincided with the Age of Discovery and was complicated by a political change that crystallized from the somewhat shapeless medieval political structure a new firm political form—the nation. It was further complicated by a social transformation that brought to a new position of power and usefulness in the world a new class—the middle class—which found in the Protestant religion with its accent on individual responsibility, industry and sobriety a congenial faith.

The Reformation was one of those fierce pulsations of the mind and spirit through which, in the turbulence and tragedy of growth, Western civilization has repeatedly released great circles of liberating and irradiating energy. In retrospect the Age of the Reformation seems like one of those portentous panoramas which Tintoretto was painting in Venice (for the late Renaissance was also in full swing) in which the violence of the movement of rushing masses of men is caught up and intensified in the violence of the swirling and livid sky.

For this age knew massacres that resembled battles—like that of St. Bartholomew's day in France when Catholics murdered more than 10,000 Protestants at the signal of the tocsin that still clangs shudderingly down the centuries. It knew persecutions that in duration, brutality and numbers of victims resembled serial massacres. It knew wars, civil wars and rebellions. It saw the revolt of the Dutch Protestants against King Philip II, and the rise of the Dutch republic. It saw the war between Protestant England and Catholic Spain and the epic repulse of the Armada. It saw prolonged civil wars in Scotland, France, Switzerland and later in England, where the drama was heightened by the execution of a king (Charles I). In Germany civil war turned into a Thirty Years' War and became general when most of Europe joined in. And above the rush of armies and the crash of cannon were heard the groans of martyrs and the awesome invective of bigots.

It has been observed that in the name of religion the Reformation caused more death and destruction than the Huns. For when men are resolved to test in agony the three insights that constitute their highest manhood—love of truth, love of freedom and that love of God from which alone the other two derive their meaning—horror is an inevitable reflex of humanity at strife. Nor does this horror impair at all that prayer in which the whole aspiration of the age was condensed, in which both sides might have united and to which John Milton, the Reformation's greatest poet, gave voice:

> "What in me is dark
> Illumine, what is low raise and support;
> That, to the highth of this great argument,
> I may assert Eternal Providence,
> And justify the ways of God to men."

A curious ecclesiastical deal, cynical even for that age, touched off the great charge. Prince Albert of Brandenburg, already Archbishop of Magdeburg and Bishop of Halberstadt, had in 1514 secured the Archbishopric of Mainz. But canon law forbade one man to hold three bishoprics. So the great 16th Century banking house of Fugger lent Albert the money for the bribe which he would pay Pope Leo X to confirm him in his three offices. Representatives of both parties met formally and discussed the bribe. The Pope's deputies asked for 12,000 ducats—a thousand for each of the 12 apostles. Albert's men said 7,000 ducats—a thousand for each of the seven deadly sins. A compromise was reached on 10,000 ducats.

To make sure that the obligation would be met, Pope Leo X had granted to Albert the privilege of selling indulgences. Indulgences were promises by the Pope to remit punishment in Purgatory for sins committed in this world. They were sold on a sliding scale of prices adjusted to the sinner's means and the grossness of his sin. Half the proceeds of the sale would go to Albert to repay the Fuggers. Half would go to the Pope. He needed the money badly, for he was rebuilding St. Peter's Church in Rome.

As pious Catholics, many Germans found the indulgences shocking. As Germans, they found it infuriating. The Catholic Church owned more than a third of all the land in Germany. Germans were tired of seeing their wealth drained away to foot the high cost of Renaissance living in Rome.

Then one day in 1517 Martin Luther, an Augustinian monk and theologian at the Saxon University of Wittenberg, nailed to the door of the church 95 theses or propositions. Like most Germans, Luther knew nothing about the deal between the Pope and the archbishop. He knew only that the indulgence money was to be used to rebuild St. Peter's. And he believed that the indulgence was theologically and morally wrong. His theses denied the right or power of the Pope to grant indulgences at all. One of Luther's theses said:

"The Pope is not able to remit guilt except by declaring it forgiven by God or in cases reserved to himself. . . .

"It is certain that avarice is fostered by the money clinking in the chest, but to answer the prayers of the church is in the power of God alone. . . ."

Luther's was by no means the first reforming voice in Europe. The Humanists, the intellectuals of the age, steeped in the Renaissance revival of Greek and Latin letters, had long been critical of the Church. Erasmus, the greatest of them, had made its corruptions the target of his witty and elegant learning. In France the Humanist, Lefèvre d'Etaples, was developing that strain of criticism which, amplified and clarified by John Calvin, would later bring the Reformation to a new pitch of power. In Zurich, Ulrich Zwingli was also preaching reform.

But it was Luther's voice that caught the listening ear of Europe. Thousands who read his theses or heard them read, heard too in the words of the unknown monk the tone of a strong man who is acting not because he wills to but because, under God, he cannot do otherwise.

The reaction staggered Luther. It also puzzled Pope Leo X. This son of Lorenzo the Magnificent, the greatest of the great banking family of Medici, the political masters of Florence, had been tonsured at the age of 7. At 13 he became a cardinal. At 17 he voted in the papal curia. "Let us enjoy the papacy," he is reported to have said on his election as Pope, "now that God has given it to us." An astute intelligence glittering with the sectarian refinements of the Renaissance and preoccupied with the vast political designs of the Church, Leo X found it difficult to grasp the religious point of the dispute in Saxony.

Not until 1520 did Leo X issue against Luther the bull, *Exsurge Domine*, which declared Luther's opposition to indulgences heretical and called upon him to recant within 60 days or be excommunicated.

Luther decided upon a dramatic action. On a great bonfire outside Wittenberg he publicly burned the books of the canon law, signifying that he was no longer bound by it. Then he dropped into the flames the papal bull. As it sank into ashes, the millennial ideal of a united Christendom sank into ashes with it.

In three powerful pamphlets Luther formulated his position. He attacked the authority of the papacy and, in tune with the mounting spirit of nationalism that marked the age, called upon the restive German nobility to free themselves from the alien tyranny of papal power. He denied three fundamental positions of the Church: that only the Pope may interpret the Bible authoritatively; that only the Pope may call a Church council; that the priesthood is superior to the laity. These positions he denied in the name of the doctrine of the priesthood of all believers—the doctrine that spiritually every Christian is before God his own priest.

Next he attacked the Catholic sacraments. He found full justification only for the Eucharist and baptism and partial justification for penance. Confirmation, marriage, holy orders and extreme unction might be customs worthy of the Church's blessing, but he denied that they were sacraments. Yet it was by these sacraments that the Church kept men in fear.

Then he defined his own faith: that salvation is possible not by good works, as the Catholics maintained, but by faith in Christ, and faith alone.

There was to be one more great historic scene. In 1521 Charles V, recently elected Holy Roman Emperor, convoked an imperial Diet at Worms. A minor item on the agenda was "to take notice of the books and descriptions made by Friar Martin Luther against the Court of Rome." There the crowds jammed the streets and thronged the Bishop's Palace so solidly that late-comers to the Diet had to get in through the gardens of the houses in the rear. Luther was kept standing outside the door for two hours. Then he was summoned in.

At one end of the crowded, sweltering hall stood the peasant's son, freshly tonsured and wearing his black Augustinian robes.

At the other end of the hall sat the most powerful monarch in the world. It was one of the most momentous confrontations and one of the most momentous hours in history. Beyond the hall all Europe watched.

For two days Luther and the papal legates fenced theologically in Latin. At last he spoke simply and briefly: "Since Your Majesty and your Lordships ask for a plain answer, I will give you one without either horns or teeth. Unless I am convinced by Scripture or by right reason, for I trust neither in popes nor in councils, since they have often erred and contradicted themselves—unless I am thus convinced, I am bound by the texts of the Bible, my conscience is captive to the Word of God. I neither can nor will recant anything, since it is neither right nor safe to act against conscience. God help me. Amen."

The emperor rose abruptly and left the hall. Luther slipped out of the city. On the road to Wittenberg he was seized by soldiers. They were the Elector of Saxony's men. The elector had long been Luther's friend. He had Luther conducted secretly to the Castle of the Wartburg where he hid until danger of assassination should pass.

In the Wartburg Luther undertook another imperative task—the translation of the New Testament into idiomatic German. Before the Reformation the doctrines of the Catholic Church were the sole authority for what a Christian might believe. Not the Church but the Bible, Luther contended, was the sole authority for faith. Nor could any Christian who read the Bible reverently fail to understand God's word.

But in the 16th Century comparatively few Christians had read the Bible. It had been the first book printed when the new art was invented (c. 1450) and at the time of the Reformation there were more Bibles in Europe than ever before. But these were in Latin. Wycliffe, the 14th Century English reformer, had translated part of the Bible. But the Church banned the reading of vernacular translations.

Luther's powerful version was the first great work in modern German, and his vigorous, idiomatic prose influenced the German language in much the same way that the King James version influenced English.

In earlier ages the Lutheran outbreak might have been quickly suppressed. In the 16th Century nationalist feelings were stirring the German princes to resist the Holy Roman Emperor. A number of princes rallied around Luther. A meeting of the princes at Spires declared in effect that the princes were free to regulate religion in their own territories. When later this decision was repealed by Catholics, the Lutheran and Zwinglian churches protested, and it is from this protest that the new religion got its name: Protestant.

The liberating force of Luther's doctrines resulted in a social tragedy. Excited by the atmosphere of revolt, the German peasants, who lived in conditions of medieval servitude, took fire and in the course of a savage revolt committed frightful atrocities. Luther, shocked by the peasant excesses and seeing his lifework threatened by the peasants' appeal to his doctrines, urged the authorities to drown the insurrection in blood. This action helped to identify Lutheranism with civil authority, fixed its political forms and may have inhibited its inner growth and spread abroad. Scandinavia and Denmark accepted the new church. But there the Lutheran advance halted. The task of spreading Protestantism passed to another man, John Calvin.

Through Calvin the Reformation ceased to be a national movement (as Lutheranism had largely become). Inspired by his vision, expressed in all but faultless logic and infused with invincible purpose, Protestantism, in the form of Calvin's Reformed Church, would henceforth leap frontiers and convert whole nations.

Calvin, born in France in 1509, turned from the study of theology to law, returned to theology and, when only 27, produced his great work, *Institutes of the Christian Religion*. This was the most rational of all Protestant theologies.

It could meet on equal terms the profound and highly developed theology of the Roman Catholic Church. The central sun, illuminating Calvin's system, was his faith that God is infinite and perfect—infinitely good and infinitely glorious. Man, by Adam's original sin, is wholly wicked. Yet man must "aspire to the goodness which he lacks, to the liberty of which he is deprived." God commands men to fulfill the law only to make them realize that they can do nothing without Him. God merely desires men to realize their weakness so that they will rely on Him in all things.

Moreover man is predestined, and this historically is the central, dominant doctrine of Calvinism. From eternity God has foreordained every good or evil act that every man will commit. From eternity He has predestined all who are to be righteous and all who are to be sinners. The righteous are, by predestination, God's elect. The sinners are, by predestination, reprobate. Since there is no way of knowing who is elect and who is not, the Christian must use this life in doing what he can for God's greater glory.

This was a harsh and somber doctrine appropriate to an age when hundreds of Frenchmen who confessed the Protestant faith lived as fugitives in the woods or caves, and even those who did not daily faced the poignant possibilities of prison, torture or death at the stake. Yet this somber theology did not stultify men's spiritual fervor or inhibit their hope. For with its awesome accent on fearful and godly living, it released into the daily secular life of men an asceticism hitherto known only to the monastic life at its highest. Worldly activity was no longer a secular tumult apart from, and largely opposed to, the life of the spirit, but an opportunity whereby men could best demonstrate the vehemence of their faith. The Calvinist had discovered that men are as great not only as what they can do but as what they can do without. Simplicity became a style of the soul and lent it a pathos of rare beauty. Rectitude, when it did not lapse into self-righteousness, became a style of character and was allied to resolution. Rational faith, when it did not freeze into bigotry, induced a style of mind in which perfect assurance fathered enterprise.

As the new middle class rose to new power with the increase of commerce and industry that resulted from the discovery of the New World and the opening of the new trade route to India, it found in Calvinism a faith in which the characteristic middle-class virtues of initiative, thrift, prudence, probity and sober living were specifically prescribed as the way of life most pleasing to God. Calvinism sanctioned enterprise and set a tone of religious and ethical dealing that, whatever the lapses from it, became the standard for this great creative energy of men. For implicit in Calvinism was the injunction to establish the City of God on earth.

The great attempt was made in Geneva, a free Protestant city. There Calvin, passing through in 1536 on his flight from Catholic France, was urged to remain and preach. His first attempt to introduce the Calvinist scheme of the good life was a failure. The unregenerate Genevese resented his efforts to ban dancing, card-playing, drinking, sports and gay clothes. Calvin was threatened, insulted, shot at. Mobs formed and riots broke out. At last he was ordered to leave the city.

But the implacable reforms had touched the Genevese soul; he was invited back. Calvin refused to return until he was granted power to carry out his reforms. For some 20 years he was the religious and moral ruler of Geneva. He was a chronically sick man and violent opposition to him was continuous. But an inexhaustible spiritual energy disciplined his ailing body. He organized the Reformed Church and in his *Ecclesiastical Ordinances* laid down his program of reform, adapting the church to the reformed life of the people so that the city itself might become a church. He established a university so that a ministry might be properly trained to spread his gospel with learning and authority. He made Geneva a haven for Protestant refugees from other lands, so that Geneva became a citadel for defense of the faith and an arsenal for its dissemination. He did not hesitate to burn men at the stake or torture and behead them to fulfill his purpose.

From Geneva spread the invigorating waves of triumphant purpose that strengthened the Dutch in their long struggle to achieve a republic free from Spain. John Knox found a haven there and went forth to harangue Mary Queen of Scots on her queenly duties and lead a civil war that turned Scotland into a Calvinist land.

When Calvin died in 1564, he left Protestantism strong and expanding. But a new force—the Catholic Counter Reformation—had already gathered strength and would henceforth successfully oppose the Protestant advance.

No part of Western Christendom remained wholly untouched by Lutheran or Calvinist teachings. Yet throughout Europe there was a solid core of Catholic piety which might abhor abuses in the Church but abhorred even more the thought of leaving it. For such Christians the Church was "My Father's House" and in its many mansions there was peace for almost any kind of soul. Upon this piety the Church based its Counter Reformation, the great effort to purge itself of abuses and regain the souls that it had lost.

For this purpose Pope Paul III, on the suggestion of the Emperor Charles V, called a Church council at Trent. The Council of Trent began its sessions in 1545. It ended them, after several adjournments, in 1563. The council blocked any last chance of reconciliation with Lutheranism, gave the Pope authority almost unlimited in scope and unprecedented in history and set up machinery for reform.

The reform of churches and monasteries began at once. Simony, nepotism, the sale of fat posts at the papal court, the sale of justice in the papal courts, luxurious living were quickly swept away. Prelates were compelled to reside at their benefices. Great banquets, hunting parties, splendid liveries were abolished. Immorality was sternly repressed. Seminaries were opened for the proper education of priests. A new uniformity in faith and ritual was imposed.

Two great engines of authority implemented the Counter Reformation—the Inquisition and the Society of Jesus. The Inquisition was the Counter Reformation's spiritual police. It had been founded by St. Dominic in the 13th Century for the purpose of detecting heretics and bringing them to justice. It had succeeded in exterminating the Albigenses, 12th Century French heretics. It had all but wiped out the Waldenses, a 12th Century reforming group, some of whom survived to form the oldest of all Protestant churches. In the 15th Century the Inquisitor General, Torquemada, is estimated to have condemned 114,000 persons in 18 years, of whom 10,220 were burned at the stake. No such rigor was shown by the Italian Inquisition during the Counter Reformation despite the increased activity of the Holy Office. But still, to achieve justice and doctrinal conformity some people had to be burned and a colony of 4,000 Waldenses was killed or sold into slavery.

While the Inquisition policed the regenerated Church, the Society of Jesus infused into it a new moral and intellectual vigor, vitalizing its dogma and buttressing the secular power of the Pope, to whose support they were specifically dedicated.

The founder of the order, one of the world's supreme leaders of men, was Iñigo López de Recalde, better known as St. Ignatius de Loyola. Born the year before Columbus discovered the New World, in his father's castle of Loyola in Spain's Basque country, Loyola was 30 when the French invaded Navarre. During the war he was wounded in the leg and left lame for life. He was convinced that his life had been spared by the intervention of St. Peter. St. Ignatius decided to renounce the world and devote himself to defending the Roman Catholic faith.

At a Dominican monastery in Catalonia, Loyola disciplined himself cruelly. He lived on bread and water, knelt for seven hours in prayer, scourged himself three hours daily and scarcely slept at all. Sometimes he was plagued by visions. Despair engulfed him. He was tempted to suicide. During the sickness that followed he became convinced that his extreme asceticism had been folly. Angels appeared to him, showing him the road to salvation, and the saint decided to dedicate his body as well as his soul to God. For Loyola was, above all, a man of action.

He preached and gathered a group of disciples. These activities brought him to the notice of the Inquisition, which imprisoned him. Loyola cleared himself of heresy, but the Holy Office sentenced him to study theology for four years.

In time Loyola again gathered nine disciples who took oaths of poverty and chastity. He determined to form a holy order, called the Company of Jesus, a spiritual militia which was to be headed by a general, elected for life with unlimited command over the order.

Loyola became the first general and for the remaining 16 years of his life directed the order's discipline and multitudinous activities. The purpose of his mission was to strengthen the Church by penetrating European society, influencing the men of all ranks who controlled it, directing education, gaining control of the confessional and preaching the faith in ways which would appeal to the imagination and weaknesses of the time. He planned to win the world through the vices and weakness of the world.

To this end he forbade asceticism (it is better, he wrote, to strengthen the stomach and other faculties than to impair the body and enfeeble the intellect by fasting). He emphasized social arts which could ingratiate the Jesuits with people of influence. He preferred recruits "less marked by pure goodness than by firmness of character and ability in conduct of affairs. . . ." In dealing with the world the Jesuits should act like "good fishers of souls, passing over many things in silence as though these had not been observed, until the time came when the will was gained, and the character could be directed as they thought best." The Church was always right: "If she teaches that what seems white to us is black, we must declare it to be black upon the spot."

A cheerful and intelligent worldliness was the Jesuit's public face. His personal life belonged to his order. He owned nothing. He was sent where the general ordered. He could be expelled and ruined in a moment. He spied and was constantly spied on so that an enormous mass of internal intelligence reports constantly cluttered the desk of the general, who was himself subject to the surveillance of five spies of the order officially appointed for that purpose. In a generation the Jesuits had spread their organization over most of Europe. Kings, ruling groups, strategically placed persons and even whole governments (like that of Portugal) were in their hands. And though their success, power and insistence on the principle that the end justifies the means made them dreaded even by Catholics, there was no question that their martial morale and cryptic activities had rejuvenated the Church at its lowest ebb and mightily helped to check the Protestant Reformation at its height.

The Protestant revolution not only changed the religious map of Europe. The interplay of secular forces with the religious ferment remade the political and economic structure and produced at last a new emergent type of man—the political and economic individualist.

The proper service of God implied not a withdrawal from the world but an intensification of worldly activity as the highest of individual religious and moral duties. Luther had advanced the idea against monkhood. Calvin gave it dogmatic form and crusading fervor. To the new man emerging from the Protestant revolution, as to Milton's Adam and Eve expelled from Paradise, "the world was all before them." Business was ascetic discipline. Work was prayer. The new spirit of the age is epitomized in the titles of its books. *The Tradesman's Calling, The Religious Weaver, Husbandry Spiritualized, Navigation Spiritualized.*

Men born early in the 16th Century found themselves at its close living in a world as different as the Atomic from the Edwardian Age. In their boyhood the Catholic Church was the uniquely dominant spiritual power whose overthrow was inconceivable. In their old age, the Catholic Church had lost many of the western and northern nations and was reduced to a competing power even in France. In their boyhood, the uniform secular power of the Church, of which the Holy Roman Empire was one expression, extended from Gibraltar to Poland. In their old age, the idea of nationalism had congealed into the fact of nations. Men no longer thought of themselves as members of medieval communities, more or less local, but as Englishmen, Frenchmen, Dutchmen, Spaniards.

For the rising rulers of the new nations, religion became sometimes a reason and sometimes an excuse for political action. England's Henry VIII set up the Church of England because he wanted political autonomy from the Pope—as well as the Church's wealth and freedom to pursue his own matrimonial and dynastic ambitions. Queen Elizabeth waited 10 years after her accession before she decided it was the wisest for her and England to declare herself Protestant. The Reformation was utterly entangled in the big and small politics of the continent. Especially was it entangled in the glorious rise of the Dutch republic.

The Netherlands, a nation subject to Spain, had become in the Age of Discovery a commercial rival of Spain! To keep down the cocky Dutchmen, Spain put on heavier and heavier taxes. The teachings of Luther and Calvin spread quickly in the Low Countries, and with them spread revolt against Spain. Since Spain was the bastion of the Catholic Church, the rebellions and reprisals became religious wars. The wars began about 1560 and lasted nearly a century. But by 1581 the issue was settled: the Dutch had won their political, economic and religious freedom. The Dutch middle class, emerging with the new political and religious freedom, became the shining model for successful Protestantism, practising in its pursuit of wealth and satisfaction the virtues which Calvin preached.

At the beginning of the century, trade and business had been concentrated in the Mediterranean basin, and Venice was the chief funnel by which the imports from the East trickled into Europe. By the end of the century Europe had faced West, and through the open sea gate of the Atlantic poured an unprecedented volume of wealth and goods which was beginning to turn the new centers of Western Europe from predominantly agricultural to predominantly trading, commercial and industrial powers. The treasure of Asia and the New World and the increased production of European mines and looms were making possible massive concentrations of capital in the hands of the great banking companies like the Welsers, Fuggers, Meutings, Haugs and Hochstetters. Capitalism had been born. War itself was big business and the wars of faith, financed by the new capitalists, extended their control, in the form of loans, over politics. The politics of the age might seem to be made by the emperor, the Pope or the kings of the new, self-conscious nations. But these mighty figures were themselves in the hands of their brokers.

The spirit of freedom which found its religious expression in Protestantism found its secular expression in commerce. Commerce was the high adventure of the age, calling forth in a supreme degree the qualities that the new faith and the wars of faith developed—individual initiative, enterprise, vigor, perseverance. To this spirit, mysticism was meaningless and embarrassing.

With the fruits of godly living came the fruits of good living. A nice materialism rewarded and embellished secular life. The great Reformation art is art like that of the Dutch, which ceases, for the first time in European painting, to be religious and seeks to capture the spirit of simple, material things and everyday scenes.

Nor did the energy of the new spirit stop with the 16th Century or the continent of Europe. It leaped the Atlantic Ocean and prepared to clear a continental forest, eliminate the remnants of stone-age man and make an appropriate space where the new dignity of the individual, safeguarded by his new freedom of faith could, under God, build a citadel, an arsenal and an altar.

FIVE

Letters
from
Westminster

THE SANITY OF ST. BENEDICT

(*Commonweal*, SEPTEMBER 19, 1952)

QUEEN VICTORIA left this world almost at the moment that I chanced to
enter it. Her memory, when I was old enough to identify it, fell thinly
across my earliest childhood. People still spoke of "the Queen," as if in all
history there had been only one and everybody must know at once that Queen
Victoria was meant. Somewhat later, I sensed that her going had stirred a
deep-set uneasiness, as if with her a part of the mainland of human experience
had sunk into the sea and no one quite knew what further subsidences and
commotions to expect. Yet, in those far-off days, no one ever chanted to me
that grim line of the Queen's favorite poet:

And the great aeon sings in blood:

though I was not very old when I had the "Death of Arthur" read to me in full,
and, after the depressingly long glories of the winter moon, I noted with relief
that

The new sun rose, bringing the new year.

With the rest of my generation, I grew in that sun's illusory light. For the
historical skies of my boyhood were only infrequently troubled, chiefly by a
triad of figures powerful and unpredictable enough to thrill from time to time
the nerve of reality. They were, of course, in America, Theodore Roosevelt: in
England, King Edward VII: and, on the continent of Europe, bestriding it like
a self-inflated colossus, the German Kaiser. Each had a characteristic motif,
too, like a Wagnerian hero: a little repetitive phrase that set the historic mood
or forecast that each, for good or ill, was about to vault again upon the world
stage, to give some new tingling turn to the plot. Thus, from the heart of
Europe, would come characteristic variations on the Bismarckian theme of
Blut und Eisen. In America, rose blithe shouts of "Bully! It's bully!" While
Edwardian England had reversed the plea in which Swinburne exhorted Walt
Whitman to "send but a song oversea to us," and both shores of the Atlantic
rocked to the surge and thunder of Tarara-boom-de-ay.

Long before I had the slightest notion what the barbaric sounds might
mean, as language or destiny, I listened fascinated to people chanting:

257

A Brussels carpet on the floor:
An elevator at the door:
Tarara-boom-de-ay; Tarara-boom-de-ay!

It was not only because of its gayness that it embedded itself in my memory. For what others found gay, I found indefinably ominous, as fixing a tone, a touch of dissolution that, even as a sensitive child, I could not possibly have explained to myself or anybody else. But one day, much later, the echo of Tarara-boom-de-ay fused itself unexpectedly with something that would seem to have nothing to do with it—a more or less random remark by one of my college instructors in Contemporary Civilization.

Contemporary Civilization, a course required for all freshmen at Columbia College, was taught by several young men whom I remember chiefly as rather lugubrious—disillusioned veterans of the First World War, and a conscientious objector who had refused to take part in it. One day, the objector, staring at some point far beyond the backs of our heads, observed that "the world is entering upon a new Dark Age."

It was one of the few things that I carried away from Contemporary Civilization, required for all freshmen. And it was not so much the meaning of the words, which I was far too unfledged to understand, as the toneless despondency with which they were uttered that struck me. That, and their acceptance of the Dark Ages as something relevant, and possibly recurrent in history.

For under the sunlit skies of my boyhood, the Dark Ages were seldom mentioned: if at all, chiefly by way of contrast to the light of our progress. For the voice of that time was, at least as it reached me, wholly incapable of the irony with which, little more than a decade later, Jean de Bosschere would ask: *"Qui se leva pour dire que nous ne sommes pas en plein jour?"*

The Dark Ages were inexcusable and rather disreputable—a bad time when the machine of civilization in its matchless climb to the twentieth century had sheared a whole rank of king-pins and landed mankind in a centuries-long ditch. At best, it was a time when monks sat in unsanitary cells with a human skull before them, and copied and re-copied, for lack of more fruitful employment, the tattered records of a dead antiquity. That was the Dark Ages at best, which, as anybody could see, was not far from the worst.

If a bright boy, leafing through history, asked: "How did the Dark Ages come about?" he might be told that "Rome fell!"—as if a curtain simply dropped. Boys of ten or twelve, even if bright, are seldom bright enough to say to themselves: "Surely, Rome did not fall in a day." If a boy had asked: "But were there no great figures in the Dark Ages, like Teddy Roosevelt, King Edward and the Kaiser?", he might well have been suspected of something like an unhealthy interest in the habits and habitats of spiders. If he had persisted and asked: "But isn't it clear that the Dark Ages are of a piece with our age of light, that our civilization is by origin Catholic, that, in fact, we cannot understand what we have become without understanding what we came from?", he would have been suspected of something much worse than priggery—a distressing turn to Popery.

I was no such bright boy (or youth). I reached young manhood serene in the knowledge that, between the failed light of antiquity and the buzzing incandescence of our own time, there had intervened a thousand years of darkness from which the spirit of man had begun to liberate itself (intellectually) first in the riotous luminosity of the Renaissance, in Humanism, in the eighteenth century, and at last (politically) in the French Revolution. For the dividing line between the Dark Ages and the Middle Ages is not fast, and they were easily lumped together.

To be sure, even before Queen Victoria died, the pre-Raphaelites had popularized certain stage properties of the Middle Ages. And on the Continent there had been Novalis, to mention only one name (but no one in my boyhood mentioned Novalis). There had been Huysmans (we knew Huysmans, but his name was touched with decadence). There was a fad of the Gothic and figures like Viollet-le-Duc: while an obscure American, Henry Adams, was even then composing *Mont St. Michel* and *Chartres*, and indicting certain thoughts on the Virgin and the Dynamo that would echo briefly above the clink of their swizzle sticks in the patter of my generation.

I was in my twenties, a young intellectual savage in college with thousands of others, before the fact slowly dawned upon me that, for a youth always under the spell of history, the history I knew was practically no history at all. It consisted of two disjointed parts—the history of Greece and Rome, with side-trips to Egypt and the Fertile Crescent: and a history of the last four hundred years of Europe and America. Of what lay in between, what joined the parts and gave them continuity, and the pulse of life and breath of spirit, my ignorance was darker than any Dark Age. Less by intelligence than by the kind of sixth sense which makes us aware of objects ahead in the dark, I divined that a main land-mass of the history of Western civilization loomed hidden beyond my sight.

I turned briefly to medieval history. But the distinguished teachers who first guided me into the Dark Ages seemed, even to my blindness, not too sure of their own way. They knew facts, more facts than I would ever know. Yet in their understanding of the facts something was missing, something that would enable them to feel that the life of the times they were exploring was of one tissue with the life of ours, that neither could be divided from the other, without an arterial tearing, that neither could be understood without the other. Their exposition, even of so obvious a problem as the causes for the fall of the Roman West, left me with a sense of climbing railless stairs above a chasm at night.

Rome fell, I learned, because of the barbarian hordes and a series of great barbarian leaders. H. G. Wells would presently startle me with the information that the hordes had been comparative handfuls among the populations they conquered, while, somewhat later, I would come to believe that the barbarian leaders were scarcely more barbarian than the Romans, that many of them were disaffected officials of the Roman state and their conduct was not so much that of invaders as what we should now call Fifth Columnists.

Or I was taught that Rome's collapse was due in part to the disrepair of the Roman roads and the breakdown of communication. Or the resurgence of the Pontine marshes and the high incidence of malaria at Rome. Or that the conquest of the East had introduced alien and indigestible masses into the Empire, and corrupted Rome, and so it fell. But even a collegiate savage could scarcely fail to note that it was precisely the corrupt Eastern half of the Empire that survived as a political unit, and, for another eight hundred years, stood against the vigorous East, and was the bulwark of the fallen West.

There were other facts and factors. My ignorance could question them only so far, and then not their reality for the most part, but their power to explain by themselves an event so complex and so thunderous as the crash of a civilization. Some more subtle dissolvent, I sensed, must also have been, undivined, at work. I thought I had caught a hint of it in Salvianus' *moritur et ridet:* "The Roman Empire is luxurious, but it is filled with misery. It is dying but it laughs—*moritur et ridet*." But Salvian, we learned with a deflecting smile, was an extremist, though, in the hindsight of disaster, his foresight would scarcely seem overstated. What interested me was that men had smiled complacently at Salvian's words when he spoke them, and men still smiled at them complacently a thousand years later—the same kind of men, I was beginning to suspect, who smiled upon a similar turning point of history.

In any case, for me it was too late. What the missing something was in the crisis of Rome I was not to learn in classrooms. The crisis of civilization in my own time had caught me in its undertow and soon swept me far beyond that earlier Dark Ages. Not until it had cast me back upon its rocks, by grace a defeated fugitive from its forces, would I again find peace or pause to seek to determine what, if anything, that mortal experience had taught me about the history of our time, or any other.

This century was half gone, and with it more than half my life, that at that moment seemed all but to have ended in an ordeal with which my name is linked, when someone, seeking only to comfort me, once more directed my eyes to that particular point in the past from which, some thirty years before, I had abruptly taken them.

Anne Ford, my friend of many years standing, sent me from the Monastery of Gethsemani a little silver medal, blessed in my family's name and mine, by Father Louis—Thomas Merton of *The Seven-Storey Mountain*, who, as a later student, had sat in the same college classrooms, listening to some of the same instructors I had known. On the medal was an image of St. Benedict.

I found myself asking who St. Benedict had been. I knew that he had founded a monastic order, which bore his name, and that for it he had written a famous Rule.

I had once written a little news story about plans for the restoration of his monastery of Monte Cassino after its destruction in the World War of 1939. What I had written had presumably been read at least by one hundred thousand people (so much for journalism in our time). But a seeker after knowledge at any age, certainly one fifty years old, must begin by confessing that he probably knew less about St. Benedict than many a pupil in parochial school. Nor, had I asked a dozen friends, regarded as highly intelligent by themselves and the world, could one of them have told me much more about St. Benedict than I knew myself. The fact that such ignorance could exist, could be taken as a matter of course, was more stunning than the abyss of ignorance itself.

For the briefest prying must reveal that, simply in terms of history, leaving aside for a moment his sanctity, St. Benedict was a colossal figure on a scale of importance in shaping the civilization of the West against which few subsequent figures could measure. And of those who might measure in terms of historic force, almost none could measure in terms of good achieved.

Nor was St. Benedict an isolated peak. He was only one among ranges of human height that reached away from him in time in both directions, past and future, but of which, with one or two obvious exceptions, one was as ignorant as of Benedict: St. Jerome, St. Ambrose, St. Augustine, Pope St. Leo the Great, Pope St. Gregory the Great, St. Francis of Assisi, Hildebrand (Pope Gregory VII).

Clearly, a cleft cut across the body of Christendom itself, and raised an overwhelming question: What, in fact, was the civilization of the West? If it was Christendom, why had it turned its back on half its roots and meanings and become cheerfully ignorant of those who had embodied them? If it was not Christendom, what was it? And what were those values that it claimed to assert against the forces of active evil that beset it in the greatest crisis of history since the fall of Rome? Did the failure of the Western World to know what it was lie at the root of its spiritual despondency, its intellectual confusion, its moral chaos, the dissolving bonds of faith and loyalty within itself, its swift political decline in barely four decades from hegemony of the world to a demoralized rump of Europe little larger than it had been in the crash of the Roman West, and an America still disputing the nature of the crisis, its gravity, whether it existed at all, or what to do about it?

Answers to such questions could not be extemporized. At the moment, a baffled seeker could do little more than grope for St. Benedict's hand and pray in all humbleness to be led over the traces of the saint's progress to the end that he might be, if not more knowledgeable, at least less nakedly ignorant. The biographical facts were synoptic enough and chiefly to be found in the *Dialogues* of Pope St. Gregory the Great or inferred between the lines of St. Benedict's Rule.

Benedict had been born, toward the end of the fifth century, of good family in the sturdy countryside of Nursia, which lay close enough to Rome to catch the tremors of its sack, in 410, by Alaric's West Goths (the first time in eight hundred years that the City had fallen), and the shock of its sack by the Vandals, who, in 455 completed the material and human havoc that the West Goths had begun.

To a Rome darkened by such disasters, Benedict had been sent to school as a boy of fourteen or fifteen. There he was shaken by the corrupt customs of his schoolmates, it is said. But we may surely conjecture that he was touched, too, like sensitive minds in our own day, by a sense of brooding, indefinable disaster, of doom still incomplete, for the Dark Ages were scarcely more than begun.

The boy fled from Rome, or, as we might say, ran away from school, and settled with a loose-knit congregation about thirty miles from the City. There he performed his first miracle. When, as a result, men called him good, he fled again. For, though he was a boy, he was clearly old enough to fear the world, especially when it praises. This time he fled into the desert wilderness near Subiaco, where for three years he lived alone in a cave. To those who presently found him, he seemed more like a wild creature than a man. Those were the years of the saint's conquest of his flesh, his purgation, illumination and perhaps his prayerful union with God. They must also have been the years he plumbed all the perils of solitary austerities and the hermit life, by suffering them.

At any rate, the saint left Subiaco to enter on his first experience in governing a community of monks. He returned to Subiaco, and, in twelve years, organized twelve Benedictine communities. His days were filled with devotion and with labor and touched with miracles. But again human factors threatened failure. St. Benedict with a few companions withdrew to Monte Cassino, some eighty miles southeast of Rome. There he overthrew an ancient altar of Apollo (for paganism was still rooted in the countryside), and there he raised his own altar.

On those heights, he organized his community, ruled his monks, performed new miracles, distilled his holy experience in his Holy Rule. There he died at a date which is in dispute, but was probably about 547, when the campaigns of the Eastern Roman Empire to recover Italy from the East Goths had so permanently devastated the Peninsula that the irruption of the Lombards into the ruins brought a new horror rather than any novelty in havoc.

Against that night and that ruin, like a man patiently lighting a wick in a tempest, St. Benedict set his Rule. There had been other monastic Rules before—St. Pachomius' and St. Basil's, for example. St. Benedict called his the *Holy Rule*, setting it down and setting it apart from all others, with a consciousness of its singular authority that has led some biographers to speculate whether he had not been prompted by the Holy See to write it. Perhaps it is permissible to hazard that his authority need have proceeded from nothing more than that unwavering confidence which commonly sustains genius.

What was there in this little book that changed the world? To us, at first glance, it seems prosaic enough, even fairly obvious. That, indeed, is the heart of its inspiration. In an age of pillar saints and furiously competing athletes of the spirit, when men plunged by thousands into the desert, in a lunge towards God, and in revulsion from man, St. Benedict's Rule brought a saving and creative sanity. Its temper was that of moderation as against excesses of zeal, of fruitful labor as against austerities pushed to the point of fruitlessness, of discipline as against enthusiasm, of continence of spirit and conduct as against incontinence.

It has been said (by T. F. Lindsay in his sensitive and searching *St. Benedict*) that, in a shattered society, the Holy Rule, to those who submitted to its mild but strict sway, restored the discipline and power of Roman family life.

I venture that it did something else as well. For those who obeyed it, it ended three great alienations of the spirit whose action, I suspect, touched on that missing something which my instructors failed to find among the causes of the fall of Rome. The same alienations, I further suspect, can be seen at their work of dissolution among ourselves, and are perhaps among the little-noticed reasons why men turn to Communism. They are: the alienation of the spirit of man from traditional authority; his alienation from the idea of traditional order; and a crippling alienation that he feels at the point where civilization has deprived him of the joy of simple productive labor.

These alienations St. Benedict fused into a new surge of the human spirit by directing the frustrations that informed them into the disciplined service of God. At the touch of his mild inspiration, the bones of a new order stirred and clothed themselves with life, drawing to itself much of what was best and most vigorous among the ruins of man and his work in the Dark Ages, and conserving and shaping its energy for that unparalleled outburst of mind and spirit in the Middle Ages. For about the Benedictine monasteries what we, having casually lost the Christian East, now casually call the West, once before regrouped and saved itself.

So bald a summary can do little more than indicate the dimensions of the Benedictine achievement and plead for its constant re-examination. Seldom has the need been greater. For we sense, in the year 1952, that we may stand closer to the year 410 than at any other time in the centuries since. If that statement seems as extreme as any of Salvian's, three hundred million Russians, Poles, Czechs, Slovaks, East Germans, Austrians, Hungarians, and all the Christian Balkans, would tell you that it is not—would tell you if they could lift their voices through the night of the new Dark Ages that have fallen on them. For them the year 410 has already come.

IS ACADEMIC FREEDOM
IN DANGER?

(Life, JUNE 22, 1953)

THERE ARE FEW MEN, I suppose, for whom the names of the college halls among which, as undergraduates, they lived and studied do not ever after touch a special note, like the sound of clock-chimes heard in the depth of a tranquil house. So the names of the halls at Columbia University touch my memory—Hamilton and Hartley, Livingston and Furnald, Havemeyer and Schermerhorn; names not remarkable in themselves but for what they have power to evoke. For, at their sound, that campus and its structures, with all their associations, rise upon the memory, as in reality they rise above Morningside Heights—the dome of the library, the leaves of Boston ivy rattling gently on the west wall of Hartley, the hoots of students on hot spring nights breaking the hush of the campus within the encircling rumble of the city.

That is the physical university. Above it rises another college that is more lasting, for it is not built of bricks or stones but persists in each of the thousands of minds that it has in any way helped to shape. Exactly to the degree in which that second college constitutes one of the citadels of the mind, and a repository of the culture of the West, it must admit the impact of what is new, be shaken by the crisis of history in the 20th Century, which is pre-eminently a crisis of the mind, and suffer each tremor of the catastrophe.

Freedom for the play of ideas is the indispensable precondition for growth in that college of the mind. Therein lies academic freedom, which is now exercising many minds in and out of universities, and which I take to mean, at its simplest, the privilege of the mind freely to inquire into the nature of things and freely to impart (within reason) the findings of its free inquiry. Thus the college of the mind is, beyond anything that it merely teaches, an influence. Its function is above all to shape, over the years, in each of those who have known it, a maturity of mind that fearlessly meets the test which Justice Holmes held to be the mark of a civilized man—his undisconcerted power to question his own first principles.

It is this background that conditions the depth of the concern—if not the intensity of the controversy—about the threat to academic freedom, now widely held to be posed by congressional committees grubbing for Communism in the schools and colleges. Everybody is talking about it. Yet, at best,

the hubbub remains somehow puzzling and impersonal—adrift in a strato-
sphere of appeals to abstract principle and professional privilege, swept by
gales of alarm, where extremists of several kinds have managed to toss and
keep it. At worst, the hubbub seems like a political brawl, one of the obscener
rowdedows of a society whose nerves keep coming apart, threatened by the
aims and ambitions of sinister politicians, or other dull and dangerous minds
bent on making everybody else as dull and reactionary as themselves.

The cries of certain educators and their friends ring oddly shrill and out of
professional character. The uproar seems too loud for the observable facts.
The malign motives of a handful of politicians and the scale of activities of the
congressional investigating committees seem scarcely enough to explain that
shrillness or the spread of the commotion, which has become international.

For the threat to freedom in the U.S. is no longer a family secret. It has
jumped the ocean and become a shudder in London, a sneer in Paris and a
snigger in Rome. Bertrand Russell has told all England (by way of the *Manches-
ter Guardian*) that America is writhing in a "reign of terror," while he girded at
the "policemen who have professors at their mercy."

Of course, Mr. Russell, the particular hallmark of whose mind has been for
decades a drily lucid rationality, did not simply spin these alarming conclusions out of thin air. He spun them out of an air crackling with the similar
views of a highly articulate group of Americans. Few, if any, of them have
ventured to speak of a "reign of terror." They prefer the term "witch-hunt,"
perhaps as being more in the American grain, at least less liable to the
frightening charge of "un-Americanism." But reign of terror is what they
mean.

Let us listen to some of the cracklings. For it is one of the paradoxes of the
"witch-hunt" that those who are discussing it most loudly are people who for
years have freely made known their views on a variety of controversial subjects, and that what they are now freely making known is that they are being
silenced.

Here is Mr. Robert M. Hutchins, formerly president of the University of
Chicago, now dispensing the vast funds of the Ford Foundation to promote
good works of a most public kind. "Everywhere in the U.S.," he says,
"university professors, whether or not they have tenure, are silenced by the
general atmosphere of repression that prevails."

Here is Mr. Bernard De Voto, one of whose chief literary charms has long
been that he advances upon almost any subject with the gait and growl of a
bear that has just spent a particularly drafty winter in a particularly uncom-
fortable cave. He holds that "fuzzy-minded nincompoops and very clear-
minded bastards are going to agitate for the dismissal of every college teacher
who expresses an idea that would not have made Roscoe Conkling blush for its
conservatism."

Here is Professor Henry Steele Commager, of Columbia University: "We are now embarked upon a campaign of repression and suppression more violent, more reckless, more dangerous than any in our history. Already teachers fear to discuss certain subjects in the classroom."

Not all these warnings are current. One of them, Mr. De Voto's, is some three years old. For the hubbub is not new. The academic freedom issue is new; at least it has newly come to the fore. But the hubbub is a continuing commotion. Those voices of alarm, or others much like them, have been loudly swelling the chorus of fear ever since it undertook to explain the Hiss case to the groundlings—rather misleadingly, it turned out. It has had other heroes (discreetly laid by) and other issues (expediently recessed).

Those cries are, of course, the voices of the liberal neurosis, which sustains a similar shock whenever a move is made at any point to expose the Communist conspiracy. That is not because liberals are Communists. Communists may turn such fears to their own purposes. Here and there, a Communist may conceal himself among liberals. But liberals are not Communists, and a mind would have to be grossly undiscriminating, or inflamed by a passion for absurdity, if it supposed that they were.

The roots of the liberal neurosis are complicated and cannot be explored here beyond saying this: the neurosis springs from a deep political insecurity. In part, this is due to the necessity, as a tactic of practical politics, for reforming liberals to seem not to be something that they are—to seem to be liberals instead of un-Marxian socialists the focus of whose hopes and plans is the welfare state on a national and international scale. In part, that insecurity is due to their fear of being mistaken for something that they are not—Communists.

For, of course, there is a strong family resemblance between the Communist state and the welfare state. The ends each has in view have much in common. But the methods proposed for reaching them radically differ. Each is, in fact, in direct competition with the other, since each offers itself as an alternative solution for the crisis of the 20th Century; and Fabian Britain has at last supplanted Soviet Russia in the eyes of political liberals when they look abroad. Nevertheless, that family resemblance is nerve-wearing, since all the minds that note it are not equally discriminating, especially in a nation that has only just become conscious of Communism and still rejects socialism. So, at every move against Communism, liberal nerves come unglued, and liberal voices go shrill, fearing that, by design or error, the move may be against themselves.

Liberal nerves have been frayed for some time by the loyalty oaths which teachers are fighting rather successfully in some states, and by the probes that state legislatures (notably California's) have long been making into Communism in schools and colleges within their state lines. But, above all, liberal minds are doom-haunted by two figures, always incongruously locked together in their nightmare: Senator Joseph R. McCarthy and Mr. Owen Lattimore.

It was a trick of fate in a low comedy mood that Senator McCarthy should first have bounded into public view dragging the unlikely and protesting person of Mr. Lattimore to share with him a historic spotlight so grateful to the one and so acutely unwanted by the other. It was a trick of fate that, in the case of each, has led to some serious confusions. For it led to the translation of Senator McCarthy into the symbol of a national snallygaster (a winged hobgoblin used to frighten naughty children in parts of rural Maryland), instead of one of the two things that he obviously is: an instinctive politician of a kind fairly common in our history, in which case the uproar he inspires is a phenomenon much more arresting than the senator; or a politician of a kind wholly new in our history, in which case he merits the most cautious and cold-blooded appraisal.

Neither can Mr. Lattimore be translated into a symbol of the calm, secluded scholar, or champion of academic freedom, by anything less than a violent wrench of the mind or the facts. He happened to be a professor (he holds no academic degree) at the Walter Hines Page School of International Relations at Johns Hopkins University. His present plight has nothing to do with his academic activities. It bears solely on what part, if any, Mr. Lattimore may have played in shaping American policy in Asia toward a national catastrophe—the Communist conquest of China—retrievable, if at all, only at an incalculable cost in life and treasure.

In any case, Senator McCarthy has nothing to do with investigating Communism in education. Nor, after his first fierce *entre-chats*, did he have much to do with the further adventures of Owen Lattimore. Lattimore's current indictment (for perjury) was wholly the result of prolonged hearings before a Senate committee of which Senator McCarthy was not a member.

The mass of Americans, who vehemently made known their views in (and during) a recent general election, know perfectly well that they are not living in a reign of terror and that they seldom look behind a door for anything more frightening than an umbrella. They need not be judged too harshly if they ask for less fear and more fact. Of course, everybody has heard about the bullying and bumbling methods of the congressional committees and about the completely innocent victim who, on the unsupported word of an informer, or for no reason at all, has been haled before the committees and mercilessly grilled while his public degradation was topped by economic ruin when he lost his job.

But that victim, when sought, remains elusive. The one instantly verifiable fact of the witch-hunt is this: of more than 50 people questioned before congressional committees in the last five years about active participation in a secret Communist conspiracy within the United States Government (often including espionage), only two have ever been prosecuted. Yet only a handful has denied the charges. Most of them have refused to answer any questions on the ground that their answers might incriminate them.

In the absence of firm facts, it is scarcely strange if, to many Americans, the gusts of strident liberal fear suggest a persecution delusion in which the unhappy victim is sincerely terrified, by nobody in particular, but by a vaguely menacing "they." *They* are after him. *They* are about to subpoena him. *They* are silencing him.

Yet facts are readily available. The official transcripts of the congressional hearings that deal with Communism in education run to some thousand pages. In them can be read, in all the spare coldness of an official court record, word by word, act by act, just what was said and done at every public hearing. But those transcripts are among the most secret of government documents. That is not because the congressional committees keep them secret. Anybody can have them for the asking. But comparatively few people ever ask for them.

Reading them may not convince everyone that no threat to academic freedom exists, though it may suggest to some that the threat is not exclusively the one they supposed it to be. But it seems unlikely that any mind whose unprejudiced purpose is to get at the facts in the case could read them without radically rearranging its ideas about the congressional committees investigating Communism in education, what they are up to, how and why.

First, some facts about those committees. There are two, and only two, of them. One is the subcommittee of the Senate's Committee on the Judiciary (chairman: Senator William E. Jenner). This is the same committee which, under the chairmanship of Senator Pat McCarran, carried through the complicated and circumspect hearings into the Institute of Pacific Relations (available in 14 volumes, more than 5,000 pages, to anybody who wants to investigate it).

The other committee is the old House Committee on Un-American Activities (chairman: Congressman Harold H. Velde). This is the committee that first brought Miss Elizabeth Bentley to repeat her startling disclosures within the hearing of the nation, and which initiated and, in a large measure, made possible the Hiss Case.

With neither of these committees does Senator McCarthy have anything to do. He is chairman of the Senate's Permanent Subcommittee on Investigations.

Neither of these committees is solely interested in investigating Communism in education. Their work in that field is only one phase (not the most important) of a much wider investigation into the pattern, personnel and activities of the Communist conspiracy in the U.S. Both committees have stressed the academic field only within the last twelvemonth. The Un-American Activities Committee has held public hearings in education only since last February.

The Senate's subcommittee does not even engage the services of an investigator. It does not need to. Its files are bulging with pertinent information.

Indeed, its interest in the schools and colleges was first stirred by the fact that so many of those cited in connection with the larger Communist conspiracy in Government came more or less directly out of leading universities, or still remained in them.

Some of this information is sworn testimony of former Communists or others. In the case of the Un-American Activities Committee, some of it is developed by direct investigation. Some of it is hearsay. The committees are engaged quite properly in trying to sift and verify it, and, in doing so, they follow a simple procedure. They first subpoena a witness in executive (secret) session and ask questions based on their researches. If a witness refuses to answer questions on the ground that his answers may incriminate him, he is given a public hearing where he can make his position a matter of public record. Witnesses who deny all allegations in executive session are seldom, if ever, taken into public hearings. Their appearance in executive session receives no publicity whatever.

No witness is ever subpoenaed unless, in the opinion of the committee members and their staffs, good grounds exist for calling him. The myth of congressmen indiscriminately subpoenaing witnesses for the delight of inconveniencing, tormenting or ruining them belongs strictly to the folklore of the intellectuals. To do so would be political suicide. Both committees have worked for years in the full glare of a prevailingly hostile press and, until some six months ago, against the obstruction and outspoken criticism of powerful elements in the Government, notably the Executive.

There is no evidence in the transcripts that the congressional committees are trying to impair academic or personal freedom by consistently probing any witness's general views. There are specific disclaimers by Chairmen Jenner and Velde that their one and only concern is to trace the Communist trail. The record bears them out. Where occasional probings beyond that main line do occur, they are less probings than pawings: a sign of bafflement and aimlessness rather than calculation.

This is not to say that the committees never make mistakes or that their members are unfailingly detached, tactful, imaginative or adroit in handling testimony or witnesses. Sometimes the evasiveness or impudence of a witness moves some members to outbursts neither admirable nor judicious. But few facts in the official transcripts are more at odds with the witch-hunting theme than those passages in which one congressman admonishes another that his questions are unfair, or that he is pressing a witness too hard; or in which a senator carefully reminds a hesitant witness that he may consult his attorney before answering.

The simple fact is that the work of the congressional committees is a response to a situation new in history—the spread of the Communist conspiracy. Within the nation, groups of its own citizens are secretly organized to sap and subvert its laws and institutions, while seeking the protection of the same laws and institutions to shield themselves when suspected or caught. From this technique, those laws and institutions are no longer fully able to protect themselves by traditional means. The congressional committees measure this problem and provide a partial answer to it.

But let us turn to those transcripts. For nothing else gives the picture so simply.

They asked the witness to stand and be sworn and give his name and occupation. He said that his name was Wendell Hinckle Furry, that he was an associate professor of physics at Harvard University, and had been since 1934, "except for two years' leave of absence during the war." *They* asked him if he had been in the Armed Services during those two years, and he said no, that he had been engaged in special work with radar at the radiation laboratory of the Massachusetts Institute of Technology.

They, in this case, was the House Committee on Un-American Activities. They were questioning Professor Furry at a public hearing in Washington, D.C. *They* asked him: "Are you now a member of the Communist party?" Professor Furry said: "I refuse to answer that on the grounds I have stated before." The privilege he was invoking is the fifth amendment to the Constitution, and the ground was that his answer might incriminate him.

They asked him: "If you were granted immunity, would you answer the question?" He said: "If I could be granted immunity sufficiently—sufficient immunity to remove my grounds for answering the question, I will answer it." *They* said: "What are the grounds for asking immunity then?" He said: "I am not asking for immunity." *They* said: "I say—what would be the grounds? You said if it was broad enough, you would answer the question. Now what is it you are afraid of, sir?" And another of *them* added: "You may confer with counsel." For Professor Furry had his lawyer with him. Professor Furry (without consulting counsel): "Well, I must refuse to answer that on the grounds I have already stated."

Presently the chair admonished his prying colleagues in a fashion puzzling enough in a "campaign of repression and suppression," and ruled that certain questions to the witness "are not fair and are improper."

But *they* also asked Professor Furry: "Do you believe that membership in the Communist party today is inimical to the interests of the U.S.?" He answered: "Sir, that is a matter about which I am perhaps not certain." *They* asked: "Can you give me an answer 'Yes' or 'No'?" He answered: "Doesn't a citizen have a right to be uncertain about a matter of public interest?" *They* asked: "How can you be uncertain about Korea?" He said: "I don't think the Communist party of the U.S. started that Korean business." *They* asked: "Do you make a distinction in your mind as between one who seeks the overthrow of the government of the United States by force and violence in this country, and one in the lines of North Korea who seeks the overthrow of the United States by force and violence in Korea?"

The professor answered: "Well, I am not sure that either one is seeking the overthrow of the United States Government by force and violence. The man in Korea is seeking control of some Korean territory." *They* said: "The Communist in Korea is seeking world domination by the Soviet Union to the same extent and in the same degree that a dedicated Communist in this country seeks the same goal. I am disappointed, frankly, that there are American citizens today who distinguish as between shades of Communism, knowing that the Communist in Korea and the Communist in this country follow the same directives, read the same textbooks and are dedicated to the same ends."

The committee had already heard relevant testimony concerning Professor Furry from two other witnesses. One was Robert Gorham Davis, Professor of English at Smith College, who had received his A.B. and M.A. from Harvard University, where he had also taught for 10 years. The other was Granville Hicks, a writer and literary critic of discrimination and probity. He had also received his A.B. from Harvard College, then studied at the Harvard Theological School, then received his M.A. from Harvard where he had been a teaching fellow. Both witnesses testified that, while teaching at Harvard, they had been members of a Communist party cell, and that Professor Furry had also been a member of the same cell.

Some three months later, Harvard University made an official announcement about Professor Furry and two other members of its faculty, all of whom had refused to say under oath whether or not they had been members of the Communist party, or to answer related questions, on the ground that their answers might incriminate them. The Harvard Corporation announced that all three would remain on the faculty.

They also asked another witness to stand, be sworn and give his name. This time *they* was the subcommittee of the Senate's Committee on the Judiciary with Senator Jenner in the chair. The hearing was held in Boston's Federal Building last March. The witness said that his name was Maurice Halperin and that he had received his A.B. degree from Harvard College, his M.A. from the University of Oklahoma and his Ph.D. from the University of Paris. He had taught at the University of Oklahoma for some 12 years and for three years at Boston University, where he was chairman of its Department of Latin American Regional Studies. *They* asked him what he had done before that and he said that he had been employed by the U.S. Government, first as an analyst with the Coordinator of Information; later as chief of the Latin American Division of the Office of Strategic Services (OSS); later still with the State Department. They asked him if he had also been chairman of a "Special Joint Army-Navy-OSS Intelligence project under the direction of the Joint Chiefs of Staff" and had addressed a plenary session of the Inter-American Defense Board. He said that he had. They asked him if he had lectured at the Military Government School at the University of Virginia. He said that he had. They asked him if he had lectured at the Military Government School at the

University of Virginia. He said that he had. They asked him if he had participated in the San Francisco organizing conference (headed by Alger Hiss) of the U.N. and had later been an "observer and consultant with the Economic and Social Council of the U.N." maintaining "liaison with the Department of State, including direct contact with the Secretary of State." He said that he believed so.

They asked him: "Are you now a member of the Communist party?" He answered: "The same answer for the same reason. That will save time, won't it, Mr. Jenner?" By same answer Mr. Halperin meant that he refused to answer the question. By same reason he meant that he refused on the ground that his answer might incriminate him.

They asked him: "Mr. Halperin, were you a member of an espionage ring, Communist espionage ring, that was directed by one Elizabeth Bentley and which operated during the war?" He answered: "I refuse to answer that question, sir, but I also want to preface that by saying that I have not committed any crime against the United States Government. I refuse to answer it by invoking the fifth amendment."

At about that point, Mr. Halperin gave a somewhat faltering answer, as if he were not sure about its legal implications. Senator Jenner interjected: "I'd like to state at this time, for the benefit of the attorney present, it's perfectly proper for the witness to ask permission to talk to his counsel. . . ."

Then *they* asked Mr. Halperin if while consultant to the Economic and Social Council of the U.N., and while he was liaison with the State Department, he had been a Communist. He refused to answer. *They* asked him: "In connection with your work at the U.N., did you ever meet Alger Hiss?" He said: "I refuse to answer that question, sir, for the same reason." *They* asked him if, while he was Division Chief of the OSS, and while he was with the State Department, he had been a Communist. He said: "I refuse to answer that question, sir, for the same reason."

They asked him if, while chairman of Boston University's Latin American Regional Studies Department, he had ever tried to recruit students into the Young Communist League or the Communist party. He answered: "I would like to preface that remark by saying that at no time in any way whatsoever have I tried to influence the political, philosophical or religious or social thinking of any of my students. With respect to the specific question, I refuse to answer because of the fifth amendment." *They* said: "Now will you answer the question? Did you actually engage in recruiting work among your students—that's recruiting for the Communist party among the students of Boston University?" He answered: "I've answered that. I have answered by saying that I refuse to answer for the same reason."

About a month after this hearing, the Senate subcommittee's chief counsel, Mr. Morris, received a telephone call from President Harold C. Case of Boston University. President Case asked if the subcommittee had any *evidence* about

Mr. Halperin and a conversation much like this ensued. "Evidence?" said the somewhat baffled chief counsel. "What evidence? You have the official transcript of the hearing." "That's not good enough," said President Case. "We need documentary evidence." As of this date, Boston University has announced no action with respect to the chairman of its Department of Latin American Regional Studies.

The temptation is to go on and on with these strange hearings, not only because the official transcripts which report them are documents of imminent historical import, but because they are fascinating human documents. Through the bare bones of question and answer, men's lives are glimpsed for an hour or two emerging from an anonymity to which most of them are audibly craving to return. There are glimpses of snarled hope and faith half seen, and tangled motives half guessed at. There is comedy, checked by the context it occurs in, and pathos, also checked by sinister matters that just peep through it.

Of such stuff is made what I shall call the Case of the Five Little Men. There may have been more than five, but it is part of their pathos that that does not matter at all. For these witnesses were not among the great ones. Most of them had been lesser instructors at the College of the City of New York. There, some 13 years ago, the Rapp-Coudert investigation had found them. One of them denied flatly then that he was a Communist. But they were worried, and another of them, a bolder spirit, decided to give up teaching. He got a job in the laboratory of a small private company. Then he brought in one of the others, and the others brought the others. Soon all, or most of them, were together again, working on lenses for the U.S. Navy in wartime; and it might be thought that they would have been happy to settle back quietly in that providential haven where their employer knew the allegations against them, but out of kindness or self-interest, or both, was willing to give them work.

But something else had also happened to the Five Little Men. One of them had changed his mind and decided to break with the Communist party. Then the Senate subcommittee found the Five Little Men and called four of them as witnesses. Not even one of them any longer chose to deny Communist party membership since one of them admitted that he had been a Communist and testified that they had too. So the others are seen, shifting and huddling behind the fifth amendment.

The last of them but one to reach the stand is Mr. Morris U. Cohen. *They* ask him, simply as a matter of routine, where he lives, and he answers, also as a matter of routine, that he lives on Mermaid Avenue. The unrecorded titters ripple from the page, but *they* are already pressing the next question. The little man is a Ph.D. from Columbia University, but it appears that nobody wants to give him a job now; he is self-employed. In his house on Mermaid Avenue, he is a chemist. *They* ask: "Who are your clients, Mr. Cohen?"

He answers: "I decline to answer that question." *They* ask: "Why is that, Mr. Cohen?" He says: "I understand that under the fifth amendment I am protected against self-incrimination." *They* ask: "Do you mean, Mr. Cohen, that if you answered that question, as to who your clients are, you would incriminate yourself?"—and the witness consults his lawyer. "It may tend to incriminate me," he says. *They* ask him if he was a member of the Communist cell at the College of the City of New York. He says, "Same answer."

They persist: "Now, without naming your clients, I want you to tell me whether or not those clients are in war work for the government of the United States or for any branch of the military service of the U.S." He says: "I must decline to answer that question, senator." *They* ask: "Have you passed on information that you have received on work of your clients to the Soviet secret service?" He says: "I must decline to answer that question." *They* ask: "Have you been guilty of espionage for the Communist government of Russia?" He says, "I must decline to answer." *They* say: "Let me ask you this question: Are you now a spy for the Soviet Union?" Mr. Cohen: "I must certainly decline to answer that."

That "*certainly*" is too much for one of the senators. He says: "You must certainly decline to answer that question, and the reason is that, if you were, you would be guilty of treason. That is the reason for your putting the emphasis there, that you must 'certainly' decline to answer that question?"

Unlike the senator, the rest of us are expressly denied the right, by the whole tradition of American law and justice, to draw any conclusions as to the guilt or innocence of Mr. Morris U. Cohen or any other witness who seeks refuge behind the fifth amendment. But one conclusion we are permitted to draw: In the face of such testimony, any government which did not pursue such investigations by every means in its power, including congressional committees, would have abdicated one of the duties for which government exists.

And one conclusion the exasperated senator and his colleagues are also permitted to draw. When deep-sea divers, cautiously probing the rocks and wreckage in the murk undersea, suddenly find themselves enveloped in a cloud of blinding ink, they may not conclude, if they are divers of a rigorously impartial mind, that they are in the presence of an octopus. In the name of justice and fair play they must decline to make any heady assumptions about the nature of that blinding ink, or its source. But one conclusion they may draw, and must, unless they are criminally negligent of their own security and their fellows'. They must conclude that they are in the presence of something that does not wish to be seen.

Some 80 educators have refused to tell the Senate subcommittee whether they are, or have been, Communists on the ground that their answer might incriminate them. Some of them have also refused, also on the ground of self-incrimination, to answer related questions, including questions about Communist espionage. Of these "fifth amendment" educators, some 50 have lost their jobs in consequence, or been suspended, not of course by the Senate's subcommittee, but by the educational institutions employing them. In the case of most colleges and universities, that has happened only after a careful, often prolonged, weighing of evidence and other factors.

Only 20 educators have refused to answer the same questions for the same reason before the Un-American Activities Committee. Of these, two appear to have lost their jobs. A number have been suspended. But the Un-American Activities Committee is so little concerned with persecuting witnesses that it is not sure how many suspensions there have been because it has never checked.

In short, about 100 educators have appeared before both committees and pled self-incrimination. But there are considerably more than one million educators—professors, instructors, teachers—in the U.S. This would seem to be a figure great enough to convince the most avid witch-hunter that the overwhelming mass of American educators is loyal beyond question. By contrast, the figure of 100 recalcitrant witnesses called by two Congressional committees seems grotesquely small. Indeed, it is sometimes cited to prove how unnecessary congressional investigations are. It does not prove that, and the committee's files and findings indicate something exactly contrary.

But one thing those oddly discrepant figures do prove. They prove, at least to minds still susceptible to simple arithmetic, that about 150 teachers called as witnesses, out of more than one million teachers in the nation, scarcely adds up to a witch-hunt.

Yet there is no such thing as 150 *witnesses*. Witnesses are not paving blocks to be grossed by the hundred. They are human souls about whom, ultimately, the most important fact is not what they look like or how they act, what they say or refuse to say, or even the degree of their innocence or guilt, but what degree of serenity they guard before the mysteries of life and death.

If 150 witnesses, in this sense, are called unfairly before congressional committees, I suffer a violence as great as if one were called unfairly—no more, no less. For I will have been wounded in something that goes much deeper, but which, for the sake of brevity, we may call an important freedom—and so will every other man alive on earth.

During Granville Hicks's public hearing before the Un-American Activities Committee, the following dialog took place. Congressman Kearny: "No matter which way it [action against the Communist party] was done, somebody would be bound to be hurt?" Mr. Hicks: "Somebody will be hurt. There's no getting around it. I mean, innocent people will be hurt."

I happen to disagree with Mr. Hicks about this point, as I often do about many points, while keeping always a great respect for the tolerant integrity of his mind.

I have read thousands of pages of official transcripts of such public hearings and have participated in a good many of them myself. I have yet to see one witness called before a congressional hearing who could be called "innocent"—or in a way that could be called "unfairly"—in the sense that he had no connection whatever with the matters under scrutiny, had never been involved or touched by them in any way, so that he had no contribution whatever to make to the record while his presence was a gratuitous inconvenience and humiliation to him.

But Mr. Hicks's comments lead to a noteworthy point. It is that when people like him look at congressional hearings, and when a great many other people look at them, though they see exactly the same spectacle, they do not always see the same things. Those thousands of Americans who watch their TV screens on the infrequent occasions when congressional hearings are televised in full—they may see what Mr. Hicks sees, but many of them also see something else. They see not only the plight of the witnesses. They also see the purpose of the congressmen and senators whom they have elected, in part to pursue such investigations. And while they too may be aware that in any fight innocent people may always be hurt, they also know that in the fight against Communism not all the people being hurt are witnesses before congressional committees.

Sherman Flanagan is a former magistrate of Westminster, Md., a former president of its Rotary Club, a former teacher who holds an M.A. in education. Now he sells some insurance and dabbles in politics and the marketing of the tomato crop. He is an almost typical American. A somewhat dry man, he is given to telling drily humorous stories that usually turn on quirks of human character—not an emotional man. But Sherman Flanagan has a son who went from college to become a jet pilot. Sherman Flanagan sat by my sickbed recently and drily said, "What I don't understand is just how a father goes on living when he knows, day after day, that his son is 40,000 feet up in the air over there."

Those thousands quietly watching the congressional hearings by their TV screens—I submit that that is the way they feel. Whatever may be at the forefront of their minds, at the back of many of them lies some form of Sherman Flanagan's question: "Just how do you go on living when you know, day after day, that he is 40,000 feet up in the air over there?"

They are not unmindful or careless of academic freedom, if only because education is an essential part of the American dream, just as academic freedom is central to those education institutions which exist to shape the minds of their children who fill them. Or did fill them. For a good many of the boys are no longer there. Like Sherman Flanagan's son, they have gone directly from college into the armed services, or been drafted from it, or before they ever got there, to fight a war against Communism in the name of a freedom, which also includes academic freedom. And they sense, those watchers, like the congressmen who questioned Professor Furry, that there is a connection between the war in Korea and the war against Communism at home. They sense, too, perhaps without being able or willing to spell it out for themselves, or you, that if Communism succeeds in winning that larger war of which both of those inseparable wars is part, all freedom will have become academic, merely academic.

THE END OF A DARK AGE
USHERS IN NEW DANGERS
(*Life*, APRIL 30, 1956)

At the 20th Congress of the Communist party two months ago Nikita Khrushchev electrified the world by denouncing the Communist demigod Stalin. Stalin, he declared, was not an all-wise patriot but a mad criminal who ruled by terror; many of those who perished in his purges were patriotic Communists whose reputations were to be posthumously rehabilitated. Since then the free world has been debating the reason for this tremendous Communist reversal and its significance. In this article the meaning of the new line is interpreted by Whittaker Chambers, onetime underground functionary of the party in the U.S., who unmasked Alger Hiss as a Communist agent and wrote Witness, *one of the most eloquent autobiographies of our time.*

THERE ARE TWO stories about the 20th Congress of the Soviet Communist party. One is about what is happening now, at this moment, throughout international Communism and within the Communist empire (including the dissolution last week of the Cominform). The other is about the political meaning of those events for the West. The first is the latest act of a bloody tragedy that has not its like in history. The second has momentous meanings for us all. Together they spell peril for the West. But the peril is blurred because the political meanings of the second story are in danger of becoming lost in the sensational developments of the first.

The first is the story of the "reverse purge"—the posthumous liquidation of Stalin and Stalinism—proclaimed at the 20th Congress. Purge, liquidation, Stalinism, Communism, party—these are mere words. There is no language that can utter the agony which those words stand for but cannot wholly convey. But there is a scene in Moussorgsky's opera, *Boris Godunov,* where music that is scarcely any longer music, and sound that is incoherent, mindless anguish, do reach the mind and soul with what is otherwise incommunicable. It is the scene in which the idiot cries out against injustice. His throat utters those animal sounds that have not their like in tragedy:

"Aooh! Aooh! Aooh! Aooh!"

You may have thought that the words of the enslaved women that close Euripides' *Trojan Women* utter as much about defeat and suffering as speech or mind can bear: "Wrath in the earth, and quaking, and a flood that sweepeth all—and passeth on." But they are words and they have rational meaning.

The idiot utters his sounds for the immeasurable, irrational evil and suffering that lie at the heart of life itself. His cry is the utmost that can be said about the meanings of those words which stand for: Great Purge, Reverse Purge, Communist Revolution, Communist party, the Communist experience as it has tempted or tormented millions of mankind. They were the lucky ones who died.

I cannot pretend to write about these matters objectively. I lived through the Great Purge, almost to its end, within the ranks of the Communist party. No one who did not live through that special experience of our time can know what is now going on in the Communist empire, just as no man who has not been tortured can know what torture is though he has collated all the descriptive details. I lived through the purge outside Russia, but in a secret cell of the Red army from whose underground walls every tremor of the purge reverberated. The Red army was the last great pool of resistance to Stalin. My closest comrades were military Communists. Most of them were killed in Communist prisons, or have since been dying by inches in Communist concentration camps.

Within the three decades, 1920 to 1950, roughly from the 10th Congress of the Soviet Communist party to the Communist mopup of mainland China, Communism's will to change history was personified in one man—the late Josef Stalin. To become the embodiment of the revolutionary idea in history Stalin had to corrupt Communism absolutely. He justified his acts by the necessities of that history and the needs of that infallible party which all Communists serve. In their name he asserted that what was true was a lie and what was a lie was truth. He sustained this corruption by a blend of cunning and brute force. History knows nothing similar on such a scale.

They say that when he came to the part of his secret speech to the 20th Congress in which he detailed Stalin's lies and crimes, Nikita Khrushchev repeatedly wept. So must many others have done: men, once his comrades, now his enemies, reading the scraps and paraphrases of his words, in other languages, other lands, and having no illusions about his purposes. They wept, not as we weep from pain or strain, but as by the opening of an unstanchable wound, so old and deep that some of them, perhaps, supposed that it no longer existed.

All over the world tonight, as I write these words, Communists and former Communists are examining the past and their consciences with a fierceness of scrutiny that has not had its like in our times. Millions of others are taking fresh hope from the demolition that may go with it. It is these millions that Khrushchev and his men are angling for.

This great turn in Communist tactics, which takes the form of the liquidation of Stalinism, opens an unparalleled struggle for men's minds. Communism is bidding for the allegiance of all those in the West who are in any way affected by its doctrine, its power or its spell. The West could make no greater mistake than to exaggerate first impressions or read into this move simply another scramble for personal power among the Kremlin masters.

The Communists are realists. They will count on the long pull. And the pull will presently be intense in the minds of millions. With Stalin down, the force of Communist attraction will be great, on many levels, and with a play of appeals that the West will not readily understand. That is why I have gone into my personal reaction at length, and why I wish to stay with it a little longer.

Three books powerfully influenced my break with Communism. When, in 1937, the slow separation of my mind from Communism, like the detaching of live tissue, had brought me to the point where I dared to read books forbidden Communists to read—dared, that is, not out of fear of the party but against my own voluntary compulsion to obey it—then I read these three books: Vladimir Tchernavin's *I Speak for the Silent;* Eugene Lyons' *Assignment in Utopia;* Victor Serge's *Russia 20 Years After.* In the years since, I have, in the course of editing news, glanced at passages in all three books. But I never read one of them through again. I did not read them because I could not stand the pain they caused me. But when I finished the report of Anastas Mikoyan's speech to the 20th Congress, the first speech in which I found an outright assault on Stalin, and when the names of the revindicated Bolsheviks began to appear—Bela Kun, Stanislav Kossior, Antonov-Avseenko—I heard my mind saying to itself in these words from *Macbeth,*

> *The times have been*
> *That, when the brains were out, the man would die,*
> *And there an end; but now they rise again. . . .*

I took up Victor Serge and lived back, line by line, over the struggle I had known in 1937 and the forepart of 1938. Let Serge give his own version of the remembered horror that is now exploding in the minds of Communists:

"As a rule, the condemned is called upon at night to quit his cell. He does not know where he is going, the turnkey does not know where he is conducting him. The elevator brings him down to the main floor. There, when he is made to take a cement staircase, powerfully illuminated, he begins to understand. . . . He follows a cement corridor bordered by gutters. He knows nothing; as a rule, he does not even know that he has been condemned to die, if the G.P.U. has invoked the death penalty administratively. A man—who himself knows only one thing and that is that he must kill the one who is being brought to him—emerges behind him on padded feet and sends a bullet through his head. The water spouts are opened, the body rolls into a trap or is pushed into a recess. . . . No witnesses; the cellar smothers all sounds; a few reliable executioners act without knowing anything exactly. Silence, secrecy. I was confined in the Lubianka when the thirty-five functionaries of the Commissariat of Agriculture were executed there for a bizarre affair of sabotage and intelligence with Poland (March, 1935). No sound disturbed the silence of the perfect prison." Stalin made Communism itself this perfect prison.

But there is something else. Serge feels the impossibility of bringing to the mind of the West, which will not hear, let alone understand, this great drama of history that bears directly on its fate. He writes: "These pages, I feel, are depressingly monotonous. All these dismal destinies seem to repeat themselves, all these men move about in a hopeless greyness. . . . Yes, this struggle of revolutionists against the machine that grinds down everything has about it something depressing when you think of it in that way, in the abstract, without seeing the simple and shrewd faces, without being well acquainted with their lives. . . . I would like to efface this impression. Everyone of these men has his true grandeur. They are not vanquished, they are resisters, and they often have victorious souls."

They often have victorious souls. . . . It is those victorious souls that Communism is now calling to its side for a last struggle against the West. They may prove more effective than armies. They will not only revitalize Communism from which the spirit had all but died, leaving only the barren executive will, the habit of command or blind submission, both locked in an unspoken hypocrisy. They will speak to others who can hear them within the West. They will speak in many voices, on many ranges of feeling and of logic. But the resonance, haunting everything they say, and giving it special force, will be, even though unspoken, a single line of Lenin's wife's: "Those who have not lived through the revolution cannot imagine its grand solemn beauty."

The West will have to match that resonance from some depths within itself. Therein lies the threat to it of the great turn, the drama, now playing out among its inveterate enemies. For this turn was made in relation to a political situation involving the West; and it is that situation that is now in danger of being lost sight of in the more sensational development.

Why now? How did it happen that this great zigzag came in the year 1956, at the 20th Congress of the Soviet Communist party? The answers have to do with an international situation that is reasonably open to survey, and an internal Soviet situation, including a power struggle in the Kremlin, where lack of exact information, or conflicting information, takes us into the realm of astrology. Everybody is guessing. I would guess, too, if there seemed any urgent reason to. I prefer to center on the international situation, that dealing directly with the West, since it has seemed to me from the first that it was chiefly that the zigzag at the 20th Congress was meant to deal with. First, a word about congresses and zigzags.

Nothing is any longer decided *at* these great Communist congresses. They simply register important decisions, taken in the highest Communist echelons, out of sight and sound of the party masses, and probably some time before they are announced.

This is especially necessary because of the frequent zigzags of the party line. Zigzags are much misunderstood. But there is nothing inherently irrational about them. Communism has one fixed purpose: to take over the rest of the world. That purpose never changes. Only the tactics for effecting it change. Given the fixed purpose, the tactics can change endlessly, can change, at need, into the very opposite of what they have been, and sometimes overnight, or so it seems.

A violent zigzag in the party line is a sign that Communism, in its perpetual assessment of the balance of forces, the power pattern in the world, has concluded that the power pattern has changed in such a way as to indicate that a rather definite stage of history is ending and a new one is beginning. A new power pattern commonly calls for new tactics in order for Communism to work successfully in it.

The 20th Congress met at what Communists suppose to be an ultimate, or penultimate, stage of this century's history. It met to register the general line of a new tactic whose end result, if successful, would foreclose that stage of history in a world wholly Communist, or on the point of becoming so. New tactics were enjoined by the new power pattern, the changed balance of force between Communism and the West. This new balance of forces was revealed—but not caused—by last year's Geneva conferences. The actual shift in the power balance had occurred several years before. But after the Geneva conferences a zigzag in the party line became a certainty.

On many in the West last year's Geneva conferences had an almost physically stunning effect. Of the two, the first (Summit) conference, which fed the illusion of "the Geneva spirit," was more stunning than the second conference which seemed to bury it. Except in fairly limited circles, the shock was not due to the fact that President Eisenhower lent the prestige of his presence to the Summit conference. As statesman he had little choice. The bull market in popular illusion showed clearly enough how narrow had been his margin of practical maneuver.

Geneva disclosed how little, vis-à-vis the Communist empire, the West had left to bargain with. The West had nothing that the Communists wanted enough (short of total or piecemeal submission), nothing they feared enough (short of total atomic war). And total atomic war they knew they need not really fear.

Thus the U.S. found itself, in one annex to Geneva, sitting down (with a

representative of the unrecognized Peking government) to interminable talks
(still unterminated) in order to spring a comparative handful of its citizens,
unlawfully held by the Chinese Communists, from jails where many of them
are still unlawfully held.

Thus, too, the West's chief strategic friend in Europe, Chancellor Adenauer
of the German Federal Republic, soon after found himself forced to make
grave concessions simply for the release by the Soviet government of a few
thousand German war prisoners.

Western diplomacy, not through stupidity but because of a new adverse
balance of real power in the world, found itself obliged to treat with Communism at a level no higher than that of a family dealing with kidnapers for its
stolen children. Yet the meaning of this shift in power balance, which in
history is of somewhat the same order as the sinking of land masses into the sea
would be in nature, seemed scarcely to dent the West's awareness.

Behind the shift lay two interlocking situations, one technological, one
political. The technological one was the open secret, which the Geneva conferences dramatized, that the atom bomb is no longer, at least in the sense that Sir
Winston Churchill meant, the shield of the free world. Both sides possessed
retaliatory power deadly enough to make resort to atomic war mutually
suicidal.

But behind the deadlocked weapons situation lay a political situation ultimately much graver for the West. The key to this situation had been China.

"My statesmanship," wrote Henry Adams in 1903 (the date is noteworthy),
"is still all in China, where the last struggle for power is to come. . . . The only
country now on the spot is Russia, and if Russia organizes China as an
economical power, the little drama of history will end in the overthrow of our
clumsy Western civilization. . . . In that event, I allow till 1950 to run our race
out." This target date, too, is of interest. In fact, when the 20th Congress met,
Communist China had been for some time engaged in the mass collectivization of its peasants—the kind of human bulldozing that marks the first step in
organizing a socialist country into a modern industrial power. It was the fall of
China that finally shifted the basic power balance in the world and so gravely
complicated the problems of the West.

It is scarcely 35 years since Russia's then shaky Communist government
convened at Baku, in Soviet Georgia, a great "Congress of Peoples of the East."
There the Communist leaders of that day had called on the Far Eastern, Indian
and Moslem masses to war against imperialism. The incredible shape of things
to come was shadowed forth by a proclamation calling for a "Holy War under
the banner of the Comintern."

Even Communists liked to smile at that one in their private gatherings. But
they labored unsmilingly to give force to Lenin's strategy on the "Colonial
Question." Its end purpose: to strike at the West from the rear, and, by rousing

Asia, Africa and Latin America, to add their force to Communism, while depriving the West of overseas markets and sources of raw material which are a foreign base of its economic life. Thus in time, Communism hoped, the rising waters of disaffection might leave the powers of Europe and North America like rooftops, islanded in a flood. The final conflict would then be narrowed to this question: who is to control the rooftops?

No doubt Soviet Foreign Minister Vyacheslav Molotov knew at Geneva that a Soviet arms deal with Egypt would soon lift that flood (in the form of aroused Arab nationalism) against the West. He knew, too, that the rise of the Soviet Union as an industrial power, re-enforced by the production and the scientific and technological brains of half of Germany and all of Czechoslovakia, would enable those Bolshevik businessmen, Khrushchev and Bulganin, to take the road into the colonial markets and initiate a trade competition which must necessarily have a political face. It could all be done, too, under the shield of the atomic bomb. This, grossly oversimplified, was the international power pattern, the new balance of forces, which enjoined the new tactics proclaimed by the 20th Congress.

There must have come a moment, possibly some time before Stalin's death, when the keen eyes of Communism, ranging over the West and non-Communist Asia, were caught by a stunning insight which may be summed up in the phrase: those who are not against us are for us. In other words, for Communism the problem was how to convert the amorphous sentiments called "internationalism" or "neutralism" from negative to positive forces, from forces merely dividing the West's will to resist Communism into its marching allies. The answer was to refine the cruder forms of Communist aggression, which had produced the favorable power balance, into subtler forms of aggression which the power balance both required and made possible. This is the chief point and thrust of the tactics set forth at the 20th Congress.

As Secretary of the Communist party, Nikita S. Khrushchev keynoted this tactical shift. His speech runs to several thousand words. Its sense, once pried out of the foam rubber mufflings peculiar to Communist oratory, spells out the steps of the new tactic: 1) peaceful coexistence; 2) peaceful trade competition with the West; 3) revival of the popular front; 4) collective Communist leadership in contrast to Stalin's one-man rule. Their core meaning can be stripped from thousands of words to four words: no third world war.

How seriously the Communists mean this, how deep-going the zigzag is, can be glimpsed from the fact that to make it at all it was necessary, as Khrushchev expressly noted, to rethink certain of Lenin's conclusions. In *Imperialism*, hitherto a basic Communist text, written by Lenin during World War I, he offered the proposition that capitalism will finally commit suicide in a general war. It is this view that has just been updated.

Three of Khrushchev's points require special notice:

1) He claimed that Communism now spoke for a majority of mankind. He reached this score by counting on the Communist side, in particular, the friendly masses of India. In this he was stretching the elastic only a little thin. It has long been clear that the swing to Communism of one more population mass—Indonesia, for example—would give it something like an even break in any count of the world's noses.

2) Khrushchev was explicit in his popular front come-on. He put it this way: "Here cooperation also with sections of the socialist movement adhering to other views than ours in the question of the transition to socialism [*i.e.*, those differing chiefly about the advisability of violent revolution] is possible and necessary. Today many Social Democrats [*i.e.*, socialists and left liberals in the American sense] are for an active struggle against the war danger and militarism, for closer relations with socialist [*i.e.*, Communist] countries, and for unity of the labor movement. We sincerely welcome the Social Democrats and are ready to do everything possible to unite our efforts," etc. etc.

3) Khrushchev was careful to emphasize that Communism is still militantly revolutionary. There may still remain, he is saying even after the soughing of the warm peace winds and the disintegrating action of popular fronts, some strongholds of opposition in the West so intractable that they can be brought to reason (*i.e.*, Communism) only by the use of revolutionary violence. The U.S. is chiefly meant.

In effect Khrushchev is saying, "See, the Bomb is not going off. We are now extracting the detonator—a ticklish business. Surely all men of goodwill want to lend us a hand." To give this tactic force and mass, it is necessary to revive the popular front. To give it a semblance of plausibility, especially in view of the recent past, it is necessary to de-emphasize the cold war. For both it is expedient to liquidate Josef Stalin. For Stalin by his cynical pact with Hitler was not only the destroyer of the old popular front of the 1930s. He showed himself to be also the chief master of cold war.

Let us glance for a moment at cold war. In a sense Communism has always pursued a policy of cold war. It is a specialty of the house. But Communism was able to mount this policy on a world scale only after World War II. Then, the meaning of cold war came home to the incredulous West. Cold war is, in fact, the true brink of war policy, and whoever stands up to it finds himself willy-nilly playing brink of war. For its blackmailing effect depends on crowding an opponent to that brink so that any effort at resistance must make the brink seem more dizzily inevitable. Secretary of State John Foster Dulles was describing the experience with simple literalness in his much-abused phrase. Adlai Stevenson, too, described it more aptly than he knew because he was firing at the wrong target when he called it "Russian roulette."

Cold war, of course, involved a real risk. And the first man in the West who had the hardihood to make a brink of war stand, namely former President Harry S. Truman, took the Communists over the brink. That spoiled the game. The United States lost the Korean war because it was afraid of the threat of a bigger war with which Communism continued to play Russian roulette. The West was afraid. But the Communists must have been terrified, and with better reasons. The last thing in the world Communism could want was world war.

Thus, the initial American reaction in the Korean war must have brought the Communists to an agonizing reappraisal of cold war policy even before Stalin died, even though his powerful influence may have continued to hold them to that course. For, of course, policies develop an inertia, a momentum, that keeps them going even after their logic is impugned and the risks disclosed. And, of course, the West made a fool of itself in Korea, throwing away almost at once, out of its fear of general war, what its original initiative, General Douglas MacArthur's strategy and the courage of American men had won for it.

How quickly, too, the Communists in the full tide of victory settled for a mere half of Vietnam. What restraint, despite the bloodcurdling war whoops and tossing of stinkpots, has so far characterized Chinese Communist action around the Formosa Strait. No doubt this restraint, like that in Vietnam, reflects China's all-out exertion at collectivization and industrialization. This, in turn, bears directly on the current Communist peace strategy, which, among other items, is buying time for mainland China to emerge as a new Communist industrial massif.

Even during the cold war, at the time of the Stockholm peace pledge, Communists called for the organization of "partisans of peace." That term was meant to verbalize the fact that peace, as waged by Communists, is a form of weaponless war. It looked ahead to the time when the "partisans of peace" might eventually serve as the rallying core of armed partisan groups.

What the new Communist strategy envisages is the mounting, on a world scale, of a vast partisans of peace movement. Its formations will be the popular front. But something much more pervasive is foreshadowed; a radical change of the whole political climate of the West, going far beyond mere popular fronts, which, however manipulable, have manifest limits. Not only the political but the emotional preconditions for that change of climate exist. The whole world craves peace. All that is best in the West—most intelligent, humane, creative—abhors the thought of war. It is even simpler than that: men and women simply look at their children and grandchildren and think, it must not be. This is the absolute precondition for a change of climate. Practically all that is necessary to change the weather is for the Communist blizzard to stop freezing men's hopes, for a warm and melting sun to rise above the steppes. It is not necessary for Communism to liquidate the threat of Communism. It is only necessary for Communism to liquidate the threat of war.

Thus the tactical problem for Communism was not greatly different from that of the wind and the sun in Aesop's parable; competing to make a man take off his overcoat. To make the man—the West—take off his coat, it was only necessary for Communism to let the sun shine. The difference with the parable lay in the fact that, hitherto, Communism could not let the sun shine. It could not for a number of overriding historical reasons embodied in the person and the official mythology of Josef Stalin. He personified those memories which, in varying degrees of distrust, aversion or horror, scarify the mind of the West with respect to Communism, and even the minds of thousands of Communists.

Lenin and Stalin—"the gruesome twosome" they were sometimes referred to when their embalmed corpses peacefully coexisted in the tomb on Moscow's Red Square. Yet it is probable that even the most devout Stalinist, in the recesses of his mind, always sets some distinctive pause between the names of Stalin and of Lenin. After all, the devout were serving Communism rather than Stalinism, and were serving Stalin chiefly as he seemed to serve Communism. Many have forgotten, over the years, that before the revolution Lenin hailed Stalin as a "wonderful Georgian." Anti-Stalinists, in particular, have preferred to remember that, as he watched Stalin's machination two years before he died, the stricken Lenin told the 11th Congress: "The machine is slipping out of your hands." Perhaps he had forgotten, as so many others have, that it was he, Lenin, who put Stalin's hand on the controls.

It happened at the 10th Congress of the Soviet Communist party in 1921. Lenin himself had announced the historic turning point: henceforth there would be no more organized opposition to the majority view of the party. Lenin said, "We do not need any opposition now, comrades, it's not the time for it. . . . It is no good reproaching me, it follows from the state of affairs."

The organizational changes that followed that act of the 10th Congress brought Stalin closer to power and raised up certain of his followers, two of whom, Vyacheslav Molotov and Kliment Voroshilov, are still members of the Communist party's ruling presidium. This obscure bit of Communist history is of high importance in understanding the meaning of the 20th Congress. It reveals the continuity of the Communist pattern of action, the degree to which the more Communism changes the more it is the same thing.

Like Lenin in 1921, Stalin could later claim for his worst acts: "It is no good reproaching me, it follows from the state of affairs." The state of affairs through which Stalin pyramided the Communist empire to power included the collectivization of the peasants and the industrialization of the Soviet Union. To buy time for this, amidst the threatening international situation,

Stalin betrayed the Spanish Republic during its civil war, the popular front
and the German Communist party. For this, he wooed Hitler ardently and
signed a nonaggression pact, thereby making possible World War II so that the
West could destroy itself more effectually and quicker than Communism
could ever hope to destroy it. He almost lost his gamble when the Germans
turned on him in turn. Yet even that near-disaster Stalin turned into a triumph, winning back by the success of Soviet arms much of the goodwill he
had lost in the West.

Meanwhile, in a series of great giveaway conferences—Tehran, Yalta,
Potsdam—he outwitted or outmaneuvered the statesmen of the West, bringing the Communist frontiers into the heart of Europe and crowning his work
with the Communist conquest of China. That is why the men who are now
liquidating Stalin dead followed Stalin alive. And that is why they must now
liquidate his memory. For to achieve his successes, Stalin had terrorized the
Communist party, crucified the Soviet peoples and committed crimes which
alienated him from the human race—crimes which make his liquidation, in
changed circumstances, a prerequisite for Communist advance in a new age.
But it is also necessary to remember that in his appalling figure Communism
found one of its supreme manifestations. The Communists whom Stalin
liquidated make up the smallest part of his kill. But it is these chiefly that the
20th Congress is lamenting. It is these that the West is chiefly reacting to. But
there also lie between Stalin and the West, to cite only one item, three to six
million peasants whom Stalin (that is to say, Stalin and the Communist party)
killed as a matter of deliberate policy, by withholding food from them. What of
these dead?

In the mid-1920s chance threw me together with the last military attaché of
the czar's Washington embassy. A common love of Russian music sometimes
took us together to watch the idiot in *Boris Godunov.* I remember that patient
military exile telling me once, from the depths of his longing for the Russian
land which he did not live to see again, how, after the interminable winter, the
ice begins to break up in the Russian rivers. Then the peasant boys run along
the banks, trying to keep pace with the clashing floes; and, as they run, they
shout *"Lyot idyot"*—"the ice is going out!" It is just such an effect that the
action of the 20th Congress has had upon those minds who have lived, at all
deeply, the tragedy of our age wherever Communism has touched it.

I think the West will fail again to measure the full meaning of that effect if it
notes only that the men who have brought it about were former collaborators
with Stalin in his evil deeds, or supposes that they are merely cynical in their
crafty plans, whose guile is not, therefore, questioned. I, for one, do not
believe that when Khrushchev wept before Congress delegates those were
simulated tears, or that simulated tears could possibly have affected such an
audience, or that Khrushchev could have dreamed they could. This is some-

thing more: *lyot idyot*—the ice is going out, the ice that froze and paralyzed the messianic spirit of Communism during the long but (in Communist terms) justifiable Stalinist nightmare. Communism is likely to become more, not less, dangerous. It is this that gives us the sensation of passing in a fortnight from one age into another.

Communism has not changed. The dictatorship of the Communist party will not end. (The 20th Congress has acted to strengthen it.) It is unlikely that the slave labor camps will go or even shrink much. (Slave labor plays too important a part in the Communist economy and the victims of the reverse purge, or anybody at all who resists, will soon replace such political prisoners as may be released now.) Communist aggression against the West will not end. The 20th Congress has acted to give such aggression new, subtler, massive forms whose disintegrating energies are beamed first at specific soft spots around Communism's continental frontiers and far across them—at West Germany, France, Italy, Britain, India, Burma, Indonesia. Yugoslavia is already doing a "slow dissolve" back into the Soviet system—a homecoming which Moscow's official disbanding of the Cominform is intended to promote. For the Cominform, an organization of satellite and West European Communist parties, was used by Stalin chiefly to combat Marshal Tito and his special brand of heresy.

But, above all, it is the smashing of the Stalinist big lie that will change the climate, exerting its influence far beyond mere orthodox Communist lines, upon the internationalist and neutralist opinion of the West. With the smashing of the dark idol of Stalin, Communism can hope to compete again for the allegiance of men's minds, especially among the youth where its influence had fallen almost to zero. What the 20th Congress meant to do, and may well succeed in doing, was to make Communism radioactive again.

SOVIET STRATEGY
IN THE MIDDLE EAST

(*National Review,* OCTOBER 26, 1957)

Westminster, Md.

TALK, HERE IN the farmlands, is chiefly of the heaviest frost of this date in a decade, and what it may have done to stands of late corn. Yet it cannot be said that we are wholly out of touch with the capitals of the mysterious East—Cairo, Damascus, Baghdad, New York. Thus, a friend, a state legislator, dropped by, a month or so ago, to discuss a matter that was plainly burning a hole in one of the multiple pockets of his mind. Another legislator (from a Western state) had dreamed up a see-it-yourself plan. Paying their own way, a group of lawmakers from all over the country would, one day soon, step into a plane at Idlewild, and, hours later, put down in turn at Cairo, Tel Aviv, Damascus, Baghdad; then, veering north, and again east, at Belgrade and Moscow. Back to the West, if I remember rightly, by way of Warsaw. Everywhere, they hoped to see what eyes can see. In the capitals, they would talk with the makers and shakers. Should he go along? my friend asked.

Looking for the question behind the question, I took it to be: Was there any exceptional danger involved; did I think he could get in and out of the enemy compounds, Cairo, Damascus, Moscow, with a whole skin? Of course, I thought my friend should go along. I thought, too, in passing, that he was his own version of the American dream. Fifty years ago, he had been a farm boy in these same cornlands, hauling his father's crops to market in a horse-drawn wagon. Now, by hard work, and the exercise of a shrewd functional intelligence, he was a man of affairs, entitled to race the speed of sound through space to bespeak other men of affairs in lands far away, though not, unhappily, far enough away. "And what advice will you give Nikita (Khrushchev)?" I asked. The pre-autumn stillness blotted up his laugh.

If I urged my friend to go along, it is not because I set any great store by such excursions, but because others do. Henceforth, this trip would be among my friend's credentials. This is the age of the eye-witness and the first-personer: "I Watched the End of the World." The editor of the *Saturday Evening Post* once told me that it made a difference of thousands of readers if an article carried a title, beginning with the magic words: "I was" or "I did." I did not doubt it. But I doubted something else. That skepticism had set firm in wartime days, when, as a foreign editor, I read with hair-curling depression the reports of old China hands, observing on the spot, and singing in close harmony, that the Chinese Communists were "agrarian liberals." I knew that the Chinese Communists were not agrarian liberals, that, after Hitler's mop-up of the German Communist Party, they were the No. 2 section of the Communist International. But what right did I have to know it? I was not on the spot. How could I presume to pit my view against the close-up of the man on the scene? So I urged my friend: go.

Yet I remain of the opinion that the peering mind, peering even from a cow pasture, even in the jet age, still commands resources of a kind such as carried Dante once as far as Hell and Heaven. So I have sought to pace my friend in his flight, supposing, even, that though earthbound I had some advantages. For the mind has a way of getting into places to which the scheduled flights have been cancelled without advance notice.

I doubt, for example, that my friend made it into Damascus. Since he left, something fairly tremendous has happened in the Middle East, turning around Damascus as a hurricane turns on its eye. Last night, there appeared on the TV screen the face of the Arab King, Ibn Saud, the Ali Baba of the oil pools, and Washington's late, greatly salaamed guest. A most thought-provoking mask it was at this turn of events, tempting us to say of the man behind it—as Bismarck said of Napoleon III: "A sphinx without a secret." Yet the big Hollywood dark-glasses, vacuous under the Arab headgear, were belied by the royal smile, playing finely on the lips of the long lower face.

King Saud's face was there because he had just left the conference at Damascus, where it had been decided that Syria's Leftist government, Communist inspired, moneyed, munitioned (though largely, it would seem, Socialist-manned) poses no threat to Syria's Arab neighbors. In short, all the Washington blandishments had failed, as yet, to detach this king-pin completely, or really to dent the Arab front. I waited for the commentator to say: Something pretty tremendous has happened. But the press does not editorialize all the news at once, and where it feels least sure of itself is most likely to "report objectively." Last night, we were editorializing the woes of James Hoffa and Little Rock—cleverly, too; that is, not openly, but by selective emphasis. About Syria and Ibn Saud we got the news unchewed.

For once, this seemed a pity. In the sum of things, Hoffa and even Little Rock are comparatively pipsqueak. It is Syria that touches home. It is a great upset—not necessarily irreversible, or in the grand style, but sufficient unto Communism's strategy of the hour. It means that, at its second important test of containing Communism, the Eisenhower Doctrine has contained chiefly a mirage. It means that the Comrade has taken his longest stride across the Western encirclement, and squats outside it, smiling effacively, from a Mediterranean lodgement, with the condoning Arab lands spread out beyond, inviting mischief.

Picture the lewd delight,
Under the bridge tonight.

Any bridge, that is, across the Moskva River.

Whose is the fault? Not the Administration's, I think. Certainly not Mr. Dulles', though he is always the handy whipping-boy, never more so than for those who shout loudly that something has gone wrong while sighing with covert relief when such mischance also means that another crisis will abate. Possibly, with the Arab sanction, this particular Syrian crisis will abate, however bumpingly, because we are flummoxed, because Communism has gained its position, and, for the moment, does not need to push so hard; needs, in fact, a breathing-spell for consolidation and the next advance, which will mount the next crisis. How can it be otherwise, given the Middle East? Before the British-French-Israeli descent on Egypt, I wrote to the editor of this magazine—differing sharply, as I sometimes do, with its reading of events—somewhat like this: "The great hook, which Communism has contrived for us in the Middle East, is that no matter what we do will be wrong. If we back Britain against Egypt [Nasser had seized the Suez Canal], we rally Arab Asia and Africa against us. If we let Nasser get away with it, Communism gets away with it. Yet, on the whole, it seems to me that, of two bad alternatives, Dulles has chosen the slightly better one."

It is necessary to try to grasp 1) what Communist Middle East strategy implies over-all, and 2) how heavily the basic situation there is weighted against us. After the Egyptian dust-up, that strategy was interrupted for a time, not only, or perhaps even chiefly, by the stiffness of the American challenge to it, or the commotion in the Soviet satellites. Hesitation in the Middle East more probably reflected resistance in Moscow, on the part of a faction that we call (loosely) Stalinist. What ensued was a new crest of what we call (even more loosely) "the power struggle in the Kremlin." That power struggle must have taken the form, in part, of a ferocious debate over Middle East strategy. And matters must have been immensely confused when Dmitri Shepilov, until then a front runner of that strategy, supposing that he saw the hunt going against him, began to tiptoe to the Stalinist side. As we know, he supposed wrong. The Stalinists lost out, though how completely, or for how long, even Khrushchev may not know much better than we do. But, with that, the Communist Middle East strategy was back with us. We are told that, in the great Kremlin debate, it was described as an "icebreaker" strategy. Of course, the strategy is new only in its specific application in the changed circumstances of 1957—namely, to overleap the military-political encirclement with which the West has ringed Communist aggression as with an ice-barrier: to overleap that, and set fire to inflammable nations and continents beyond. In this sense, it is a revolutionary icebreaker.

It is a strategy of great imaginative boldness. It is two-pronged. It strikes (*inter alia*) at 1) the Arab oil pools; it promotes 2) Communism's advance along the North African land-bridge. (How long that takes, using how many false faces, about-faces, how much sinuous indirection—those are tactical problems.) The North African thrust is itself at least two-pronged. One prong aims to soften up Europe in several ways, by pinching the arteries of its oil-fed industry (we saw the threat hang poised during the Egyptian crisis; and in this case it is not true, as Nietzsche said, that "Damocles never danced better than under a sword"). Eventually, the same prong hopes to face Europe with a second front, no farther off than the width of a Mediterranean, no longer "Our Sea," but a sea where we co-exist with *them*.

The second prong is headed much farther West, toward the Atlantic gap, where the bulge of Africa approaches the bulge of South America. (Communism loves contiguity and easy overland routes, with the narrowest possible water-jumps.) Most of us do not think much or often about Latin America, except, perhaps, as the cut-rate vacationland of the colored airline ads. We may be absolutely sure that Moscow thinks a great deal about it, and quite differently. From time to time, we have seen spastic specimens of that thinking, attempting to become deed, in Argentina, Chile, Brazil, Colombia, Guatemala, and (acutely at the moment) in British Guiana. We may also be sure that what Moscow sees looks something like this: a continental human mass, where the solvent community is stretched, taut and thin as a polyethylene film, over impoverished millions who barely manage to subsist at a level of backward misery all but unimaginable to us, in the land of: "Just add hot water and serve." In the western hemisphere, Latin America reproduces, with its own variants, most of the social inflammabilities of Asia. Latin America is Asia in our own back yard. It is this lode of social cordite that Communism's trans-African prong has in view. No doubt we are tired of hearing that the road to Paris runs through Peking. The road to Washington runs through Rio de Janeiro and Mexico City. But first it runs through Damascus, Cairo and Algiers. It is the prospective path along which travels a little fuse, a mere sputter yet, toward the high explosives of the Western world. In this sense, Communist Middle East strategy implies the beginning of a direct assault on the United States.

But a strategic concept is still far from a strategic reality? And Russians are not ten feet tall? Forty years ago, most of Communism was a handful of seedy outlaws, piling their plates with cigarette stubs during endless wrangles in the Swiss equivalent of beaneries. But they were wrangling in terms of the world. They now control a third of it, and even (since I began writing this) overlook the rest from space, from that mechanical moon whose circlings must be seen as the latest outcome of those circling Swiss wrangles. I beg you, do not underrate the energy of the Communist will or the sweep of its strategic vision, simply because it seems improbable to you.

If for no other reason, the need to pinch that Communist fuse close to the quick, and at a stroke, justified the Eisenhower Doctrine, all its risks and inadequacies at once conceded. The same need justified the repudiation of our old friends, Britain and France, during their Egyptian descent. And that, quite apart from the high moral phrases—no doubt devoutly believed in by the phrasers—which helped to transfigure (and to blur) what was, when cut to the bone, a necessity of raw power; the necessity to block the Communist thrust before it got galloping. Moral turpitude—how bizarre the words sound by Communist contrast, by contrast with the overarching provocation (and its implications) that triggered the Anglo-French act. Against Egypt, moral turpitude was the least of the sins of Britain and France, whose chief sin was the one for which history gives no absolution—the sin against reality. Reality was defined here by a debility of will, enacted in a debility of performance, of those two quondam powers, bled white and exhausted in two world wars and their consequences, so that they could no longer strike, even in concert, with a force which would redeem its risks in the world's one universal coin: success, for they could not act at all without inciting that rally of Asia and Africa against the West, which, in the context of the Communist conflict, was a dated luxury that the West could no longer afford.

We might do worse than glance at the reminder that Mommsen set at the threshold of this age: "History has a Nemesis for every sin: for the will to freedom that fails in force, as well as for the pride of mind that fails in understanding." So the Egyptian crisis disclosed, as its core meaning, chiefly this: that leadership of the West had at last to become one with where real power in the West alone lay—in the United States. This, regardless of what anybody might want or of the quality of leadership.

The same need justified our philanderings with Ibn Saud, unseemly to some, preposterous to others. Who else was there to philander with? Mr. Dulles could have had few illusions. It is scarcely three years since King Saud had his finance minister's right hand chopped off (it had made away with some $3 million of the royal oil receipts), and nailed up in a public square of the capital. If this seems an exotic trifle in an age when great European governments, claiming to be civilized, have organized the planned massacre of millions, it is a trifle which stands for much that must be intensely repugnant to Mr. Dulles, who would not willingly see even Mr. Harold Stassen's right hand nailed to a desk in Foggy Bottom. But history gives you certain pieces to work with, and gives no others. It gave Mr. Dulles Ibn Saud.

In the Middle East, we are in the presence of two energies, which, for convenience, we may separate, but which, in fact, interlock. The first of those energies is political revolution, express in Egypt and Syria, smouldering everywhere. It takes the diverse forms of Arab Nationalism. For historical reasons that we all know, it is prevailingly, often fiercely, anti-Western. Yet for a variety of reasons, Arab Nationalism is constrained to work with the West. For a variety of reasons, of which two—our need to pump out Arab oil, and our need to contain Communism—are foremost, the West is constrained to work with Arab Nationalism.

In doing so, in replacing Britain as the paramount power in the Middle East, and seeking to contain Communism there in the gambles and gambols of power politics, we deal, perforce, with a spectrum of sheiks of varying shapes and sizes. The Kings, Ibn Saud and Hussein of Jordan, may be taken to stand close to one end of that spectrum. Toward the other end, stand the Christian Arab leaders (a rather different breed) of the Lebanon, the main American beachhead. Somewhere in between, stand the Iraqis. Everywhere, the coin we deal in is Arab Nationalism, supplemented (one hopes, at least) by our skill in dispensing much more tangible coin, as we should because we must. It is a game that requires the utmost in tact, steadiness of nerve, and experience, which, as newcomers, we must gain largely by doing. It is a game, too, in which we may expect only partial or impermanent successes (Jordan looks, at the moment, to be one of these).

We are now up, now down; nothing is final; all is in flux. And we are not the only player on the field. At this level, Communism can play the game, too, and adroitly. It has, besides, the advantage of a master piece, which it can use in ways denied to us. Wherever we seek to regroup Arab Nationalism in the interest of the West, Communism advances that disruptive master piece. We all know what it is, though no one likes to mention it. It is the State of Israel. At once, it becomes necessary to define our intentions clearly. A filthy anti-Semitism afflicts many minds in the West. Nothing is gained by denying it. So let us say flatly: in Christendom, no mind can claim to be civilized and, at the same time, be anti-Semitic, any more than an American mind can claim to be civilized and be anti-Negro. For all Christians, regardless of creed, the Vatican has defined the position once for all: "Spiritually, we are Semites." Moreover, an immense compassion—mere good will is too genderless a term—before the spectacle of the Jewish tragedy in our century, must move our hourly understanding of what the State of Israel means in terms of a hope fired by such suffering.

Let us be quite sure that we know this. For it is also necessary to look at Israel in terms of Middle East reality. Communism may lose friendly Egypt or Syria; it will look for purchasable pawns elsewhere. It is Israel, as an enemy, that Communism cannot afford to lose. Israel is Communism's indispensable piece in the Middle East, so that a firm Israeli-Arab settlement would be the greatest disaster that could befall Communism in that region. The crux of the problem is not chiefly, as we so often hear, the question of resettling the Arabs displaced from Palestine. The crux is the Arab fear of Israeli expansion. Communism has only to tweak that nerve of Arab fear, and, at the touch, Arab Nationalism closes ranks, despite our utmost effort, despite the ferocious animosities sometimes dividing the Arab leaders themselves. Thus, at the power-political level, the Middle East situation is weighted against us by this all but unsolvable problem.

Yet Israel is chiefly useful to Communism at that level, and, perhaps, chiefly at this stage. Over the long haul, the Middle East is weighted against us by something much deeper-going. That something is an incipient social revolution whose makings are everywhere. It is the fermenting energies of that revolution that Communism counts on. If we think little about Latin America in such terms, most of us think scarcely at all about the Middle East.

Imagine a vast region, most of it empty desert, where cities are few, where thousands live in caves, or, at a higher level, in hovels or slums, though these words of ours scarcely convey the Arab reality. Here, an illimitable poverty is the norm, a poverty made sodden by endemic disease, dark by endemic illiteracy and by an absence of hope that may best be called hereditary. Where, among millions, the daily struggle to eat at all is the term in which the possibility of hope first presents itself, hope turns easily to social revolution. Anything serves to turn it. Arab Nationalism turns it, and cannot anywhere mount its political revolution without at the same time stirring the energies of the social revolt, and blending with them, until political and social revolution tend to become one. At that fusion point is bred the Arab Communist, a comparatively new development. It is on such native shock troops that Communism counts; and, as usual with Communism, it is not numbers, but a certain kind of knowing fanaticism, resolute and resourceful, that matters.

How easy it is for Communism to work with those social revolutionary energies, which it needs only to set in motion in order to win half its battle. How much easier than for the West, which does not want them set in motion, which, in so far as it works with such energies at all, must work to moderate, restrain and channel them toward peaceable development, while helping these destitute populations to reach a level of minimum well-being, which may act as a brake on revolution. That takes time. It also takes capital. It is surprising, is it not? to see revolution turning on a question of capital. Yet so it is in the Middle East. This is, of course, one of the aspects of foreign aid; and those who set themselves most implacably against it, might brood upon this context. For what is needed here are the irrigation ditch, the factory, and the dam that supplies the ditch and powers the factory, and all the enterprise the factory feeds and stands for.

There are only two sources of such capital—the West and the Communist Empire. Presumably, the West has a good deal more capital to invest, or even to expend, than Communism has. But, again, how much easier it is for

Communism. Western capital must, in the nature of things, expect a proper return on its loans, both in the form of interest and tangible advantages, chiefly political, which are a justified collateral. But to the Arab of all classes, therefore, the West appears, or can easily be made to appear, as the niggard banker, whose prudent doles serve to replace a political imperialism, of which the memory is green, by an economic imperialism which the Arabs fear is the other side of the political coin.

How different Communism looks. If its imperialism is of an enslaving frightfulness unknown since Rome's, the Arabs have no direct experience of it. If Communism has less than the West to give, it needs to give less; and it can dole out its credits at rates of interest that radically undercut the West. For, with Communism, capital is the exclusive property of the State, which can assign it where it best promotes Communism's political purposes. Nor does Communism need to disperse its bounty to gain its ends. It can spot it for best effect. Easy credits to Egypt or to Syria, and these places become show-windows in the great Middle East bazaar, to which all eyes are drawn. Moreover, these are down-payment on a promise that need not be kept. If the situation develops favorably to Communism, it will not be kept. But if the West interferes with those who accept the Communist bounty, the West appears to be interfering with the promise. No doubt King Saud's action at Damascus was motivated, at least in part, by this realization, and his fear of the effect which our interference might have, in such terms, on Arab minds. For the Communist promise, though largely unfulfilled, is lure enough. And it is cheaper than foreign aid.

Not all, or even a great many, of the Arabs who take Communist cash, can be Communists. But "O, take the cash and let the credit go" is an Eastern admonishment. It is also the impulse of the needy anywhere. The literate Arab, who is not yet a Communist, can have few illusions about what he is doing. He knows that to play with Communism is a dangerous game. He has weighed the risks and discounted them. Meanwhile, he has the credits to buy the guns (yonder lies Israel!), and to finance at least some small beginnings of the irrigation ditch, the dam and the factory.

And the illiterate Arab, in his miserable millions, what does he think? How can anyone know? But there is evidence that a whisper has run through the caves and hovels, as far south as the Sultanate of Oman and Muscat, and the Saudi wastes, that help has come from that great Power in the steppes, where—praise be to Allah!—the workers have seized the factories and the peasants divided the land—or so the prophets have said. Let us remember that it was a Nobel Prize winner of the West, who, after the Communist-planned massacre by famine of some four million peasants, still hailed the Soviet Union as: "That great light in the East." Should we be surprised if a ragged fellah knows no more?

* * *

But have not these wretched Arabs heard, too, that in Soviet Siberia several million of their co-religionists exist in a misery not much different from their own? Possibly they have heard. Radio has put everybody in the next room from everybody else. The air is crisscrossed invisibly at all hours by warning and hectoring voices. Moreover, and particularly in illiterate lands, news of this kind travels with surprising speed, nobody quite knows how. So perhaps they have heard. But "Russia is wide and the Tsar is far away" was a peasant saying even in our boyhoods. It is extremely difficult to imagine a reality other than our own; and, if our own is desperate, the feat becomes almost impossible, and, in addition, pointless. We need not be too surprised, perhaps, if there is vaguely taking form at the back of the eyes that watch from the slums and the deserts, a vision that has little to do with reality, which distance itself has stripped of the monstrous reality—a vision of Moscow as a mythical Tsarigrad, the symbol of present power, credits, but, above all, of hope.

And where are Washington, New York and London? No screening distance has mercy on them. The wretched Arab sees their tokens all about him in shapes financed by oil profits (and others) of the West's necessary allies. He sees them in the dusty flash of a royal Cadillac, steaming past the mud huts, in the $90 million palace which King Saud has conjured up from the unirrigated sands.

This is the picture I see, peering from my cow-pasture. It is stroked in, of necessity, in gross shorthand, with gross omissions and simplifications. All I have meant to do is to suggest certain considerations which, it seems to me, are somewhat overlooked, but which would seem to bear heavily on the outcome of history in the Middle East. I am curious to learn what first-hand impressions my legislative friend brings back from his Eastern travels, to correct my own.

THE COMING STRUGGLE
FOR OUTER SPACE

(*National Review*, NOVEMBER 2, 1957)

TV UTILIZED a break in a Braves-Yankees broadcast to amplify the first, skeptical announcement of a day or so before that Sputnik really was up there. Listening to the somewhat breathless confirmation ("it says: 'Beep! Beep!'"), I laughed. Neighbors, who happened to be present, asked why. I could only answer: "I find the end of the world extremely funny." "What's funny about that?" one asked. What could I answer: that men always defy with laughter what they can do absolutely nothing else about? Beyond that, any explanation I attempted would have been as puzzling as my reaction seemed.

I think I should have had to begin something like this. In 1923, I was sitting in a restaurant on the Kurfuerstendamm, in Berlin. What did the mark then stand at—40 million to the dollar? The exact ratio of catastrophe is unimportant. In Germany, inflation had wiped out all small and middle bank accounts, and the value of all wages, pensions, payments, as completely and inexplicably as if the top floor of a skyscraper had collapsed and dropped the whole nation to the ground. Germany, in 1923, was a madhouse of stunned, desperate, tormented millions.

On the sidewalk beyond my table, there walked past a handsomely dressed, extremely dignified woman. It would miss something to say that she was crying. Tears were streaming down her face—tears which she made no effort to conceal, which, in flowing, did not even distort her features. She simply walked slowly past, proudly erect, unconcerned about any spectacle she made. And here is what is nightmarish: nobody paid the slightest attention to her. The catastrophe was universal. Everybody knew what she signified. Nobody had anything left over from his own disaster to notice hers.

She became one of my symbols of history in our time. About this unknown, slowly walking, weeping woman, as about certain other things, no more momentous, that were around me in those days, I came to feel at length as Karl Barth said of something else: "At that moment, I found my hand upon the rope, and the great bell of prophecy began to toll." I began then (along with thousands of others) to draw certain conclusions about the crisis of history in this time that I can merely sketch in like this: 1) the crisis was total (in the end, none would be spared its lash); 2) its solution would fill the lifetime of my generation and the next ones; 3) the one certainty about the solution was that the stages by which it was reached must be frightful, whatever the solution itself turned out to be.

Does it sound wildly irrational to say that, when the newscaster broke into the ball game, I also laughed because that woman walked again across my mind's eye? It is so. With her began the prophecy; the circling of the scientific moon was implicit in her slow walk-past (though neither she nor I could know that). Yet to have lived with this prospect of reality for more than thirty years, and to have been unable to communicate it convincingly to others—that is the heart of loneliness for any mind. Cassandra knew.

It works out, too, in the simplest, most immediate ways. As soon as my wife and I were alone, I said: "They still do not see the point. The satellite is not the first point. The first point is the rocket that must have launched it." Of course, the scientists and the military chiefs grasped this obvious implication at once. But it took three or four days for anybody to say so, in my hearing.

In short, the struggle for space has been joined: But this was only the immediate, military meaning. Widen it with this datum: the satellite passed over Washington, sixty miles away. One minute later, it passed over New York. We have entered a new dimension. Like Goethe after the battle of Valmy, we can note in our journals: "From this day and from this place, begins a new epoch in the history of the world; and you can say that you were there."

There is a wonderful passage in the Journal of the Goncourt Brothers, wonderful, in part, for its date, which cannot be later than 1896. I shall not be able to quote it exactly from memory, but it goes much like this: "We have just been at the Academy, where a scientist explained the atom to us. As we came away, we had the impression that the good God was about to say to mankind, as the usher says at four o'clock at the Louvre: 'Closing time, gentlemen.'" None of us supposes that this moon means closing time. None of us can fail to see, either, that closing time is a distinct possibility. Again, the point is not that we do not yet have the ICBM fully developed; we will. The point is that the new weapons are, of their nature, foreclosing weapons, and, whether or not they are all presently in our hands, too, they are in the hands of others over whom we have no control. That is what I meant by "end of the world." Only those who do not know, or who do not permit their minds to know, the annihilative power of the new weapons, will find anything excessive in the statement. "Nine H-Bombs dropped with a proper pattern of dispersal" was a figure given me, three or so years ago, as the number required to dispose of "everything East of the Mississippi River." Whether the figure is accurate to a bomb or a square mile is indifferent. Any approximation of it speaks for itself.

* * *

Unlike Goethe, I doubt that any of us can feel a particular elation in being able to say: "And you were there." I suspect that about the best we can muster will be like the historic first words said to have been uttered by the King of Greece, on landing there after the German occupation in World War II and the ruinous civil war. "Nice weather for this time of year, isn't it?"

In those words, the end of dynastic Europe is, once for all, self-proclaimed. Their staggering inconsequence is not stupidity, but something much more final: the inability of a mind any longer to feel or know the reality which, by position, it should be shaping. Such a mind is no longer equal to the meaning of what is happening to it or to anybody else. Is not this condition growing on all of us? Is there not a deliberate will to inconsequence—a will not to know, not to see, the dimensions of what we are caught up in—a will to make ourselves, and our vision, small, in the child's hope that, if we work hard enough at it, we can make the tremendum enclosing us as small as we are? Perhaps, if we do not look, it will go away, leaving us with the Edsel and the split-level house. How else explain the fact that, born into a century unprecedented in scale, depth and violence of disruption (the two world wars and the new energy sources are instance enough), we nevertheless manage so successfully not to know its total meaning, but to see its shock piecemeal, as a disjointed, meaninglessly recurrent hodgepodge? The attitude is fixed in a habit of minimizing complacency, commonly couched as a posture of strength. But since it does not conform to the scale of real events, it is irrational, and leads, invariably, to those equally irrational spasms of extravagant jitter or extravagant optimism (such a wave as swept the West after the Geneva Summit Conference), whose inevitable recession in the face of the facts, plunges us into deepest puzzlement.

It is a late and tired habit of mind, which we seek to glorify by twining about it the rather dry and lifeless vine-leaves called: reasonableness, the calm view, common sense, the injunction never, under any circumstances, to feel strongly about anything (which, among other things, is blighting the energy of our youth at the source). "I believe," the little old man of twenty-one who was his college's most brilliant political science major, explained to me, "that the tendency, nowadays, is to see everything quantitatively." "Yes," agreed the Fulbright fellow who was with him, neither approving nor disapproving, merely baffled, but, above all, by my extraordinary question: "Doesn't the student mind ever get excited about anything any more?" It is a positive will not to admit or permit greatness in event or men. But, since will itself implies a suspect energy, it takes form as a vague distaste, discomfort, distrust, relieved by a preference for the commonplace, the conforming, the small, the minutely (hence safely) measurable, the quantitative—method and dissection replacing life and imagination.

Whatever else Sputnik is or means, the handwriting that it traces on our sky writes against that attitude the word: Challenge. It means that, for the first time, men are looking back *from outside*, upon those "vast edges drear and naked shingles of the world" which Arnold reached in imagination. In imagination—which is the creative beginning of everything (God Himself had first to imagine the world), the one indispensable faculty that has brought man bursting into space from that primitive point of time he shamblingly set out from. That breakthrough (all political considerations apart) touches us with a little of the chill of interstellar space, and perhaps a foreboding chill of destiny—a word too big with unchartable meanings to be anything but distasteful to our frame of mind. For it is inconceivable that what happens henceforth in, and in consequence of, space, will not also be decisive for what happens on the earth beneath. In short, Sputnik has put what was useful and effective in method and dissection once more at the service of imagination. It is the war of imagination that, first of all, we lost. It is in terms of imagination that the Russians chiefly won something. The issue has only been joined. Nothing is final yet. But it is joined in space, and it is at that cold height that henceforth we will go forward, or go nowhere. There is no turning back.

Before this illimitable prospect, humility of mind might seem the beginning of reality of mind. As starter, we might first disabuse ourselves of that comforting, but, in the end, self-defeating, notion that Russian science, or even the Communist mind in general, hangs from treetops by its tail.

A WESTMINSTER LETTER:
THE LEFT UNDERSTANDS THE LEFT
(*National Review*, NOVEMBER 16, 1957)

THE WORLD IS randomly streaked with comings and goings—the evidence of an intense activity, taking place largely out of sight. Sometimes, we catch glimpses of its passage. They are curiously suggestive. Usually they ask more than they tell. The comers and goers are, in general, public persons, but not, as a rule, official; though they may have been official a few moments ago, and may be official again a few minutes later. Such a public figure goes privately from America to India or Yugoslavia, for example—and sees whom; and what was said? A Soviet national comes to the United States in some unnoticed delegation, or one that is scarcely noticed, and, in any case, almost instantly forgotten. And, again, sees whom; and what was said? We are unlikely ever to know.

These half-glimpsed fittings fascinate by all they suggest, but do not tell. We can do little more than note them, though we may guess that, in the course of them, some little thread has been connected with some other thread, which, if we could see the whole web of the history of our time, might bear surprisingly on much that puzzles the mind about the underlying design.

Not long ago, I came on a little news item, dropped in more or less as filler—the brief news that Mr. Aneurin Bevan, on a recent trip to the Crimea, had been the house-guest of Mrs. Nikita Khrushchev. Presumably it was treated more fully elsewhere, but this was all that came my way. I found it a little nugget—one of those unnoticed bits of living history (unnoticed, certainly, by thousands living around me), which, like a bead of radium, lights up shoals of darkness, though the nature of radium remains a riddle, and what we see by its glow chiefly perplexes.

Mrs. Khrushchev perplexes. She is the wife of a man whose name, a year or so ago, was all but unknown to the West, but who in some six months has emerged as one of the most powerful men alive. The West knows so little about his wife that the discovery that she exists at all was something of a scoop. It is said that—another victim of "the cult of personality"—she passed some years in a Siberian slave labor camp. Khrushchev, meanwhile, stayed at home, as Stalin's Paramount Chief in the Ukraine or in the powerful Moscow Party section. He seems to have been able, or willing, to rescue his wife only after the Georgian's death. Some link this large restraint with the gossip that makes Elena Furtseva Mrs. Khrushchev's great rival. It seems to be true that Khrushchev moved his wife back from Siberia not long before he moved Furtseva into the Praesidium of the Soviet Communist Party.

Such Suetonian tales, perhaps a little true and largely silly, usually predispose us toward the wife. So does Mrs. Khrushchev's apolitical appearance. She looks like the type of peasant woman whom a Russian once described to me as: "A meal sack with a rope tied round the middle." (Of course, *that* Russian was not a Communist, but a Socialist Revolutionist; as solemn heads everywhere know, humor is the seed of heresy.)

Mrs. Khrushchev is burlier than the type, which tends to softness. In that plain, earthy face is read a vigor of the twofold kind that will rush in tears to rescue a kitten drowning in a rain-barrel, while snatching up, on her way, a chicken whose head she will, without pausing in her rush, tweak off, with the evening meal in mind. Of course, there is nothing exclusively Russian in that; peasants everywhere act much alike. Yet the Russian peasant does seem to have a special dialectic talent for combining opposites. A Yiddish writer summed it up to me this way: "A Russian peasant is a man who will go to endless pains to murder his grandmother by burning her alive in her hut. But then he remembers that the canary is also inside, and, at peril of his life, plunges into the flames to save the bird." A good deal that happens inside Russia is scarcely comprehensible in any other terms.

Yet I prefer something else. A former Russian anarchist, then old and gravely ailing, once showed me a little photograph of himself, taken in Tsarist days when he was in Siberian exile. In it, the sick man, stooping beside me over the picture, was seen as a youth, seated by a window filled with potted plants, in a Siberian *isba*. He was wearing a collared Russian blouse, and the lightly melancholy smile proper to his age, and to the revolutionist of that other age. The old man beside me mused: "The Siberians are not a mellow people, like the Russians. But, you see—there are flowers in the window. So, you see"—and here his voice dropped into that dying fall in which the Russian voice catches at times the weight of all this weary, unintelligible world—"so, you see, there is something gentle in those people, too."

Perhaps there is something gentle in Mrs. Khrushchev, too, if you are lucky enough not to be a chicken at meal time. What suffering she must have known and seen—revolution, civil war, famine, purges, murder of classes, nations, friends, world war, terror, terror, terror, such as hunting and hunted animals live in hourly—and, at last, a slave. This Lady Macbeth from Mtsensk might also say: "I have supped full with horrors." Is that what she said to Aneurin Bevan?

For, of course, it was his entrance under her battlements that made the news item seem to me a nugget. What was he doing in that galley? What was said across the *pertsovkas*? Aneurin Bevan, it is generally supposed, will be Britain's foreign minister—perhaps its next one—if the Labor Party comes to power, as it may do in two years time or less. (In Britain, prices are up 50 per cent in seven years; interest rates as high as 7, some say 8 per cent; gold and dollar reserves down $517 million in two months; good growing weather for Socialism.) Did they talk about that? Language would have been no barrier; they share a basic language. Keynes is a dialect of Marx not too greatly different than Slovene, say, is from Russian.

Did they talk about what, as foreign minister, Bevan might do to shoehorn Communist China into the UN; to pluck some feathers from the mutually detested conservative, the German Chancellor Adenauer; to coax American air bases out of Britain; to curb American thermonuclear prowess? It all falls under the plausible head of "relieving world tensions."

Or did they discuss common housekeeping details—the theoretical developments now being argued, heatedly within Western socialism, violently within Communism? The nub of that debate is the question of how some individual freedom can still be had, and how much, while still having socialism. The degree to which Communism and socialism can approach each other over that bridge underlies one of the strategies implied in the theses of the 20th Congress of the Soviet Communist Party.

Did they discuss the tactical shift within British socialism whereby the Labor Party, with an eye to votes and much else, has shelved outright nationalization, at least for a while, in favor of a Socialist government's buying into key industry as majority stockholder; thus letting the old managers continue to do the work they do, in general, so much better than Socialist bureaucrats—namely, that of managing their own business, but as hirelings of the Socialist State? We can only guess. We are unlikely ever to know.

But we know this: Aneurin Bevan has long been a spokesman of that section of British socialism which has shrilly demanded that Britain's Conservative Government cease its development of thermonuclear weapons. "I see no purpose," Bevan recently (and shrilly) confided to Prime Minister Nehru about the H-Bomb, "in Britain arming herself with that useless weapon."

We live and learn, especially if we have been to Mrs. Khrushchev's. After his Russian visit, Mr. Bevan reversed his field to such effect that a motion putting the Labor Party on record against thermonuclear development was voted down 5 to 1 at the Party's latest Congress, with Mr. Bevan himself steering the steamroller amidst shouts of: "Turncoat," "Traitor," from that plangent minority which never learns that to gain power is what political parties first of all exist for. Why this turnabout? Well, you can scarcely expect an average Briton to vote for you as Socialist if, by doing so, he must also vote against his own thermonuclear self-defense. We are also told that, in Russia, Khrushchev gave Britain's presumptive foreign minister some specific Socialist advice: "Don't give up your Bomb and leave a vacuum." A vacuum? That is to say: Don't leave the United States, the one great power uncommitted to socialism, as the one thermonuclear power in the West.

Beyond that, what does this mean? I can only tell you what I think it means. Around 1951, one of the British Socialist leaders—Mr. Hugh Dalton, if I remember rightly—was urging on a Labor Party gathering a more concilia- tory line toward the Soviet Union. In clinching his plea, he said: "The Left understands the Left." Yes, that is the crux of the matter. It is to say that, in the showdown, despite all brotherly invective and despite all brotherly arm- twisting, socialism still has more in common with Communism than either of these two has with conservatism. "Do not give up your Bomb and leave a vacuum." How that might work out with Mr. Bevan as foreign minister, in some tearing crisis of the East-West conflict, none of us knows. Neither is it at all difficult to imagine how it might work in terms of a Britain disposed by a justifiable self-interest to neutrality, and disposed by a Socialist government to conciliate Communism. The Left understands the Left.

A WESTMINSTER LETTER:
"TO TEMPORIZE IS DEATH"
(*National Review*, NOVEMBER 23, 1957)

"THIS TIME last year," I thought. For the voice, asking its rather staggering questions over the long-distance wire, yesterday, was the same voice that had telephoned this time last year, almost to a day. It belongs to a friend who has spent a good many years in public life and public service. There was the same tenseness in his voice now as there had been a year before, but for reasons as different as if, in the meantime, the world had spun over on its axis and reversed its poles. Then the voice had seemed to me curiously optimistic (the Hungarian revolt was on). Now it seemed to be speaking from the bottom of a pit (Sputnik II had been launched the day before). Until that moment, I had not realized, could scarcely have believed possible, the degree of alarm that the second Communist moon had stirred in the West.

The voice said: "Suppose the Russians have one hundred rockets of the thrust that launched the second Sputnik, and that the rockets have hydrogen warheads. Suppose they are trained on the United States. Will the Russians first give us an ultimatum in the hope of taking our technology intact? Or will they launch the rockets without any ultimatum? Certain quarters," the voice went on, "have put that question to their Communist experts. What would your answer be?" As put to me, it was a purely personal, unofficial question; I am not a Communist expert. Perhaps that is why, instead of reaching for a graph, I thought: "This time last year . . ." Let us remember that time a little, because it bears both on my friend's question and my answer.

This time last year, I came out of my workroom, one morning, to find my wife waiting, shaken and distracted, just outside. "They've come back," she said. "They're bombing the city. It's horrible." It was Sunday, November 4, 1956. The Soviet armor had wheeled back on Budapest. We listened to the pleas for help from the Hungarian resistance radios, boosted, rebroadcast or paraphrased by the stations of the West. One appeal broke off: "May God help you and help us." "At that point, the Hungarian station went off the air," said the American announcer's Sunday voice—comes out like a ribbon, lies flat on the brush. At that point, in fact, the man with the tommy-gun had kicked in the door, and it required no imagination at all to know what had happened next in that Hungarian studio. My wife burst out: "Why don't they stop those horrible commercials! Why don't all the stations pray, why doesn't everyone simply pray to God to help the Hungarians? Poor people, oh, poor, poor people!" She rocked back and forth silently in order not to give way further to her grief.

I said nothing. I was thinking of what the West would do, or, as I surmised, would not do, with this historic opportunity. I was remembering certain words of Lenin's at the great turning-point of this century. He was warning his sluggard henchmen that history sometimes gives men one chance, and that it seldom gives them a second chance; that, for resolute and intelligent men, given that chance, not to seize and act upon it is "crime"; that "to temporize is like death," "to temporize *is* death."

This time last year, the temporizing UN was trying to try to push through a resolution condemning the Hungarian horror; was screaming moral indignation, though somewhat like the duck in *Peter and the Wolf*, "from the middle of the pond." This time last year, the voice that telephoned me yesterday called from Washington to ask hopefully: "What do you think? Will we intervene in Hungary?" I said: "No intervention. The people are afraid it means world war. If you could put it to a vote, you would not get one thousand votes for intervention in the whole country." The figure might just as well have been one million votes without in any way changing the fact.

This time last year, I wrote, to try to fix, first of all, the physical image of those events while they were happening, and then certain of their wider meanings, but also, perhaps, out of the need that sometimes makes men scrawl last-minute notes that may never be read and set them adrift in bottles that may never be found. So I wrote: "There are names that belong to the language of destiny, and one of them is Budapest—Budapest of the November days. In hallways, civilians huddled over machine-guns—men as watery with fear, you may be sure, as all others who have gone against Communism, not with words only, but with acts. On the streets, half-grown boys, darting bare-handed against Soviet armor, to stuff flaming rags in the tank vents. Patrolling the shattered housefronts, children with slung rifle and tormented faces. On the public squares, the ranged bodies of the fallen, already nondescript in death, and stared at by the nondescript living of a kind that always clots around the raw edges of action. A late autumn landscape of an age that certainly supposes itself to be some kind of summit of accomplishment."

This time last year, I wrote: "Here, on the Hungarian and on the Polish plain, history is struggling to break in two. A phase has been arrested, which (visibly) from Teheran and Yalta through the Communist conquest of China, and (incalculably) in every direction beyond, has been one of piecemeal disaster to mankind. In its stead, there has opened the possibility of a phase of hope, still highly unstable and inconclusive. In this new region of experience, the Hungarians hold the first heights of meaning. The mind cannot enter here from the West except by way of Hungary, any more than you can enter

Thermopylae from the south without passing that marker which, after two thousand years, still says to those who may have forgotten every other fact about the Persian Wars: Stranger, tell the Lacedemonians that we lie here, obeying their command.

"This is not because the center of political gravity in the satellite situation lies in Hungary. Events are likely to disclose that it lies, as it has from the first, in Poland and in the Germanies (West as well as East). Least of all is it, as we have so often heard of late, because Soviet action in Hungary has at last stripped the mask from Communism and revealed its true face. Anybody who had to wait for Budapest to tell him that does not know what century he has been born into. Nothing has happened in Hungary by way of horror that has not happened repeatedly within the Communist Empire, and more horribly. Millions of Russians (let us remember) have already been destroyed, defying Communism. Their struggle and their cries were lost in the distances of Euro-Asia. But we *heard* the Hungarians, and they tore at least at our nerves.

"Those cries command our attention first to a challenge that is as simple as it is timeless. All other factors change or fade—the politics, economics or their catchwords that men defied or defended. But resistance enacts a human meaning that is always the same. It says that when man, the sufferer, rises by courage above the odds of pain, he liberates by his act the one force that brute power, destroying all else, is powerless to destroy. There is more. To the exact degree in which brute power is most incontinently brutal, those who resist compel it to collaborate in dramatizing that meaning. That done, resistance, though it can be crushed, cannot be defeated. Disaster is not defeat. Resistance outlives disaster because the sons remember the fathers, and that memory is caught at again and again by others who suffer, and whom it moves to dream of resisting in their turn. This is the dialectic of hope; it stirs in darkness."

This time last year, I wrote: "But there is not just one challenge. There are two of them. It is not only Soviet power that the Hungarians have challenged. They also confront the West with a challenge equal to, or greater than, their challenge to Communism. The history of the past forty years has been marked by this incongruity: that Communism, permanently strife-torn and precarious, and weak in most material ways beyond anything imaginable to the average experience of the West, has repeatedly stood off or scored off a West in most material ways immensely more powerful. Until Communism detonated its A and H Bombs, it was never a question of comparative power. Power, on the part of the West, was never lacking. Will was lacking. And that failure of will was matched by a failure of intelligence, taking form as an inert complacency, varied recurrently by sweeps of illusion that Communism was about to change into the exact opposite of what it is, into the opposite of all that has given it power and empire, into something more like that image that the West cherishes of the West, something more eligible for the garden party guest-list.

This of the most consistently implacable revolution in history. It is to that failure of will and intelligence in the West that the Hungarians have cried: 'Halt!', challenging it to reverse its forty-year retreat by giving it precisely what most it dreads—an opportunity."

But at last I pushed those pages to one side. Who, in the West, would read in them anything but overblown feeling; as if revolution for Communism or against it, were ever made by anything less than feeling, running molten under the pressures of necessity. But feeling does not, as one of our fondest notions has it, keep the measuring mind from measuring narrowly the reality of what it feels about. I knew before I had finished writing that, within weeks, what I was writing about would be as dated as if it dealt with another age.

The opportunity had been given and it had gone. Autumn had frozen into winter. The Hungarian revolution had passed into the stricken twitchings of the general strike. The West continued to babble about it—some jumble of initials or words that meant that a second revolt might occur in the spring. What does the West know of the pathology of revolution, let alone the pathology of a revolution defeated, which converts at once into mean commonplaces of a kind that make no colorful news stories—the helplessness, grief and induced terror of those who have had the mischance to survive fathers, brothers, sons, who have been shot, jailed, or have simply "disappeared"? Or the unheroic monotony of no food, fuel, gas, electricity; the grimy misery of cold, continual, sapping cold; and the colder knowledge, gained by so hideous a trial and error, that no help is coming from anywhere, not in time, not in any way that counts. The defeated almost never revolt twice—not in quick succession. Nor did we need any expert to tell us this. One Hungarian resistance fighter had packed it all into one sentence; not bitterly, either, but with the simple statement of fact which is more impaling. He said: "You did not organize even a gun-running service for us."

So, yesterday, one year later, I answered to this effect the startling question of the voice that had asked so different a question, this time last year: "If the Russians have one hundred ICBMs trained on us and mean to use them— then, in my fallible opinion, you can be quite sure that there will be no ultimatum. The Russians will launch the rockets first and talk afterwards, if there is anybody left worth talking to. On the other hand, again in my fallible opinion, the Russians do not have one hundred such rockets trained on us. Nor do I believe that such saturation attack forms any part of over-all Communist strategy at this time. Communist strategy seems to me to have quite different procedures and ends in view, geared to a close, forty-year scrutiny and experience of the West."

"For once," said the voice, brightening, "you are more hopeful than I am." I said: "That is not hope." I meant this: Budapest convinced me that the will and intelligence of the West are still unequal to what besets them, and this regardless of the sumptuousness of our retaliatory power. What price retaliatory power if, having it, you must stand by, lacking the will or ingenuity to improvise "even a gun-running service for us"? I take it to be a matter of simple fact that the retaliatory power of the Strategic Air Command still offsets any temporary thrustahead of Communist rocket prowess—as the President has assured us in the first of his "chins-up" talks. Retaliatory power is a simple necessity of survival. But retaliatory power keeps rocketing into ever more terrifying stages of stalemate. And there is probably a limit, not easy for the layman to grasp, beyond which these sprints into progressive stalemate can sprint no farther. Even now, neither side dares break the relative stalemate except in the certainty of consequences so frightful that imagination rejects as pointless the effort to picture them.

Forward motion in either direction would seem, therefore, to lie outside the central stalemate. This is a revolutionary conflict we are locked in, and, in it, we are, perforce, compelled to act as much as revolutionists as the enemy, though in a different way.

For victory must presumably go to him who succeeds in overleaping or by-passing the weapons stalemate, and swinging to his side decisive population masses and their economies now beyond his control. This is the strategic thrust of the theses of the 20th Congress of the Soviet Communist Party, now personified in the leadership of Nikita Khrushchev. That is what, at the moment, the Middle East is about. This is why what I can see by Sputnik II's dim light alarms me less than it alarmed my telephoning friend and millions of others. It is why, instead, I look back from Sputnik II to Hungary, this time last year.

Some years ago, I met in an unlikely executive office, high in a New York skyscraper, a little group of men, introduced namelessly as leaders in America of a Hungarian resistance movement. I did not know why we had met and I do not know now. The modern world is like that. But suddenly the spokesman for the rest asked me: "Do you know what is America's secret weapon?" I said: no. He brought his hand with unexpected force against his chest as he answered: "We, *we* are your secret weapon."

In the days of Budapest, I thought often of that odd conversation. I thought, too, that, if we were holding it again, I should have put a question in my turn. I should have asked: "Do you think we shall know how to use our secret weapon?" But I should have spared them from answering by answering myself: "Neither do I." The moment when the West, by action, has made that answer untrue, will, I suspect, mark a turn in history quite as decisive in its way as Sputnik II.

BIG SISTER IS WATCHING YOU

(*National Review*, DECEMBER 28, 1957)

SEVERAL YEARS AGO, Miss Ayn Rand wrote *The Fountainhead*. Despite a generally poor press, it is said to have sold some four hundred thousand copies. Thus, it became a wonder of the book trade of a kind that publishers dream about after taxes. So *Atlas Shrugged* (Random House, $6.95) had a first printing of one hundred thousand copies. It appears to be slowly climbing the best-seller lists.

The news about this book seems to me to be that any ordinarily sensible head could possibly take it seriously, and that, apparently, a good many do. Somebody has called it: "Excruciatingly awful." I find it a remarkably silly book. It is certainly a bumptious one. Its story is preposterous. It reports the final stages of a final conflict (locale: chiefly the United States, some indefinite years hence) between the harried ranks of free enterprise and the "looters." These are proponents of proscriptive taxes, government ownership, Labor, etc. etc. The mischief here is that the author, dodging into fiction, nevertheless counts on your reading it as political reality. "This," she is saying in effect, "is how things really are. These are the real issues, the real sides. Only your blindness keeps you from seeing it, which, happily, I have come to rescue you from."

Since a great many of us dislike much that Miss Rand dislikes, quite as heartily as she does, many incline to take her at her word. It is the more persuasive, in some quarters, because the author deals wholly in the blackest blacks and the whitest whites. In this fiction everything, everybody, is either all good or all bad, without any of those intermediate shades which, in life, complicate reality and perplex the eye that seeks to probe it truly. This kind of simplifying pattern, of course, gives charm to most primitive story-telling. And, in fact, the somewhat ferro-concrete fairy tale the author pours here is, basically, the old one known as: The War between the Children of Light and the Children of Darkness. In modern dress, it is a class war. Both sides to it are caricatures.

The Children of Light are largely operatic caricatures. In so far as any of them suggests anything known to the business community, they resemble the occasional curmudgeon millionaire, tales about whose outrageously crude and shrewd eccentricities sometimes provide the lighter moments in Board rooms. Otherwise, the Children of Light are geniuses. One of them is named (the only

smile you see will be your own): Francisco Domingo Carlos Andres Sebastian
d'Antonio. This electrifying youth is the world's biggest copper tycoon.
Another, no less electrifying, is named: Ragnar Danesjöld. He becomes a
twentieth-century pirate. All Miss Rand's chief heroes are also breathtakingly
beautiful. So is her heroine (she is rather fetchingly vice-president in charge of
management of a transcontinental railroad). So much radiant energy might
seem to serve an eugenic purpose. For, in this story as in Mark Twain's, "all the
knights marry the princess"—though without benefit of clergy. Yet from the
impromptu and surprisingly gymnastic matings of the heroine and three of
the heroes, no children—it suddenly strikes you—ever result. The possibility
is never entertained. And, indeed, the strenuously sterile world of *Atlas
Shrugged* is scarcely a place for children. You speculate that, in life, children
probably irk the author and may make her uneasy. How could it be otherwise
when she admiringly names a banker character (by what seems to me a
humorless master-stroke): Midas Mulligan? You may fool some adults, you
can't fool little boys and girls with such stuff—not for long. They may not
know just what is out of line, but they stir uneasily.

The Children of Darkness are caricatures, too; and they are really oozy. But at
least they are caricatures of something identifiable. Their archetypes are Left
Liberals, New Dealers, Welfare Statists, One Worlders, or, at any rate, such
ogreish semblances of these as may stalk the nightmares of those who think
little about people as people, but tend to think a great deal in labels and
effigies. (And neither Right nor Left, be it noted in passing, has a monopoly of
such dreamers, though the horrors in their nightmares wear radically different
masks and labels.)
    In *Atlas Shrugged*, all this debased inhuman riffraff is lumped as "looters."
This is a fairly inspired epithet. It enables the author to skewer on one
invective word everything and everybody that she fears and hates. This spares
her the plaguy business of performing one service that her fiction might have
performed, namely: that of examining in human depth how so feeble a lot
came to exist at all, let alone be powerful enough to be worth hating and
fearing. Instead, she bundles them into one undifferentiated damnation.
    "Looters" loot because they believe in Robin Hood, and have got a lot of
other people believing in him, too. Robin Hood is the author's image of
absolute evil—robbing the strong (and hence good) to give to the weak (and
hence no good). All "looters" are base, envious, twisted, malignant minds,
motivated wholly by greed for power, combined with the lust of the weak to
tear down the strong, out of a deep-seated hatred of life and secret longing for
destruction and death. There happens to be a tiny (repeat: tiny) seed of truth
in this. The full clinical diagnosis can be read in the pages of Friedrich
Nietzsche. (Here I must break in with an aside. Miss Rand acknowledges a
grudging debt to one, and only one, earlier philosopher: Aristotle. I submit

that she is indebted, and much more heavily, to Nietzsche. Just as her operatic businessmen are, in fact, Nietzschean supermen, so her ulcerous Leftists are Nietzsche's "last men," both deformed in a way to sicken the fastidious recluse of Sils Maria. And much else comes, consciously or not, from the same source.) Happily, in *Atlas Shrugged* (though not in life), all the Children of Darkness are utterly incompetent.

So the Children of Light win handily by declaring a general strike of brains, of which they have a monopoly, letting the world go, literally, to smash. In the end, they troop out of their Rocky Mountain hideaway to repossess the ruins. It is then, in the book's last line, that a character traces in the air, "over the desolate earth," the Sign of the Dollar, in lieu of the Sign of the Cross, and in token that a suitably prostrate mankind is at last ready, for its sins, to be redeemed from the related evils of religion and social reform (the "mysticism of mind" and the "mysticism of muscle").

That Dollar Sign is not merely provocative, though we sense a sophomoric intent to raise the pious hair on susceptible heads. More importantly, it is meant to seal the fact that mankind is ready to submit abjectly to an elite of technocrats, and their accessories, in a New Order, enlightened and instructed by Miss Rand's ideas that the good life is one which "has resolved personal worth into exchange value," "has left no other nexus between man and man than naked self-interest, than callous 'cash-payment.' " The author is explicit, in fact deafening, about these prerequisites. Lest you should be in any doubt after 1168 pages, she assures you with a final stamp of the foot in a postscript: "And I mean it." But the words quoted above are those of Karl Marx. He, too, admired "naked self-interest" (in its time and place), and for much the same reasons as Miss Rand: because, he believed, it cleared away the cobwebs of religion and led to prodigies of industrial and cognate accomplishment.

The overlap is not as incongruous as it looks. *Atlas Shrugged* can be called a novel only by devaluing the term. It is a massive tract for the times. Its story merely serves Miss Rand to get the customers inside the tent, and as a soapbox for delivering her Message. The Message is the thing. It is, in sum, a forthright philosophic materialism. Upperclassmen might incline to sniff and say that the author has, with vast effort, contrived a simple materialist system, one, intellectually, at about the stage of the oxcart, though without mastering the principle of the wheel. Like any consistent materialism, this one begins by rejecting God, religion, original sin, etc. etc. (This book's aggressive atheism and rather unbuttoned "higher morality," which chiefly outrage some readers, are, in fact, secondary ripples, and result inevitably from its underpinning premises.) Thus, Randian Man, like Marxian Man, is made the center of a godless world.

At that point, in any materialism, the main possibilities open up to Man. 1) His tragic fate becomes, without God, more tragic and much lonelier. In general, the tragedy deepens according to the degree of pessimism or stoicism with which he conducts his "hopeless encounter between human questioning and the silent universe." Or, 2) Man's fate ceases to be tragic at all. Tragedy is bypassed by the pursuit of happiness. Tragedy is henceforth pointless. Henceforth man's fate, without God, is up to him, and to him alone. His happiness, in strict materialist terms, lies with his own workaday hands and ingenious brain. His happiness becomes, in Miss Rand's words, "the moral purpose of his life." Here occurs a little rub whose effects are just as observable in a free enterprise system, which is in practice materialist (whatever else it claims or supposes itself to be), as they would be under an atheist Socialism, if one were ever to deliver that material abundance that all promise. The rub is that the pursuit of happiness, as an end in itself, tends automatically, and widely, to be replaced by the pursuit of pleasure with a consequent general softening of the fibers of will, intelligence, spirit. No doubt, Miss Rand has brooded upon that little rub. Hence, in part, I presume, her insistence on "man as a heroic being" "with productive achievement as his noblest activity." For, if Man's "heroism" (some will prefer to say: "human dignity") no longer derives from God, or is not a function of that godless integrity which was a root of Nietzsche's anguish, then Man becomes merely the most consuming of animals, with glut as the condition of his happiness and its replenishment his foremost activity. So Randian Man, at least in his ruling caste, has to be held "heroic" in order not to be beastly. And this, of course, suits the author's economics and the politics that must arise from them.

For politics, of course, arise, though the author of *Atlas Shrugged* stares stonily past them, as if this book were not what, in fact, it is, essentially—a political book. And here begins mischief. Systems of philosophic materialism, so long as they merely circle outside this world's atmosphere, matter little to most of us. The trouble is that they keep coming down to earth. It is when a system of materialist ideas presumes to give positive answers to real problems of our real life that mischief starts. In an age like ours, in which a highly complex technological society is everywhere in a high state of instability, such answers, however philosophic, translate quickly into political realities. And in the degree to which problems of complexity and instability are most bewildering to masses of men, a temptation sets in to let some species of Big Brother solve and supervise them.

One Big Brother is, of course, a socializing elite (as we know, several cut-rate brands are on the shelves). Miss Rand, as the enemy of any socializing force, calls in a Big Brother of her own contriving to do battle with the other. In the name of free enterprise, therefore, she plumps for a technocratic elite (I find no more inclusive word than technocratic to bracket the industrial-financial-engineering caste she seems to have in mind). When she calls "productive achievement" man's "noblest activity," she means, almost exclusively, technological achievement, supervised by such a managerial political bureau. She might object that she means much, much more; and we can freely entertain her objections. But, in sum, that is just what she means. For that is what, in reality, it works out to. And in reality, too, by contrast with fiction, this can only head into a dictatorship, however benign, living and acting beyond good and evil, a law unto itself (as Miss Rand believes it should be), and feeling any restraint on itself as, in practice, criminal, and, in morals, vicious—as Miss Rand clearly feels it to be. Of course, Miss Rand nowhere calls for a dictatorship. I take her to be calling for an aristocracy of talents. We cannot labor here why, in the modern world, the pre-conditions for aristocracy, an organic growth, no longer exist, so that impulse toward aristocracy always emerges now in the form of dictatorship.

Nor has the author, apparently, brooded on the degree to which, in a wicked world, a materialism of the Right and a materialism of the Left, first surprisingly resemble, then, in action, tend to blend each with each, because, while differing at the top in avowed purpose, and possibly in conflict there, at bottom they are much the same thing. The embarrassing similarities between Hitler's National Socialism and Stalin's brand of Communism are familiar. For the world, as seen in materialist view from the Right, scarcely differs from the same world seen in materialist view from the Left. The question becomes chiefly: who is to run that world in whose interests, or perhaps, at best, who can run it more efficiently?

Something of this implication is fixed in the book's dictatorial tone, which is much its most striking feature. Out of a lifetime of reading, I can recall no other book in which a tone of overriding arrogance was so implacably sustained. Its shrillness is without reprieve. Its dogmatism is without appeal. In addition, the mind, which finds this tone natural to it, shares other characteristics of its type. 1) It consistently mistakes raw force for strength, and the rawer the force, the more reverent the posture of the mind before it. 2) It supposes itself to be the bringer of a final revelation. Therefore, resistance to the Message cannot be tolerated because disagreement can never be merely honest, prudent or just humanly fallible. Dissent from revelation so final (because, the author would say, so reasonable) can only be willfully wicked. There are ways of dealing with such wickedness, and, in fact, right reason itself enjoins them. From almost any page of *Atlas Shrugged*, a voice can be heard, from painful necessity, commanding: "To a gas chamber—go!" The same inflexibly self-righteous stance results, too (in the total absence of any saving humor), in odd extravagances of inflection and gesture—that Dollar Sign, for example. At first, we try to tell ourselves that these are just lapses, that this mind has, somehow, mislaid the discriminating knack that most of us pray will warn us in time of the difference between what is effective and firm, and what is wildly grotesque and excessive. Soon we suspect something worse. We suspect that this mind finds, precisely in extravagance, some exalting merit; feels a surging release of power and passion precisely in smashing up the house. A tornado might feel this way, or Carrie Nation.

We struggle to be just. For we cannot help feel at least a sympathetic pain before the sheer labor, discipline and patient craftsmanship that went to making this mountain of words. But the words keep shouting us down. In the end that tone dominates. But it should be its own antidote, warning us that anything it shouts is best taken with the usual reservations with which we might sip a patent medicine. Some may like the flavor. In any case, the brew is probably without lasting ill effects. But it is not a cure for anything. Nor would we, ordinarily, place much confidence in the diagnosis of a doctor who supposes that the Hippocratic Oath is a kind of curse.

A WESTMINSTER LETTER:
SPRINGHEAD TO SPRINGHEAD

(*National Review*, MAY 31, 1958)

AFTER WINTER'S long, cold enemy occupation, spring is back; no longer halting and promissory, but true, irreversible spring. Now the spring-heads, dried up in last summer's fierce drought and long silent, burst out again, refilled by this spring's plentiful moisture, and rush on their way to the sea with a chance of drowning babble in babble as they pour past Washington (we are in the Potomac watershed). Now the voices of the fertilizer and lime purveyor and the farm implement hucksters are heard louder than the voice of the turtle in the land. "Make five blades of corn grow where one grew before," they coo. "Let 140 bushels an acre (with fertilizers) swell farm surpluses which 40 bushels (without fertilizer) could never swell so prosperously. Let one man do (with machines) the work that three could scarcely do (without). So dis-employment thrives." Of course, they do not really say these things; this is only the logic of what they say.

And, as throughout nature in the spring voice answers voice, their voices are answered by others. These are the voices of the Agriculture Department's employees, and other official and semi-official farmers' helpmeets. There are enough of these turtles in the land so that, if there were time at this season to count noses, I suspect that the bureaucratic nose count in almost any farm county would fill you with wonder at how they manage without colliding. In part, they manage by a division of labor. While some (bringing, often, a good deal of expert knowledge and patient solicitude to jobs, in general, poorly paid) are helping you multiply yields—others (the land-bankers and that ilk) are exhorting you to decrease yields. They will pay you for it, too; and so painlessly that some scarcely notice that the hand which reaches for the payment is thereafter meshed in the controls. Since few seem to mind this, or to notice the gaping paradox—the coos of increase cancelling the coos of decrease—perhaps it hardly matters. Yet history, glancing back, may be struck by another paradox and wonder if, in America, it was not in the countryside that socialism first took firm root and stooled.

It has been a carefully nurtured growth. The earlier controls (Roosevelt and Wallace *consulibus*) were rather flirtatious things. Bureaucracy was chiefly

feeling out the land to see how many inches it could take before reaching for a
mile. On this farm, we were always careful to plant less than the official wheat
allotment. But the great tactic (it is almost a reflex) of the bureaucrat mind is to
keep things unsettled, to keep you off balance, to make you feel unsure. So I
was not surprised when, one day years ago, a small character knocked at the
door to say that he was the wheat inspector, that he had been looking over our
fields (of course, without asking), and that we were overplanted. His thin,
sidewise smile tried to hint at least hanging at sunrise. It disturbed my wife.
But I knew that we were not overplanted, and I thought I knew what silver
cord connects bureaucracy and politics. "Elections are coming up," I said to
her. "You can be absolutely sure that nothing more will be heard of this."
Nothing was, of course.

But, shortly afterwards, I happened in on a neighbor who is made of sterner
stuff. It was hog-feeding time, and he approached with a pail of slop in each
hand. I asked: "Did that fellow look over your fields?" My neighbor set down
each pail, somewhat with the air of a President laying a State of the Union
message on a lectern; and eyed me for a moment of dense silence. Then he
said: "You know he's a black-hearted skunk," adding with immense relish: "I
run 'im." I thought I heard the fifes of '76.

You will not hear them now, or, I think, again. Those days, around Pearl
Harbor, were a simpler, sweeter time. Besides, the Second World War, with
mass armies and half a world to feed, made nonsense of controls. It remained
for this Administration to weld them on. I have never known on just what
remote, snow-capped Olympus the wheat allotments were alloted. Official
notice of how much (or how little) wheat you could henceforth lawfully plant
just arrived, one day, in the mail. But, if you had been alloted less than fifteen
acres (most of us were), you could not afterwards vote about continuing or
discontinuing this control. Voting about that was henceforth the privilege
of the bigger planters. Those under fifteen acres were henceforth stripped
of a vote in this rather relevant matter. Moreover, if you planted above your
official allotment, even if the yield of the overplant was not for sale, was used
wholly to feed your own stock or poultry, you still had to pay a penalty for
growing it. Moreover, government surveyors could come into your fields at
any time, to measure your wheat acreage and determine what penalty you
must pay. This, you will see, went considerably beyond controls in the earlier
sense, which most farmers had been content to abide by if only, by doing so,
they would be let alone; while some, in the vain hope that the surest way to be
let alone was not to take even the subsidies to which controls entitled them,
refused these.

So it happened, now, that a few such farmers, who held that their land was
inviolable, and that the day of the *kolkhoz* had not yet arrived made known their
temperatures by running up, at the entrance to their farms, signs which read:

"Government agents keep out!" There was a tiny farm revolt hereabouts, with some strong feelings and words between embattled farmers and officials. And these farmers were certainly mistaken; at least about what hour of history it is. The years of bureaucratic feeling-out were over. The day of submission-or-else had come. The Administration moved swiftly against the resisters in a legal action known (ironically enough, it seemed to some) as: *The People v. Morelock*.

You can read about this particular Morelock in *Witness*, where I wrote of him and his family: "Names to be written rather high, I think, on the column which is headed: 'And thy neighbor as thyself.' " In sum, the charge was interfering with government agents in pursuit of their duty. Mr. Morelock and his fellow defendants won that action, on a technicality, rather, I suspect, to the relief of the bureaucracy, which wanted no martyrs; and whose chief purpose, after all, was not to harass or penalize farmers. What was wanted was to seal on controls and cut surpluses, and this the resistance threatened over-all.

It was a silly, hot-headed, inconsequential resistance? It did not reflect the feelings of masses of farmers anywhere? There is a point of view—nowadays we tend to exalt it as "reasonable"—from which any spontaneous resistance on principle, and against odds, is seen always to be silly. And such struggles often appear inconsequential enough at the time. Those who make them are few in number if only because those who react fiercely on principle are, in the nature of men, likely to be few. Nor are they, in the nature of themselves, likely to be worldlywise, to have thought out in crisp detail all the implications of their action. If they could do this, presumably they could not act. For their drive to act is organic and instinctive, not neatly cerebral. So their opponent finds it easy to dismiss them as crackpots and extremists; and, in general, his strength is defined by the degree to which he can afford to dismiss them with the derisive smile. The smile mantles power.

Perhaps I should make a point clear: I was not directly concerned by any of this. Some time before, when we saw that controls were coming to stay, we simply stopped planting wheat. But I could not bear to see my friends mauled. So I spoke privately to the wife of one embattled farmer. I went to the wife because I did not wish to sustain the man's hurt or blazing anger at what I had to say. In effect I said: "Urge him to stop. He cannot win. He will only destroy himself, and for nothing. This cause was lost before it began." These people are strong human types of a kind little known among the mystic circles of the intellectuals. They hate a quitter, and they do not make a quick distinction between a faint heart and the coldly measuring glance. I saw dawning in this woman's eyes, first shock that I, of all people, should say this; then a tinge of just-repressed contempt. "That is not what you did in the Hiss Case," she said. I said: "No. That is why I am saying this to you. Do not destroy your lives for nothing."

Then I went away. I did not return until the action was over; all had simmered down, and reality had taught what words seldom can. For these people have a strong grasp of reality, a simple wisdom of the earth, where ten minutes of unseasonable hail will tear to ribbons a year's corn—but you go on from there. By then, they knew (whether or not they would admit the fact in words) that they were the defeated. They were proud to have made the effort; and I think that this pride was about in ratio to their realization that they could only have been defeated; no other issue was possible. It was their pride to have acted, anyway. Into that pride they retreated. This was no retreat from principle. The retreat was into silent conformity to superior force, the force of the way things are, which compels compliance, but convinces no one. In ending their resistance, they yielded to that force, but from their silence they looked out at it with unyielding scorn.

I asked the woman to whom I had first spoken: "What now?" She answered that, when the Republican Party was first organized, her forebears (they had always lived on this same farm) had voted for Fremont. When, just before and during the War Between The States, Maryland was rent, they had twice voted for Lincoln. They were Black Republicans; in the whole history of the line, they had never voted anything but Republican. She said: "We will never vote for a Republican again." I said: "What do you gain by that? Do you suppose those others [the Democrats] will not give you more and tighter controls?" She said: "Then we will never vote again at all." Never is a long word. But, in so far as anything can be certain in an uncertain world, I think it is certain that these people—they are of the breed of those who built the nation from the un-peopled earth—will never vote again. They have silently seceded, not so much from the electorate (that is only the form the gesture takes), but from what they believe to be betrayal of basic principle, without which their world surrenders a part of its meaning. That principle is the inviolability of a man's land from invasion even by the State, the right of a man to grow for his own use (unpenalized by the State) a harvest which his labor and skill wrings from the earth, and which could not otherwise exist. Freedom was at stake, of which the inviolable land and its harvest were symbol and safeguard. The word "indivisible" is not one that these people commonly think or speak with. So they do not think or say: "Freedom is indivisible." But that is what they sensed and that is why they acted. It was not controls, but coercion, they resisted.

Do not misunderstand me. I do not suppose that wheat allotments, or similar controls, are inherently wicked, or that government's action in enforcing them was wrong—given our reality. I believe them to be inescapable, which is something different. The problem of farm surpluses is, of course, a symptom of a crisis of abundance. It is the gift of science and technology—improved machines, fertilizers, sprays, antibiotic drugs, and a general rising efficiency of know-how. The big farm, constantly swallowing its smaller neighbors, is a logical resultant of those factors (big machines are fully efficient only on big acreages). Surpluses follow. So does the price trend of farm real estate, steadily creeping upward for decades. So does the downtrend of the farm population (it has fallen by a million in about two decades).

If farmers really meant to resist these trends, to be conservative, to conserve "a way of life" (as they often say), they would smash their tractors with sledges, and go back to the horse-drawn plow. Of course, they have no intention of doing anything so prankish, and, moreover, would not be let do it if they tried. Controls would appear at that point, too. For the cities, which dominate this society, are dependent on machine-efficient yields. So the State would have to act to prevent the farmer from preserving "a way of life," just as it has to act by controlling, in the field, an agriculture of anarchic abundance. Both are actions against anarchy. Controls of one kind or another are here to stay so long as science and technology are with us; or, until the ability of farmers to produce and the ability of the rest of us to consume their product is again in some rough balance, thus ending the problem. That balance will be restored, presumably, in the course of a survival of the fittest, in which efficiency determines survival. And efficiency is itself the result of a number of factors, one of which is almost certainly size of operation. In short, the farm unit tends to grow bigger and more efficient, as the farmers, growing more efficient, too, grow drastically fewer in necessary numbers.

This is the only *solution* of the farm problem; one that is obviously impersonal and rather inhuman (and in that it is exactly like any other comparable development in history, for example the development of the factory system). Short of that solution, no man or party can solve the farm problem. They can only contrive palliatives. All that men and parties can do is to try to mitigate and soften, in human terms, the plight of the farmer in the course of heading toward that impersonal solution which science and technology impose. Hence controls and the incipient socialism of the countryside which controls imply and impose. This is the basic situation, however much incidental factors may disguise, blur, or even arrest it for longer or shorter terms. That is why the mass of farmers go along with controls which, almost without exception, they loathe. Who will say that they are not right?

Yet neither do I believe my neighbors were wrong to resist. I believe they were right, too—and on a plane which lies beyond controls. In my heart, I believe that no resistance on principle, where freedom is the principle involved, is ever meaningless, or ever quite hopeless, even though history has fated it to fail. For it speaks, not to the present reality, but to the generations and the future. And, in so far as it speaks for freedom, it speaks for hope.

Freedom and hope—they are the heart of our strength, and what we truly have to offer mankind in the larger conflict with Communism that we are also locked in.

It was not the initial resistance that I was urging my neighbors against in this case, but an unwise persistence in it. I thought that resistance, once enacted, was well done and full of meaning for us all. I thought that, thereafter, swift disengagement was simple common sense, since neither the battle nor the war could be won—not in this season of history. The fewness of the resisters, their summary defeat, the way in which their struggle passed largely unnoticed and was quickly forgotten, seemed to bear out this view.

It also chilled me. It seemed to me that, with the defeat of these farmers, a retaining wall had fallen out. And this not only in the sense that hereby the enveloping State had made a new envelopment, and that, to that extent, the whole outwork of individual freedom and its safeguards was weakened. The real portent was the complacent consensus that it scarcely mattered. No one was stirred. No one really cared. No one rose to say that when, at any point, the steadily advancing State retrenches the rights and freedom of any group, however small, however justified the retrenchment is in terms of impersonal reality, every man's security is breached. That tells us what hour of day it is.

That is why, I think, it is not wholly cranky or idle to remember, with each returning spring, this episode. Not that I think it will be forgotten. The land has a long, long memory. Nothing is much more thought-provoking than to listen—in barns where men meet and talk on days too wet to work, in farm kitchens on winter nights—and hear the names of men and women long dead (names which, in life, were scarcely known beyond a radius of 30 miles) come to life in conversation. They live again in most precise detail—tricks of manner, speech, dress, foibles, follies, generosities, integrities, courage, defeats. Often such recollections are laced, in the telling, with much human malice. Yet even this, at its worst, has the effect of brushing the grass on many an otherwise neglected grave. And, by that touch, is restored a great continuity—the same from the beginning of the earth, through the mentioned dead, to those who mention them. A nation is also its dead. As if any of us lived otherwise than on the graves of those who gave us life, who, so long as we conserve them in memory, constitute that generative continuity. Among such memories, surely, will remain, like a germ in a seed, the little farmers' resistance. Perhaps in some more fully socialized spring to come, someone, listening to that recollection, will pause over it long enough to ask himself: "What was the principle of freedom that these farmers stood for? Why was the world in which this happened heedless or wholly unconcerned? Why did they fail?"

Perhaps he will not be able, in that regimented time, to find or frame an answer. Perhaps he will not need to. For perhaps the memory of those men and women will surprise him simply as with an unfamiliar, but arresting sound—

the sound of springheads, long dried up and silent in a fierce drought, suddenly burst out and rushing freely to the sea. It may remind him of a continuity that outlives all lives, fears, perplexities, contrivings, hopes, defeats; so that he is moved to reach down and touch again for strength, as if he were its first discoverer, the changeless thing—the undeluding, undenying earth.

SOME UNTIMELY JOTTINGS

(*National Review*, SEPTEMBER 27, 1958)

WITH MILLIONS of other TV-viewers, I watched the President give his UN address on Arab slum clearance; a well-organized speech, and rather gallantly delivered, besides—only, almost wholly irrelevant. The rate at which things are moving is glimpsed in the fact that nothing whatever had been settled about the crisis in the Middle East, before we put it largely out of mind in favor of the current crisis in the Far East, which had overtaken it. Later, Mr. Eisenhower gave us his views on that one.

Groping for the sense behind the President's words, I came up with nothing better than: didn't say he would, didn't say he wouldn't. Since the speech was beamed to Moscow and Peking, quite as much as to you and me, this, I presume, was exactly the effect intended: keep them guessing. Alas, they are rather good at guessing. Besides, they know the secret in the daisy, the secret in each crisis. Seldom has a secret been less of a riddle. The rhetorical issues in each crisis are almost never the point. Neither the freedom of the Lebanon nor the title deeds to Quemoy is the point. In each crisis, there is only one point to be settled, and it is always the same point: whether or not the West has resolved at last to stop the Communist advance in the only way it can be stopped: by a decision to make war at need.

Of course such war, at this stage of stalemated history, could only be in the nature of an adventure. Doubtless there are those, on both sides, who are impatient to end the intolerable stalemate by risking the adventure. But, since the consequences to both sides are foreseeably apocalyptic, it seems unlikely that the adventurers will have their way. For nobody needs to guess about the thermonuclear consequences.

It is this that leaves the veteran guessers in Moscow and Peking free to guess (like the President) that there will be no world war over Quemoy. Hence the wrenching pathos which is what I, for one, chiefly carried away from both the President's addresses, namely: a sense that he and his advisers, doing the very best they know how, could still, in effect, do so little. Never imagine that their plausible critics could do more. Those critics might do it all somewhat differently. That is to say—unless they, too, had taken firmly the frightful decision for war at need—they might conduct the alternative retreat more gracefully, trippingly, wittily in the style of the Adlai-an adlib. It is unlikely that they could accomplish anything more effective in a situation whose extremity is defined by its two alternatives: fight or retreat. That is the only secret in the daisy.

If this is true, but there is to be no war—what then? Mercifully, I am not required to guess.

But I should like to stick my neck out interspatially by guessing about something else, lest, one of these months, we suffer another Sputnik-type alarm at the expectable. I should like to guess that the Russians are fairly content to leave to us the vast cost and effort of shooting the moon. Instead, I should guess that the Russians are investing every available resource of mind, material, money, in getting men into space and back again, alive. Like the rest of us, they have heard that whoever first learns to commute to and from space, and to man something or other up there, will presumably control space, and much else besides.

War on the scale of the worlds, annihilation, space and its command, a visible nearness to the brink of unheard-of disaster. We know that it is scarcely farther away than an initiating impulse in the whorls of a brain responsible for ordering a responsible hand to push a button, and so set in motion the marvelous mechanisms for inflicting or resisting chaos. We are continually told about it. We listen, and in part believe. In larger part, the reality passes us by; it passes our imagination. Too big. Too big truly to grasp. One day, a meaning of it comes home in a form we can grasp—the distress of a single human creature and his reflections on it. A friend writes: "Up at 5 A.M. today to get some hot coffee into my son and drive him to his draft board in time (for the Army vehicle which was picking up the quota). If the time should ever come (as I pray it never will), when you have to take this journey with your son, I think you will consider with a quite new urgency what Jaspers meant in writing: 'Quietly, something enormous has happened in the reality of Western man: a destruction of all authority, a radical disillusionment in an over-confident reason, and a dissolution of bonds that makes anything, absolutely anything, seem possible. . . . Philosophizing, to be authentic, must grow out of our new reality, and there take its stand.'"

"Quietly, something enormous has happened in the reality of Western man." I am constantly baffled because so few seem to grasp this enormity of our situation, which is defined by the certainty that there is no way out of it that can possibly be simple, easy, familiar, usual, in terms of anything we have known before. Whether the resolution of our total crisis is to be unimaginably violent, or what, at this moment, seems even less imaginable, a massive peaceful settlement, what comes next can only be tremendous. We are visibly at a point of change, a turning point, which has not its like in history. Henceforth, peace implies consequences almost as staggering as war.

LETTER FROM WESTMINSTER:
A REMINDER

(*National Review*, NOVEMBER 8, 1958)

A WATCHFUL READER notes that I closed a recent piece in this magazine by saying: "We have visibly reached a point of change, a turning-point, which has not its like in history." He also recalls that I used the same phrase several years ago, in an article (about the 20th Congress of the Soviet Communist Party) in *Life* magazine. "You rang several changes on it then," he writes. "Does this phrase have some mystic meaning for you, not known to the rest of us? Is it an incantation? Or is it just that you can't think of anything else to say?"

I suppose that, in a way, it *is* an incantation, in the sense that it is meant to evoke something—to be a reminder of something though it is never identified—so that readers, coming on it, may feel a little uneasily: That theme again. I have used it deliberately somewhat like that leitmotif which, now and again, stirs under the dense overcast of Wagnerian sounds to remind us that Fate is still at work.

Though we late-comers are scarcely any longer aware of it, one of Christianity's tidings of great joy was that it had banished Fate from the world. No longer was a man's Fate fixed and shaped irreversibly by the stars he happened to be born under, so that his life was predestined to be just so, and not otherwise. The moving finger writ, and all his piety and wit could not cancel out one fated circumstance; so that the noblest posture, for slave (Epictetus) and Emperor (Marcus Aurelius) alike, was a stoic resignation. This was the glad tidings—that Fate was overthrown. The hopeless entrapping ring was broken. Man himself could break it, since every individual soul was divinely precious. Armed with this knowledge, man was free at last, first of all from Fate; then free to make of his destiny what he would and could.

In our century, Fate has returned to the world, and possessed the minds of millions who, submitting to its thrall or acting in its name, seek to extend its dominion. This time, Fate has returned in the guise of History. It may be put (very loosely) like this: History is shaped by the action and interaction of great impersonal forces. Men merely enact it. If they act, prevailingly, in the direction of the main lines of force, its momentum carries them along to success; and we are invited to call such men great, wise, and even good. Those who, out of folly, ignorance or stubborn principle, resist the main lines of force, History exterminates mercilessly. They are in the way; and what does a ragweed, for example, have to do with mercy, when a million pollen grains may be wasted to bring a single seed to fruition? The process is impersonal.

There is grandeur in this concept. It is idle to fancy that we can dismiss it with a snap of the fingers or by snapping shut our minds against it. Nor can we easily frown it down by a stately assurance which, very often, is not truly assured. For we see the main design and workings of the concept enacted on all sides of us, in Nature. Why should Man be the exception? Prove it. Nor is this concept at home only in the Communist East. It exists widely throughout the West, nameless, or under various distracting names, as a floating ambience, breeding a climate.

Thus, at a basic point of issue, the mind of the West is divided against itself; and this basic division is repeatedly rubbed raw as it is touched by each of our recurrent crises, at all levels. For this is the basic cleavage. It is this which, behind the teeming crises, the overtoppling threat of great disaster, not only in the form of bombs and missiles, gives to our mood a hovering sense of finality that no amount of rationalizing quite dispels. It is this which sometimes makes us feel as if there were occurring in the general mind of man something like a molecular rearrangement of particles; that man is about to become something other than he is, if he does not perish in the process. Behind all events and all appearances, *this* choice is presented: Fate or Freedom. And it is presented as an issue that must be decided—now. It is this which gives us that sense of living through a time which has not its like in history.

The phrase is not mine. It was spoken in our own lifetime, by a particular, fateful man in the spin of this century's moment of decision. I am assuming that the Russian Revolution was the decisive action of the century's first half, in the sense that, directly or indirectly, it affected everything of importance that came after. I should like to identify the man and the moment as I felt their impact close to the time when both converged. What follows is from an unpublished manuscript:

I was thirteen years old when Sir Edward Grey, then Britain's Foreign Secretary, stared into the dusk of the day in 1914 when England declared war on Germany, and summed up for his age: "The lights are going out all over Europe tonight. They will not be lit again in our time."

I was sixteen when, on an October day in Petrograd—the rain-wind beating in from the Finland Gulf—Antonov-Avseenko, at the head of the Red Guard, rushed the Winter Palace. Therewith, all power in the former empire of the Czars fell to Communism. In the Petrograd Soviet Leon Trotsky rose to report the revolutionary victory. As if (for once) at a loss for language, he stared for a moment through his glasses at the mass of capped, greatcoated, high-booted men who stared back at him. Then he found the words equal to the event:

"Comrades of the Soviet of Workers' and Soldiers' Deputies, we have this day begun an experiment that has not its like in history."

This is where the phrase comes from. This is the formal announcement that Fate had returned to the world in the guise of History. This is why I use the fateful phrase, from time to time, to remind others, without expressly laboring it, of a choice that it will surely be granted to each of us to make in this time, first in our mind, then in our acts: Fate or Freedom.

A REPUBLICAN LOOKS
AT HIS VOTE

(*National Review,* NOVEMBER 22, 1958)

THE HOUSEWIFE ahead of us was in the polling booth so long, I thought she could not just be splitting her ballot; she must be emulsifying it. It turned out that she was trapped (voting machines are still something of a novelty with us). When she pushed the lever to the right, the curtains had closed behind her. She could not remember how you open them again. She could not call out (decorum forbade); and she could not get out (panic was taking over). I missed the big moment of her liberation by a bipartisan rescue team. I was watching the voting queue.

Something was noticeable in the faces of the voters—a peculiarly braced sobriety. They seemed to me the faces of people who had, some time before, firmly and finally made up their minds, and were here to do something about it. I had not the slightest doubt as to what most of them meant to do.

Nevertheless, I would vote with my Party. I always vote like a Democrat—that is to say, I always vote a straight Party ticket, but Republican. In that way, I understand myself to be furthering, at least until it becomes simple historical idiocy to do so, certain general propositions about the world—propositions which, on this most recent election day, seemed remarkably remote and unreal.

So voting did not take me a minute. I read only one name (J. Glenn Beall) to locate the Republican line. I snapped down all the Republican keys and left the booth, feeling as if I had thrown my vote into the gutter.

No doubt, a man who seeks to act in and on reality, rather than to stand still and watch from some fastidious sideline, must, of necessity and more than once in his life, consciously throw something very precious in a gutter.

I took my little self-disgust, which was only the private face of a larger concern, out into the golden autumn weather that was so ironically like the weather of election day, 1952. Our naive fervors of 1952 appear wildly comical in the disenchanted light of 1958. The discrepancy helps to measure, I think, where six years of "middle of the road" (or twilight sleep) Republicanism have brought some of us.

The morning before that other election day I was ill. There was a family hubbub. We all knew what was wrong. But we were also deeply concerned about something else. We supposed that the vote between General Eisenhower and Adlai Stevenson might be close, and we felt that Stevenson's election would be a disaster. Therefore, every vote counted. Perhaps you must have gone through the school of the Revolution to take voting so seriously as we do; to feel that, in a sense, there is no longer such a thing as a merely American election because every election and its outcome here is an event in the world conflict. Every vote contributes to a cumulative outcome that bears directly on the fate of hundreds of millions of people elsewhere, as well as our own.

So that day in 1952, somebody said: "But you can't have a heart attack *now*. You've got to vote tomorrow if we have to take you there on a stretcher." As I walked away from the polling place in that same autumn sunlight, I was struck down.

By evening, an ambulance had got me to a hospital, which, by one of those wonderful fumbles that occur, turned out to be the wrong hospital. While everybody tore inside to straighten matters out, my stretcher lay on the ramp; and I could hear voices close by, talking election. A blanket had been pulled (prematurely) over my face. Later, I clawed my way through drugs and made out foggily a small bare room and a little nurse, sitting in one corner. When I stirred, she jumped up and asked if there was anything she could do for me. I said: "Tell me how the election turned out." She hesitated, disappeared, reappeared almost at once, and said: "A landslide for Eisenhower." I stopped fighting the sedative and fell most peacefully asleep.

On this last election night, we sat—my wife, my son and I—listening to the remarkable TV coverage. My son, who had just cast his first vote, was clearly exhilarated by the scale of the event he was witness to. He knew, at least in a general way, that he was seeing the incipient third phase of that American social revolution of which the New and Fair Deals had been rocket stages one and two. My wife, as the returns piled up, huddled deeper in her chair. "Gloom" could not possibly cover what she felt. It was rather that she knew she was watching the Republicans epitomize one of the Bible's most cruelly piercing insights: "To him who hath shall be given. But from him who hath not, even that little which he hath shall be taken away." I was almost wholly unmoved. I had "discounted" the news. "It is not Fortune that governs the world," Montesquieu has told us. "There are general causes, moral and physical, which operate in every monarchy, raise it, maintain it, or over-turn it."

If this is true of monarchies, it is also true of parties. The Republicans had lost touch with reality in all directions, and in all groupings, until domestic policy resembled irresolution tempered by expediency, and foreign policy more and more resembled something like eccentricity. They had been handed a disaster.

SOME WESTMINSTER NOTES

(*National Review*, JANUARY 31, 1959)

SOMEBODY SAID, the other day, when we were talking about the new jet service to Europe, that in twenty or thirty years people will be traveling abroad by rocket. New York will then be fifteen minutes from Paris, or closer than the Empire State Building seems ever likely to be to Rockefeller Center by Fifth Avenue bus. Nobody saw anything wildly improbable in the notion.

Still, the mind is not yet committed to the shortest distance between two points as invariably the best of all possible ways to get somewhere. The mulish mind may still prefer detours, precisely because they digress.

Just before Christmas, somebody sent me a French book, part of whose leisurely title reads: *Five Essays on the History of Ideas in Russia and Europe*. Essay I begins: "Between 1758 and 1762, Koenigsberg was occupied by Russian troops under General Fermor. In the old Collegium Albertinum—as the university was called—a thirty-five-year-old professor, of somewhat timid appearance, announced a course in physics for 'Messieurs, the Russian officers.'"

This was news to me and I found it fascinating. As if the author invited us to peer into the least likely of peepholes, and what we saw, incredulously, was the dark backward and abysm of time, with (somewhere down below) the greatest of all human centuries (I mean, of course, our own), squirming, germlike, at one of its countless, forgotten points of origin—Koenigsberg, 1758.

This is not just because Koenigsberg, easternmost of provincial German towns, has lately been next-door neighbor to Peenemunde, the experimental rocket base. Nor is it because, even more lately, we have seen Koenigsberg become Kaliningrad, not merely Russian-occupied this time, but annexed outright as the westernmost of Soviet cities. Nor is it that the timid-looking science teacher was Immanuel Kant, "unknown as yet even in Germany"—the author (to be) of *The Critique of Pure Reason*, schoolmastering the forerunners of the enveloping East. What arrests is rather (with the Sputniks in mind) the thought of Russian officers, enlivening the tedium of that earlier occupation by getting up their physics. And, indeed, physics and politics have been in curious (and often violently unstable) mixture throughout the last 200 years. Not only in Koenigsberg—or, see your morning newspaper.

And with that, the mind is off on a little ramble. With the Koenigsberg classroom as center, it scans the horizon of that time in search of anything else that may be curiously lurking in it. The mind stops, arbitrarily, with a child.

In 1758, Lazare Carnot was only five years old. Who gives a thought to

Carnot today, though he was an engineering and military head of the first
rank, of whose achievements Napoleon made full use, but whose genius
Napoleon's masks, somewhat as Bach's so long masked Buxtehude's? It would
be some years after Koenigsberg before Carnot whipped up his first important
paper: *Essay on Machines in General*. A few years more, and he would organize
from scratch, and in one year, the French Revolution's fourteen armies; and,
almost singlehanded, elaborate their innovating strategy and tactics. Accomplishment enough so that, when the many tongues that wag in the many heads
that do not think, cried out for his arrest during some terrorist spasm, they
could be silenced by a single voice which asked: "Would you dare to lay hands
on the organizer of victory?" So Fate, who now and again prefers irony to the
knife, let Carnot live, to die an exile in Schoolmaster Kant's Germany.

To Lavoisier, who is on the Koenigsberg horizon, too—his first interest
physics, like Kant's Russian officers'—Fate turned the cutting edge. That
brilliant brain was canceled at the neck by the guillotine—the murderous
technical improvement that the Revolution contributed to progress, along
with certain other innovations that are with us still. For example, conscription,
mass armies, the concept of the nation in arms (in part Carnot's brainchild, and
necessity's).

True, in our day some have sought to undo that business of mass armies.
Among them, a master of French prose and author of a treatise, celebrated
chiefly among specialists: *Vers une Armée de Métier—Toward a Professional Army*.
The master of prose (and of much else French at the moment) is, of course,
General Charles de Gaulle.

With that the circling mind has circled back to the thoroughfare of here and
now. And just in time for some sensational traffic. For while I was shuffling
these bits and pieces, the Russians sent up that rocket which, missing the
moon, has gone on, they tell us, to orbit the sun. 1758 to 1958 plus two.
Lunik, Kant (of all people), facing an all but forgotten roomful of Russian
officers. At last the impulse takes form in a trajectory that bursts Earth's
gravitational field. A wall has fallen. Nobody knows how many other walls, of
the mind, of reality, fell with it, unnoticed. Which reminds me that, in the far-
off 1920s, one of my fellow undergraduates had this to say of (and to) his age:

> *Once in unpeopled Nineveh,*
> *Where no one heard the sound,*
> *The human-headed bull of god,*
> *Crashed outward to the ground.*
>
> *Such ways, the solitary mind*
> *Strains backward, year on year.*
> *Are all the walls at Nineveh*
> *Whose crash we do not hear?*

MISSILES, BRAINS AND MIND

(*National Review,* FEBRUARY 28, 1959)

THOUSANDS, PERHAPS millions, of us have been following, as closely as possible, the great weapons debate whose epicenter is in the Congress. That debate breathes a rancid tone of political partisanship. This is extremely disquieting. On the other hand, without that political animus it is possible that there would be no debate. That would be more disquieting still. I, for one, hold the belief that at least a majority of literate men and women are pretty shrewd at separating what is politically motivated (or distorted) from the reality of the situation which emerges from the argument. And it is this reality that none of us can afford to miss or widely misunderstand.

This debate goes (as Germans say) *um Tòd und Leben*—for life or death. Not only is the basic reality of the situation it evokes awesome; it is peculiarly perilous because the reality is so novel that many cannot credit it. They simply cannot take it seriously. That reality is, of course, that, for the first time in our history, the nation as a whole is coming under the possibility of direct, annihilative attack. Our continental fortress is no longer unreachable; our ocean moats have shrunk or may serve to float toward us the submarine conveyors of disaster. The rockets have done this.

Therefore, what we are truly debating is our survival as a people that wills to remain sovereign and not subject—as the people that we are and will to be, and not what someone else wills to make us. Let us, for the moment, table all brave talk about our special breed of freedom and this or that high moral issue, as all luxuries go overboard in combat, which, in the resolving clinch, never turns on these, but on the necessity for raw survival. This is what we are debating: survival.

The debate is especially difficult for most of us to follow efficiently because: 1) much of it concerns regions of science and technology which, as laymen, we are simply not competent to grasp; and 2) much of it turns on scraps and echoes of conflicting information which, for good reasons, we are not permitted to know in full, and, again, might well not be competent to evaluate if we did know it. But most of us feel competent to see that the conflict forks out from two main Intelligence questions.

One of them is what our Intelligence tells us about the state of Soviet weapons progress. The other concerns our own rate of progress, past, present and tomorrow. Neither is clear. In addition, opinions about these matters

cannot be simple. Naturally, they involve many more (and much more complex) factors than whether the Russians are ahead of us in certain respects and
behind in others; whether, at this moment, they can match us rocket for
rocket, or outmatch us, etc., etc., etc. But the oldest, simplest rule of war
would seem to dispose of much of this part of the debate. The rule is: never
underrate your mortal enemy. Do not, if you can help it, overrate him; but far
better to overrate than underrate.

Just here, there emerges from the debate another point which almost any
literate layman can claim competence to see and call decisive. The point is this:
whatever the precise state of Russian rocketry and missile production, or our
own, the Russians have achieved approximate destructive parity with us. This
would seem to mean that, whether or not either nation has the power to inflict
near-total extinction on the other, each has the power to ruin the other. And
that would seem, to those who may lie under such ruins or inherit them, to be
about all that is necessary.

As someone has remarked, the real horror of an atomic war is not the fate of
millions who may be fried in a flash; the real horror will be the fate of those
who survive to haunt the ruins. If, as seems to be the case, people exist who
still fail to grasp what this apocalypse implies, perhaps it is well to remind
them of a colloquy (on TV, several months ago) between Mr. Dave Garroway
and one of the top-ranking generals responsible for giving the signal to retaliate
in event of atomic attack on us. The Q. and A. went much like this:

MR. GARROWAY: "General, in your opinion could we survive such an
attack?"

THE GENERAL: "Yes, I think so."

MR. GARROWAY: "How long would it take us, after such an attack, to get
back to where we are now?"

THE GENERAL: "Perhaps a couple of hundred years."

They were not trying to frighten little children. They were trying to make
big children face reality.

Approximate destructive parity would seem to be all that is necessary for
another reason. I happen to be one of those who believe that, barring hideous
folly or human failure, these ruins will never come to pass. I cannot possibly
document this belief; and neither can anybody else who holds (extremely
tentatively, of course) this view. But it is not just fantasy. It derives from
conclusions (drawn from Communist theory and decades of Soviet strategy
and tactics in action) that Russian missiles are primarily political, not primarily military, weapons. The last thing, in my tentative opinion, that the Russians want to do with their missiles *at this time* is to launch them against the
United States. For parity, by definition, works both ways. The Russians are
not romantics, and have no greater whim than we have to become a continental
ruin—especially since the ruins after an atomic war will not even be worth
looking at.

The purpose of the Soviet missiles is, first, to erect a deterrent fence around the Communist heartland. For some reason, some of us seem unable to realize that the Russians are also afraid of us. But, finally, and much more important, the purpose of the Soviet missiles is to impose on the West a truce of exhaustion, taking form in one or another degree of atomic disarmament. No need to recap here the perils for the West of such a truce. My colleague, James Burnham, has long and patiently pointed them out in explicit detail. On the other hand, the depth and ferocity of the world crisis is measured by the fact that the atomic stalemate forced the East-West conflict into space in order to continue it on the scale of that new, fluid dimension.

The question is inescapable: How long can this go on, how far, and to what end? I find no comfort, because I put little credence, in the complacency of those who say: We can outlast and outplay the Russians at this game. This seems to me to overlook (among others) two instantly visible points. It assumes 1) that the Russians are competing only in the rocket field, and not in others, where, in general, they have been more successful than we have been to date. It overlooks 2) that a formidable enemy, seeing itself dangerously outclassed, might be driven to desperation. In that case, the rockets might, at that moment, cease to be primarily political, and become in fact primarily military weapons. With that we are back at those ruins.

The larger probability would seem to be that neither power can long sustain a decisive over-all weapons headway of the other; but that, by spurts, now one, now the other, will draw ahead in some feature of this mortal race. Of course, this leaves out the possibility of the development of a defense, at least partially effective, against rockets. I am told, pretty reliably I believe, that we are in fact hopefully engaged in such a project. If this is true, you can be reasonably sure that so is the vigilant enemy. But such defense, too, works both ways, and would seem again to bring us to a point of partial standoff without, however, ending the weapons and space race.

Obviously, this cannot be ended while either side is racing. For if it is true that Soviet missiles are primarily political, we cannot therefore cease trying to catch up and overtake Soviet progress. To do so would also be hideous folly; would again, instantly, and more certainly than any desperation, convert the Soviet rockets from political to prime offensive weapons of immediate aggression. We can only do our utmost to outmatch the presumed Soviet lead. In this matter, I find myself thinking more like a Democrat than like many of my more tranquilized fellow-Republicans; and this, both as to belief in the necessity of supposing that a Soviet lead exists and may widen, and the necessity of sparing no effort or cost to close the weapons gap.

But, at that unsparing point, certain consequences also appear, which my mind refuses not to face as part of our total reality. As the weapons and space race climbs ever more steeply in cost and effort over years, it is scarcely conceivable that the pull should not begin to be felt by every American in constrictive ways, which, if pushed (and there are plenty of pushers around, gleefully waiting for a pretext) must radically transform our way of life. The Russian missile and space program is paid for directly out of the pockets, hide and hopes of the Soviet citizen. True, Russia began from hunger while we still have wads of affluent fat to melt off before the pinch is cruel; and the strong-arm State must enforce those ultimate sacrifices which State power exists to enforce. Is it conceivable that it will not come to this, even among us? It will be simple necessity; and necessity is its own imperative sanction.

I submit that this is one reason why certain businessmen, who sense clearly enough the grim shape of things to come, appeared to listen with closer attention than did certain hopefully socializing labor leaders, to what Anastas Mikoyan flew so far to tell us, namely: that Russia wants to end the Cold War. I submit, too, that this was what Mikoyan chiefly came to say, and that all else— verbal ticklings of the German question; or talk of trade contingent on credits; or the relaxing of our restrictions on certain exports; or a passionate interest in supermarketing and the packaging of potato chips—was incidental to that one simple statement: Russia wants to end the Cold War. The commissar had only to repeat it as frequently and publicly as possible since, above all, he was saying it over the heads of the Administration to the people as a whole. Nor was this just a random tactic of divisive mischief. This kind of deception applies a tactic rooted in Communist theory and successfully tested in four decades of Soviet practice.

But the prospect of political and economic changes among us is not the only transformation we might bear in mind as an ultimate consequence of the space and weapons race. There is another transformation, which is much more certain, and certain to come much faster. Usually, this one is discussed in terms of American education and its inadequacies. In some circles, it has become almost a sport to cite the discrepant figures which tend to show how many more scientists, engineers, etc., etc. the Russians are yearly graduating than are we. It is a deadly sport. For, if the figures are generally accurate (and, again, for our own skins' sake it is well to assume that they are), they spell out a portent. It is, of course, that in a comparatively short time the Russians will have produced a massively outnumbering elite of the kind on which the security and progress of modern States depend. Nor is this, again, a sudden, spastic lunge on the Russians' part. Again, the development of such an elite derives directly from Communist theory and the Communist world-view. Those who would like to glimpse what the enemy is up to, could do worse than dip (for a starter) into Friedrich Engels' polemical work commonly called the *Anti-Duehring*.

In general, the problem appears to be viewed as simply one of education, in an almost automatic sense. "Give us the funds, the necessary physical plant and the proper teachers' pay," goes the refrain in which can be heard the deep hunting bay of the Education lobby in full cry—"Give us these, and we will mass-produce the brains." And, certainly, these needs must be met if brains are to be mass-processed.

Yet it seems possible, too, that the problem does not turn wholly on the academic processing of what we loosely call "brains." It would seem to turn, at least as critically, on the much more difficult problem of what we loosely call "mind." I suggest that the implied presence in the latter word of reflective and creative imagination, rare and elusive as a trace metal, measures some difference of meaning between the two terms. Practical brains we have always had, and of an organizing genius whose scale and audacity have made America one of the wonders of history. Mind, in the sense I have suggested, is something else again, not, perhaps, because it is necessarily in short supply, but because something like a national revolution in our attitude to it must occur before it can become effective.

Almost a decade ago, Henry Regnery, the publisher, and I sat with some others in (appropriately, perhaps) the Douglas MacArthur suite of a Midwest hotel. There were no Sputniks in the sky that year. Yet there was a shared feeling that something was radically wrong in the land, which the conversation tried, fumblingly, to get at. Somebody said: "America has always secretly despised the mind. Now mind is taking its revenge. We need it desperately; and it simply isn't there." A sweeping criticism, but not nearly so critical or so sweeping as the evidence which has since crested in our missiles lag. The energy of practical brains, backed by the immense resources of our technology, may make good that lag, which, in default of sovereign and imaginative mind, was not foreseen—together with much else. It is a basic attitude toward mind, quite as much as education, that needs transforming. Such basic transformations are, admittedly, harder to make, and take longer, than mass-processing a dozen campus generations, or even closing a missiles gap. But there seems no valid reason to suppose that necessity will not breed what survival requires. That is one root challenge of our ordeal.

While we are mastering it, we might do worse than curb those recurrent twinges of fear that secretly (and sometimes openly) beset us, by fixing in our heads the insight that the great diagnostician of this age added to the grammar of courage: "What does not destroy me, makes me stronger."

THE HISSIAD: A CORRECTION

(*National Review*, MAY 9, 1959)

THE EVER-HELPFUL press has been at it again, this time in the matter of Alger Hiss' decision to go to Europe, and the State Department's decision to issue him a passport for the purpose. Press treatment of this news reached a fine blossom in the paragraph with which *Newsweek* (April 20) wound up its story about the Hissiad: "At the weekend, endorsement of Hiss' travel plans came from an unexpected source. 'Alger Hiss is an American citizen who has paid his penalty for the crime of perjury,' said Whittaker Chambers. 'He has every right to apply for and receive a passport.' "

Whatever the intention, the effect of this paragraph is mischievous. Still, left to myself, I should probably have let it pass without comment. Why single out one item more than another from the quota of distortion that daily passes for news? But good friends insist that this one will deeply puzzle, and even dismay, many people. I am afraid that anybody of whom this may be true is in for a good deal of nervous shock, though for better cause, before this century ends. But I also agree that there are matters about which people have a right not to be puzzled and dismayed unnecessarily. So, for what good it may do, here goes.

Newsweek's paragraph begins with a fumble ("endorsement"), and ends, I am afraid, with a misquotation. Perhaps it can be said of *government* that it "endorsed" "Hiss' travel plans" to the extent that issuance of a passport supposes a considered decision. It cannot possibly be said of me. I have no competence whatever to "endorse" the Hiss plans, no means, no desire; nor, for that matter, any particular interest in a project about which I know nothing beyond the wispy report. I may (and do) speculate that this journey was a predictable next step in that public reorbiting of Mr. Hiss which is so precious a cause to his partisans, among them certain fairly formidable national figures. Beyond that speculation, the report that Alger Hiss is going abroad excites me no more than the news that several thousand other tourists are, even now, poised for the annual pilgrimage ("Ah, Venice—the Leaning Tower!").

Of course, I was aware from the first buzz what fanciful chigger would be inflaming the press just below the skin. For have we, even yet, learned anything that matters about these things, and how they work, and why? I seriously doubt it. Anyway, telephoning newsmen promptly produced the expected chigger in the form of the expected question: "Is *he* going behind 'the Iron Curtain'?" I said: "Of course, *he* isn't going behind 'the Iron Curtain'." Question: "Why do you say that?" Answer: "I must ask you not to press me on the point. You can easily figure it out for yourself." In short, if, for a decade, and in spite of everything, you had been insisting that you never were a Communist, you would scarcely, at first chance, streak for the Communist Empire. Mr. Hiss could find little that would serve his turn in going to Moscow; and neither would Moscow.

My guess would be that Hiss will home on London, to lay a wreath (figurative, at least) on the grave of the late Lord Chief Justice, who, for somewhat cryptic cause, was moved to write a handsomely slanted book in his favor. In Britain, Hiss has long had many partisans, literate, righteous, opinionated, and, in this case, completely muddled, as only clever English minds can sometimes be. There will be an epergne on the luncheon table.

Now to that part of *Newsweek*'s paragraph in which I claim to be misquoted. It consists of the words: "[Alger Hiss] has paid his penalty for the crime of perjury." I do not believe that I said this because I do not believe it (except in the shallowest legalistic sense) to be true. So I am as certain as anyone can be, in the absence of transcript, that I could not have said it, even in the haste and annoyance of answering foolish questions. That is not the way the matter presents itself to my mind.

History and a lengthening lifetime have left me too uncertain on the general subject of society, and the question of debts to it, or penalties, for me to have put the case like that. Society and the least man in it are too bafflingly manifold, the chances of birth and heredity, of time, place, environment and history, too incalculable, for such easy packaging. Moreover, the Scriptural injunction not to judge is not only compassionate; it is almost self-servingly prudent. We never pass judgment on anything or anybody without, by that act, in the same instant, defining our own human limitation. The act of judging always, mercilessly, judges, first of all, ourselves.

Of course, it is true—life does not permit us to live, for the most part, in such terms. We live on the world's terms, and act within their web of reverend compromises. But, in those terms, I can think of few men of whom it seems to me less possible to say that he has paid any effective penalty than Alger Hiss. In his case, a penalty was exacted, and a suffering was incurred. But the horror of it derives only in the last instance (though it sounds heartless to say so) from Hiss' suffering as an individual man. The true horror of it lies in the fact that, on his side, the penalty and the suffering were sheer waste. There is only one main debt, and one possible payment of it, as I see it, in his case. It is to speak the truth. That, to this hour, he has defiantly refused to do. Worse, he has spent much time and contrivance to undo the truth.

If this were a matter touching only him and me, it might be of little moment. Obviously, it goes far beyond any individual man. We are not playing games; we are dealing with the lives of "children's children" in the world we are preparing for them. There are insurrectionists of the 1956 revolt, sitting in Hungarian jails, and in the night that falls when hope fails absolutely, whose fate is touched by Hiss' defiance. And I find it difficult in the extreme to understand how certain of his perfervid partisans can pay lip-service to those resisters and their cause, and not make the basic equation between his defiance and their suffering. Beside it, his own, however immeasurable, loses scale. "With every dawn," Camus tells us of our time, "masked assassins slip into some cell; murder is the question before us." An historic lie on this scale helps turn the key that lets the murderers in.

But we do not need to travel so far as Budapest. That celebrated defiance touches much closer home. It divides the minds of some of the best men and women among us at a point on which, in this juncture of the human crisis, they need to be (and we need that they should be) most clear: the point of truth. Hiss' defiance perpetuates and keeps from healing a fracture in the community as a whole. And this is particularly true of that part of the community which is (or should be) the custodian and articulator of its collective virtue, i.e., its mind. For when you accept a lie and call it truth, you have poisoned truth at the source, and everything else is sickened with a little of that poison. If you are looking for its monument, look around you.

You may say that all this is past and tiresome, try to sweep it largely out of sight and mind, and resolve briskly to get on to more pressing things. Your resolution remains chiefly bustle. The least, brushing touch (like this of Hiss' travels) shows that the wound is there, and fresh, and that its poisons continue to drain through the system. That is why the Hiss Case, though it has become modish in certain circles to glance away, though its dimensions in themselves are small among so many greater lesions, remains a central lesion of our time. That is why, ultimately, I cannot say (however differently I should prefer to get at it, at another level) that Alger Hiss has paid any effective penalty. For precisely he can end the lesion at any moment that he chooses, with half a dozen words.

So much for that part of the direct quotation which I claim to be misquoted, and which, in any case, does not reflect my view. The rest of the quotation is fairly reported: "Alger Hiss is an American citizen. He has every right to apply for and receive a passport." This *does* reflect my view, though it was chiefly chance that it was said about Alger Hiss. I suspect that the misleading words were inserted (no doubt, with the best intention) by some newsman, trying to explain, for his own heart's ease, and his readers', how so bizarre a view came to be held by me.

The reason, if dismaying to some, is simpler than the one dreamed up. I am a bug on the question of unrestricted travel, as I am against the obscenities of wire-tapping, mail tampering, and related mischiefs that, in the name of good intention, are helping to pave the road that leads to 1984. I hold strongly that it is a right of man and of the citizen to travel freely where and when he will, and that any extensive restriction of that right is among the usurpations that feed the Total State. Of course, I know the arguments from expediency; here security is "the question before us." I have seen scarcely a shred of evidence, by contrast with the many sweeping arguments, that convinces me on this score. It is not the known Communists whose travels need greatly alarm us. Let them travel where they will, and let us observe their travels. They will take us to their leader, and possibly many NCO's en route. A dozen secret services, not only ours, must exist to watch them. It is the unknown Communist (or sympathizer) whose travels may work us harm; and to him a passport would be issued without question, in any case, because we do not know who or what he is.

So strong has this argument from expediency (or fear) become, that we have all but forgotten how recent travel restriction is. My generation grew up in an almost passportless world. In those days, the Russian Autocracy and the Turkish Sultanate were considered semi-barbarous, in part because almost alone, they inflicted on their nationals the uncivilized indignity of passports. To me, travel restriction seems chiefly to multiply the files behind which bureaucracies always gratefully barricade and entrench their positions, and fiercely defend them.

No doubt, in some quarters on the Right, such views will put me in a lonely minority. I can only urge most careful reflection on the matter. A little shift in the political weather, and it may be the spokesmen of the Right whose freedom of travel is restricted—with a certain smugness. The grounds will be expediency, of course. The precedent will be almost unassailable. Anti-Communists will have promoted it.

I think I can hear a crescent rumble rising: "Why, the man is talking like a Liberal." I have scarcely any interest in invective tags. My concern is not for the political geography of this or that position, but whether or not the position taken makes sense, and is, to that degree, as we say: justified. And of course I know too: Woe to those who grope for reality, and any approximate truth that may be generalized from it, in the No Man's Land between incensed camps. History and certain personal experiences leave me in little doubt about the fate of such seekers. They are fair game to the snipers of both sides, and it is always open season. But while Mr. Hiss hurries to his plane or ship, and the snipers wait for the man to reach, in his groping, the point where the hairlines cross on their sights, I may still have time to sort the dead cats into tidy piles—those from one camp, here; those from the other, there. As one of my great contemporaries put it: "Anybody looking for a quiet life has picked the wrong century to be born in." The remark must be allowed a certain authority, I think, since the century clinched the point by mauling with an axe the brain that framed it.

FOOT IN THE DOOR

(*National Review*, JUNE 20, 1959)

IT LOOKS TO ME as if The George Washington University (in Washington, D.C.) were helping to pioneer something whose long-range implications may be pretty important for a lot of us. What it implies, if I am right about it, is the beginning of the breakthrough in mass education, by using television. Of course, other institutions have been experimenting with television education, and on a grander scale. But George Washington's project happens to be the one that I have seen close up; so I shall limit myself to it. The larger significance of this development seems scarcely possible to overrate. Among other mercies, if time and a fuller curriculum justify the general use of TV for teaching, that would seem to thrust a formidable foot into the Closing College Door.

By now, there cannot be many of us who are unfamiliar with that implacably Closing Door. Daily, and sometimes several times a day, it has been threatening to slam in our faces, or our children's or grandchildren's. The problem posed by the Closing College Door is due not only to our population explosion, but to the realization, abruptly brought home by those sky-writing Sputniks, etc., that: 1) a lot more Americans are going to have to be educated a lot better and more quickly than in the past; and that 2) henceforth education bears directly on national security and possibly national survival. On the TV screen, we see a flutter of black and white flakes, rather like snow mixed with soot. This is radioactive fallout; and, any day now, an accompanying voice tells us, we may find ourselves in the midst of it. The voice is unruffled, almost cozy—*nil desperandum Teucro duce et auspice Teucro*—as if you and I or the commentator were the kind of people who would ever let ourselves show surprise at a little radioactive fallout.

Behold the contrast with the Closing College Door. Nothing lulling about this one. The accompanying voice is that of the Education Lobby. The scene on the TV screen is full of pathos, too. We see Willie, gowned in his high school graduation togs, clutching his diploma, all set for the next step: going to College. Heartbreak: Willie isn't going anywhere, except that he is fated to go forever un-higher-educated. For—a Delphic voice warns us—by 1984 (or whatever the fateful deadline is) the Closing College Door will have slammed shut in Willie's eager face. Googols of secondary school graduates will be besieging the gates of campuses, quite futilely, since college facilities will be totally inadequate to cope with such hordes. (In case you do not yet realize what age you have been born into, a googol is shorthand for a digit followed by one hundred zeros.) We are invited to write for a leaflet, setting forth these matters more fully, from an address sufficiently pseudonymous to stir a surmise that this is an air-hole of the Education Lobby, or one of its isotopes.

The problem of the Closing College Door is beyond question a real one. And it would be impermissible to treat Willie and his plight so lightly, if this particular presentation of it did not remind us uneasily of the commercials which try to persuade us that virility is inseparable from smoking certain brands of cigarettes. In each case, we resent a sneak assault on good sense. In Willie's case, it takes no great wits to guess what we are expected to do next: shake out what is left in our lank wallets while we pressure our legislators (themselves, paradoxically, not always beacons of literacy) to syphon federal taxes into higher education. Parents are not, apparently, presumed to be educated (or natively bright) enough to perceive that federal aid to education is their own tax-ravaged and inflated dollars fed into academic tills by other-directed and coercive means.

Perhaps it will come to this. But let us not delude ourselves about what it is we shall have come to. This is the age of euphemism, because this is the age of the Total State that is dawning, more or less everywhere, though under various softening and dissembling names and forms, on various impressive pretexts or necessities. But it is not deemed expedient that we should grasp what age it really is—at least, not all at once, or all of us at once. So, perhaps, of necessity, the State must soon be into the Business of Education, as the witty and bracingly arrogant Professor J.K. Galbraith assured us, only the other day, that it must.

But must it? It is just here that that formidable foot I mentioned may have got into the Closing College Door. Which brings us back to The George Washington University and its television project. Early this year, the University's College of Special Studies, in cooperation with Station WTOP (the *Washington Post*), offered a TV course in Russian for beginners. Within a fortnight or so, some 3,400 students had paid their fees (up to $75), and enrolled for the course. Perhaps it is worth remembering that Russian (like English) is one of the most difficult of the great cultural languages; and that, until recently, those who struggled with it had to rise before daybreak for the lectures which go on the air at 6:30 A.M. That invisibly listening 3,400 must form one of the biggest classrooms anywhere. They equal the entire population of many a college campus. Bear in mind, too, that they are being taught by a single instructor—the very competent Mr. Vladimir Tolstoy. One mind efficiently instructing a formally enrolled class of 3,400 other minds—it is at that point that the possibilities of television education begin to open out. When this is possible and comparatively simple, why need the Closing College Door close, or be held open chiefly by the strong-arm State? Why cannot a comparatively small faculty (and a highly select one at that) instruct millions just as well as 3,400?

I am not an educator, so that the reasons why not do not leap to my mind as fleetly as I have no doubt they will leap to authoritative minds. Some of the objections must certainly be well taken, if only on grounds of ca' canny. Some, we may feel reasonably sure, will be simple obstruction, not perhaps consciously identified as such by the obstructors. For here we run up against the rooted human reluctance to innovation (a reluctance for which, at times, there is something to be said), but which, perhaps rather more often, amounts to a dense inertia. We also get into the preserves of vested academic interest. And I incline to the view that Fafnir, grunting and belching over the Niebelung Hoard, was a tame and temperate dragon compared to schoolmen, guarding academic interests to which they have staked claims during dedicated lifetimes, with little enough recognition, and few of this world's rewards.

Here, too, we can only brush the powerful forces, which we lump loosely as the Education Lobby, and which appear, in general, to be bound by the most tender, consanguine ties to vaster, more powerful forces that look to the State as the sovereign solvent of our social (and most other) problems. And this, not because such heads are peculiarly mischievous, wicked or (as an otherwise intelligent Conservative said to me recently) "immoral." Mischief and malignity might be comparatively easy to deal with. But these folk are, in general, intelligent, articulate, and intellectually effective, to the degree in which, having looked into the problem and sounded its complexities in depth, they find no agency but the State adequate to solving it on such a scale. It is this, precisely, that gives them a quite unbearable moral presumption. They also note that, given the general pattern of the age, the whole momentum of historical forces, quite apart from what anybody might want to do, or not to do, about it, is working to strengthen the State. And their sense of riding this irresistible momentum is precisely what gives them an insufferable self-righteousness. Since anything that magnifies the power of the State hastens a process, which is deemed inevitable, whatever tends to speed it up shortens it, and is, to that degree, beneficent. Anything that slows it down is unintelligent, maleficent, and, in such terms, "immoral." That is to say, much the same judgment reached by my Conservative friend, but reached from the other direction by reading the same terms in a reverse sense.

Since the Closing College Door tends to strengthen the State, that Door is a godsend to such folk, and they may be expected to put their full and ululant weight behind it, and against anything that might keep it ajar. They do not necessarily think of it this way. But we are not speaking here about what individual heads think, but about relationships of forces and interests, and what happens when individual men are drawn by them into action, which has a way of depersonalizing most of us. In any event, if televised education really threatens to thrust a foot in the Closing College Door, we may well see some plain and fancy surgery to sever the foot at the ankle.

One line of surgery seems obvious. While talking with the head of the Slavic Department and others at George Washington, I thought I caught the whine of the whetstone just behind their backs. The same sound seemed phrased in a question on the form that many TV students filled out for the College of Special Studies: "Can Education be successfully given over TV?" My answer: "No question whatever about it; it can."

Another line of attack is easily foreseen. Presumably, it would go much like this. Suppose you are televising not just a single course; and one, too, about which there is, admittedly, a touch of fad. Suppose you are televising a full semester's high school or college work, especially to younger students. When they are put on their own, largely removed from the hourly discipline of class attendance and supervision, what grounds have you for expecting, what right have you to expect, that the mass of such students would do the necessary work? My reaction to that one is brief, blunt, and to many, I should think, abhorrent: about this the Russians seem to me unquestionably right. Those who cannot learn should be spared the ordeal. Those who will not learn should be spared the privilege. If they will not learn, and, while learning, keep to a certain standard of progress—into the factories with them, or stores, or any occupation that will usefully employ (and train) their hands and heads, without making undue demands upon their minds. At the same time, every effort should be made to help out of routine, stultifying jobs young (and older) people who can, and *will*, use their minds, but are prevented from learning by the need to earn. No use to say that this is undemocratic. This selective process, and only this one, is truly democratic, drawing out of the fecund, unranked body of the nation, the forces on which, when trained, depends the well-being of the community as a whole.

In the past, our slackness about learning did not matter. At least, it did not matter enough to justify so drastic a stand. But the past and its easy ways (which I, personally, prefer to anything that is likely to take their place) helps us little or nothing now. We are visibly on a historical turning-point which is all but certain to determine the human condition for an unforeseeable reach of time. How that turning-point comes out for us, turns, in a much more foreseeable degree, on what the oncoming generations make of their minds. And not only the oncoming generations. There are plenty of adult minds (a sizable arsenal of them, one suspects) whose efficiency a little easily accessible education would greatly step up, probably to their own considerable exhilaration.

I am not suggesting, of course, that televised education can replace (or displace) Harvard—letting that name stand, *in excelsis*, for many others. No merely functional teaching is likely to be a substitute for a campus education with its celebrated intangibles, dedicated to shaping, as we are reminded at almost any Commencement exercises, "the whole man." There is also a fairly dreary waste (which also has its justifying arguments) in any college education. Ninety windows smashed in one fraternity house in one glorious night (to cite an item of rather recent personal recollection) scarcely seem indispensable to shaping "the whole man." Nor is all the waste on the side of the students, as anybody knows who has been exposed to the enshrined prejudices, posturings and crotchets of certain old faculty boys of nostalgic memory. These, too, have their justifications, though one cannot help wondering how those antics might go over on a TV screen under the sobering stare of millions.

I am not suggesting, either, that televised education is coming tomorrow, or that it does not pose its own order of grave and complex problems; or that it is a cure-all for our educational plight. I am saying only that the need is great, pressing, and generally conceded; that, in television, a means to meet the need, at least in part, appears to be at hand; that it is comparatively inexpensive and need not involve the State. What is required next would seem to be the will to mate the means and the need; to work out organizational and other problems, which, however difficult, are likely to be somewhat less so than those of splitting the atom or orbiting a rocket around the sun. I venture that, if need and means were brought together, the public response might be at least as startling as the response to The George Washington University's Russian course.

In fact, the problem's thrust outstrips all such terms. It is clear that mankind may, within a rather short time, blow itself into a poisonous powder and lie dusting a vaster putrefaction. I happen to believe that the odds, though touch and go, are rather against apocalypse. If this proves true, it seems to me that, for a century or so, the energies of mankind will be increasingly directed to, and absorbed, with an exclusive and unparalleled intensity, in raising the level of human material well-being, *i.e.*, social wealth, and in solving certain related problems. One of the beneficent side-effects of the crisis of the twentieth century as a whole, is a dawning realization, not so much that the mass of mankind is degradingly poor, as that there will be no peace for the islands of relative plenty until the continents of proliferating poverty have been lifted to something like the general material level of the islanders. It is this perfectly practical challenge, abetted by a sound self-interest, which must engross the energies of mankind, and more and more, perhaps, inspire it as a perfectly realizable vision. Especially, I should think, it would inspire Americans, who, in a sense, invented abundance; and who appear to feel what other nations have felt as a sense of destiny, only in the generous act of bringing their abundance, and the know-how behind it, to less fortunate breeds.

But the world is also degradingly ignorant—and by no means only in Africa. Unless the general level of mind is raised at the same time as the level of material well-being, and not too many steps behind, we shall all risk resembling those savages whom, within living memory, civilizers introduced to the splendor of top hats and tight shoes, for the greater glory of their extremities, leaving unredeemed the loin-cloth of their middle zones, and the wits between their ears.

In fact, we shall have little choice but to raise the level. A modern economy of abundance cannot be sustained, cannot even be organized, without also organizing (*i.e.*, educating) the brains to run it. At the point where such brains must number millions, education must almost certainly take to the air. It seems extremely doubtful that the old local centers of learning, however expanded, can cope with twenty-first century needs. They will doubtless long retain their glory, which will draw to them the élite of the élite for the refinement of knowledge. But the educational scale of the future would seem to require solutions in something approaching googol terms.

Still, men are incurably traditional, no doubt because they are irremediably mortal—a circumstance that no amount of material wellbeing is likely to change much. So every revolution prepares a conservatism of new forms. Patterns of convention, symbol, ritual reassert themselves to provide a comfort and a reassuring hand-hold on the slowly sinking ship, which, since each of us always dies, each of us always is. So perhaps, when the great television universities of the future go on the air, beaming their courses from satellite stations orbited in space, students in Katmandu or Cochabamba, before tuning in, may bow three times ceremoniously toward Cambridge (U.K. or Mass.) and the University of California at Los Angeles, though they may no longer know or care just why they make this ritual gesture. Only the oldest old boys may mumble, between their stainless steel teeth, of a legend that, in the centuries BTE (Before Television Education), Oxford, Princeton, Yale, and the like, were names for high places of the mind by which the wonder came.

INDEX

Adams, Henry: influences WC's generation, 259; on China and Russia, 284

Adenauer, Konrad, 284, 306

Aeschylus, 175

Agee, James, ix, xiii, xix, xxiii; personal similarities to WC, xxi

Aiken, Conrad, *The Coming Forth by Day of Osiris Jones*, 64–65

Albert, Prince of Brandenburg, 244–45

Alberti, Leon, 215

Alinsky, Saul D.: WC's review of *Reveille for Radicals*, 123–25

American Mercury, The, xxiv

Amery, John, 159

Anderson, Marian, xxiii, xxix; WC on, 134–40

Anti-Semitism, 77–78, 92, 296

Aquinas, Saint Thomas, 197–98, 199, 200, 227; WC on *Summa Theologica*, 201–02; *Summa Contra Gentiles*, 201

Aristotle, 202, 314

Arnold, Matthew, 303

Arvin, Newton, 61

Atkinson, Brooks, 107–08

Augustine, Saint, 63

Bacon, Roger, 198

Bakunin, Mikhail, 179

Barth, Karl, 186–87, 300

Barzun, Jacques, xxiv

Baudelaire, Pierre, 169

Beach, Sylvia, 54

Beard, Charles: WC's review of *The Republic*, 74–77; *An Economic Interpretation of the Constitution of the United States* "laid an axe to a view of morality," 75–76

Beckett, Samuel, 64

Beethoven, Ludwig van, Violin Concerto, Op. 61, 137–38

Benedict XV, Pope, 66, 72

Benedict, Saint, xxv; WC on, 261–64

Bentley, Elizabeth, 269

Benton, Thomas Hart, 117

Bevan, Aneurin, 304–07

Biddle, Nicholas, 116–17

Bismarck, Otto von, 292; foresees nature of Marxist society, 177–78

Book-of-the-Month Club: chooses WC's *Witness* as a main selection, xxv

Borgese, G. A., 95; WC's review of *Common Cause*, 80–81; *Goliath: The March of Fascism*, 80

Bosschere, Jean de, 258

Brod, Max: WC's review of *Franz Kafka*, ix, 150–55

Buckley, William F. Jr., x, xxvi–xxviii; meets WC, xxvi; on WC's character, xv; on WC's pessimism, xxviii; on WC and Henry Luce, xxv; on WC's prose, xxix; denies influence of WC, xxviii; *God and Man at Yale*, xxvi

Bukharin, Nikolai Ivanovich, 161–62

Bunyan, John, *Pilgrim's Progress*, 150

Burke, Edmund, *Reflections on the Revolution in France*, ix

Burnham, James, 337

Caldwell, Erskine, 61

Calvin, John, 245, 247–49; WC on *Institutes of the Christian Religion*, 247–48

Camus, Albert, 342

Cantwell, Robert: recommends WC for a job at *Time*, xviii

Capitalism: as an alternative to Marxism, 183

Carnegie, Andrew, 231

Carnot, Lazare, *Essay on Machines in General*, 333–34

Carradine, John, 58–59

Chambers, Whittaker, biography: early life, xvi–xvii, 86, 257–60, 300; goes to work for *Time*, xviii; writes first *Time* cover story, xx; edits *Time*'s "Foreign News" section, xxi–xxiii; writes "The Ghosts on the Roof," xxii–xxiii; forms *Time*'s "Special Projects" unit with James Agee, xxiii; writes *Life*'s "History of Western Culture" series, xxiv; testifies before HUAC, xv, xxiv; resigns from Time Inc., xxv; writes *Witness*, xxv; later relations with Henry Luce, xxv; and *National Review*, xxvi–xxvii; dies, xxviii; posthumously awarded Medal of Freedom, xiv

Chambers, Whittaker, personal qualities, attitudes and habits: dislike of having his magazine pieces edited, x; acceptance of *Time* style, x; religious roots of his anti-Communism, xxi; working habits described, xxiv; pessimism, xxiv, xxviii, 74, 97, 258, 300–01; final judgment on Henry Luce, xxv; attitudes toward conservatism, xxvi–xxvii, 82–83; influence on William F. Buckley, Jr., and the conservative movement, xxviii

Chambers, Whittaker, books: *Cold Friday*, ix, x, xiv, xxviii; *Odyssey of a Friend*, ix, x, xiv; *The Third Rome* (unfinished), xxviii;

Witness, ix, x, xiv, xvi, xx, xxv, xxvi, 321

Chanson de Roland, 198

Charlemagne, 199

Chesterton, G. K., 225

Chiang Kai-shek, xxii; WC on, 104–10

Churchill, Winston, 101, 114

Clemens, Samuel (Mark Twain), 314

Cohen, Morris U.: testifies before Senate subcommittee, 274–75

Coigny, Mademoiselle de, 217

Colum, Padraic, 63

Columbus, Christopher, 233; WC on, 237–39

Commager, Henry Steele, 266–67

Communism: as practical answer to crisis of faith, xvi; and fascism, 60–61, 95–96, 317; appeal to intellectuals, xvi, 60–62, 83; relationship to liberalism, 71; in China, 106–10, 284; in Central Europe, 113–15; prospects in U.S. and Great Britain, 115; practical consequences of its spread, 177–78; as a religion, 178; origins, 179; and alienation, 263; effects of Khrushchev's "secret speech" on, 279–90, 312

Conservatism: and pragmatism, xxvi; and the social revolution, 82–83; vulnerability to liberalism, 86; threatened by the alternatives of totalitarian fascism and totalitarian communism, 97

Cooper, Thomas Haller, 158–59

Coudenhove, Count Richard N.: WC's review of *Crusade for Pan-Europe*, 74, 77–79

Cowley, Malcolm: "craved only to be left in peace to lick his spiritual wounds" after 1940, 61

Crichton, Kyle (Robert Forsythe), 61

cummings, e. e., 56

Daily Worker, xv; WC on, xvi

Dalton, Hugh, 307

D'Annunzio, Gabriele, 54

Dante, x, 197, 200, 212, 213, 216; The Divine Comedy, 73, 198; WC on, 202–03

Darwell, Jane: WC's review of her performance in The Grapes of Wrath, 58–59

Davis, Robert Gorham: testifies before HUAC, 272

Deffand, Madame du, 220

De Gaulle, Charles, Vers une Armée de Métier, 334

Democracy: and the Founding Fathers, 74–77; and the Jacksonian Revolution, 116–18; prospects for revitalization through radicalism, 123–24

Depretis, Agostino, 93–94

De Voto, Bernard, 266–67

Diderot, Denis: his "all-embracing influence" on France, 221–22

Dostoevsky, Feodor: finds "no solution for the problem of evil," 186; The Brothers Karamazov, 186; The Idiot, 186; The Possessed, ix, 186

Douglas, Melvyn: WC's review of his performance in Ninotchka, 56–57

Dreams: WC on their significance, 50, 53

Drucker, Peter: on Henry Luce as manager, xix

Dulles, John Foster, 286, 293, 295

Edward, Kenneth, 157

Edward VII, King, 232, 257; WC on, 223–30

Einstein, Albert: WC on, 127–33

Eisenhower, Dwight, xxvi, 326, 332; Eisenhower Doctrine, 292, 295

Engels, Friedrich, 179; his eulogy of Marx, 180–82; Anti-Dühring, 338; Condition of the Working Classes in England, 99

Enlightenment: WC on, 218–19; fulfilled by the Edwardians, 224

Epictetus, 328

Erskine, John, 162–63

Euripides, The Trojan Women, 280

Fadiman, Clifton, xvi

Farm policy, U.S.: as an instrument of "nationwide social change," 82; WC on, 319–25

Fascism: American intellectuals fail to see its relationship to Communism, 60–61; Italian fascism as "a historical paradigm worth examining," 92–97

Fearing, Kenneth, The Big Clock, xviii–xix

Federalist, The, 74

Feudalism: WC on, 204–08

Fitzgerald, Robert: on Time's "Books" section, xix

Flexner, Abraham, 132

Flynn, John T.: WC's review of As We Go Marching, 92–97

Fonda, Henry: WC's review of his performance in The Grapes of Wrath, 58–59

Ford, John: WC's review of The Grapes of Wrath, 58–59

Fortune, xviii, xix

Franco, Gen. Francisco, 70

Frank, Waldo: explains why he was a fellow traveler, 61; Chart for Rough Water, 62

Freud, Sigmund, 230–31
Furry, Wendell Hinckle: testifies before HUAC, 271–72

Galbraith, John Kenneth, 346
Gandhi, Mahatma, 148
Garbo, Greta: WC's review of her performance in *Ninotchka*, 56–57
Gardner, Mona: WC's review of *The Menacing Sun*, 49
Garibaldi, Giuseppe, 92
Garroway, Dave, 336
George, Herbert, 158
Gibbs, Wolcott: his *New Yorker* profile of Henry Luce, x, xviii
Gilbert, Stuart, 55
Goethe, 301–02; *Conversations*, 64
Gold, Michael: his "low growls" at apostate left-wing intellectuals, 61
Golden Legend, The, 197
Goncourt, Edmond and Jules de: predict the effects of atomic energy in their *Journal*, 133, 301
Gosse, Edmund, 54
Gramont, Madame de, 222
Grapes of Wrath, The (motion picture): WC's review of, 58–59
Grapewin, Charley: WC's review of his performance in *The Grapes of Wrath*, 58–59
Grey, Sir Edward, 143, 329
Gropper, William, 61

Halperin, Maurice: testifies before Senate subcommittee, 272–74
Hamilton, Alexander, 74–75
Hammett, Dashiell, 61
Hawthorne, Nathaniel, 52–53
Hegel, Georg Wilhelm Friedrich, 178
Hellman, Lillian, 61
Henry the Navigator, Prince, 235–36

Hersey, John: on WC's prose style, ix
Hicks, Granville: discovers that "Communism was daily growing more like fascism," 61; testifies before HUAC, 272, 276–77
High Time (newsletter published by *Time*'s Communist staffers), xx
Hiss, Alger, xiii, xiv, xv, xxv; WC on his right to apply for a passport, 340–44
History, theories of: WC on, 141–49
Hoffa, James, 292
Holmes, Oliver Wendell Jr., 265
Hopkins, Harry, 117
Hurok, Sol, 135–36
Hutchins, Robert M., 266

Ibn Saud, King, 292, 295, 296
Ibsen, Henrik, *Rosmerholm*, 162
Ignatius de Loyola, Saint: WC on, 250–51
Informer, The (motion picture), 58
Intellectuals, American: their attitudes toward Communism, 60–62

Jackson, Andrew: WC on, 116–18
Jaspers, Karl, 327
Jenner, William E., 269, 272
Jerome, V. J.: writes "a pamphlet (*Intellectuals and the War*) tearing his old friends to pieces," 61
Jesus Christ: WC on, 148
Johnson, Nunnally: WC's review of his script for *The Grapes of Wrath*, 58–59
Jolas, Eugene and Maria, 55, 63–65
Josephson, Matthew, 61
Joyce, James: WC's review of *Finnegans Wake*, 50–55; WC's obituary of, 63–65; *Exiles*, 54; *Finnegans Wake*, xiv, xx, 63–65; *Portrait of the Artist as a Young Man*, 50; *Ulysses*, 50, 53, 54, 55, 63, 65

Joyce, William (Lord Haw Haw), 160–61

Judd, Walter H., 104

Judis, John B., xxvii; *William F. Buckley, Jr.: Patron Saint of the Conservatives*, xxviii

Jully, Madame de, 221

Jung, Carl, 231

Kafka, Franz: WC on, 150–55; "The Burrow," 153; *The Castle*, 150–51, 152, 187; *The Great Wall of China*, 150, 152; "The Hunter Gracchus," ix; "Investigations of a Dog," 153; "Metamorphosis," 150, 153; *Parables and Paradoxes*, ix; *The Trial*, 150, 152, 153–55

Kant, Immanuel, 217, 334; *Critique of Pure Reason*, 131, 333

Kendall, Amos, 117–18

Keppel, Mrs. George, 229

Khrushchev, Nikita, 291, 293, 304–05, 312; his "secret speech" on Stalin, 279–90

Khrushchev, Mrs. Nikita, 304–07

Kierkegaard, Sören: influences Kafka, 153; "haunted by the tragic sense of life," 186; on the state of temptation, 189; his influence on Reinhold Niebuhr's doctrine of original sin, 190

Koestler, Arthur: on WC's HUAC testimony, xxiv; reacts to WC's death, xxviii; WC's review of *Arrival and Departure*, 80, 83–85; *Darkness at Noon*, 83–84

Kronenberger, Louis: initial impressions of WC, xx

Langtry, Lily, 228

Lattimore, Owen, 268

Lenin, 54, 148; on intellectuals, 60–62;

his pursuit of power, 182–83; WC's description of, 225; and Stalin, 288; warns that "to temporize is death," 309; *Imperialism*, 285

Leo X, Pope, 244–45

Leo XIII, Pope, 67

Léon, Paul, 64

Lewis, C. S., *The Screwtape Letters*, xxiv, 168

Liberalism: its relationship to Communism, 71, 267; its power to undermine conservative values, 86; and religious skepticism, 169–70; inadequacy in the 20th century, 185–86

Life, ix, x, xiii, xiv, xv, xviii, xix, xxiv, xxv, xxviii, 328

Lindsay, T. F., *St. Benedict*, 263

Lippmann, Walter, *The Good Society*, 71; *U.S. Foreign Policy: Shield of the Republic*, 109

Lovestone, Jay, xvi

Low, David, 163

Luce, Clare Boothe (ed.), *Saints for Now*, xxv

Luce, Henry, xv, xviii–xix, xx; admiration of WC, xx–xxi, xxiv; later relations with WC, xxv

Ludd, Ned, 176

Luther, Martin, 169; WC on, 245–47

Lyons, Eugene, *Assignment in Utopia*, 281

MacArthur, Gen. Douglas, 287

Macdonald, Dwight, xix

Maclean, Fitzroy, 101

MacLeish, Archibald, xix, 61

Malraux, André, xviii

Mann, Thomas, 80, 153

Manning, Cardinal, 69

March of Time (newsreel), xix

Marcus Aurelius, 328

Maritain, Jacques, 124

Marquand, John P.: on WC's *Witness*, xiv

Marx, Karl, 225; Marxism contrasted with the Roman Catholic Church, 71; would have shuddered at the "naive economic determinism" of Beard's *Economic Interpretation*, 76; *Das Kapital* less appealing than Sorel's *Reflections on Violence*, 95; his theory of class struggle compared to that of Arthur Schlesinger, Jr., 118; WC on, 175–83; and Ayn Rand, 315; *The Communist Manifesto*, 175, 177, 183; *Das Kapital*, 142, 177, 181

Materialism: in *Atlas Shrugged*, 315–17

Matthews, T. S., x, xxv; hires WC as *Time* book reviewer, xviii; describes WC's personal demeanor and working habits, xx–xxi; makes WC *Time's* "Foreign News" editor, xxi; publishes WC's "The Ghosts on the Roof," xxiii; *Angels Unawares*, xviii

May, Alan Nunn, 159–60

Mazzini, Giuseppe, 92

McAlmon, Robert, 54

McCarran, Pat, 269

McCarthy, Joseph R., 268, 269

McKenney, Ruth, *My Sister Eileen*, 61

McWilliams, Carey, 82

Medieval life and thought: WC on, 197–203

Merton, Thomas, xxv; *The Seven-Storey Mountain*, 261

Mikoyan, Anastas, 338

Miller, Henry, *Tropic of Cancer*, xix; *Tropic of Capricorn*, xix

Milton, John, x, 63, 159, 244, 251

Mirepoix, Maréchale de, 220–21

Mola, Gen. Emilio, 156

Molotov, Vyacheslav, 106, 285, 288

Mommsen, Theodor: *History of Rome* describes precursors of fascism, 92;

warns that history "has a Nemesis for every sin," 295

Montesquieu, 220; *De L'Esprit des Lois*, 221

Moore, George, 54

Morningside, The, ix

Mosley, Sir Oswald, 158, 161

Mozart, Wolfgang Amadeus, 219

Mumford, Lewis: considers his casual fellow-traveling "one of the shames of my life," 61; *Faith for Living*, 62

Murray, Gilbert, 143

Mussolini, Benito, 68, 70, 96; archetype of "the children of hate," 182

Mussorgsky, Modest, *Boris Godunov*, 279–80, 289

Napoleon, 216

Nasser, Gamal Abdul, 293

Nation, The, 60

National Review, ix, x, xiv; WC's relations with, xxvi–xxvii

New Masses, ix, xiv, xv, 61

New Republic, The, 60

New Yorker, The, 156, 164

Newsweek, 340–41

Newton, Sir Isaac, 128, 218; *Principia Mathematica*, 170–71

Nicholas II, Czar, xxii; WC imagines his posthumous conversion to Marxism, 111–15

Niebuhr, Reinhold, xiv, 168; WC on, 185–93; *The Nature and Destiny of Man*, 168, 186, 187–91, 192

Nietzsche, Friedrich, 294; Ayn Rand's debt to, 314–16

Ninotchka (motion picture): WC's review of, 56–57

Nixon, Richard, xxvi

Norton-Taylor, Duncan: edits WC's *Cold Friday*, xxviii

Orwell, George, xxviii

Pan-Europeanism, 77–79
Parker, Dorothy, 61
Paul III, Pope, 249
Pegler, Westbrook, x
Pétain, Marshal Philippe, 70
Pineau, André, *Marie-Thérèse Noblet, Servant of Our Lord in Papua*, 169
Pius XII, Pope: WC on, 66–73
Plato, *The Republic*, 74
Polignac, Marquise de, 220
Pope, Alexander, 218
Pound, Ezra, 54
Progress, idea of: its "bland influence" on modern man, 185; in the Enlightenment and the Edwardian era, 224
Prokofiev, Serge, *Peter and the Wolf*, 309
Proust, Marcel, 63

Quadragesimo Anno (papal encyclical), 71

Race relations in America, 140
Rand, Ayn: WC's review of *Atlas Shrugged*, xxvii, 313–18; *The Fountainhead*, 313
Rawlings, Marjorie Kinnan: praises WC's *Time* cover story on Marian Anderson, xxiv
Reagan, Ronald: posthumously confers Medal of Freedom on WC, xiv
Regnery, Henry, 339
Religion: irreconcilability of belief in God and belief in man, xxi, 83; possible renewal through the American Negro Church, 140; as an active force in history, 142, 145, 147–48; modern man's need to deny God, 150, 152–53; treason as a

response to the loss of faith, 162; decline of belief in Satan and Hell, 167–74; man's unending effort to know God, 184; the paradox of sin, 188–91; and materialism, 315–16; and belief in fate, 328–30
Renaissance: WC on, 214–15, 219
Rerum Novarum (papal encyclical), 67; WC on, 71–72
Respighi, Ottorino, *The Fountains of Rome*, 81
Roman Catholic Church: WC on, 66–73; in the Middle Ages, 199; and the Reformation, 242–52
Roosevelt, Eleanor, 136
Roosevelt, Franklin D., 68, 104, 110, 111, 117, 127, 319
Roosevelt, Theodore, 257
Ross, Harold, 164
Rougemont, Denis de, 168
Rousseau, Jean-Jacques, *Le contrat social*, 222
Rusher, William: on WC's joviality, xxvii
Russell, Bertrand, 266

Santayana, George: WC's review of *Persons and Places*, 86–91; *The Last Puritan*, 86
Satan: WC on, 166–74
Saturday Evening Post, 291–92; serializes *Witness*, xxv
Schapiro, Meyer, xvi
Schlamm, Willi, xxvi
Schlesinger, Arthur Jr.: WC's review of *The Age of Jackson*, 116–18
Schuman, Frederick L.: WC's review of *Soviet Politics*, 123–25
Scothinus, Saint, 197
Serge, Victor, *Russia Twenty Years After*, 281–82

Shakespeare, William, 65, 214; *Coriolanus*, ix; *Macbeth*, 281

Shaw, George Bernard, 111, 163

Sheen, Bishop Fulton, 168

Sibelius, Jean, 135

Simpson, Russell: WC reviews his performance in *The Grapes of Wrath*, 58–59

Smedley, Agnes, 108

Snow, Edgar, 108

Sorel, Georges: "had the knife between his teeth" in *Reflections on Violence*, 95

Soule, George, 61

Soviet Union: as portrayed in *Ninotchka*, 56–57; postwar intentions, 113–15; "solves" the problems of economic and political liberty, 124; effects of Khrushchev's "secret speech" on, 279–90; Middle East strategy in the 1950s, 291–99

Space, U.S.-Soviet race for: WC on, 300–03, 308

Spengler, Oswald: quoted by Charles Beard, 76–77; his "bracing pessimism about the age," 133; *Der Untergang des Abendlandes* compared to Toynbee's *A Study of History*, 142

Spirituals: WC on, 134, 137–40

Stalin, Josef, 83, 112–15, 279–80

Stassen, Harold, 295

Steinbeck, John, 61; *The Grapes of Wrath*, xx, 58

Stevenson, Adlai, 286, 326, 332

Stewart, Donald Ogden, 61

Stilwell, Gen. Joseph, xxii; WC on, 104–10

Sun Yat-sen, 22

Swanberg, W. A., xix

Swinburne, Algernon Charles, 223, 257

Sylvester II, Pope, 204

Szilard, Leo, 127

Taney, Roger B., 117

Taylor, John, *An Enquiry into the Principles and Policy of the Government of the United States*, 118

Tchernavin, Vladimir, *I Speak for the Silent*, 281

Technology: the key element of 20th-century civilization, 127; and destruction, 185; faith in as a liberating agent, 231

Teller, Walter Magnes (with P. Alston Waring): WC's review of *Roots in the Earth*, 80, 82

Tencine, Madame de, 220

Tennyson, Alfred Lord: his "silly" optimism, 185

Tertullian, 188

Thompson, Craig: on WC's tenure as *Time*'s "Foreign News" editor, xxii

Thucydides, *The Peloponnesian War*, 144

Time, ix, x, xiii, xiv, xv, xviii–xxvi; extent of its influence on American opinion, xix; prevalence of left-wing staffers during Forties, xx; official responses to revelations about WC's Communist past, xxv; obituary of WC, xxviii

Tintoretto, 243

Tito, Marshal Josip Broz, 290; WC on, 98–103

Toller, Ernst: and WC's generation, 82–83

Torquemada, 250

Toscanini, Arturo, 134

Toynbee, Arnold: 140, 172; WC's review of *A Study of History*, 141–49

transition, 55

Treason: 20th-century manifestations of, 156–62

Trilling, Lionel: on WC's early writings,

xvi; on WC's *New Masses* stories and later writings, xvii; *Matthew Arnold*, xiii

Trotsky, Leon, 114, 329–30, 344

Truman, Harry S., 287

Unamuno, Miguel de: on "the God-ache," 152–53; on the comparative value of religion and philosophy, 191

Urban II, Pope, 207

Van Buren, Martin, 117

Victoria, Queen, 223, 228, 257

Virgil, 203

Voltaire, 217; WC on, 222

Wallace, Henry, 96, 106, 319

Wang Shih-wei, "Wild Artichoke," 108–09

Waring, P. Alston (with Walter Magnes Teller): WC's review of *Roots in the Earth*, 80, 82

Waugh, Evelyn, xxv

Weaver, Harriet, 54

Webb, Sidney (Lord Passfield) and Beatrice, 162, 225; *History of the English Poor Law*, 182

Weinstein, Allen, *Perjury: The Hiss-Chambers Case*, ix, xv, xvi

Wells, H. G., 163, 260

Werfel, Franz, 152

West, Dame Rebecca, xxv; *Black Lamb and Grey Falcon*, 157, 163; WC's review of *The Meaning of Treason*, 156–65; *The Strange Necessity*, 157, 163; *The Thinking Reed*, 157, 163

White, Rawlins, 242–43

White, Theodore: dissatisfaction with WC's editing, xxii; *In Search of History*, xxii

Wierus, Johannes, *Concerning the Artifices of Demons*, 169

Willkie, Wendell, 97

Wilson, Edmund, *Axel's Castle*, 51, 52

Wordsworth, William, 191, 216

Yeats, W. B., 54

Zanuck, Darryl, 58

Zukofsky, Louis, xvi

About the Editor

TERRY TEACHOUT is a member of the editorial board of the New York *Daily News*. His writing appears in *The American Scholar, The American Spectator, Commentary, High Fidelity, Musical America, National Review, The New Criterion, The New Dance Review* and *The Wall Street Journal*.